D0081430

FILE STRUCTURES
USING PASCAL

The Benjamin/Cummings Series in Computer Science

G. Booch
Software Engineering with Ada, Second Edition (1987)

G. Booch
Software Components with Ada: Structures, Tools, and Subsystems (1987)

G. Brookshear
Computer Science: An Overview (1985)

D.M. Etter
Structured FORTRAN 77 for Engineers and Scientists, Second Edition (1987)

D.M. Etter
Problem Solving with Structured FORTRAN 77 (1984)

P. Helman and B. Veroff
Intermediate Problem Solving and Data Structures: Walls and Mirrors (1986)

A. Kelley and I. Pohl
C by Dissection: The Essentials of C Programming (1987)

A. Kelley and I. Pohl
A Book on C (1984)

R. Lamb
Pascal: Structure and Style (1986)

N. Miller
File Structures Using Pascal (1987)

W. Savitch
Pascal: An Introduction to the Art and Science of Programming, Second Edition (1987)

W. Savitch
An Introduction to the Art and Science of Programming: TURBO Pascal Edition (1986)

M. Sobell
A Practical Guide to the UNIX System (1984)

M. Sobell
A Practical Guide to UNIX System V (1985)

FILE STRUCTURES USING PASCAL

Nancy E. Miller
Mississippi State University

The Benjamin/Cummings Publishing Company, Inc.
Menlo Park, California • Reading, Massachusetts
Don Mills, Ontario • Wokingham, U.K. • Amsterdam • Sydney
Singapore • Tokyo • Madrid • Bogota • Santiago • San Juan

Sponsoring Editor: Alan Apt
Production Editor: Richard Mason
Copy Editor: Toni Murray
Cover and Consulting Designer: Hal Lockwood
Illustration and Composition: Graphic Typesetting Service

The basic text of this book was designed using the Modular Design System, as developed by Wendy Earl and Design Office Bruce Kortebein.

Library of Congress Cataloging in Publication Data

Miller, Nancy, 1951–
  File structures using Pascal.

  Bibliography: p.
  Includes index.
  1. File organization (Computer science)
2. PASCAL (Computer program language)   I. Title.
QA76.9.F5M55   1987   005.74   86–21641
ISBN 0-8053-7082-X

BCDEFGHIJ-DO-8987

The Benjamin/Cummings Publishing Company, Inc.
2727 Sand Hill Road
Menlo Park, California 94025

Contents

PART I   FILE PROCESSING ENVIRONMENT   1

v

PART II   SEQUENTIAL ACCESS   127

PART III   RANDOM ACCESS   203

PART IV   TREE-STRUCTURED FILE ORGANIZATION   267

PART V   LIST-STRUCTURED FILE ORGANIZATION 397

Preface

MOTIVATION

After teaching file processing courses for years using COBOL as the vehicle language, I concluded that students do learn to use COBOL for a variety of file organizations (sequential, indexed sequential, and relative) but do not gain an understanding of the data structures involved in implementing the more complex file structures such as direct files and indexed sequential files. A programming language with less support for file organizations than COBOL allows students to gain greater in-depth knowledge about the implementation of routines that access data structures on external files. Pascal, with its support for relative files, fills this need.

GOAL

This textbook meets the requirements of The Association for Computing Machinery (ACM) course CS5 as defined in the ACM curriculum guidelines. The goal of the book is to study the external data structures necessary for implementing different file organizations. Most texts currently available present file processing by using languages such as COBOL or PL/1, which have built-in support for direct access and indexed sequential access. Pascal does not have this built-in support. Instead, this language can be used in a more practical, pedagogical way by allowing students to gain more in-depth file implementation experience as they analyze data structures for efficiency and write their own access routines.

The algorithms in this book are presented in a Pascal-like pseudocode, which provides students with a familiar environment in which to study the key concepts and structures necessary to implement a variety of file organizations. Data structures such as trees, linked lists, stacks, and queues are studied and analyzed for efficient use in the implementation of various file organizations. By using a superior pedagogical language such as Pascal and analyzing key data structures, students will gain a better understanding of design analysis and the implementation of file organizations.

LEVEL/AUDIENCE/PREREQUISITES

The prerequisites for the course addressed by this book, CS5, are two semesters of Pascal; in other words students should already have taken ACM CS1 and CS2 courses. Third-semester Computer Science majors constitute the primary audience for this book.

ORGANIZATION AND COVERAGE

Chapter 1 presents a conceptual overview of the file-processing environment, including discussions of common file organizations, file types and characteristics, and different ways of manipulating files as factors that affect file design. Several of the examples of file applications in this chapter are referenced in later chapters.

Chapter 2 reviews the syntax for declaring and using records and for declaring and accessing files in Pascal. This chapter may be omitted for those students with a good understanding of Pascal records and files.

Chapter 3 deals with the topics of blocking and buffering of records in a file. The central theme of the chapter is the fewer I/O operations required for a program that accesses a blocked file and the reduction of the time that the CPU waits for an I/O operation to be completed when using a buffered file. Interfacing algorithms for record blocking and deblocking are also presented in this chapter. Quantitative measures of the effects of blocking and buffering are given solely in terms of the number of I/O accesses.

Chapter 4 describes external storage devices as a background for understanding the impact of storage devices on file design and manipulation. Quantitative measures of the effects of blocking and buffering (similar to those in Chapter 3) are repeated in terms of physical access time using various blocking factors and different numbers of buffers.

Chapter 5 deals with the design and maintenance of sequential files on both sequential and random-access storage devices. Algorithms for maintenance of sequential files stored on sequential devices are contrasted with algorithms for maintenance of sequential files stored on random-access devices. Sample data for a car-rental agency are used for implementing a sequential file. Quantitative measures of access times are given.

Chapter 6 describes external sort/merge techniques, which are necessary for sorting very large sequential files. Sorting is a common file-processing task, especially for manipulating sequential files. Sorting methods discussed at length are the two-way merge, the balanced k-way merge, and the polyphase merge. These methods are compared in terms of the number of merge cycles and external storage devices needed for several example data sets.

Chapter 7 begins with a discussion of the basic structures of direct files. A variety of techniques are presented for obtaining random access to data files, including the use of hashing. Examples are used to illustrate several methods for handling hashing collisions. Also included are some algorithms for creating and maintaining random-access files in versions of Pascal with the random-access file extension. In order to compare random and sequential access, the car-rental agency data used in Chapter 5 are stored in a random-access file and quantitative measures of access times are computed.

Chapter 8 describes several types of tree structures that are used to access random-access files sequentially. The most important tree structure is the B-tree, and ways of representing and manipulating the B-tree are discussed along with accompanying algorithms. The chapter also discusses the application of trees that allow sequential and random access to the car-rental agency data file created in Chapter 7.

Chapter 9 describes common implementations of indexed sequential organization, including implementations that use a tree structure, such as a B-tree, for the indexes. The chapter studies Scope Indexed Sequential files used on CDC computers, cylinder-and-surface-indexed sequential files (ISAM) used on IBM computers, and VSAM file organization used on IBM computers. Also included are algorithms for implementing indexed sequential files using a variety of data structures. Applications include the car-rental agency data, and access times for sequential, random, and indexed sequential files are compared.

Chapter 10 investigates other types of file organization that use linked lists or tree structures to provide multiple-key access to random-access data files. Included in this chapter is a discussion of inverted files and multilist files along with creation and manipulation algorithms. The car-rental agency data are implemented as an inverted file and multilist file to provide access by several keys. Quantitative measures of access times are given by comparing these file organizations with others discussed previously.

OUTSTANDING FEATURES

Pedagogy

Case Studies   Chapter 5 introduces a case study based on an actual car-rental agency, and this case study is used throughout the book as an ongoing example illustrating practical file concepts and issues.

Additional practical, real-world case studies are presented in Chapter 2. They include discussions of an inventory of products, student class schedules, and the assignment of course grades for a class.

Examples/Illustrations   Throughout the book there are a variety of examples and algorithms accompanied by numerous figures and tables. Students have found these to be very helpful for independent study.

Algorithms/Exercises   Throughout this book algorithms are presented in a Pascal-like pseudocode. Students learn best by working with files of varying organizations rather than just reading about them. A variety of exercises and programming projects have been provided that illustrate the creation and manipulation of files for each type of organization. Students can implement the algorithms from the book in a hands-on, file organization programming environment, thus gaining experience and greater knowledge of all the key concepts. The program solutions for these exercises are provided to the instructor in the Instructor's Guide. Solutions to odd-numbered exercises are provided at the back of the book.

Glossary/Key Terms   Key terms are highlighted and defined as they occur in the text, and are also included in the glossary at the end of the book.

Class Tested   This book was thoroughly class tested for six semesters in a sophomore-level file structures course. The readability of the book was greatly enhanced because of student and reviewer feedback over the course of several drafts.

The Use of Pascal

Chapter 2 reviews the Pascal syntax for declaring, using, and accessing Pascal records and files. This chapter can be omitted for those students with a good understanding of Pascal.

The Pascal syntax for linked lists and trees is included in corresponding sections. The first two sections of the book (I and II) reference the ISO standard Pascal, while sections III and IV require random-access files, which are not included in the ISO standard. Most versions of Pascal have been extended to allow random access (OMSI Pascal, TURBO Pascal, UCSD P-System Pascal, and VAX-11 Pascal, to name a few). Appendix A includes a sequential simulation of random access using arrays in internal memory as an easy alternative to those versions of Pascal without random access. The syntax for random access for various versions of Pascal is included in Appendix B.

INSTRUCTOR'S GUIDE

The accompanying Instructor's Guide includes:

- guidelines for presenting the material in each chapter
- additional examples for classroom use, including points to be emphasized
- solutions to all even-numbered exercises
- solutions to all programming problems with appropriate Pascal programs
- transparency masters of various illustrations and tables from the book
- quizzes for each chapter.

SOFTWARE

A tape or disk of all programs from the book is available from the author for a nominal fee.

ACKNOWLEDGMENTS

I am grateful to the numerous individuals who have helped me in preparing this book. I am indebted to the faculty of the Computer Science Department of Mississippi State University for providing equipment and an environment conducive to writing a book. My thanks also go to the reviewers: James D. Schoeffler, Cleveland State University; Rayno D. Niemi, Rochester Institute of Technology; James Blahnik, St. Norbert's College; Medhi Owrand, University of Oklahoma; Robert Uzgalis, University of California at Los Angeles; and Walter Scacchi, University of Southern California.

Special thanks go to the students in my classes who corrected typing errors in earlier versions of the book. I express my appreciation to my editor, Alan Apt, and to all those individuals at Benjamin/Cummings who have organized the reviewing and production of this book. Finally, I thank my husband for his continued support, encouragement, and understanding.

Nancy E. Miller

FILE STRUCTURES
USING PASCAL

PART I

FILE PROCESSING ENVIRONMENT

Chapter 1
Overview of Files

Chapter 2
Pascal Records and Files

Chapter 3
Blocking and Buffering

Chapter 4
Secondary Storage Devices

Chapter 1

CHAPTER CONTENTS

Overview of Files

PREVIEW

THIS CHAPTER PRESENTS AN OVERVIEW of file organization, file types, access methods, and ways of manipulation as a background for the detailed discussion of traditional file organization in Parts II through V. The remainder of Part I describes the file processing environment which is necessary to fully understand the data structures and analyses of the traditional file organizations presented in the rest of the book.

FILE DESIGN

The study of file structures involves the investigation of the data structures used to organize a large collection of data into one or more external files that are stored on secondary storage devices. A programmer must have a good understanding of file structures to organize data in a way that facilitates efficient storage and access. Just as the success or failure of a program depends on the choice of the structure for storing the data in internal memory, the accessibility of data stored on external storage devices depends on efficient file organization.

A **file** is a collection of related data—a payroll file contains data concerning employee pay schedules and a student file contains data about all the enrolled students. To allow easy access to all the data about one employee, all the relevant data in the payroll file is usually stored in contiguous memory locations in a record. Files of records of related data are stored on external storage devices for a number of reasons. First, the collection of data is usually too large to fit into internal memory. Second, the entire collection of data need not be stored internally since only a small portion of the file (one record of data) is accessed at a time. Third, the collection of data needs to be retained in a permanent form for access by more than one program.

In a file of records, it is necessary to be able to identify a particular record. The technique for identifying a record involves choosing as the identifier a data item from the record of data that has a unique value. Such an identifier is the **key field** of the record. For a payroll file, the key to a record of data for an employee might be the employee's social security number. Since each record has a unique key value, the file might be logically ordered in ascending key order. A library might need a more complicated arrangement to organize records of the books in the library. A computerized library system might arrange records by the author's last name (one key) and by the subject area (a second key) so that a user could access information by author or by subject.

A programmer must consider several factors when designing a file: the organization of the file (a choice that involves selecting proper data structures); the type of function each file plays in an information system; and the characteristics of a file. A programmer must also consider the manipulations necessary to keep the file current and to extract information from it. The rest of this chapter will show how these considerations apply to file design.

File Organization

File organization refers to the way in which records are stored in an external file. To put it another way, the term *file organization* refers to the data structures used for organizing the data. The type of access to records available on an external file depends on file organization and storage media. This chapter presents four common file organizations that we will discuss in later chapters at greater length:

1. sequential
2. random
3. indexed sequential
4. multikey

When a programmer arranges a file with **sequential file organization**, records are written consecutively—in sequence from beginning to end—and must be accessed in the same manner. The tenth record of the file can be accessed only after the first nine records have been read. Searching for a particular record requires the same process. Often the records in a sequentially organized file are stored in ascending or descending order according to a key field. The result is the ability to search rapidly for the key value. On the average, if records are arranged in the file by the key field, half of the records in the file must be searched in order to locate a particular record. A sequentially organized file is easier to maintain than other organizations—especially in terms of adding and deleting records—since the entire file must be copied in order to update it. Unfortunately, the fact that a sequentially organized file can *only* be accessed sequentially means that its records cannot usually be updated in place; the user must copy the file to another file during updating. (This limitation does not apply to other file organizations.) The fact that sequential files are limited to sequential access also gives them an advantage, however: namely, the programmer can use records of varying length. Part II contains an extensive discussion of the manipulation of sequentially organized files.

Random file organization implies a predictable relationship between the key used to identify an individual record and that record's location in an external file. This organization is described as random because it is possible to access a record without searching sequentially through the file. Instead, a random search considers the key and directly computes the location of the record. The logical ordering of the records need not have any relationship to their physical sequence.

A **relative file** is a common implementation of random file organization and is available in most high-level programming languages. The document that officially defines Pascal (ISO Pascal Standard) does not include random-access files, but many implementations (OMSI Pascal, Turbo Pascal, UCSD Pascal, and VAX-11 Pascal) have been extended to allow random-access files. Once a key-position relationship is established, the position of the record in the file is specified as a record number relative to the beginning of the file. (The first record is numbered 0 or 1 depending upon the implementation.) Each address is computed according to the following equation:

$$\text{record's address} = (\text{relative record number} \times \text{fixed record length})$$
$$+ \text{ beginning of file}$$

Note that the equation specifies that the length of records in a relative random-access file must be fixed. The limitation also imparts an advantage, however: the file can be updated in place.

Relative files can also be accessed sequentially. The user specifies the relative record numbers in order from 0 or 1 (depending on the Pascal implementation) to n, the last record on the file. Sequential access to a relative file defines the physical ordering of records, which is usually meaningless since the record's address is computed. A retrieval of records ordered by the record keys is usually provided by some sort of index structure. Part III contains a detailed discussion of the organization and manipulation of random-access files.

Indexed sequential file organization combines sequential access and ordering with the capabilities of random access. An indexed sequential file contains two parts:

1. A collection of records stored in contiguous locations within blocks in a relative file and ordered by a key field.

2. An index (a hierarchical structure of record keys and relative block numbers) to the file of ordered records.

The blocks of records in the file are not necessarily stored in sequential order; the index indicates the order in which the blocks should be accessed to achieve sequential order by record keys. Since records are stored in blocks, variable-length records may be used as long as the blocks have a fixed length for random access. A search of the index of record keys retrieves the relative record number of a block containing a record, then the relative file of records is accessed randomly. Chapter 8 presents a detailed discussion of B-trees, which are the most common indexing structure used to implement indexed sequential organization.

Indexed sequential access is relatively rapid, although it is not quite as fast as random access since the index must be searched before the record is retrieved. The relative file can be accessed sequentially, using the index, to retrieve the file of records in order by the key field. The relative file can also be accessed randomly to update the records in place. Chapter 9 contains detailed discussions of three common implementations of indexed sequential file organization.

Multikey file organization allows access to a data file by several different key fields. A library file that requires access by author and by subject matter is a good example of a multikey file. Indexed sequential file organization uses indexes to provide random access by one key field. Multikey organization uses an indexing structure and includes the data file of records and an index for each different key field that will be used to access individual records. For example, a file of employee records might be accessed by employee number, by the job code, or by the number of vacation days accumulated. Multikey organization will be investigated at length and implemented using B-trees in Chapter 10.

Data File Types

The collection of data for a particular information system (a payroll information system, for example) usually resides in several types of files. The files in an information system are classified by the function they serve. There are six types of files in an information system:

1. master file
2. transaction file
3. table file
4. report file
5. control file
6. history file

Most files fall into only one of these six categories. A **master file** contains records of permanent data that are updated by adding, deleting, or changing data. For example, a payroll master file contains an employee's social security number, the rate of pay, marital status, number of exemptions claimed, and year-to-date deductions and earnings. Individual records are added as new employees are hired and records are deleted as employees leave. Changes to rate of pay are made as employees receive pay raises. The master file must be maintained to keep the data up to date. The organization of the master file is usually sequential, random, indexed sequential, or multikey, in order to provide the required fast and efficient access to the permanent data in that master file.

A **transaction file** contains records of changes, additions, and deletions made to a master file. One or more fields of individual records in a master file may be changed, or individual records may be added or deleted. Instead of containing updated data, a transaction file contains data that will be summarized before storage in the master file. For example, a transaction file for the payroll system may contain data about hours worked during a pay period. These transactions are then applied to the payroll master file to generate payroll checks and update year-to-date earnings and deductions on the master file. The number of hours worked during each pay period is not stored in the master file; rather, the data increment the year-to-date earnings field of the master file.

Figure 1.1
Sample table file

Product code	Product description	Product price

Figure 1.2
Inventory master file records

Product code	Quantity on hand	Quantity on order	Reorder point

Figure 1.3
Customer orders master file records

Customer number	Customer name	Product code	Quantity ordered	Total sales

Figure 1.4
Production division's master file records

Product code	Number made this month	Number made previous month	Number made 2nd previous month	Number made this year to date	Number made last year to date

```
 Inventory Master File Maintenance Audit Listing          Page 1

  Update   Product   Quantity   Quantity   Reorder
   Code     Code     On Hand    On Order    Point      ------ACTION-------

     A     DR1112      400         50        400      Addition
     C     DR2000      350                            Change -- Qty on hand
     A     DR3814      239          0        200      Addition
     A     DR3914      150          0         50      Addition
     D     DR4000                                     Deletion
     C     GR5000                 100                 Change -- Qty on order
     C     GR5014                             45      Change -- Reorder point
     A     SA3012      100         25        110      Addition
     C     SA4310      125                            Change -- Qty on hand
```

Figure 1.5
Sample page of an audit listing of a maintenance run

A **table file** consists of a table of data, such as a price list, a tax rate table, or some other form of reference data that is static and is referenced by one of the other types of files. For example, a table file contains records of product codes, product descriptions, and product prices. (Figure 1.1 shows the contents of such a file.) Accompanying master files in this case are an inventory master file (Figure 1.2), a customer orders master file (Figure 1.3), and a manufacturing division's production master file (Figure 1.4). All the master files reference the product by product code. The table file must be referenced by all these master files in order to include product description and price on any reports. This represents a savings in space for the master file since each of the master files need not store product code, description, and price; the master files must only store product codes. Redundancy is eliminated, and the user makes changes in the product descriptions and prices in one place, the table file. The changes are reflected in all the files that reference the table.

A **report file** contains information that has been prepared for the user. The report file may be spooled to a printer to yield a hard copy, or be displayed on a cathode ray tube (CRT). The report file may be an audit listing of a maintenance run (Figure 1.5), an error listing of mismatches from a maintenance run (Figure 1.6), a listing of the entire master file (Figure 1.7), or a summary report of information on the master file (Figure 1.8).

A **control file** is another output from a maintenance run. The control file is small and contains information concerning a particular maintenance run, such as the date of the run; the number of master records read, added, deleted, and written; and the number of transaction records read, processed,

```
Inventory Master File Maintenance Error Listing                               Page 1

Update   Product   Quantity   Quantity   Reorder
  Code     Code     On Hand    On Order    Point    --------ERROR MESSAGE--------

   D      DR3000                                     Invalid Delete--Master Not On File
   C      GR5013      100                            Invalid Change--Master Not On File
   A      HM1032      125         0         75       Invalid Add--Master Already On File
   X      HM1308                                     Invalid Update Code
   Y      SA3014                                     Invalid Update Code
   A      SA4201       50         0         30       Invalid Add--Master Already On File
   D      SD1103                                     Invalid Delete--Master Not On File
```

Figure 1.6
Sample page of an error listing of a maintenance run

```
Inventory  Master  File  Listing                    Page 1

Product      Quantity      Quantity      Reorder
Code         On Hand       On Order      Point

DR1015          25             0            30
DR1112         400            50           400
DR2000         350            25           375
DR3814         239             0           200
DR3914         150             0            50
GR2001          74            10            80
GR3034          25            10            30
GR5000         500           100           525
GR5014          45             0            45
HM1032         123             0           120
HM1308          75             0           102
SA3012         100            25           110
SA4201          50             0            30
SA4310         125             0           100
SA5012           3             0             5
```

Figure 1.7
Sample listing of
master file

```
Inventory Master File Listing of Records With       Page 1
        Quantity On Hand BELOW Reorder Point

Product      Quantity      Quantity      Reorder
Code         On Hand       On Order      Point

DR1015          25             0            30
HM1308          75             0           102
SA5012           3             0             5
```

Figure 1.8
Sample page of sum-
mary report from a
master file

```
Transactions Read              578
    Adds                       461
        Processed              446
        Invalid                 15
    Changes                     87
        Processed               79
        Invalid                  8
    Deletions                   29
        Processed               27
        Invalid                  2
    Invalid Update Codes         1
    Master Records Read     28,406
    Master Records Written  28,825
```

Figure 1.9
Sample control file
contents

and in error (Figure 1.9). This information is necessary to perform the two arithmetic checks that determine the success of a maintenance run. In a successful maintenance run:

1. The number of master records read minus the number of master records deleted plus the number of new master records added equals the number of master records in the new updated master file.

2. The number of transaction records read minus the number of transaction records found to be in error equals the number of transaction records processed (the number of records that caused changes to the master file).

A **history file** simply consists of all the backup master files, transaction files, and control files from past runs. The history file stores these files to provide a trail for the programmer to recreate a master file should it and all the backups be accidentally destroyed. History files are usually stored on magnetic tape reels, which are less expensive than magnetic disk packs.

File Characteristics

The use of a file can be characterized by the activity and the volatility of a file. The **activity** of a file is a measure of the percentage of existing master records changed during a maintenance run. A file with high activity is more efficient if it is organized sequentially (assuming that random access is not required for improved response time), since each record in the file must be copied to a new file during maintenance. A low-activity file is more efficient if it employs some other organization that provides random access, so that only the records to be changed are accessed and updated.

The **volatility** of a file is a measure of the number of records added and deleted compared to the original number of records. A highly volatile sequential file is updated by a procedure that merges master file records and transaction file records into a new up-to-date master file. Without the incorporation of some form of linked organization (such as a B-tree, as Chapter 8 discusses), the efficiency of a nonsequential file deteriorates with high volatility because of the extensive reorganization that takes place to accommodate additions or deletions.

Closely related to the activity and volatility of a file is its **frequency of use** and the required response time. The frequency of use is an important factor in file design since the type of access available with a particular file organization may hamper the frequency of use. A file with only sequential access available requires more time to update on an hourly basis rather than once a day or once a week. The more frequent the required use of the file, the more necessary random access to the file becomes.

The **required response time** for accessing a file with queries or updates usually determines the type of access available to a file. If a response is required in seconds rather than hours or days, then random access will probably be the choice, and random access is not available with sequential organization. (To evaluate response time for each of the file organizations discussed in later chapters, performance of sequential files will be measured as time units necessary to read a sequential file when performing a maintenance run. Performance of random-access files will be measured in time units to access an individual record.)

The number of records in the file and the length of each record determine the **file size**. The record length (in bytes) is established when deciding what information to store in each record. The length of a record equals the sum of the length (in bytes) of each field in the record. The future (not present) file size equals the number of records that will be stored presently plus the number of records to be added in the future. The file size is a consideration in choosing adequate secondary storage hardware, as Chapter 4 explains.

FILE MANIPULATION

Once a file is created, manipulation of that file may include querying the file to extract information, merging files of related data to produce needed reports, and maintaining the file with up-to-date data.

Queries

File queries involve searching a file for records containing certain values in particular key fields. Examples of queries to the payroll master file include:

Listing the record for a particular employee
Listing all employees that have worked more than 40 hours in the preceding week
Listing all employees within a certain department
Listing all female employees who are in managerial positions.

The user queries the inventory master file (Figure 1.2) to identify all products for which the quantity on hand is less than the reorder point or to list all products for which an order has been placed. The user queries the inventory table file (Figure 1.1) to retrieve the current price to charge a customer.

File queries also involve searching the file of data for records that match a set of key values. The set of key values may contain:

Only one value in one field (a particular product code)

Several unique values in one field (all students majoring in computer science, mathematics, or statistics)

Unique values in several fields (all books in the library where author = Knuth and subject = data structures).

The program developer must anticipate the types of queries and organize the file to facilitate them.

Merging

Data often need to be extracted from more than one file of a particular information system to produce a summary report. A report summarizing the total inventory on hand and a listing for each product in the inventory (the product code, description, quantity on hand, and price) requires that the inventory table file containing individual descriptions and prices merge with the inventory master file, which contains quantity on hand. Assuming that both files are in ascending key order, the records from the two files can be input, and the product codes (the key) matched to produce the report. Merging these two files provides a check that determines if each product in the current inventory has a record of data in both files (and not just one).

Maintenance

File maintenance involves updating a master file with transactions to keep the data in the master file up-to-date. Transactions consist of the addition of new records to the master file, changing data in existing records, and the deletion of existing records from the file. A one-character update code represents each type of transaction: A for an add transaction, C for a change transaction, and D for a delete transaction. The transaction data need to be validated to ensure that the update code field is valid and to ensure that the transactions are in the same sequence (ascending order, in most cases) as the master file. The transaction file can be edited in a separate front-end editing program prior to the execution of the maintenance program or as part of the maintenance program. If the editing is performed in a separate program, each record must be accessed to validate the transactions, then each valid transaction in the transaction file is accessed again by the maintenance program to apply the transactions to the master file. Often the maintenance program performs the editing so that each record in the transaction file is accessed only once instead of twice.

The **file maintenance program** is the basic file-merging program that determines if transactions match existing master records. If the transaction duplicates an existing master record, it becomes a change or deletion, and if the transaction does not match existing records, it becomes an addition. If no transactions apply to an existing master record, there is no change. The file maintenance program performs a sequential update or a random update depending on the organization of the master file. In a sequential master file update, all the master records are input, matched to the transactions, and copied to a new, updated master file. The transactions must be sorted in the same key sequence as the master file records. (Chapter 5 presents the algorithm that describes the process of updating a sequential master file.) The file maintenance program performs a random master file update on files with relative and indexed sequential organization. A random update causes only the master records that match transactions to be input, modified, and rewritten to the same master file. Since the transactions are applied randomly, they need not be sorted, but the physical access time needed to perform the maintenance can be reduced if they are sorted. (Chapter 7 presents the algorithm that describes the update of a random-access file, and Chapter 4 discusses physical access time and secondary storage devices.)

When considering file maintenance, the programmer must remember that, in many cases, permanent data are stored on several master files, not just one. For example, as Figures 1.1 through 1.4 show, an inventory information system may contain four master files of permanent data. The table file contains a product description and price information that is referenced along with the other master files. The product code is listed in each master file to indicate how information that resides in four different master files corresponds. The program that prints customer bills from the customer orders master file (Figure 1.2) would also have to access the table file (Figure 1.1) in order to print the description and unit price. A summary report of inventory holdings might require that the table file of Figure 1.1, the inventory master file of Figure 1.2, and the production master file of Figure 1.4 all be accessed.

Multifile information systems, such as the inventory system, are designed to reduce duplication of information. The price and description stored in one table file is referenced at the same time as another file; the user does not have to store the price and description in each file. Storing the price in one file also makes it easier for the user to keep price information up to date. However, the fact that more than one file must be accessed to retrieve all the information concerning a particular product can be a disadvantage in some cases. Each file in the multifile system has a different format, and users of the files must be aware of the file formats to retrieve information. The structure of records in a file (fields within a record) is usually not apparent to the operating system that performs that file's I/O operations. The I/O operations simply access the required number of bytes—the user must be aware of the record formats. The developer must provide special retrieval programs to access records with different record formats.

A database is a multifile system in which the user need not be aware of the different file formats. The database management system, unlike master files, does contain information pertaining to the record structures (formats) of all files within the database. The user interacts with a database management system that serves as a software interface between the master data files in the system and the user. The database management system allows the user to retrieve all the information concerning a particular product in the database without specifying which one of the several master files contains that information; the user must specify only the pertinent fields. A program that executes through the database management system may actually reference several of the permanent data files that make up the database. This book outlines the traditional file organizations used in single-file information systems; it does not cover database file designs for the implementation of multifile information systems.

SUMMARY

Files are a useful data structure for storing large collections of data on nonvolatile secondary storage devices. In designing files to match the desired access, a program developer must consider several factors:

The type of the file (master, transaction, table, report, control, history)
The organization of the file (sequential, random, indexed sequential, multikey)
The characteristics of the file (in terms of activity and volatility).

The design of the file should also accommodate the required file manipulations: querying, file merging, and file maintenance.

Key Terms

activity
control file
file maintenance program
file organization
file size
frequency of use
history file
indexed sequential file organization
key field

master file
multikey file organization
random file organization
report file
relative file
sequential file organization
table file
transaction file
volatility

Exercises

Match the following terms with the definitions in exercises 1 through 9:

a. master file
b. transaction file
c. control file
d. table file
e. report file

f. history file
g. activity of a file
h. volatility of a file
i. file size

1. What contains updates (additions, changes, and deletions) to be applied to the master file?

2. What contains a limited number of records that consist of program statistics, record counts, and the like from a maintenance run?

3. What refers to the percentage of master records changed during a maintenance run?

4. What contains current permanent information?

5. What refers to the percentage of additions or deletions made to a master file during a maintenance run?

6. What is a collection of the old master files, old transaction files, and control files from past maintenance runs?

7. What is determined by the number of components in the file and the length (in bytes) of each component?

8. What contains information drawn from a master file that has been prepared for a user?

9. What contains a table of information that is static and referenced by other files?

Match the following file organizations with the definitions in exercises 10 through 13:

a. indexed sequential file organization
b. multikey file organization
c. sequential file organization
d. random file organization

10. Name an organization in which a predictable relationship exists between the key that identifies an individual component and that component's location in an external file of this organization.

11. Name an organization that combines the sequential access and ordering of components provided in sequential file organization and the random-access capabilities of random file organization.

12. Name an organization in which file components are written and accessed consecutively.

13. Which organization allows access to a data file by several different key fields?

14. What types of file organization methods are usually available?

15. What options exist for data access? What are the differences among these access methods?

16. List reasons for structuring a collection of records as a file on a secondary storage device rather than as a data structure in main memory?

17. Why do computer systems usually support several file organization techniques?

For each application described in questions 18 through 22, name an appropriate file organization. Justify your answer.

18. The employee payroll file is accessed once a week to calculate the company's payroll and to issue paychecks. Each record in an employee payroll master file contains the employee identification number, pay rate, and withholding information. The master file is accessed in order by employee number. A transaction file containing data from weekly time cards updates between 90 and 95 percent of the records in the master file. What organization should the employee payroll file employ?

19. An airline reservation file contains flight information used in booking passengers and issuing tickets. Each record in the airline reservation file contains a flight number, the name of the airline, the departure time, the arrival time, the maximum number of seats in the airplane, and the number of seats booked. The file is accessed by flight number. Rapid access to the file is required so that customers can receive flight information while they wait at reservation counters or on the telephone. Bookings take place immediately, and the flight records are updated as soon as passengers ask for reservations. What organization should the airline reservation file employ?

20. An inventory file contains production information about all merchandise in stock. Each record contains a product number, a product description, a product price, the quantity on hand, and the reorder point. The inventory file is updated when an item of merchandise is withdrawn from the stock to sell to a customer and when stock is replenished with a new shipment. It is important that the updates take place immediately to maintain a current record of product availability. Periodic inventory reports are prepared for management. The reports are in sequence by product number and indicate the quantities of merchandise in inventory. Customers' queries about the availability of stock require that the product records be accessible immediately through on-line terminals. What organization would be best for the inventory file?

21. A table file of federal withholding tax tables is used for determining withholding amounts during payroll processing. The table file is loaded

into tables in main memory when the payroll program is run. The payroll program searches the tables in memory to locate withholding amounts. No maintenance is required since the table is a reference file that is built one time at the beginning of the year. What organization should the table file employ?

22. An on-line maintenance program adds, changes, and deletes records in a master file interactively through on-line terminals. Each transaction is recorded in a transaction log file as part of on-line master file maintenance. Each record in the log file contains the date on which the modification took place, an identification (a key) of the master record that was affected, the type of maintenance activity applied (add, change, or delete), and the master record field that was modified. The log file provides an audit trail through which the transaction can be traced from origin to current appearance in the master file. What organization should the log file employ?

Chapter 2

CHAPTER CONTENTS

Pascal Records and Files

PREVIEW

THIS CHAPTER REVIEWS THE SYNTAX for declaring and accessing Pascal records and record variants. The chapter also reviews the syntax of external Pascal files; it explains the syntax for declaring them and the statements and standard procedures for creating and accessing them.

RECORD DATA TYPE

Many programming languages provide data types for representing data structures. Some programming languages, such as FORTRAN and BASIC, provide little beyond arrays and files for this purpose. Other programming languages, such as COBOL, PL/1, and Pascal, provide records in addition to arrays and files as data types.

Arrays are a useful structure for storing data of the same type; a single identifier and an index will access an array. **Parallel arrays** are the only facility available in FORTRAN and BASIC for storing data of differing types, and accessing parallel arrays is more complicated than accessing records. Each array must be accessed separately with the same index range to retrieve related information of different types. For example, a collection of inventory data might consist of a code, description, and price for each product. (Figure 2.1 shows such a collection.)

The inventory data could not be stored using multidimensional arrays because some items are character data, some are real data, and some are integer data. By implementing parallel arrays, however, each column of inventory data becomes a single one-dimensional array, and the same index range accesses all three arrays (columns) of data.

The declarations in Pascal for storing the inventory data of 50 entries using parallel arrays are as follows:

```
TYPE
    Name_20 = Packed Array [1..20] of Char;
VAR
    product_code          : Array [1..50] of Integer;
    product_description : Array [1..50] of Name_20;
    product_price         : Array [1..50] of Real;
```

The declarations allocate the memory as shown in Figure 2.2. The 50 product codes are stored in contiguous memory locations followed by 50 product descriptions followed by 50 product prices. The ith element of each array references the data about a particular product found in the ith row of the inventory table.

The Pascal statements needed to initialize the parallel arrays with the first entry of the inventory table are as follows:

```
product_code [1]          := 754;
product_description [1] := 'carburetor              ';
product_price [1]         := 12.95;
```

Figure 2.3 shows the result of initialization on memory. All the data in the parallel arrays could be printed in columnar form by implementing the following Pascal statements.

Product code	Product description	Product price
754	Carburetor	12.95
863	Muffler	51.95
915	Air filter	5.45

Figure 2.1
Collection of inventory data

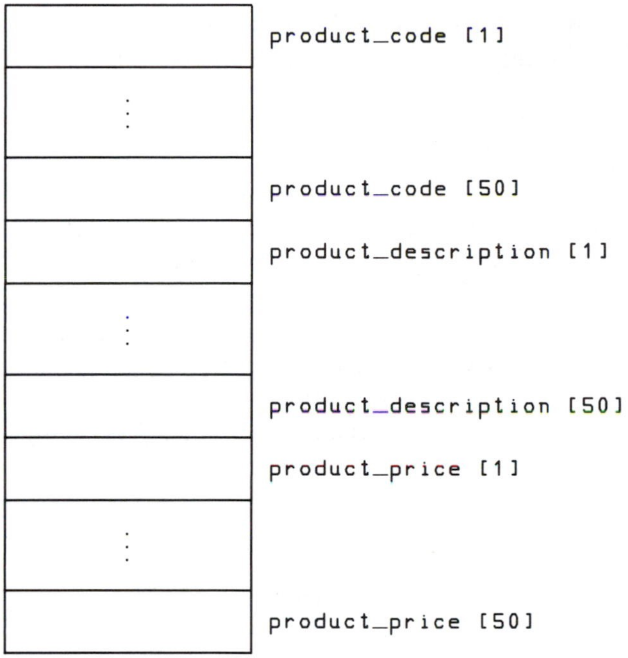

product_code [1]

⋮

product_code [50]

product_description [1]

⋮

product_description [50]

product_price [1]

⋮

product_price [50]

Figure 2.2
The inventory data in memory as parallel arrays

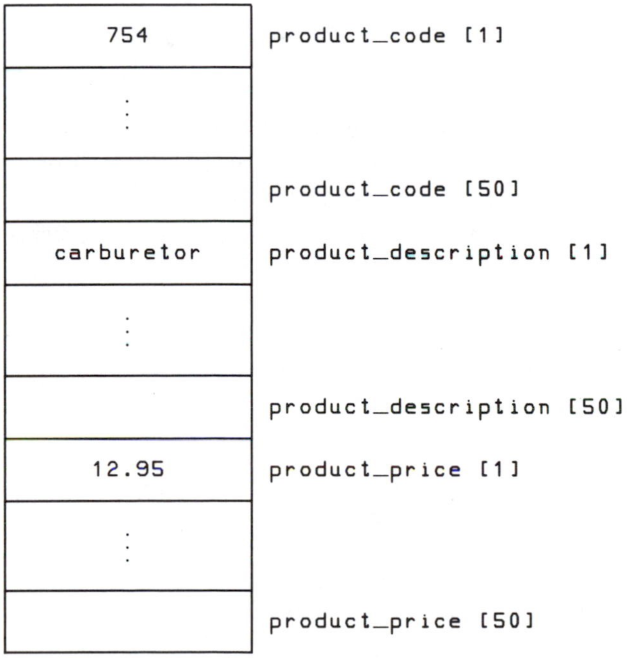

754	product_code [1]
⋮	
	product_code [50]
carburetor	product_description [1]
⋮	
	product_description [50]
12.95	product_price [1]
⋮	
	product_price [50]

Figure 2.3
The parallel arrays with one entry

```
For i := 1 To 50 Do
    Writeln (product_code [i],
                product_description [i],
                product_price [i]);
```

Since each identifier with a different data type is stored in a separate but parallel array, each identifier must be accessed using an index.

Definition

The **record data type** available in COBOL, PL/1, and Pascal allows the inventory data to be stored so that all data related to a particular product is in contiguous memory locations as one group of data. A reference to one record allows access to any piece of data about a particular product.

The **record data structure** is a collection of data items of different types accessed by a single name.

The format for the record data type in Pascal is as follows:

```
TYPE
    Record_Name =
        Record
            field_name_1 : Type;
            field_name_2 : Type;
                    .
                    .
                    .
            field_name_n : Type
        End;
```

Record_Name is a valid identifier name, field_name_i ($i = 1, \ldots, n$) is a valid identifier name and one of the components of the record data structure, and Type is any Pascal data type.

The declarations for storing the inventory data using the record data type are

```
TYPE
    Name_20 = Packed Array [1..20] of Char;
    Record_Entry =
        Record
            code        : Integer;
            description : Name_20;
            price       : Real;
        End;
VAR
    product : Record_Entry;
```

Operation on Records

The general form for reference to a field of the record consists of

```
Record_Name.field_name_i
```

where `Record_Name` is a valid record name, and `field_name_i` is the name of the ith component in the record data structure known as `Record_name`. The following Pascal code references the fields within the record and initializes the record data structure.

```
Read (product.code);
For i := 1 To 20 Do
    Read (product.description [i]);
Read (product.price);
```

Instead of parallel arrays an array of records would be more appropriate for storing the inventory data.

```
VAR
     products : Array [1..50] of Record_entry;
```

allocates storage for an inventory table of 50 entries. As Figure 2.4 shows, each entry consists of a product code (integer), a product description (20 characters), and a product price (real).

The general form for reference to a single record in the array

```
Record_Name [index]
```

allows access to all information about a particular product. Access to the ith field of a single record is the result of

```
Record_Name [index].field_name_i
```

The following valid Pascal statements initialize the first entry in the inventory table.

```
products [1].code        := 754;
products [1].description := 'carburetor
products [1].price       := 12.95;
```

Figure 2.5 shows the resulting memory. An array of records stores the inventory data about a product in contiguous memory locations (Figures 2.4 and 2.5). Parallel arrays store each piece of information in a different

Figure 2.4
The inventory data
stored as an array of
records

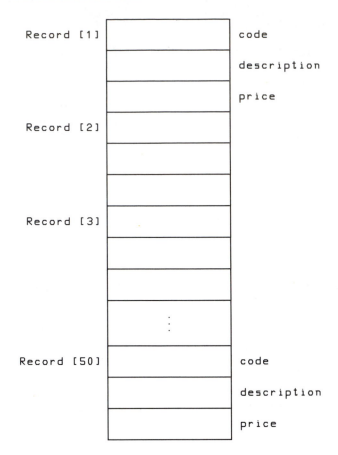

but parallel array; information is spread out over memory (Figures 2.2 and 2.3).

One of the advantages of the record data type for storing the inventory data over parallel arrays is that a record variable may be assigned to another record variable of the same type. For example, with the additional declaration

```
VAR
      new_record : Record_Entry;
```

the following Pascal statements input all the information concerning a new part into new_record:

```
Read  (new_record.code);
For i := 1 To 20 Do
     Read (new_record.description [i]);
Read (new_record.price);
```

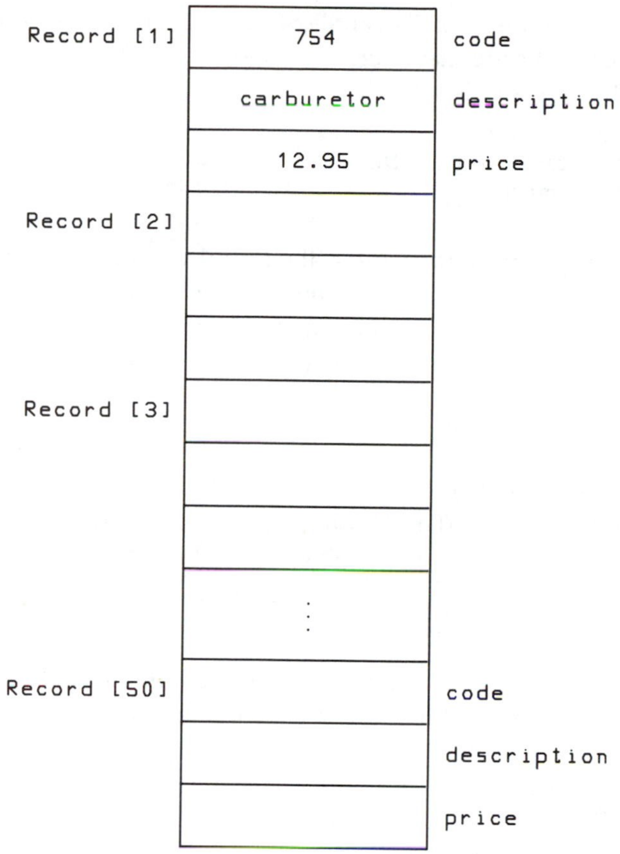

Record [1]	754	code
	carburetor	description
	12.95	price

Record [2]

Record [3]

⋮

Record [50]   code

description

price

Figure 2.5
The array of records
with one entry

The single assignment statement below stores the whole record of data in the array products:

```
products [i] := new_record;
```

The fact that the record data type allows the user to move a group of related data with a single reference makes records one of the most common data structures for storing related data.

With Statement

The advantage an array of records provides—being able to store a group of related data items of different types in contiguous memory locations— is offset by one glaring disadvantage: A reference to a particular data item becomes

```
Record_Name [ index ].field_name_i
```

The **With** statement in Pascal allows the record name to be specified once for a block of code that references fields within the record. The format for the With statement is

```
With Record_Name  Do
      statement
```

In the With format `Record_Name` is the record variable and may be indexed, and `statement` is any Pascal statement that includes references to a component of the record by using only the field name. The With statement can then be used to simplify references to the record `new_record`.

```
With new_record Do
Begin
     Read (code);
     For i := 1 To 20 Do
          Read (description [i]);
     Read (price);
End
```

The references to field names in the Read statements are components of the record `new_record` that the With statement specifies.

Scope of Identifiers

When references to more than one record variable inside the With block are necessary, the code must qualify the reference. For example, in the following Pascal code the assignment statement assigns to `code` in record `products [1]` the `code` in the record `new_record`.

```
With new_record Do
Begin
     Read (code);
     For i := 1 To 20 Do
          Read (description [i]);
     Read (price);
     products [1].code := code
End
```

Had the assignment statement been

```
code := code;
```

`new_record` would have been the record for both; therefore,

```
new_record.code := new_record.code
```

is redundant. The indexed record name `products [1]` had to be added as a qualifier to override the assumed record name stated in the With statement, `new_record`.

Since the record name listed in the With statement may be indexed, the initialization of the first entry of the symbol table is simplified:

```
With products [1] Do
Begin
    code := 754;
    description := 'carburetor          ';
    price := 12.95
End
```

Notice that the indexed record name is specified at the beginning of the block using the With statement and is assumed for all field name references within the block of code.

The following prints the entire symbol table:

```
For i := 1 To 50 Do
    With products [i] Do
        Writeln(code,
                description,
                price)
```

The For statement sets the value of i, and the With statement inside the For statement uses the current value of i. If the programmer transposed the For and With statements:

```
With products [i] Do
    For i := 1 To 50 Do
        Writeln(code,
                description,
                price)
```

an error would result since the value of i in the With statement would be undefined.

EXAMPLE 1: RECORDS

The ABC Company wishes to keep an inventory of all the products they sell. For each product the data to be stored includes a five-character product code, a 15-character product description, an integer indicating the quantity on hand, the unit price in dollars and cents, the reorder point as an integer, and an integer indicating the size of an outstanding order made to the manufacturer. A value of zero for outstanding order indicates that no outstanding order exists. The record description for each product is

```
TYPE
    Product =
        Record
            code                     : Packed Array [1..5] of Char;
            description              : Packed Array [1..15] of Char;
            quantity_on_hand         : Integer;
            unit_price               : Real;
            reorder_point            : Integer;
            outstanding_order_size   : Integer
        End;
```

If the ABC Company sells 10,000 different products, then an array of Product records is needed. The following is the declaration of the array.

```
VAR
        inventory : Array [1..10000] of Product;
```

Assuming each character uses 1 byte of memory, each integer uses 2 bytes of memory, and each real uses 4 bytes of memory, each record will use the following amounts of memory.

COMPONENT	SIZE IN BYTES
code	5
description	15
quantity_on_hand	2
unit_price	4
reorder_point	2
outstanding_order_size	2
	30

Each record will contain 30 bytes for each product. A total of 300,000 bytes will be needed to store information for 10,000 products. Should the requirement be larger than the main memory available, the programmer would have to store all 10,000 records on external storage devices, using files, with the result that the main memory would store only one record at a time. Files will be discussed at length later in this chapter.

EXAMPLE 2: RECORDS

Suppose the record data structure is used to store data concerning college students. Data on one student may consist of the student's name, address, and phone number. A sample declaration is

```
TYPE
     Student =
          Record
               name             : Packed Array [1..31] of Char;
               address          : Packed Array [1..50] of Char;
               phone_number  :  Integer
          End;
VAR
     one_student  :  Student;
```

The declaration allows 31 characters in name for last name, first name, and middle initial; address contains 50 characters, and phone_number stores the telephone number as an integer.

Since this is information about a college student, the record would probably contain two addresses: a home address and a campus address. The declaration of address should allow both addresses to be stored, and each address should contain up to 50 characters. A record data structure is appropriate for both addresses.

```
TYPE
     Addresses =
          Record
               home    :  Packed Array [1..50] of Char;
               campus  :  Packed Array [1..50] of Char
          End;
```

The record type, Student, is

```
TYPE
     Student =
          Record
               name             : Packed Array [1..31] of Char;
               address          : Addresses;
               phone_number  :  Integer
          End;
VAR
     one_student  :  Student;
```

Moving the type declaration Addresses inside the Student record declaration provides a clearer picture of the record being declared and the arrangement of components in memory. The following structure offers additional improvements.

```
TYPE
    Student =
        Record
            name      : Packed Array [1..31] of Char;
            address :
                Record
                    home    : Packed Array [1..50] of Char;
                    campus : Packed Array [1..50] of Char
                End;
            phone_number : Integer
        End;
VAR
    one_student : Student;
```

The record containing both home and campus addresses is nested inside the record data type, Student. The home and campus addresses would be accessed as a group with

```
    one_student.address
```

or individually accessed with

```
    one_student.address.home
    one_student.address.campus
```

The record name one_student contains the component address which in turn is a record name containing the components home and campus. These relationships hold true whether the nested record data structure is used literally or the type Addresses is defined and used.

The component name could also be viewed as a group of three components: a last name of 15 characters, a first name of 15 characters, and a middle initial. Consider substituting the following record data structure for the declaration of name:

```
    name :
        Record
            last    : Packed Array [1..15] of Char;
            first   : Packed Array [1..15] of Char;
            middle : Char
        End;
```

If the programmer uses nested records, the record declaration would look like this:

```
TYPE
    Student =
        Record
            name :
                Record
                    last    : Packed Array [1..15] of Char;
                    first   : Packed Array [1..15] of Char;
                    middle : Char
                End;
            address :
                Record
                    home   : Packed Array [1..50] of Char;
                    campus : Packed Array [1..50] of Char
                End;
            phone_number : Integer
        End;
VAR
    one_student : Student;
```

The resulting description consists of three components: name, address, and phone_number. The first two components are groups of components. The component name, for example, is a group containing three components: last, first, and middle. The following accesses the three components.

```
one_student.name.last
one_student.name.first
one_student.name.middle
```

The address component is a record of two components: home and campus which are accessed by

```
one_student.address.home
one_student.address.campus
```

Some computers do not allow the data type Integer to contain the 10 decimal digits necessary for the phone number. In this case the programmer declares a record to contain the three-digit area code, the three-digit exchange, and the four-digit number.

```
phone_number :
    Record
        area_code : Integer;
        exchange  : Integer;
        number    : Integer
    End;
```

The record description `Student` with the expanded phone number is now

```
TYPE
    Student =
        Record
            name :
                Record
                    last    : Packed Array [1..15] of Char;
                    first   : Packed Array [1..15] of Char;
                    middle  : Char
                End;
            address :
                Record
                    home    : Packed Array [1..50] of Char;
                    campus  : Packed Array [1..50] of Char
                End;
            phone_number :
                Record
                    area_code  : Integer;
                    exchange   : Integer;
                    number     : Integer
                End;
        End;
```

The following are valid Pascal accesses of the phone number components.

```
one_student.phone_number.area_code
one_student.phone_number.exchange
one_student.phone_number.number
```

The nested record declarations could be broken apart or modularized to facilitate parameter passage of a record structure and declaration of more than one variable of the same record type. Using this technique on `Student` results in a `Type` declaration for each component of `one_student` that is referenced from within the declaration of `Student`.

```
TYPE
    Names =
        Record
            last    : Packed Array [1..15] of Char;
            first   : Packed Array [1..15] of Char;
            middle  : Char
        End;
    Addresses =
        Record
            home    : Packed Array [1..50] of Char;
            campus  : Packed Array [1..50] of Char
        End;
```

```
     Phone =
         Record
             area_code  :  Integer;
             exchange   :  Integer;
             number     :  Integer
         End;
     Student =
         Record
             name           :  Names;
             address        :  Addresses;
             phone_number   :  Phone
         End;
 VAR
     one_student  :  Student;
```

The declarations allow the types Names, Addresses, Phone, and Student to be referenced easily in formal parameter lists and to be referenced several times in the VAR section of the program. All accesses to components must include the record name of all nested records to produce a fully qualified reference.

To make Student an appropriate data structure for storing information about a college student, the programmer must allocate additional memory within the record to store the student's class schedule. Suppose a college student may enroll for as many as six courses, and the data concerning each course includes a course number (six characters), a room number (four characters), and a meeting time (an integer). An appropriate data structure for storing the class schedule is an array of six records where each record contains data pertaining to a course. The following is the declaration for one class.

```
 TYPE
     Class =
         Record
             course_number  :  Packed Array [1..6] of Char;
             room_number    :  Packed Array [1..4] of Char;
             meeting_time   :  Integer
         End;
```

The class schedule could be added as the fourth component of the record Student in this manner:

```
 TYPE
     Student =
         Record
             name           :  Names;
             address        :  Addresses;
             phone_number   :  Phone;
             classes        :  Array [1..6] of Class
         End;
```

```
VAR
     one_student : Student;
```

The valid form for referencing data pertaining to the ith course is:

```
one_student.classes [i].course_number
one_student.classes [i].room_number
one_student.classes [i].meeting_time
```

Record Size

The declaration

```
VAR
     one_student : Student;
```

allocates storage for data concerning only one student but totals several bytes. Assuming each character uses 1 byte of memory and each integer uses 2 bytes of memory, the four components of one_student use the following amounts of memory.

COMPONENT	SIZE IN BYTES
name	31
address	100
phone_number	6
classes	72
	209

Consider the array that would result if data were collected for 10,000 college students.

```
VAR
     all_students : Array [1..10000] of Student;
```

This array of 10,000 records would require 2,090,000 bytes of memory! Computers with limited memory capacities would not be able to allocate an array of 10,000 records; the programmer would have to use files to store the records on external storage, and only data concerning one student could be brought into main memory at a time. Files would also provide permanent storage for the 10,000 records. Recall that main memory is volatile. If the array of 10,000 records is not stored in files, the records are lost after the program that allocated the array is executed.

Variant Records

Sometimes additional fields are required in some records in the file but not in others. The presence of these additional fields depends on the value of other fields within the record. For example, in Record Example 2, home address and campus address would be the same for students living at home. Why store the same address twice? For those students with the same address for home and campus, only one address need be stored; for all other students, both the home and campus address is required. Variant record types in Pascal allow for additional fields (the **variant part** of the record) to be specified according to the value of another field in the record. A record containing a variant part is a **variant record**.

The variant part of a record, which must follow the fixed part, is specified using a version of the Case statement. The format for the variant record type in Pascal is

```
Case identifier : Type of
    variant_1;
    variant_2;
    variant_3;
        .
        .
        .
    variant_i
```

The tag field `identifier` is the data type tested in the Case and determines which `variant_i` is present within the record. One or more constants followed by a list of declarations in parentheses characterize `variant_i`.

```
constant_1 [,constant_i]... : ( [field_list] )
```

A valid constant, `constant_i` is of the type listed in the Case. The `field-list`, if present, consists of any Pascal declarations, including variant record types. Notice that no corresponding End statement is required for the Case; a record may have only one variant part so no other declarations may follow a variant part.

The record type `Addresses` from Record Example 2 was a fixed record type.

```
TYPE
    Addresses =
        Record
            home    : Packed Array [1..50] of Char;
            campus  : Packed Array [1..50] of Char
        End;
```

To alter `Addresses` to contain a fixed part of the home address and a variant part of campus address is simple. In the alteration that follows, the variant part is present only if the home and campus addresses are not the same.

```
TYPE
    Addresses =
        Record
            home : Packed Array [1..50] of Char;
            Case same_as_campus : Boolean of
                TRUE  : ();
                FALSE : (campus : Packed Array [1..50] of Char)
        End;
```

The variant part depends on the value of `same_as_campus`, which is the **tag field**. If the value of `same_as_campus` is TRUE, the record contains only the fixed part, `home`, as indicated by the empty parentheses; otherwise, the record contains the fixed part, `home`, and the variant part, `campus`. The tag field, `same_as_campus`, is part of the record and must be initialized to one of the values in the Case constant list before being written to a file. The value of the tag field must be interrogated before the fields in the variant part may be accessed.

EXAMPLE 3: RECORDS

A record structure describing people would include some fixed fields—name, sex, date of birth, number of dependents, and marital status—as well as some variant fields that were dependent on marital status. If the person is married, for example, the record might include the spouse's name. If the person is single, the spouse's name would not be included.

```
TYPE
    Mmddyy      = Packed Array [1..6] of Char;
    Name_Type   = Packed Array [1..25] of Char;
    Status_type = (DIVORCED, MARRIED, SINGLE, WIDOWED);
    Person =
        Record
            name                  : Name_Type;
            sex                   : (FEMALE, MALE);
            date_of_birth         : Mmddyy;
            number_of_dependents  : Integer;
            Case marital_status   : Status_Type of
                MARRIED  : (spouse_name : Name_Type);
                DIVORCED : (date_of_divorce : Mmddyy);
                SINGLE   : ();
                WIDOWED  : (date_of_death : Mmddyy)
        End;
```

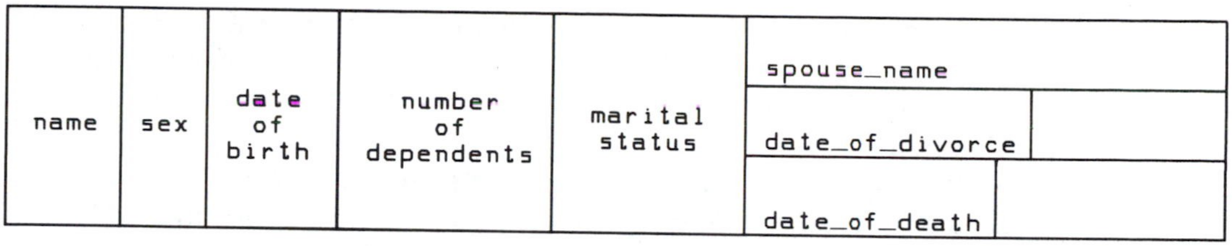

name	sex	date of birth	number of dependents	marital status	spouse_name	
					date_of_divorce	
					date_of_death	

Figure 2.6
The physical view of storage for a variant record

This record structure determines that the description of a married person contains six elements:

1. `name`
2. `sex`
3. `date_of_birth`
4. `number_of_dependents`
5. `marital_status = MARRIED`
6. `spouse_name`

The description of a single person contains only five elements:

1. `name`
2. `sex`
3. `date_of_birth`
4. `number_of_dependents`
5. `marital_status = SINGLE`

Figure 2.6 provides a physical view of the storage requirements for the record `Person`. Storage is allocated for every identifier in the record. The storage for each constant in the variant part of the record is overlayed to conserve storage space. As a result the tag field should be checked before attempting to access any data; checking the tag field ensures that the data will be interpreted as the correct type of data. In this example, a test of the tag field, `marital_status`, would need to yield `MARRIED` before the user could reference the variant field `spouse_name`.

CASE STUDY 2.1

Problem

Write a program that will read test scores and scores for programming assignments (programs scores) for a class. The input will be in the form of student identification (four characters), exam 1 score, exam 2 score, and programs score. A -1 for exam 1 score, exam 2 score, and programs score indicates that the student has dropped the class. Store all of the information in an array. Include a field for total score, which your program will compute. Do not include -1 scores in the total.

Write a function that, when passed a score and an average for the set of scores, will return a letter grade based on the average for the total score. Assign

A to all who are at least 13% above the average
B to those who are above the average but who do not merit As
C to those who are above 19% below the average but who do not merit As or Bs
D to those who are above 26% below the average but who do not merit As, Bs, or Cs
F to those below the D cutoff.

The program will print the identification, the exam 1 score, the exam 2 score, the programs score, the total score, and the letter grade for each student. Print out the average for the total scores. There will be no more than 200 sets of scores in the input file.

Top-Down Design

Input Input no more than 200 sets of students scores consisting of identification, exam 1 score, exam 2 score, and programs score.

Output The output should contain identification, exam 1 score, exam 2 score, programs score, total score, and letter grade for each student. Also compute the total score average.

Data Structures Allocate an array of records to store identification, exam 1 scores, exam 2 scores, programs scores, and total scores.

Pseudocode

```
Level 0
    sum_of_total_scores ← 0
    number_of_students ← 0
While not Eof and arrays not full
    Get id, exam_1_score, exam_2_score, programs_score
    Add_Up_Total_Score
    Sum_Total_Scores
average ← sum_of_total_scores / number_of_students
```

For number_of_students
    Find_Grade (score, average)
    Print id, exam _1_score, exam_2_score, programs_score,
      total_score, grade

Level 1

Add_Up_Total_Score
total_score ← 0
If exam_1_score not = −1
Then total_score ← total_score + exam_1_score
If exam_ 2 _score not = −1
Then total_score ← total_score + exam_2_score
If programs_score not = −1
Then total_score ← total_score + programs_score

Sum_Total_Scores
number_of_students ← number_of_students +1
sum_of_total_scores ← sum_of_total_scores + total_score

Find Grade
For number_of_students
    If score > 13% above average
    Then grade ← 'A'
    Else If score > average
        Then grade ← 'B'
        Else If score > 19% below average
            Then grade ← 'C'
            Else If score > 26% below average
                Then grade ← 'D'
                Else grade ← 'F'

Solution

The following program, which uses an array of records as the data structures, is the solution to this problem.

```
PROGRAM Grading(input,output);
TYPE
    Char_Array = Packed Array[1..4] of Char;
    Student =
        Record
            exam_1_score,
            exam_2_score   : Integer;
            identification : Char_Array;
            program_score,
            total_score    : Integer
        End;
```

```pascal
VAR
    class               : Array [1..200] of Student;
    count               : Integer;
    grade               : Char;
    i                   : Integer;
    number_of_students  : Integer;
    sum                 : Integer;
    total_average       : Real;
    FUNCTION Find_Grade(score : Integer; average : Real):Char;
    BEGIN { Find_Grade }
        If score >= (1.13 * average) Then
            Find_Grade := 'A'
        Else
            If score > average Then
                Find_Grade := 'B'
            Else
                If score > (average - (0.19 * average)) Then
                    Find_Grade := 'C'
                Else
                    If score > (average - (0.26 * average)) Then
                        Find_Grade := 'D'
                    Else
                        Find_Grade := 'F'
    END; { Find_Grade }

BEGIN { Grading }
    Write('ID':5,'EXAM 1':12,'EXAM 2':10,'PROGRAMS':11);
    Writeln('TOTAL':9,'GRADE':8);
    Writeln;
    count := 0;
    sum := 0;
    While (count <= 200)
    And Not Eof Do
    Begin
        count := count + 1;
        With class [count] Do
        Begin
            For i := 1 To 4 Do
                Read(identification [i]);
            Readln(exam_1_score, exam_2_score, program_score);
            total_score := 0;
            If exam_1_score <> -1 Then
                total_score := total_score + exam_1_score;
            If exam_2_score <> -1 Then
                total_score := total_score + exam _2_score;
            If program_score <> -1 Then
                total_score := total_score + program_score;
            sum := sum + total_score
        End
    End;
```

```
number_of_students := count;
total_average := sum / count;
For count := 1 To number_of_students Do
     With class [count] Do
     Begin
          grade := Find_Grade (total_score, total_average);
          Writeln(' ':2, identification:4,
                  ' ':7,exam_1_score:2,
                  ' ':8,exam_2_score:2,
                  ' ':8,program_score:2,
                  ' ':8,total_score:3,
                  ' ':8,grade);
     End
END. { Grading }
```

In the program Grading, which uses an array of records, the reference to a particular record contains an index. The index is specified once at the beginning of the With statement, so all references within the block of code are to the field name only.

FILES

The amount of main memory necessary to store large amounts of data within a program is often larger than the memory available. Data that are stored in a program are volatile; the data will remain in main memory only while the program is running. When the program is finished running, the memory space is allocated to another program—all data stored in the first program are lost. The amount of storage within a program is limited by the size of main memory (unless virtual memory is available). For these reasons, a large collection of data is often stored on **external files,** secondary storage devices that are nonvolatile. The external file is a collection of data in which each element is of the same type. External files may be thought of as arrays stored on secondary storage devices. Unlike arrays, however, only one element of the file can be accessed at any one time; the number of elements in the file may vary and need not be specified in the declarations.

A Pascal file is a collection of components having the same structure and is terminated by an end-of-file marker (⟨eof⟩). A file may consist of characters, integers, reals, arrays, or records. A Pascal file is read or written one component at a time. Two types of file access are available in most versions of Pascal: sequential (ISO standard) and random (nonstandard). Sequential access means that the elements of the file can only be accessed in sequential order from beginning to end. Random access, which is not part of the Pascal ISO standard but is available in many versions of Pascal, means that the elements of the file can be accessed in any order. This chapter illustrates sequential access, and Part II offers detailed discussion of this concept. Part III covers random access at length.

Format Definition

The declaration of a file in Pascal is

```
VAR
      file_identifier : File of type;
```

In the declaration type may be Integer, Real, Char, Boolean, Array, Packed Array, Set, or Record. The type describes one element or **component** of the file.

The following declaration

```
VAR
      exam_scores : File of Integer;
```

declares a file named exam_scores in which each component is an integer representing one exam score. To complete the declaration the file identifier, exam_scores, must also appear in the program header.

```
PROGRAM Sample (exam_scores);
```

Since a file is stored on secondary storage devices, the declaration does not specify length as the declaration of an array does. In a file declaration only the type of each component is specified.

The same formats store data in an external file on a secondary storage device and in main memory. For example, if an integer data item is stored in a word of main memory, a file declared as a File of Integer will have a word of storage for each file component. If a real data item occupies two words of main memory, a file declared as a File of Real will have two words of storage for each file component. All data types stored in an external file are stored using the same format as data items stored internally in main memory. External files are, therefore, an extension of main memory.

Operations on Files

All input/output commands use a **location indicator** that specifies the current component of the file being accessed and a **file buffer**, which is a variable in main memory that contains the current component that may be accessed at any time. The file buffer may be accessed as a variable as **file_identifier^**, where **file_identifier** is the name of the declared file. A file is empty when created; it contains no file components, only an ⟨eof⟩ marker. Components may be added to the file, they may be examined, and—if random access is available—the components may be modified.

An empty file is created by the standard Pascal procedure Rewrite:

```
Rewrite (file_identifier)
```

The `Rewrite` opens the file named `file_identifier` as an output file, places an ⟨eof⟩ marker in the empty file with the location indicator positioned at the ⟨eof⟩ marker, and allocates storage for a file buffer variable. The storage allocated for the file buffer is the size of one component of the file. The result of the execution of `Rewrite` is shown in Figure 2.7.

The file `exam_scores`, declared earlier as `File of Integer` may be created as an empty file by the statement

```
Rewrite (exam_scores)
```

The file buffer variable, `exam_scores^`, is allocated storage for one integer (the component type). If the file `exam_scores` had been used before and contained any components, the file contents would be erased by this command.

Once the empty file is created, a component may be added at the end of the file immediately prior to the ⟨eof⟩ marker. `Rewrite` correctly positions the location indicator at the ⟨eof⟩ marker; the empty file is now ready for insertions.

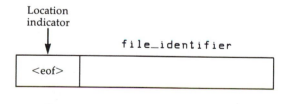

Location
indicator

file_identifier

⟨eof⟩

File
buffer

Figure 2.7
Result of `Rewrite`
`(file_identifier)`

Adding a component to the file involves the file buffer variable (file_identifier^) and the standard Pascal output procedure Put in a two-step process:

1. The data to be output to the file, whose type is the same as a component of the output file, must be stored in the file buffer variable (file_identifier^).

2. The data in the file buffer variable (one component of the file) is written to the external file.

The first step—loading the data into the file buffer variable—is accomplished by the assignment statement

```
file_identifier^ := data
```

The type of data is the same as the component type of the declared file named file_identifier. Figure 2.8(a) depicts the movement of data into the file buffer variable.

The second step—physically transferring the file buffer contents to the external file on a secondary storage device—involves the output procedure Put.

```
Put (file_identifier)
```

The file buffer contents are written to the file, the location indicator is advanced, and the ⟨eof⟩ marker is placed at the end of the file again. Figure 2.8(b) depicts the movement of the buffer contents to the external file. Each time a new element is written, it is written to the end of the file. The location indicator advances, and the ⟨eof⟩ marker is placed at the end of the file.

A component (the integer 92) may be added to the declared file exam_scores with two statements:

```
exam_scores^ := 92;
Put (exam_scores)
```

The results are shown in Figure 2.9. The integer 92 is stored in the file buffer with the assignment statement (Figure 2.9a). Put copies the file buffer contents to the file (Figure 2.9b). The file buffer variable, exam_scores^, is undefined after execution of Put.

Once a file has been created and components added, the file must be closed. The close operation is automatic in many versions of Pascal but must be issued explicitly in others. Some versions of Pascal use a standard procedure, Close, to accomplish this operation. The procedure Close sets the

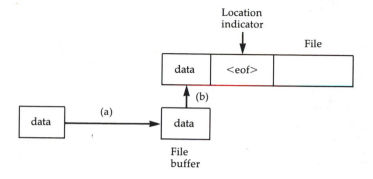

Figure 2.8
File output operations

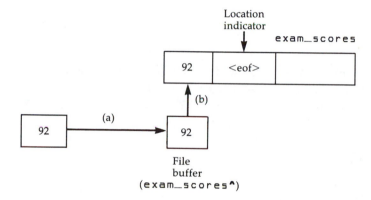

specified input or output text files to a closed state, thus disabling further input or output associated with the file until a subsequent Reset or Rewrite is performed. Close is available on some Pascal compilers and may be required between a Rewrite and subsequent Reset issued to the same file. Standard Pascal will allow consecutive Rewrite and Reset calls to the same file without Close between them. (Reset checks to see if the file is already open and issues Close before performing Reset.) On all Pascal compilers, Close is issued automatically for all files open at program termination. Close records the file name in the file directory so that it may be located later.

A Pascal file may be input using the standard Pascal procedure Reset.

```
Reset (file_identifier)
```

Reset opens the file named `file_identifier` for access, positions the location indicator at the first component of the file, copies the first component of the file into the file buffer variable (`file_identifier^`), and

Figure 2.10
Result of Reset
(file_identifier)

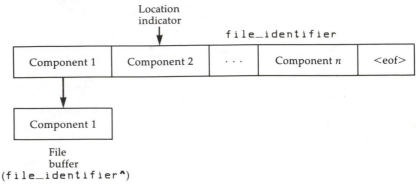

moves the location indicator to the second component of the file. The result of the execution of the Reset is shown in Figure 2.10.

The file exam_scores, which has one component (as Figure 2.9 shows), may be opened for access by the statement

```
Reset (exam_scores)
```

As a result the first component of the file (92) is copied to the file buffer, and the location indicator moves to the second component (the ⟨eof⟩ marker). Figure 2.11 shows the result of the execution of this statement.

After a file has been reset, the file may be accessed to input one component at a time. The program must incorporate two steps to input a component from a file:

1. The contents of the file buffer variable in main memory must move into a variable in the variable list in the program.

2. The next component from the file must move into the file buffer variable.

The Reset procedure loads the first component of the file into the file buffer. The first step of the input process copies the first component from the file buffer into a variable in the program using the assignment statement

```
variable_identifier := file_identifier^
```

The declared variable variable_identifier is the same type as the file component. Figure 2.12(a) illustrates the input of data from the file buffer.

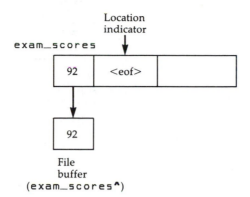

Figure 2.11
Result of Reset
(exam_scores)

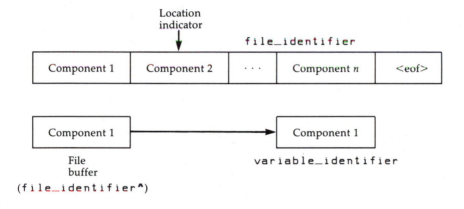

(a) First step of input operation

Figure 2.12
File input operation

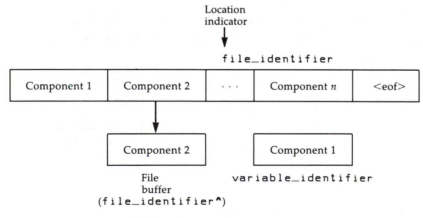

(b) Second step of input operation

Figure 2.13
File input operation
for file
`exam_scores`

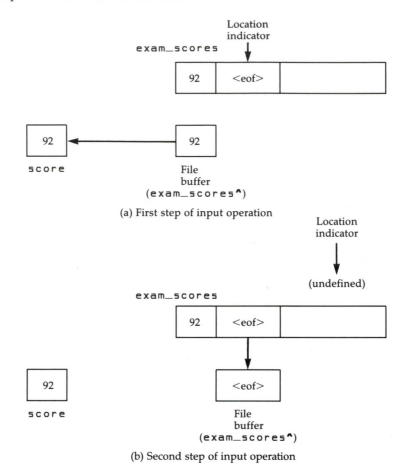

(a) First step of input operation

(b) Second step of input operation

The second step of the input process uses the standard Pascal procedure `Get` to copy the next component indicated by the location indicator into the file buffer.

```
Get (file_identifier)
```

Figure 2.12(b) illustrates how the file buffer is refreshed during input. `Get` leaves the file buffer ready for the repeat of the two-step input process.

After the file `exam_scores` has been reset, a component (an integer) may be accessed with the two statements

```
score := exam_scores^;
Get (exam_scores)
```

Note that `score` has been declared an integer—the same as the file component type. The results of the execution are shown in Figure 2.13(a). Reset loads the first component into the file buffer variable and positions the location indicator to the second component of the file. The first step of the input operation (assignment statement) copies the file buffer contents into the variable `score`. In Figure 2.13(b) `Get` fills the file buffer with the component indicated by the location indicator (the second component) and moves the location indicator to the next component of the file. If there is no next component, the location indicator is undefined.

A program that is reading a file needs to be able to detect when the end of the file has been reached. The standard Pascal Boolean function Eof checks the contents of the file buffer variable.

```
Eof (file_identifier)
```

If the file buffer contains the ⟨eof⟩ marker, which indicates that the last component of the file has been accessed, the function `Eof` returns `TRUE`; otherwise, function `Eof` returns `FALSE`. For example, in Figure 2.13, after the first component of the file `exam_scores` has been input, the file buffer contains ⟨eof⟩. The following program segment uses the function `Eof` to determine when the last component has been accessed.

```
   PROGRAM Sample (exam_scores);
   VAR
        exam_scores : File of Integer;
        score        : Integer;
   BEGIN
1       Reset (exam_scores);
2       While Not Eof (exam_scores) Do
3       Begin
4           score := exam_scores^;
5           Get (exam_scores);
6       End
   END.
```

`Reset` in line 1 fills the file buffer with the first component (92) and positions the location indicator at the second component (⟨eof⟩). The function `Eof` in line 2 looks in the file buffer and does not find the ⟨eof⟩ marker; `Eof` returns `FALSE`. The `While` loop is entered, the file buffer contents are copied into `score` (line 4), and the file buffer is filled with the next component (⟨eof⟩). The result is that the location indicator (line 5) is undefined. The function `Eof` (line 2) is called again and returns `TRUE` since the file buffer does contain ⟨eof⟩. The `While` loop terminates.

Text Files

One standard file type, Text, exists in Pascal and is defined as

```
Type
     Text = File of Char;
```

Pascal provides two standard files that are predeclared as Text files: input and output. Input is the standard input medium to Pascal programs (the keyboard), and output is the standard output medium from Pascal programs (the CRT screen or printer). The standard files, input and output, need not be declared, because they are predeclared files in Pascal, but they must appear in the program header when used.

```
PROGRAM Sample (input, output);
```

When input is in the program heading, a Reset is automatically issued for the file. Similarly, when output is listed in the program heading, a Rewrite is automatically issued for the file. The standard procedures Reset and Rewrite must not be used with the two standard files input and output; the procedures are called automatically.

The data in a **text** file, regardless of data type, are stored as characters; the data stored in a **non-text** file are stored according to the internal storage formats for each data type. The characters in a text file are organized into lines that are much like the lines of data on a CRT screen. An end of line marker (⟨eoln⟩) is stored after each line of data. The end of a file is marked with an end of file marker (⟨eof⟩). That is, the last line of data is followed by an ⟨eoln⟩ marker, then an ⟨eof⟩ marker.

Additional text files may be declared using the predefined type Text.

```
VAR
     new_file : Text;
```

The program heading must also contain new_file.

```
Program Sample (input, output, new_file);
```

Several standard procedures and functions are available in Pascal for accessing text files only.

```
Write (file_identifier, output_list)
Read (file_identifier, variable_list)
Writeln (file_identifier, output_list)
Readln (file_identifier, variable_list)
Eoln (file_identifier)
```

The parameter output_list is a list of variables, constants, or expressions of information to output; variable_list is a list of variables (not constants or expressions) that are to be initialized during input.

The two steps required during an output operation can be abbreviated for text files by using Write,

```
Write (file_identifier, data)
```

which by definition is equivalent to

```
file_identifier^ := data converted to characters;
Put (file_identifier)
```

The data written to a text file must be character data because the definition of text is File of Char. Since the items listed in the output_list may be of any type, the noncharacter data listed in the output list are converted from internal to character form before being stored in the buffer. The statements

```
Rewrite (new_text);
Write (new_text, 95)
```

will create new_text as an empty file, automatically convert the integer 95 to the character string '95', and output to new_text.

The two steps performed during an input operation can be abbreviated for text files by using Read,

```
Read (file_identifier, variable)
```

which by definition is equivalent to

```
variable := character data converted to internal form;
Get (file_identifier)
```

The data input from the text file are in character form and are automatically converted to internal form according to the type of variable.

If the text file new_text is closed and opened with

```
Close (new_text);
Reset (new_text);
```

the data in the file may then be accessed with the Read procedure.

```
Read (new_text, number)
```

The variable `number` is declared as an integer. To form an integer in the variable `number`, the characters in the text file are input—one at a time—and converted to internal integers until a blank or nondigit character is found. Since the data in `new_text` are the character string '95', the character 9 is input, converted to an integer 9, then multiplied by 10. The next character, 5, is input, converted to an integer 5, and added to the previous calculation to form the integer 95 in internal format in the variable number.

`Write` and `Read` may contain a list of items rather than just one item. In that case the steps described above are repeated until all items in the list have been handled.

Since characters in a text file are grouped into lines of characters and terminated by ⟨eoln⟩, three standard Pascal procedures deal with the ⟨eoln⟩ marker. The `Writeln` procedure,

```
Writeln (file_identifier, output_list)
```

performs the same steps as `Write`. In addition `Writeln` will output an ⟨eoln⟩ marker (usually a carriage return and line feed) to the output file. This causes the next output to start on a new line in the output file. The `Readln` procedure,

```
Readln (file_identifier, variable_list)
```

performs the same steps as `Read`, and when finished it will move the location indicator in the file to the first character after the next ⟨eoln⟩ marker. The first character following the ⟨eoln⟩ is copied to the file buffer and the location indicator moves to the second character on the line. This positions the location indicator at the beginning of the next line of data. The next `Read` or `Readln` will input data using the file buffer and location indicator. A `Readln` with no variable list will move the first character following the next ⟨eoln⟩ marker to the file buffer and advance the location indicator.

A program that is reading a text file needs to determine when the end of a line of data has been reached. The standard Pascal function `Eoln`,

```
Eoln (file_identifier)
```

checks the contents of the file buffer variable. If the file buffer contains the ⟨eoln⟩ marker, which indicates that the end of this line of data has been reached, the function `Eoln` returns TRUE; otherwise, `Eoln` returns FALSE. The following program segment uses `Eoln` to read the text file `new_text` (containing 95 ⟨eoln⟩) and to determine when the last character of the line has been accessed.

```
    PROGRAM Sample (new_text);
    VAR
        ch         : Char;
        new_text : Text;
    BEGIN
1       Reset (new_text);
2       While Not Eoln (new_text) Do
3           Read (new_text, ch);
4       Close (new_text);
    END.
```

Reset in line 1 fills the file buffer with the first character (9) from the file and positions the location indicator at the second component (5). The function Eoln in line 2 looks in the file buffer and does not find the ⟨eoln⟩ marker, so it returns FALSE. The While body is entered, the file buffer contents are copied into ch, and the file buffer is filled with the next character (5). The location indicator now points to the ⟨eoln⟩ marker (line 3). The function Eoln is called again (line 2), and again it returns FALSE. The While body is entered, ch receives the '5' in the file buffer, the file buffer receives the ⟨eoln⟩ marker, and the location indicator is undefined. The function Eoln is called, and it returns FALSE since the file buffer now contains ⟨eoln⟩. The While loop terminates.

A file containing several lines of data may be accessed by a program using Reset, Read, Eof, and Eoln.

```
    PROGRAM Sample (new_text);
    VAR
        ch         : Char;
        new_text : Text;
    BEGIN
        Reset (new_text);
        While Not Eof (new_text) Do
        Begin
            While Not Eoln (new_text) Do
                Read (new_text, ch);
            Readln (new_text)
        End
    END.
```

Readln is required after the While Not Eoln loop to skip over the ⟨eoln⟩ marker, move the first character of the next line into the file buffer, and reposition the location indicator. While Not Eoln and Readln are executed until the ⟨eof⟩ marker is in the file buffer.

For the standard external files input and output, the file name need not be specified. The name input is the assumed file name for Read,

Readln, Eof, and Eoln; output is the assumed file name for Write, and Writeln. The programmer must specify the file name of additional external text files to override these defaults.

When using the standard external file input,

```
Read (file_identifier, variable_list)
Readln (file_identifier, variable_list)
Eoln (file_identifier)
Eof (file_identifier)
```

may be simplified as

```
Read (variable_list)
Readln (variable_list)
Eoln
Eof
```

Reset is performed automatically. Similarly, when using the standard external file output,

```
Write (file_identifier, output_list)
Writeln (file_identifier, output_list)
```

may be simplified as

```
Write (output_list)
Writeln (output_list)
```

Rewrite is performed automatically.

The following program inputs exam scores from the standard input and creates a non-text file of exam scores.

```
  PROGRAM Create (input, exam_scores);
  VAR
      exam_scores : File of Integer;
      one_score   : Integer;
  BEGIN
1     Rewrite (exam_scores);
2     While Not Eof Do  { Eof (input) }
3     Begin
4         Read (one_score);
5         exam_score^ := one_score;
6         Put (exam_scores)
7     End; { While }
8     Close (exam_scores)
  END.
```

Read in line 4 accepts a value in character form from the keyboard, converts it to an internal integer, and stores it in one_score. Statements 5 and 6 perform the same steps as the procedure Write for text files with the exception that no conversion is necessary. Some versions of Pascal define Write for all types of files, so lines 5 and 6 are simplified as:

```
Write (exam_scores, one_score)
```

The file exam_scores may be accessed and output to the CRT screen using the following program.

```
PROGRAM List (exam_scores, output);
VAR
     exam_scores : File of Integer;
     one_score   : Integer;
BEGIN
1     Reset (exam_scores);
2     While Not Eof (exam_scores) Do
3     Begin
4         one_score := exam_scores^;
5         Get (exam_scores);
6         Writeln (one_score)
7     End { While }
END.
```

Statements 4 and 5 input a score from the file exam_scores without conversion; it is already in internal form. Statement 6 converts the score to a character string and writes on the CRT screen.

Some versions of Pascal define the Read procedure for all types of files, so lines 4 and 5 are simplified as

```
Read (exam_scores, one_score)
```

CASE STUDY 2.2

In Record Example 2 an array of 10,000 student records required more main memory than available. A common solution is to store the 10,000 records on an external file and access each record one at a time. The declarations of a program that creates a file of records is shown overleaf.

```
TYPE
  . Names =
      Record
          last   : Packed Array [1..15] of Char;
          first  : Packed Array [1..15] of Char;
          middle : Char
      End;
    Addresses =
      Record
          home   : Packed Array [1..50] of Char;
          campus : Packed Array [1..50] of Char
      End;
    Phone =
      Record
          area_code : Integer;
          exchange  : Integer;
          number    : Integer
      End;
    Class =
      Record
          course_number : Packed Array [1..6] of Char;
          room_number   : Packed Array [1..4] of Char;
          meeting_time  : Integer
      End;
    Student =
      Record
          name         : Names;
          address      : Addresses;
          phone_number : Phone;
          classes      : Array [1..6] of Class
      End;
VAR
    student_file : File of Student;
    one_student  : Student;
```

The student file could be created from a text file (input) with the following program body.

```
BEGIN
    Rewrite (student_file);
    While Not Eof Do      { Eof(input) }
    Begin     { input info on one student }
        With one_student Do
        Begin
            With name Do
            Begin
                For i := 1 to 15 Do     { i : Integer }
                    Read (last [i]);
                For i := 1 To 15 Do
                    Read (first [i]);
```

```
                    Read(middle)
                End; { with name }

                With address Do
                Begin
                    For i := 1 To 50 Do
                        Read (home [i]);
                    For i := 1 To 50 Do
                        Read (campus [i])
                End; { with address }

                With phone_number Do
                    Read (area_code, exchange, number);
                For i := 1 To 6 Do
                    With classes [i] Do
                    Begin
                        For j := 1 To 6 Do      { j : Integer }
                            Read (course_number [j]);
                        For j := 1 To 4 Do
                            Read (room_number [j]);
                        Read (meeting_time)
                    End { with classes [i] }
            End; { with one_student }
                {
                   store one student's data in file buffer
                   variable
                }
            student_file^ := one_student;
                { write one student's data in file }
            Put (student_file)
        End; { While }
        Close (student_file)
END.
```

Once the non-text file student_file is created, another program could input the file (using Get) and copy it to a backup file. The following program is the solution.

```
PROGRAM Backup (student_file, backup_file);
TYPE
    Names =
        Record
            last    : Packed Array [1..15] of Char;
            first   : Packed Array [1..15] of Char;
            middle : Char
        End;
    Addresses =
        Record
            home   : Packed Array [1..50] of Char;
            campus : Packed Array [1..50] of Char
        End;
```

```
                Phone =
                    Record
                        area_code : Integer;
                        exchange  : Integer;
                        number    : Integer
                    End;
                Class =
                    Record
                        course_number : Packed Array [1..6] of Char;
                        room_number   : Packed Array [1..4] of Char;
                        meeting_time  : Integer
                    End;
                Student =
                    Record
                        name          : Names;
                        address       : Addresses;
                        phone_number  : Phone;
                        classes       : Array [1..6] of Class
                    End;
VAR
    backup_file,
    student_file : File of Student;
BEGIN
    Reset (student_file);
            { first component in student_file^ }
    Rewrite (backup_file);
    While Not Eof (student_file) Do
    Begin
            {
                store student_file^ in backup_file buffer
                variable
            }
        backup_file^ := student_file^;
            { write component to backup_file }
        Put (backup_file);
            { get next student }
        Get (student_file)
    End; { While }
    Close (student_file);
    Close (backup_file)
END.
```

Notice that there is no declaration of a variable of the file component type; rather, the file buffer variables are used to input a component from student _file and transfer it to backup_file. A total of 209 bytes for each record are copied from student_file to backup_file without any data conversion. Both are non-text files of the same type; the transfer is simpler and more efficient than if these were text files.

SUMMARY

Arrays are a useful data structure for storing data of the same type. Parallel arrays are the only structure available in some programming languages for storing data of differing types. Accessing parallel arrays is more complicated than accessing records. The record data structure is a collection of data of different types accessed by a single name. Arrays of records allow related data to be stored in contiguous memory locations. The entire record of related data and any individual component of the record may be referenced. The With statement simplifies the reference to a record component. The record data structure may have nested records and arrays within it. Variant records are available in Pascal. They allow the programmer to declare additional fields that depend on the value of other fields in a record.

Files are a useful data structure for storing large collections of data on nonvolatile secondary storage devices. Files allow greater flexibility in storing large data sets than arrays within a particular program. Text files in Pascal store all data—numeric and nonnumeric data—in character form in lines. Non-text files in Pascal store all data according to the internal storage formats for the data types. The component type of a file must be fixed, but a file may be any type available in Pascal.

Key Terms

array	record data type
component	tag field
external file	text file
file buffer	variant part
location indicator	variant record
non-text file	With
record data structure	

Exercises

1. Assume that a Char scalar occupies 1 byte of memory, an Integer scalar occupies 2 bytes, and a Real scalar occupies 4 bytes. Specify the total number of bytes occupied by the data structure named block as declared in parts a through d below.

   a.
```
VAR
    block :
        Record
            hunk1 : Integer;
            hunk2 : Integer
        End;
```

```
    b. VAR
          block :
                Record
                      chunk   : Array [1..10] of Char;
                      sector  : Integer;
                      section : Real
                End;
    c. VAR
          block : Array ['A' .. 'D'] of
                Record
                      portion1 : Char;
                      portion2 : Integer;
                      portion3 : Real
                End;
    d. TYPE
          Part2_Record =
                Record
                      part2_1 : Integer;
                      part2_2 : Array [1..3] of Char
                End;
        VAR
          block :
                Record
                      part1 :
                            Record
                                  part1_1 :
                                        Record
                                              part1_1_1 : Char;
                                              part1_1_2 : Integer
                                        End;
                                  part1_2 : Char
                            End;
                      part2 : Array [1..2] Of Part2_Record
                End;
```

2. Specify the number of bytes in `block.part1.part1_1` in d of question 1.

3. Specify the number of bytes in `block.part1` in d of question 1.

4. Given the following definition and declarations

```
    TYPE
        Period =
              Record
                    month,
                    days,
                    year : Integer
              End;
```

```
        Time =
            Record
                month,
                days,
                year : Integer
            End;
    VAR
        interval,
        passage : Period;
        snows_of_yesteryear : Time;
```

determine if a through e below are legal or illegal. Explain why a statement is illegal.

a. `Period := Time;`

b. `passage := interval;`

c. `snows_of_yesteryear := passage;`

d. `snows_of_yesteryear := interval;`

e. `passage := Period;`

5. Given the following declarations

```
    TYPE
        Employee =
            Record
                name : Packed Array [1..30] of Char;
                age  : Integer;
                wage : Real;
                sex  : (FEMALE, MALE);
                dept : (ACCOUNTING, LEGAL, PRODUCTION, SALES)
            End;
    VAR
        worker : Array [1..100] of Employee;
```

list the Pascal reference and the type of data referenced for each of the descriptions below.

a. all information for employee #6

b. the age of worker #13

c. the third letter of the name of worker #62

d. the entire name of worker #71

6. For the declarations used in exercise 5 above, rewrite the following code using a With statement wherever possible.

```
count := 0;
For j := 1 To 100 Do
    If (worker [j].dept = ACCOUNTING)
    And (worker [j].sex = FEMALE) Then
        count := count + 1;
Writeln (count, ' employees in accounting are female')
```

Use the declarations in exercise 5 and the following declaration to complete exercises 7 and 8.

```
TYPE
    Name_Type = Packed Array [1..30] of Char;
    Person =
        Record
            name : Name_Type;
            age  : Integer
        End;
VAR
    Family :
        Record
            man      : Person;
            woman    : Person;
            children : Array [1..20] of Name_Type
        End;
```

7. Rewrite the following code segment without using the With statement:

```
With worker [i] Do
Begin
  name := family.man.name;
  age := family.man.age;
  sex := male
End;
```

8. Why is the following code segment illegal? Rewrite the code segment so that it is legal.

```
With worker [i], family.man Do
Begin
    name := name;
    age  := age;
    sex  := MALE
End;
```

9. Code a record structure in Pascal that contains a 30-character name and a Boolean identifier named FINANCIAL_AID. Use a variant record so that two real values, CURRENT and TOTAL, will be allocated to those records when FINANCIAL_AID is TRUE.

Match the following descriptions to the appropriate term in exercises 10 through 13.

a. used to reference the entire record of information
b. a single component of a record structure
c. used to access a field within a record structure
d. a data structure in which a component of the record is an array
e. a data structure in which each element of the array is a record structure

10. record_name.field_name

11. field

12. array of records

13. record_name

14. Determine whether each statement below is true or false.

    a. A record structure declaration starts with a Begin statement.

    b. Several fields of different types may be declared within a record.

    c. The type of the fields within the record may be any standard or user-defined scalar types.

    d. The type of the fields within the record may be any data structure, such as an array or record.

    e. A record structure declaration is terminated with an End statement.

15. Study each procedure or function below. Mark TEXT if the subprogram may be used with text files and mark NONTEXT if it may be used with nontext files. Some items can be used with both.

    a. Eof   f. Readln

    b. Eoln   g. Reset

    c. Get   h. Rewrite

    d. Put   i. Write

    e. Read   j. Writeln

Match the following terms to the appropriate statement in exercises 16 through 26.

a. file   c. text files

b. file buffer   d. non-text files

16. a file stored on an external storage device that is created and used by Pascal programs only and cannot be accessed by a text editor

17. File of Char;

18. undefined when Eof (file) is TRUE

19. an identifier referenced as filename^ that holds one element of the file

20. a structured data type containing a sequence of elements of identical type with only one element available at a time

21. used when accessing components of files

22. a file containing numeric information in internal representation form rather than character form

23. accessed by procedures Get and Put

24. a file in which each line of characters is separated from the next by an end of line separator

25. a file containing numeric information in character form

26. is initialized to the first component of the file by the Reset procedure

27. Write the Pascal code segment that must be used instead of the Read procedure to input a component from a nontext file.

28. Write the Pascal code segment that must be used instead of the Write procedure to output a component to a nontext file.

Programming Problems

1. Write a program that will store and update a small telephone directory in memory in the form of a singly linked list of records. Print the original directory. Then make some insertions and deletions and print the final directory. Use any format for input and output you desire. For example, the header and the elements may be stored as follows.

	Title	Pointer
Header	Telephone Directory	2000

Location	Information			Pointer
2000	Abel, J. G.	110 Oakleaf	236-4010	2013
2013	Baker, Sue	409 Sunset	784-1182	2026
2026	Carter, L. H.	17 Bernay	785-1365	2078
2039	Minte, Al	204 Pine	236-7295	2052
2052	Pont, M. R.	1 Market	480-1027	2065
2065	Sands, T. H.	671 First	784-8240	—
2078	Lang, Al	311 Moss	236-1111	2039

To solve the problem complete the steps that follow.

a. Input an initial list. Each record should contain:

   name (last, first, middle)
   street address
   phone number

Store the input data in a singly linked list of records.

b. Produce an initial list in alphabetical order. Allow one line in each entry for name, street address, and phone number. Include the appropriate headings.

c. Input update records.

   code ('I' for insert, 'D' for delete)
   name (last, first, middle)
   street address
   phone number

Each record represents a change. Insert the entries in alphabetical order by last name.

d. Produce a list after all update records have been processed in alphabetical order. Allow one line in each entry for name, street address, and phone number. Include the appropriate headings.

2. Implement the following improvements to the program in problem 1:

a. Use double linked lists.

b. Add linked list for phone numbers in ascending order, and list output by phone number.

c. Add linked list for each exchange, and list output by exchange.

3. Write a program that, when given the taxable income for a single taxpayer, will compute the income tax for that person. Use Schedule X shown below. Assume that line 37 contains the taxable income.

Schedule X—Single Taxpayers

Use this Schedule if you checked File Status Box 1 on Form 1040.

If the amount on Form 1040, line 37 is:		Enter on Form 1040, line 38:	Of the amount over
Over	But not over		
$0	$2,300	—0—	—0—
2,300	3,400	-0- + 11%	$2,300
3,400	4,400	$121 + 13%	3,400
4,400	8,500	251 + 15%	4,400
8,500	10,800	866 + 17%	8,500
10,800	12,900	1,257 + 19%	10,800
12,900	15,000	1,656 + 21%	12,900
15,000	18,200	2,097 + 24%	15,000
18,200	23,500	2,865 + 28%	18,200
23,500	28,800	4,349 + 32%	23,500
28,800	34,100	6,045 + 36%	28,800
34,100	41,500	7,953 + 40%	34,100
41,500	55,300	10,913 + 45%	41,500
55,300	————	17,123 + 50%	55,300

Example: If the individual's taxable income is $8,192, the program should use the tax amount and percent shown in column 3 of the line for amounts over $4,400. The tax in this case is

$251.00 + 0.15 (8192.00 − 4400.00) = $819.80

The input to the program is a text file (income) with one individual's taxable income per line.

The output from the program should be the taxable income input and the total tax for each line input.

To solve the problem, store the tax table in a text file (taxrate). Set up an array of records where each record will hold the three values from one row of the tax table: the tax base, the tax percent, and the excess base (for example, $251, 15%, $4,400). The file taxrate will have three values per line (base, percent, and excess). Given the taxable income, search the excess values for the correct index to be used for the tax base and percentage.

4. Write a program that will input information about marital status and store the data in an array of variant records. Input changes in marital status, and modify the data in the array. To solve the problem, complete the steps that follow.

   a. Input data in this form, storing the data in an array of variant records:

      name (20 characters)
      age (integer)
      sex ('F' or 'M')
      marital status ('M', 'D', or 'W')
      (only for married, 'M'):
           length of marriage (integer)
           number of children (integer)
           spouse's name (20 characters)

      (only for divorced, 'D'):
           divorce date (mmddyy)

      (only for widowed, 'W'):
           year of death (mmddyy)

   b. Input the following changes:

      name (20 characters)
      new status ('M', 'D', or 'W')
      (for 'M'): length, number of children, and spouse's name
      (for 'D'): divorce date
      (for 'W'): year of death

      and make the appropriate changes to the array of records

   c. Output the array of updated information.

5. Write a program that will input student data and store an array of variant records. Input the names and graduation dates of students who have recently become seniors, and change the data in the array. To solve the problem, complete the steps that follow.

   a. Input student data in this form:

      name (20 characters)
      sex ('F' or 'M')
      classification (1, 2, 3, or 4)
      (only if freshman, 1): date first enrolled (mmddyy)
      (only if senior, 4): graduation date (mmddyy)

b. Update the data to include the following information about seniors:

    name (20 characters)
    graduation date (mmddyy)

c. Output the revised array.

6. Write a program to (a) prepare a non-text file of student records from a text file and (b) print a grade report from the non-text file.

a. Input a text file of student data containing the following information for each student:

    Student number (integer)
    Student name (22 characters)
    Number of courses (integer)
    Course 1 information:
        Course code (5 characters)
        Credit hours (integer)
        Grade (1 character)
    course 2 information
    course 3 information
    course 4 information
    course 5 information
    course 6 information
    course 7 information

Output a nontext file of student records with the same data as the text file.

b. Input the nontext file created in problem 6a.

Produce a grade report that contains the student number, name, course information, and the average (real) for each student. Assign grade points to grades as follows:

    A = 4
    B = 3
    C = 2
    D = 1
    F = 0

At the end of the report, print the number of students in the file, the percent who passed, the percent who failed, and the overall average.

7. Write a program to (a) prepare a nontext file of part records from a text file and (b) print a part report from the nontext file.

a. Input a text file of part data containing the following information for each part:

    record code (1 character)
    part number (10 characters)
    part description (26 characters)
    part price (real)

Create a nontext file of part records with the same data as the text file but omit the record code.

b. Input the nontext file created in problem 7a.

Produce a part report listing the part number, description, and price. At the end of the report, print the number of parts in the file, the lowest price in the file, the highest price in the file, and the overall average of prices in the file.

8. Write a program that will merge the salary data from a file of male employees with the salary data from a file of female employees into a third file. Retain the ascending order of employee numbers. For each employee (component) on the two input files, include an employee number (four digits), an employee name (20 characters), and an employee salary (a real number).

Input a sequential file (men) of records with salary data and a sequential file (women) of records with salary data.

For each employee (component), create a record containing the employee number, employee name, employee salary, and a letter (F or M) to indicate the sex of the employee. Output the record to a nontext file.

Produce a listing of the nontext file created with appropriate headings.

9. Write a program to input and print a text file using only the procedures Get and Put rather than Read, Readln, Write, and Writeln.

Chapter 3

CHAPTER CONTENTS

Blocking and Buffering

PREVIEW

THIS CHAPTER DISCUSSES THE EFFICIENCY of blocking and buffering. Accessing blocked files and buffered files requires fewer I/O operations and less processing time. Chapter 4 discusses the relationships among blocking and buffering, hardware, and access times. In this chapter the discussion measures efficiency only in terms of the number of I/O accesses. Chapter 3 also presents algorithms that illustrate blocking and deblocking.

BLOCKING

Components of a file are usually quite small when compared with the total capacity of most secondary storage devices. Accessing one component at a time in a Pascal program can be inefficient for the Central Processing Unit (CPU) of the computer. The time required to process a component is often much less than the time needed to read it from the file or write it to the file. Accessing secondary storage takes longer than accessing main memory—even for small components. One way to improve the execution time of a program that accesses a file is by **blocking** components on a file.

A **block** is the smallest amount of data that can be read from or written to a secondary storage device at a time. A block is simply a group of data that consists of several file components of information. By grouping several components into one block—a process called **blocking** components—several components (one block) can be accessed from the file at a time. The result? Fewer accesses retrieve the entire file of components. Reducing the number of physical accesses (input or output operations to the file) reduces the execution time of a program accessing the file.

Suppose we wish to input an entire file of 10,000 components. With a block containing only one component, 10,000 input operations would be required. If we employ a blocking factor of 10—a block containing 10 components—the entire file would contain 1,000 blocks of 10 components each and could be input with 1,000 input operations. We could enhance efficiency by employing a blocking factor of 100. In this case the file could be input with access to 100 blocks of 100 components each. Of course the most efficient way of storing the 10,000 components would be to place all 10,000 in one block; only one input operation would input the 10,000 components.

BLOCK SIZE LIMITATIONS

Obviously, the larger the blocking factor, the fewer the number of physical accesses necessary. A number of considerations affect block size, however. One of the primary limitations is the size of available main memory. The size of one block, which is the amount of data transferred to or from the file during an access, cannot exceed the amount of available main memory. As a result, storing all the components in one block is probably unrealistic unless the file has a small number of components.

The programs that use the file constitute another important consideration. Each program requires space in main memory for internal data and instructions in addition to space for one block of data. The sum of these three must not exceed the amount of main memory allocated for the execution of the program. Each program that accesses the file may vary greatly in the size of internal data and instructions. The program using the largest amount of main memory will be a determining factor in setting the block size.

The accesses to a file constitute another consideration in determining block size. When accessing a single component from a file of blocked components, the entire block that contains that single component must be accessed. If the component is updated, then the entire block must be output back to the external file. If the block size is large compared to the component size, this presents a disadvantage: we will have to access a large block of data to update one component. Suppose we plan to access several components within a short time of each other. If we group these components in one block—a practice called **clustering**—the disadvantage of accessing the entire block is diminished. When deciding whether to cluster and determining block size, consider not only the frequency of access expected for a file, but the required response time for a given access. The time to access the next block depends on how far the next block to be read is from the last block read. Ordering accesses to match the order of components in the file can reduce access time per block.

The characteristics of the external storage devices used to store a file of blocked components is the fourth consideration in determining block size. Access time to a block can be improved by making one block the same size as a track of data (if cylinder-track architecture is used) or a sector of data (if sector addressing is used). External storage devices will be discussed in detail in Chapter 4.

SINGLE BUFFERING

Blocking components in a file can decrease execution time because programs access a block of several components each time instead of accessing one component at a time. Blocking presents a problem when writing programs that access the blocked file, however, since Pascal programs access one component (usually a record from the file) at a time. A software interface reconciles blocked components with the processes of Pascal. Employing such an interface is called **buffering**.

A buffering interface is of one of two types: a deblocking routine or a blocking routine. When reading a blocked file, a **deblocking routine** is the interface that accesses one block from the file and sends one component at a time to the program. When writing to a blocked file, a **blocking routine** stores the components from the program into a buffer in main memory. The buffer is the size of one block. The act of writing the components to the block-size buffer is called a **logical write**. When the buffer is full, the block is physically output to the external file in a process called a **physical write**.

Buffering Input

The deblocking routine is executed by the I/O channel of a computer. The I/O channel directs a device control unit to input or output data for the device specified. All input/output operations are handled by the I/O channel, so the CPU simply processes data and directs the I/O channel to access a particular device. A deblocking routine includes the following steps:

1. If the buffer is not empty, go to step 6.
2. The CPU issues an input request.
3. The I/O channel signals the device controller for the device specified in the input request.
4. The device controller locates the requested information and starts reading bytes from the device and sending them to the buffer in main memory.
5. The I/O channel waits until the buffer is filled, then signals the CPU that the input operation is complete. The location indicator for the buffer is set to 1.
6. The next component to which the location indicator points is sent to the program.
7. The location indicator is incremented.
8. The CPU continues to execute the program.

Each input operation performed on the file reads one block of data. Each read is termed a **physical read** since the file is accessed physically. Each input operation issued by a program logically accesses one component of the blocked file from the buffer. The input statement, Read, issued by the program is a **logical read** since the file is not accessed physically. Rather, the next component is accessed logically from the buffer. Each Read issued by the program is a logical read from the buffer until the buffer is empty. Then the logical read is translated to a physical read. The net effect is that every nth Read (where n is the blocking factor) is translated to a physical read.

Suppose a file has 10 components in one block. The first Read issued by the program accesses the buffer logically. The buffer is empty, which causes a block to be input from the file (a physical read) into a buffer in main memory. The first component in the buffer is sent to the program. Figure 3.1 shows the result of the first logical read. The next nine Reads will simply retrieve the next component from the buffer in main memory as Figure 3.2 shows. This process is a memory access (a logical read) rather than a physical read from the external device. The deblocking routine keeps a location indicator, which points to the next component to be accessed from the buffer. The routine retrieves that component from the buffer, then passes it on to the program. When a Read is issued and all the components

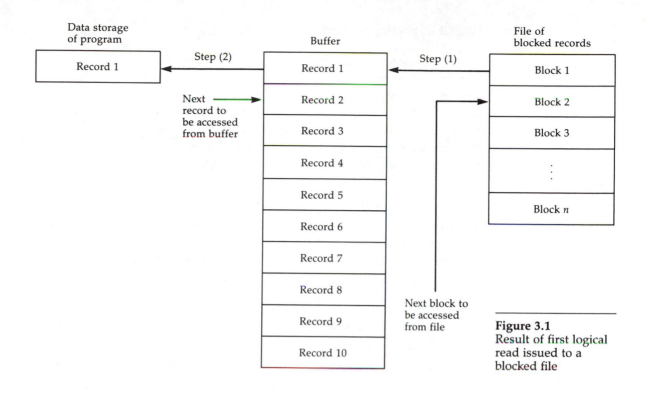

Figure 3.1
Result of first logical
read issued to a
blocked file

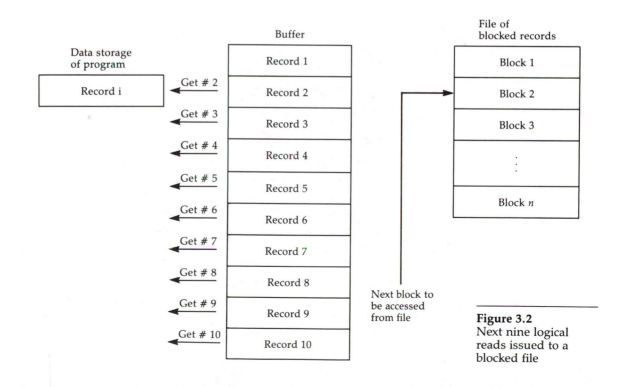

Figure 3.2
Next nine logical
reads issued to a
blocked file

in the buffer have been accessed, the next block of data from the file is input into the buffer in main memory, and the first component in the buffer is sent to the program (see Figure 3.3). The deblocking routine interfaces the storage of data on the file and the accesses of the program. As a result, we can block the components on the external file to save access time. In this example we use one physical read for 10 components, and the program accesses one component at a time using 10 logical reads.

Buffering Output

The blocking routine is executed similarly by the I/O channel. As a result, a program can output one component at a time to the buffer and block components in the file. The blocking routine includes the following steps:

1. If the buffer is not full, go to step 6.
2. The CPU issues an output request.
3. The I/O channel signals the device controller for the device specified in the output request.
4. The device controller starts writing bytes from the buffer to the device.
5. The I/O channel waits until the entire buffer is written to the device, then signals the CPU that the output operation is complete. The location indicator for the buffer is set to 1.
6. The next component from the program is stored in the buffer in the space to which the location indicator points.
7. The location indicator is incremented.
8. The CPU continues to execute the program.

Each output statement, Write, that the program issues stores components in the buffer with a logical write; the file is not accessed physically. When the buffer becomes full, a physical write outputs the buffer contents to the file physically.

For a file with a blocking factor of 10, the first nine calls to Put issued by the program will logically output data to the buffer in main memory. The logical output constitutes a memory access rather than an output operation to the external file (see Figure 3.4). The 10th Put will cause the block of 10 components to be physically output to the external file as Figure 3.5 shows. The 11th Put uses a logical write to fill the buffer with a component (see Figure 3.6). Again, the program can now output one component at a time, and with the use of a blocking routine, the components can be output as blocked components on the external file to save access time to the external device. A file with a blocking factor of 10 can be created by a Pascal program more efficiently than a file without blocking since one physical write occurs for every 10 logical writes (Puts).

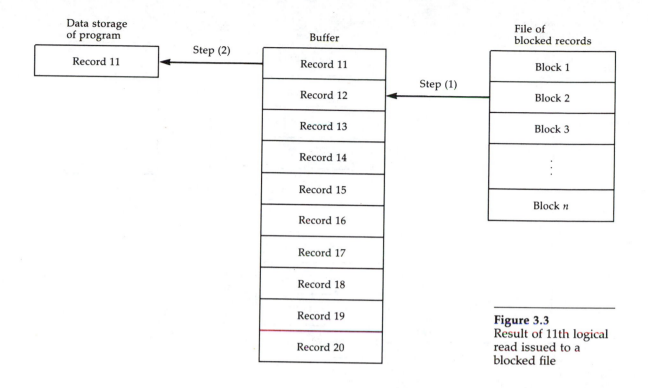

Figure 3.3
Result of 11th logical read issued to a blocked file

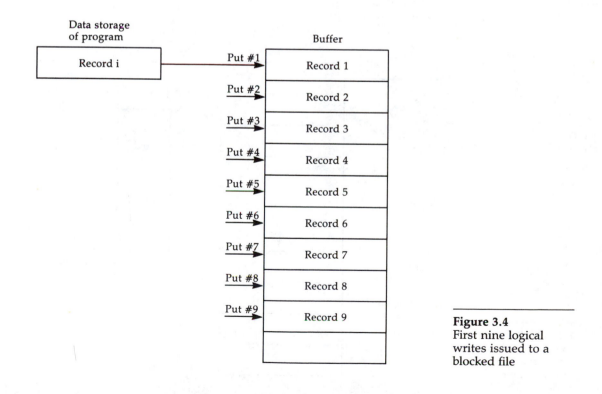

Figure 3.4
First nine logical writes issued to a blocked file

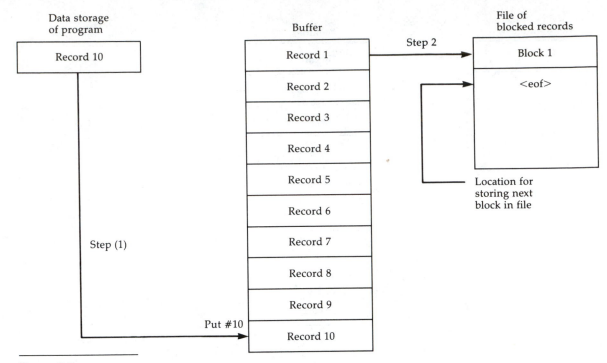

Figure 3.5
Result of 10th logical
write issued to a
blocked file

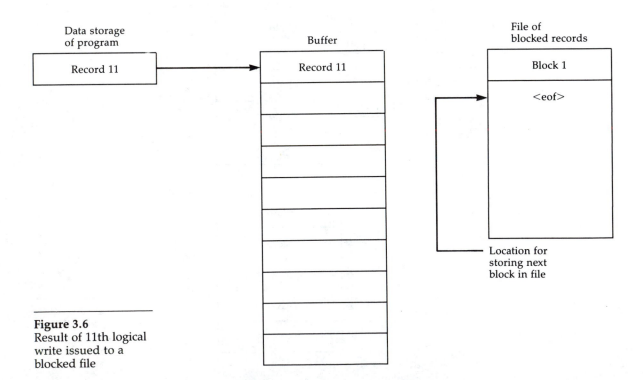

Figure 3.6
Result of 11th logical
write issued to a
blocked file

EXAMPLE 1: SINGLE BUFFERING

Suppose 2,000 records, each 100 bytes long, are stored in file A unblocked (1 record per block). File B employs a blocking factor of 25 (25 records per block). The number of blocks in file A is

$$\frac{2,000 \text{ records}}{1 \text{ record/block}} = 2,000 \text{ blocks}$$

The number of blocks in file B is smaller.

$$\frac{2,000 \text{ records}}{25 \text{ records/block}} = 80 \text{ blocks}$$

The number of physical accesses necessary to input or output each entire file is equal to the number of blocks in the file. File A can be input with 2,000 physical reads, and file B can be input with only 80 physical reads.

An examination of physical reads and writes in terms of milliseconds provides a clearer understanding of why reducing physical accesses is important. One second contains 1000 **milliseconds** (ms). Suppose 100 bytes can be transferred (from disk to CPU or vice versa) in 0.008 ms. Each physical read or write involves some overhead time in addition to the 0.008 ms per 100 bytes of data. The expensive portion of a physical access is the overhead time, which varies depending on the type of secondary storage device. (Chapter 4 compares the overhead times of specific devices.) Suppose the overhead of each physical read or write is 50 ms. As Table 3.1 indicates, each physical read or write for file A takes 50.008 ms, and each physical read or write for file B takes 50.2 ms. The total time to access all blocks in file A is

$$50.008 \text{ ms/block} \times 2,000 \text{ blocks} = 100,016 \text{ ms}$$
$$= 100.016 \text{ seconds (sec)}$$
$$= 1.667 \text{ minutes (min)}$$

Table 3.1 Impact of blocking factor on file access time

	File A	File B
Number of logical records	2,000	2,000
Record length in bytes	100	100
Blocking factor	1	25
Number of physical blocks	2,000	80
Block length in bytes	100	2,500
Time to transfer each block (ms)	0.008	0.2
Overhead time per block (ms)	50	50
Total access time for entire file (min)	16.67	0.67

The total time to access all blocks in file B is

$$50.2\,\text{ms/block} \times 80\,\text{blocks} = 4016\,\text{ms}$$
$$= 4.016\,\text{sec}$$
$$= 00.67\,\text{min}$$

The access time per block is longer for file B (50.2 ms/block) than for file A (50.008 ms/block), but file B has fewer blocks (80 blocks for file B versus 2,000 blocks for file A); therefore, file B requires fewer accesses. Buffering components into a block of components helps reduce the number of physical accesses to a file of data. Reducing the number of physical accesses to the file reduces the overhead, which is the biggest portion of total access time.

Implementation in Pascal

Programming languages such as COBOL and PL/1 contain specifications that indicate block size. These languages also have preset blocking and deblocking interface routines, and they allow the program to be written to access one component at a time after the programmer indicates the blocking factor. Pascal has no built-in facilities for accessing blocked files, so a Pascal programmer needs to write deblocking and blocking routines.

We implement blocking in Pascal by storing a block of components as an array of components. Each Pascal Get accesses one block of the file, which is a block of x components or an array of x components. Then the program accesses each of the x components in the block or array logically and one at a time. The same is true of the action of Put. Each component is stored logically in an array of x components until the array is full. Then a Pascal Put physically writes the block of x components to the file. The last block is usually not a full block in a sequential file, but on a random file several blocks may be partially filled after updates. As a result, the partially filled blocks are padded at the end with very high values, so all blocks are fixed in length. This implementation is a simulation of blocking and buffering; actual buffering routines are part of a computer's operating system.

The three algorithms that follow outline the blocking portion of buffering in Pascal.

Algorithm   Create_File

    counter ← 0

Create_File initializes the counter for the number of components in the buffer. All blocks will have a maximum value of BLOCK_SIZE for the number of components.

Algorithm   Write_To_File

    counter ← counter + 1
    buffer [counter] ← a_component
    If counter = BLOCK_SIZE { buffer full }
        Output buffer to file_name
        counter ← 0

Write_To_File moves components into the buffer one at a time, filling positions one through BLOCK_SIZE of the array. When the buffer is full, it is physically written to the external file.

Algorithm   Close_File

    If counter > 0
        For i ← counter + 1 To BLOCK_SIZE
            buffer [i] ← very high values { for padding }
        Output buffer to file_name

Close_File pads a partially filled block with very high values, and physically writes this last block to the file.

The algorithms that follow outline the deblocking portion of the buffering.

Algorithm   Open_File

    If Not Eof (file_name)
        Input first block from file into buffer
        counter ← 1
    Else
        counter ← BLOCK_SIZE + 1 { buffer empty }

Algorithm   Read_From_File

    If counter > BLOCK_SIZE
                { buffer empty }
        If Not Eof (filename)
            Input next block from file into buffer
            counter ← 1
    If counter <= BLOCK_SIZE
        a_component ← buffer [counter]
        counter ← counter + 1
        If buffer [counter] = very high values
            counter ← BLOCK_SIZE + 1

Algorithm   End_Of_File

    If Eof (file_name)
    And (counter > BLOCK_SIZE)
            { buffer empty }
        End_Of_File ← TRUE
    Else
        End_Of_File ← FALSE

Open_File fills the buffer with the first block of components from the file and initializes the counter to 1. Read_From_File fills the buffer (if empty) with the next block of components from the file and returns a component from the buffer. If the next component to be returned contains very high values, the counter is set to indicate an empty buffer. The function End_Of_File checks for an end of file condition and includes a test for an empty buffer. Once the last block is input, Eof (file_name) will be TRUE, but file processing is not complete, in this case, until all components in the last block in the buffer have been accessed.

File buffering is not available in Pascal as it is in COBOL and PL/1. Some Pascal implementations of text files may access a group of characters from the file and store them in a buffer rather than accessing them one character at a time. (In these implementations a group usually consists of 80 characters or 128 characters.) As is the case with blocking components on a file, accessing a buffer of a group of characters rather than accessing one character improves access time.

DOUBLE BUFFERING

To improve the access time to an external file, most high-level languages such as COBOL and PL/1 contain two buffer variables for each file. This attribute permits double buffering. **Double buffering** is possible when the I/O operations performed by the I/O channel and the processing operations performed by the CPU overlap in time. In the case of an input file, the first block from the file is input into buffer 1, the second block is input into buffer 2, and the first component from buffer 1 is passed to program storage. Figure 3.7 illustrates double buffering for an input file with 10 records to a block. When buffer 1 becomes empty while buffer 2 is still full, processing of record 11 from buffer 2 begins. The third block from the file is input into buffer 1 as Figure 3.8 shows. The effect is that the next block from the file has been physically accessed before the program directs the input; the information is waiting in one of the buffers. The program can access the waiting information in the buffer without having to wait for the information to be accessed.

Figure 3.9 illustrates the time frame that applies to single buffering. The CPU is idle while the first block is input in the buffer. In this illustration the time to input a block is 50 ms, and the time for the CPU to process a block of data is 25 ms. When the CPU finishes processing a block of data, it is idle for 50 ms while the buffer is filled with the next block of data. (This pattern yields 33 percent utilization of the CPU.) Total file-processing time is

$$(50 \text{ ms} + 25 \text{ ms})/\text{block} \times n \text{ blocks/file} = 75 \text{ ms/block} \times n \text{ blocks/file}$$

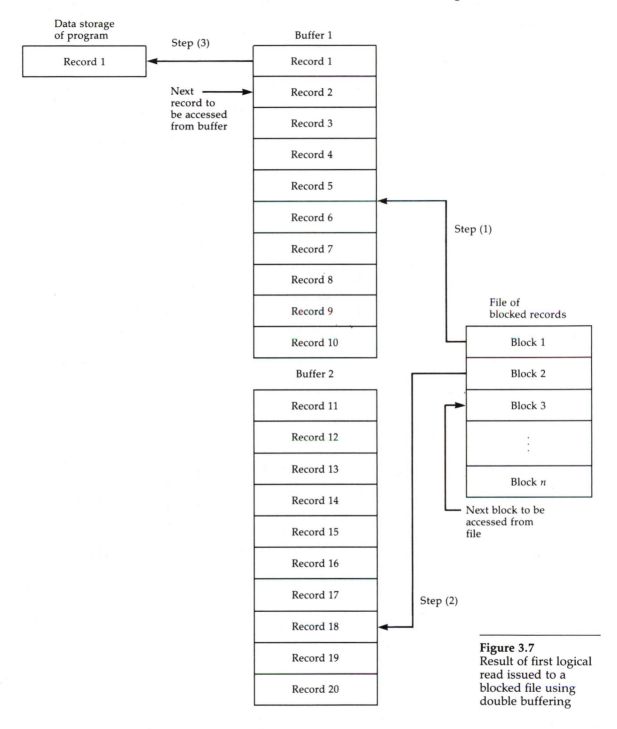

Figure 3.7
Result of first logical read issued to a blocked file using double buffering

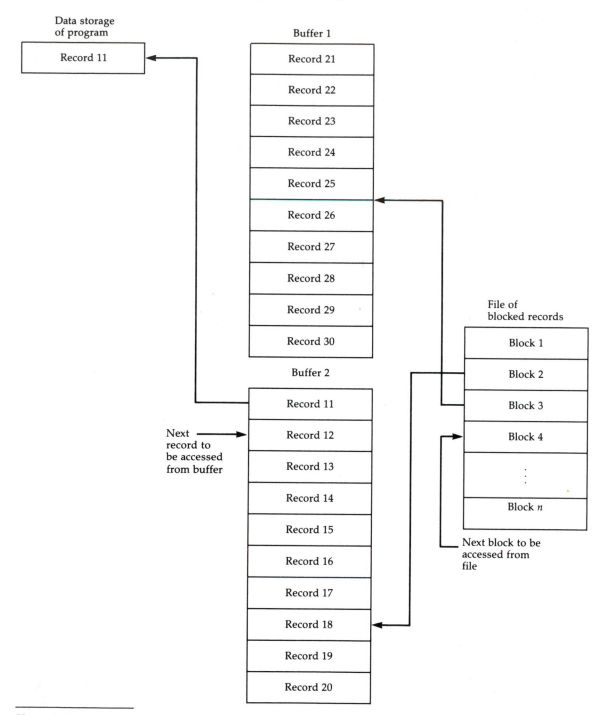

Figure 3.8
Result of 11th logical
read issued to a
blocked file using
double buffering

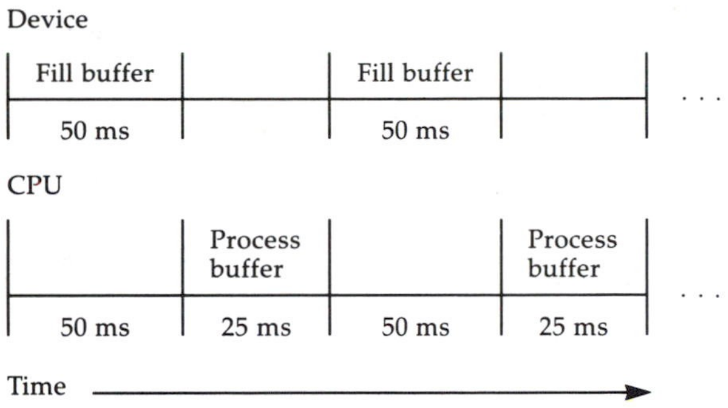

Device

Fill buffer		Fill buffer		
50 ms		50 ms		

. . .

CPU

	Process buffer		Process buffer	
50 ms	25 ms	50 ms	25 ms	

. . .

Time ⟶

Figure 3.9
Single buffering with input

Device

Fill buffer 1	Fill buffer 2	Fill buffer 1	Fill buffer 2
50 ms	50 ms	50 ms	50 ms

. . .

CPU

	Process buffer 1		Process buffer 2		Process buffer 1	
50 ms	25 ms	25 ms	25 ms	25 ms	25 ms	25 ms

. . .

Time ⟶

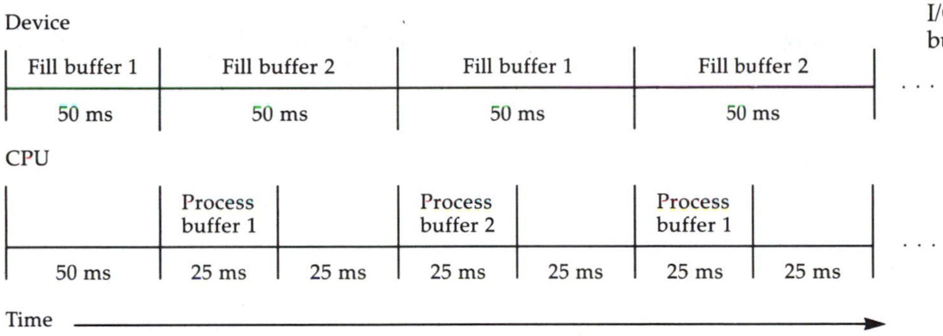

Figure 3.10
I/O-bound double buffering with input

The total time to process a file with 1,000 blocks is

$$75 \text{ ms/block} \times 1{,}000 \text{ blocks/file} = 75{,}000 \text{ ms} = 75 \text{ sec}$$

Figure 3.10 illustrates the time frame that applies to double buffering. The CPU begins to process data in buffer 1 as soon as buffer 1 is filled. At the same time, buffer 2 is being filled with the next block of data. The result is that the CPU only waits 25 ms for the other buffer to be filled before continuing to process. In this situation, where access time to input one buffer from the file is longer than process time, the implementation is said to be **I/O-bound.** The total time to process all the data in the file cannot be reduced without reducing the access time to the file. In this I/O-bound case we have achieved 50 percent utilization of the CPU. The total time to process a file is

time to input the blocks (50 ms/block)

+ 25 ms to process the last block

$= (50 \text{ ms/block} \times n \text{ blocks/file}) + 25 \text{ ms}$

Figure 3.11
Processor-bound
double buffering with
input

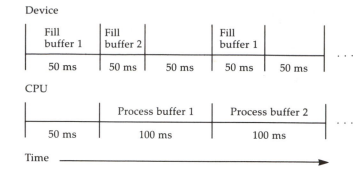

Double buffering, in this case, produces a savings of almost 25 ms/block over single buffering. The total time to process a file with 1,000 blocks using double buffering would be

$$(50 \text{ ms/block} \times 1,000 \text{ blocks/file}) + 25 \text{ ms}$$
$$= 50,025 \text{ ms}$$
$$= 50.025 \text{ sec}$$

The total processing time for a file of 1,000 blocks using double buffering is 66 percent of the total time using single buffering.

Figure 3.11 illustrates an implementation that is **processor-bound**; to fill a buffer takes 50 ms and to process a buffer takes 100 ms. Since the processing time is longer than the access time, the CPU is never idle (except while buffer 1 is being filled). The total time to process all the data in the file cannot be reduced without reducing the processing time; in other words this processor-bound implementation represents 100 percent utilization of the CPU.

Double buffering is also used for output files to decrease the time in which the CPU waits for a buffer to be emptied. Figure 3.12 illustrates double buffering to an output file with 10 components to a block. When buffer 1 becomes full and a physical write is issued to store buffer 1 contents physically in the file, the CPU need not wait for buffer 1 to be emptied; buffer 2 is empty. While buffer 1 contents are being stored in the external file, the program continues moving data into buffer 2 (see Figure 3.13). When buffer 2 becomes full, a physical write is issued to stored buffer 2 contents in the external file while the program continues to fill buffer 1 (see Figure 3.14). Alternation between buffer 1 and 2 continues; the result is diminished waiting time for the CPU.

Figure 3.15 illustrates the time frame that applies to creating an output file using only one buffer. As with the single buffering for input files, the CPU is idle while the buffer is written to the file. Double buffering for output

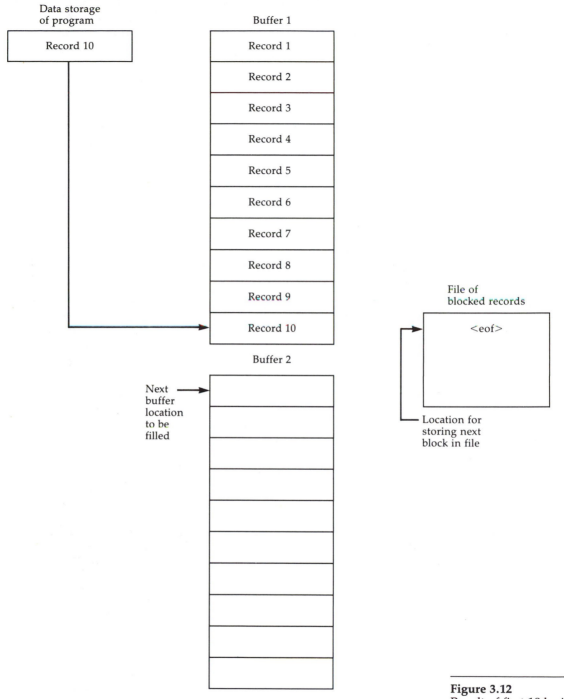

Figure 3.12
Result of first 10 logical writes issued to a blocked file using double buffering

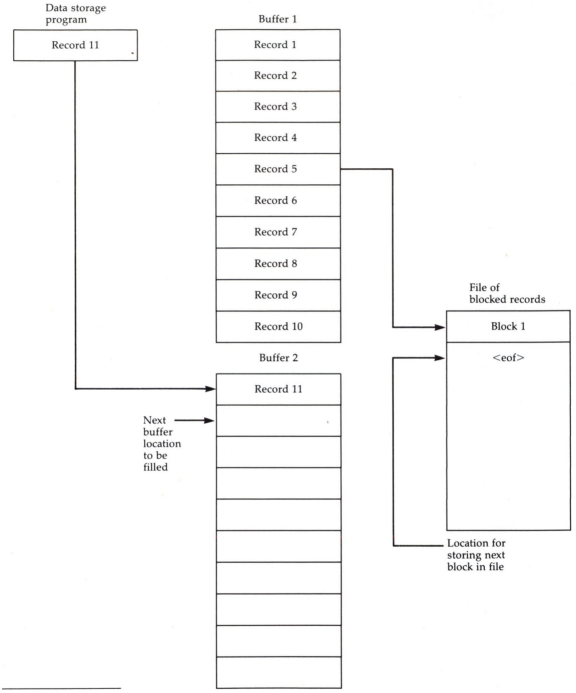

Figure 3.13
Result of 11th logical
write issued to a
blocked file using
double buffering

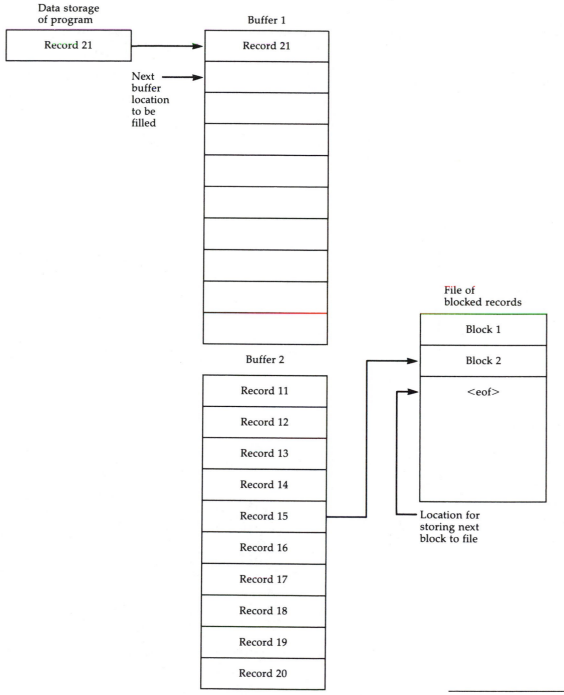

Figure 3.14
Result of issuing 21 logical writes to a blocked file using double buffering

Figure 3.15
Single buffering with
output

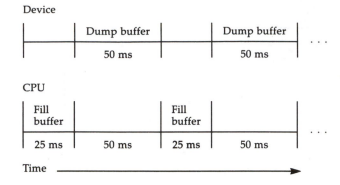

Figure 3.15
Single buffering with
output

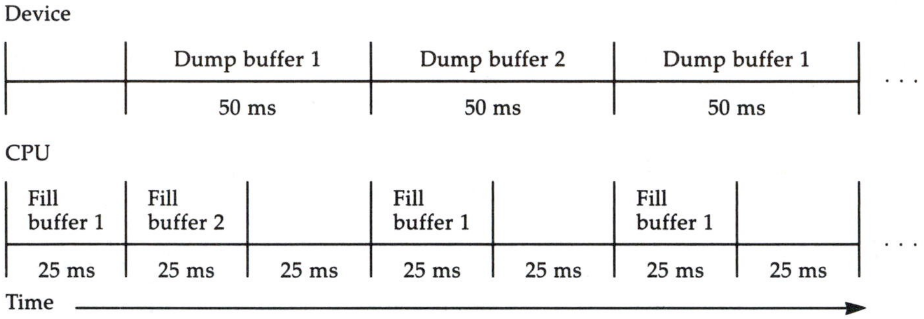

Figure 3.16
I/O-bound double
buffering with output

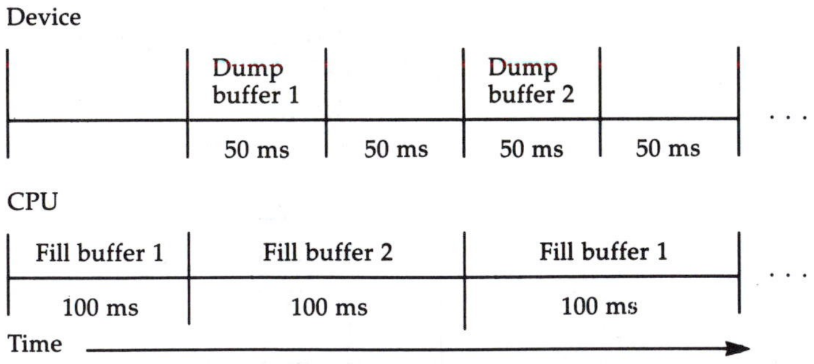

Figure 3.17
Processor-bound
double buffering with
output

files can improve CPU utilization by allowing the CPU to fill a second buffer
while the first buffer is physically written to a file. Depending on the access
time to write the buffer to the file and the time for the CPU to fill a buffer,

double buffering may be *I/O-bound* (see Figure 3.16) or *processor-bound* (see Figure 3.17).

Pascal does not usually allow read/write operations to overlap with processing because double buffering is not available. (Double buffering is available in many file-processing languages, however—in COBOL and PL/1, for example.)

SUMMARY

Blocking data on a file reduces the number of physical accesses to the file, and thereby improves the execution time of programs that access the blocked file. The block size is determined by a number of factors: the size of main memory, the size of the largest program accessing the file, the accesses to the file, and the physical characteristics of external storage devices. Buffering data to and from the file consists of blocking and deblocking interface routines that allow programs to deal logically with one component at a time while physically blocking components on the external file. Double buffering can provide an added improvement in file access time for both input and output files when overlapping of I/O and processing is possible.

Key Terms

block	I/O-bound
blocking	logical read
blocking routine	logical write
buffering	millisecond
clustering	physical read
deblocking routine	physical write
double buffering	processor-bound

Exercises

1. Describe the difference between a logical file component and a physical file component.

2. Explain file component blocking.

3. What is the purpose of blocking?

4. Why is blocking important?

5. What factors should be considered in determining block size?

6. Why is multiple buffering important?

7. What are the benefits of opening a file explicitly with the Reset or Rewrite procedure before accessing a file?

8. What are the benefits of closing a file explicitly rather than closing it implicitly at the end of program execution?

9. Does buffering use auxiliary storage or main storage?

10. Trace the sequence of steps involved in reading and processing a block of logical components using single buffers. How does the sequence change if double buffering is used?

11. If components are stored in a file with a blocking factor of 1, and there are nb blocks in the file, how many logical and physical accesses do we need to input the file?

12. If components are stored in a file with a blocking factor of nc, and there are nb blocks in the file, how many logical and physical accesses do we need to input the file? Compare the effects of this blocking factor to the effects of the blocking factor in exercise 11.

13. If a record is 120 bytes long and the blocking factor is 25, what is the block length in bytes? How large is the file buffer we need to access a file using single buffering? If double buffering is used, how large must the file buffer be?

14. Determine the maximum blocking factors for each of the files listed in a through i if 38,500 bytes of main storage are available. All blocking factors should be integers. How many blocks (physical accesses) does each file require?

    a. a file of 100,000 records of 367 bytes accessed with single buffering.

    b. a file of 100,000 records of 367 bytes accessed with double buffering. Compare the efficiency of this buffering to the efficiency of a.

    c. a file of 45,000 records of 417 bytes accessed with single buffering.

    d. a file of 45,000 records of 417 bytes accessed with double buffering. Compare the efficiency of this buffering to the efficiency of c.

    e. a file of 248,000 records of 860 bytes accessed with single buffering.

    f. a file of 248,000 records of 860 bytes accessed with double buffering. Compare the efficiency of this buffering to the efficiency of e.

    g. a file of 75,000 logical components of 120 bytes each accessed with single buffering.

    h. a file of 75,000 logical components of 120 bytes each accessed with double buffering. Compare the efficiency of this buffering to the efficiency of g.

    i. a file of 75,000 logical components of 120 bytes each accessed with triple buffering. Compare the efficiency of this buffering to the efficiency of g and h.

15. Given the following times to input a block for each file of the corresponding letter in exercise 14 (100 bytes input in 0.008 ms), and 25 ms to process a block, compute the total time to input and process each file. The applications are I/O-bound.

    a. input time = 53.05 ms

    b. input time = 51.52 ms

    c. input time = 53.07 ms

    d. input time = 51.53 ms

    e. input time = 53.02 ms

    f. input time = 51.51 ms

    g. input time = 53.07 ms

    h. input time = 51.53 ms

    i. input time = 51.01 ms

16. Change the time to process a block in exercise 15 to 100 ms. These applications are processor-bound.

Programming Problems

1. Implement the blocking routines described in the chapter as external routines to a user program.

2. Write the double buffering routines described in the chapter as external routines to a user program.

Chapter 4

CHAPTER CONTENTS

Secondary Storage Devices

PREVIEW

THIS CHAPTER DESCRIBES THE CHARACTERISTICS of external storage devices as a background for understanding the impact of storage devices on file design and manipulation. The chapter also presents quantitative measures of blocking and buffering in terms of physical access time and various blocking factors.

TYPES OF STORAGE DEVICES

Magnetic tapes and magnetic disks are the two most commonly used types of secondary storage devices that store large files of data. Anyone creating or using files for programs and data should understand how data are stored on secondary storage devices and the data transfer speeds that apply. It is also important to know the types of file organizations appropriate for each secondary storage device.

MAGNETIC TAPE

Magnetic tape is a sequential-access storage device in which blocks of data are stored serially along the length of the tape and can only be accessed in a serial manner. The tape itself is a thin strip of plastic about 0.002 inch thick and about 1/2 inch wide. The plastic is coated with a magnetic oxide. The tape is usually 2,400 feet (ft) long but the length may vary; 300-, 600-, and 1,200-feet lengths are common. Whatever the length, the tape is wound onto reels. Data are recorded as magnetic "spots" (or bits) on the magnetic oxide film in nine **tracks** that are parallel to the edges of the tape. Figure 4.1 illustrates a section of a tape with the bits shown as dots.

One character (1 byte) of data is recorded across the width of the tape and may use all nine tracks. The pattern of the magnetic spots in tracks is determined by the recording format. The two most prevalent recording formats are Extended Binary Coded Decimal Interchange Code (**EBCDIC**) and American Standard Code for Information Interchange (**ASCII**). EBCDIC is an encoding scheme for representing data in which 8 bits arranged in different patterns can represent any character in the character set. ASCII is a 7-bit code; 7 bits in varying patterns represent any character in the character set. The characters of data are stored serially along the length of the tape as are the records of data in a file.

One of the magnetic bits that comprise each character on the tape is the **parity bit**, which detects errors that occur when reading or writing data. Parity is established on a drive as either even or odd. If the convention is **odd parity**, the number of 1 bits required to represent a character must be odd. When a character is represented by an even number of 1 bits, a parity bit is added to make the number of 1 bits odd. If an even number of 1 bits is read from the tape, it must be the result of an error. The convention of **even parity** employs the parity bit to make the number of 1 bits an even number and detects errors by finding odd numbers of 1 bits.

The **recording density** of a tape is the number of characters or bytes of data that can be stored per inch. Recording densities are 200; 556; 800; 1,600; 3,200; and 6,250 characters or bytes per inch (bpi) of tape. Tapes with density

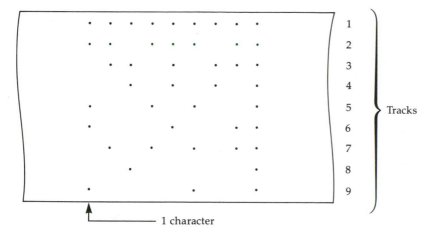

Figure 4.1
A section of magnetic tape

ratings of 800; 1,600; and 6,250 are the most common. The higher the recording density of the tape, the higher the storage capacity.

Data can be read from or written to a tape only when the tape is moving at a specific, fixed speed past the read/write heads (see Figure 4.2). The amount of data that can be transferred at any one access is a block of data. A block of data is sometimes called a **physical record**. A block may contain one or more logical records as Chapter 3 discussed.

When a request to read or write a block of data is issued, the tape drive must start the tape moving, accelerate to a fixed speed in order to read or write a block, then decelerate to a stop. Physical records or blocks must be separated by **interblock gaps (IBGs)** that provide space in which the tape can start and stop between read or write requests. IBGs are also called **interrecord gaps (IRGs),** and they are unused spaces on the tape that pass under the read/write heads during acceleration and deceleration so the block of data passes under the read/write heads at the proper speed. Figure 4.3 shows blocks of data separated by IBGs.

These gaps are usually between 0.6 inch and 0.75 inch, but the size may vary with tape densities. IBGs decrease the amount of space on the tape available for storage of data. For example, suppose a record of 80 characters is stored on a nine-track tape with a density of 1,600 bpi and a gap of 0.6 inch. If the record is stored as one block of data, an IBG precedes and follows the record on the tape.

Figure 4.4 shows the size of the 80-character record relative to the size of the gaps. The 80-character record uses 80/1,600 inch of the tape, or 0.05 inch of the tape. Each gap uses 0.6 inch of the tape, or 12 times the space that the record uses.

In addition to the advantages of blocking discussed in Chapter 3, blocking records on tape provides a physical advantage; blocking on tape reduces the number of IBGs and allows more data to be stored on a tape. Storing

Figure 4.2
A schematic drawing
of a tape drive

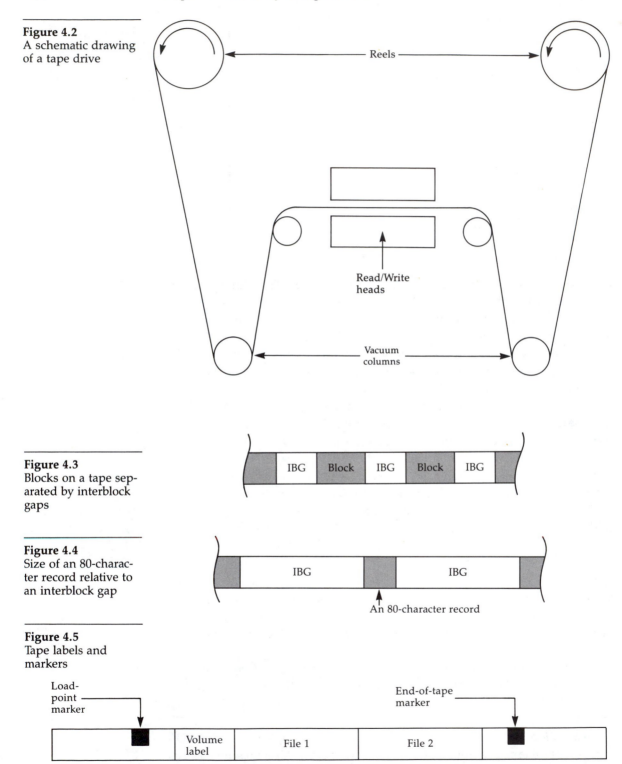

Figure 4.3
Blocks on a tape sep-
arated by interblock
gaps

Figure 4.4
Size of an 80-charac-
ter record relative to
an interblock gap

Figure 4.5
Tape labels and
markers

Data file

File header label	IBG	Block 1	IBG	Block 2	. . .	Block n	IBG	File trailer label

Figure 4.6
A data file with labels

12 of these 80-character records in a block results in one gap for every 12 records rather than one gap for each record. In other words, blocking results in one-twelfth the number of IBGs or eleven-twelfths more space for data.

Figure 4.5 shows other characteristics of magnetic tape: the **end-of-tape markers** at each end of the tape and the labels at the beginning of the tape and at the beginning and end of each file. The beginning of a tape has a leader section followed by a **load-point marker,** which is a reflective aluminum strip that the tape drive can sense. The end-of-tape marker is made of reflective aluminum that deactivates the tape drive to prevent the tape from unthreading from the reel. Data can be recorded on the tape after the load-point marker and before this end-of-tape marker.

Between the tape markers the storage of data usually consists of a volume label followed by one or more files of data. The **volume label** contains the serial number of the tape and other identifying information. Each file of data is preceded by a **file header label**, which contains file identification, and succeeded by a **file trailer label**, which contains record and block counts for the file. A tape containing two files would appear as in Figure 4.5 where each file contains the information diagrammed in Figure 4.6.

Magnetic tapes can be used for files with sequential organization only. Magnetic tape reels cost less than magnetic disk packs (about 10 times less) and are more convenient to store because reels are smaller than disk packs. For these reasons, tapes are often used for storing backup files. Table 4.1 gives the characteristics of commercial tape drives current at the time this book was written.

Table 4.1   Characteristics of current tape drives

Manufacturer and tape model	Speed (inches/sec)	Density (bpi)	Transfer rate	
CDC 626	75	800	120	KB/sec
CDC 679-7	200	6,250	1.25	MB/sec
IBM 3420-4	75	6,250	470	KB/sec
Telex 6420-66	125	6,250	780	KB/sec
Univac Uniservo 12	42.7	1,600	68	KB/sec

EXAMPLE 1: SPACE CALCULATION FOR TAPE

Consider a magnetic tape drive with the following characteristics:

density $= 1,600\,\text{bpi}$

IBG length $= 0.5\,\text{inch}$

Compute the number of inches of tape required to store 100,000 records of 100 bytes each with a blocking factor of 32.

$$\begin{aligned}
\text{block length (in bytes)} &= \text{logical record length} \times \text{blocking factor} \\
&= 100\,\text{bytes/record} \times 32\,\text{records/block} \\
&= 3,200\,\text{bytes/block}
\end{aligned}$$

Determine the number of blocks by dividing the number of records by the blocking factor.

$$\begin{aligned}
\text{number of blocks} &= \frac{\text{number of records}}{\text{blocking factor}} \\
\text{number of blocks} &= \frac{100,000\,\text{records}}{32\,\text{records/block}} \\
\text{number of blocks} &= 3,125\,\text{blocks}
\end{aligned}$$

Next divide the block length in bytes by the density (bytes/inch) to determine the length, in inches, of one block.

$$\begin{aligned}
\text{block length (in inches)} &= \frac{\text{block length in bytes}}{\text{density}} \\
&= \frac{3,200\,\text{bytes/block}}{1,600\,\text{bytes/inch}} \\
&= 2.0\,\text{inches/block}
\end{aligned}$$

Each block is surrounded by IBGs, so the length of tape to store the blocks is determined by assuming that there is one more IBG than there are blocks.

$$\begin{aligned}
\text{tape length} &= (\text{number of blocks} \times \text{block length}) \\
&\quad + (\text{number of IBGs} \times \text{IBG length}) \\
\text{tape length} &= (3,125\,\text{blocks} \times 2\,\text{inches/block}) \\
&\quad + (3,126\,\text{IBGs} \times 0.5\,\text{inch/IBG}) \\
\text{tape length} &= (6,250\,\text{inches}) + (1,563\,\text{inches}) \\
\text{tape length} &= 7,813\,\text{inches} = 651.083\,\text{ft}
\end{aligned}$$

A 600-foot tape would not be long enough; we need a 1,200-foot tape to store the file. Note that the calculation does not include space for header and trailer labels and the volume label.

EXAMPLE 2: SPACE CALCULATION FOR TAPE

Consider a magnetic tape and tape drive with the following characteristics:

length = 2,400 feet
density = 1,600 bpi
IBG = 0.5 inch
transfer speed = 50 inches/sec
start or stop time = 10 ms (0.010 sec)

Compute the number of records that can be stored on the tape if the logical record length is 80 bytes, and the blocking factor is seven records per block. Find the block length in bytes by using the record length (in bytes) and the blocking factor.

$$\begin{aligned}
\text{block length (in bytes)} &= \text{logical record length} \times \text{blocking factor} \\
&= 80\,\text{bytes/record} \times 7\,\text{records/block} \\
&= 560\,\text{bytes/block}
\end{aligned}$$

Next the block length in bytes is divided by the density (bytes/inch) to determine the length, in inches, of one block.

$$\begin{aligned}
\text{block length (in inches)} &= \frac{\text{block length in bytes}}{\text{density}} \\
&= \frac{560\,\text{bytes/block}}{1,600\,\text{bytes/inch}} \\
&= 0.35\,\text{inch/block}
\end{aligned}$$

Each block is surrounded by IBGs, so the number of blocks that can be stored on a 2,400-foot tape must be one less than the number of IBGs.

$$\begin{aligned}
\text{tape length} &= (\text{number of blocks} \times \text{block length}) \\
&\quad + ((\text{number of blocks} + 1) \times \text{IBG}) \\
2{,}400\,\text{ft} &= (\text{number of blocks} \times 0.35\,\text{inch}) \\
&\quad + ((\text{number of blocks} + 1) \times 0.5\,\text{inch}) \\
2{,}400\,\text{ft} &= (\text{number of blocks} \times 0.35\,\text{inch}) \\
&\quad + (\text{number of blocks} \times 0.5\,\text{inch}) + 0.5\,\text{inch} \\
2{,}400\,\text{ft} &= (\text{number of blocks} \times 0.85\,\text{inch}) + 0.5\,\text{inch}
\end{aligned}$$

Then find the number of blocks.

$$\begin{aligned}
\text{number of blocks} &= \frac{(12\,\text{inches/ft} \times 2{,}400\,\text{ft}) - 0.5\,\text{inch}}{0.85\,\text{inch/block}} \\
&= 33{,}881\,\text{blocks}\,[33{,}881.764\,\text{truncated}]
\end{aligned}$$

The number of blocks must be an integer because the definition of a block is the smallest amount of data the tape drive can access at any one time. Part blocks cannot be accessed.

To compute the number of records that can be stored on the tape, multiply the number of blocks by the blocking factor.

$$\text{number of records} = \text{blocking factor} \times \text{number of blocks}$$
$$= 7 \text{ records/block} \times 33{,}881 \text{ blocks}$$
$$= 237{,}167 \text{ records}$$

Assume the blocking factor is changed to 24 records. Now compute the number of records that can be stored on a 2,400-foot tape.

$$\begin{array}{l}\text{block length} \\ \text{(in bytes)}\end{array} = \text{logical record length} \times \text{blocking factor}$$
$$= 80 \text{ bytes/record} \times 24 \text{ records/block}$$
$$= 1{,}920 \text{ bytes/block}$$

$$\begin{array}{l}\text{block length} \\ \text{(in inches)}\end{array} = \frac{\text{block length in bytes}}{\text{density}}$$
$$= \frac{1{,}920 \text{ bytes/block}}{1{,}600 \text{ bytes/inch}}$$
$$= 1.2 \text{ inches/block}$$

$$\text{tape length} = (\text{number of blocks} \times \text{block length})$$
$$+ ((\text{number of blocks} + 1) \times \text{IBG})$$
$$2{,}400 \text{ ft} = (\text{number of blocks} \times 1.2 \text{ inches})$$
$$+ ((\text{number of blocks} + 1) \times 0.5 \text{ inch})$$
$$2{,}400 \text{ ft} = (\text{number of blocks} \times 1.2 \text{ inches})$$
$$+ (\text{number of blocks} \times 0.5 \text{ inch}) + 0.5 \text{ inch}$$
$$2{,}400 \text{ ft} = (\text{number of blocks} \times 1.7 \text{ inch}) + 0.5 \text{ inch}$$

$$\text{number of blocks} = \frac{(12 \text{ inches/ft} \times 2400 \text{ ft}) - 0.5 \text{ inch}}{1.7 \text{ inch/block}}$$
$$= 16{,}940 \text{ blocks } [16{,}940.882 \text{ truncated}]$$

$$\text{number of records} = \text{blocking factor} \times \text{number of blocks}$$
$$= 24 \text{ records/block} \times 16{,}940 \text{ full blocks}$$
$$= 406{,}560 \text{ records}$$

The blocking factor of 24 records per block can allow approximately $1\frac{1}{2}$ times the number of records than a blocking factor of 8 will allow (406,560 versus 237,167 records).

EXAMPLE 3: ACCESS TIME AND TAPE

Compute the time required to read the tape in the second space calculation example with a blocking factor of 7 records per block. Assume the tape stops completely after reading each block. The **start/stop time** includes the time it takes the tape to advance the IBG.

$$\begin{aligned}\text{time to read 1 block} \atop \text{(time 1 blk)} &= \frac{\text{block length in inches}}{\text{transfer speed}} + \text{start time} + \text{stop time}\\[6pt]
&= \frac{0.35\,\text{inch/block}}{50\,\text{inches/sec}} + \frac{(0.01\,\text{sec} \times 2)}{\text{block}}\\[6pt]
&= (0.007 + 0.02)\,\text{sec/block}\\[4pt]
&= 0.027\,\text{sec/block}\end{aligned}$$

$$\begin{aligned}\text{time to read tape} &= (\text{time 1 blk}) \times (\text{number of blocks})\\[4pt]
&= 0.027\,\text{sec} \times 33{,}881\,\text{blocks}\\[4pt]
&= 914.787\,\text{sec}\\[4pt]
&= 15.2\,\text{min}\end{aligned}$$

Compute the time required to read the same tape with the blocking factor of 24 records per block. Assume that the tape comes to a complete stop after reading each block.

$$\begin{aligned}\text{time to read 1 block} \atop \text{(time 1 blk)} &= \frac{\text{block length in inches}}{\text{transfer speed}} + \text{start time} + \text{stop time}\\[6pt]
&= \frac{1.2\,\text{inches/block}}{50\,\text{inches/sec}} + \frac{(0.01\,\text{sec} \times 2)}{\text{block}}\\[6pt]
&= (0.024 + 0.02)\,\text{sec/block}\\[4pt]
&= 0.044\,\text{sec/block}\end{aligned}$$

$$\begin{aligned}\text{time to read tape} &= (\text{time 1 blk}) \times (\text{number of blocks})\\[4pt]
&= 0.044\,\text{sec} \times 16{,}940\,\text{blocks}\\[4pt]
&= 745.360\,\text{sec}\\[4pt]
&= 12.4\,\text{min}\end{aligned}$$

The blocking factor of 24 allows $1\frac{1}{2}$ times the number of records (406,560 versus 237,167 records). The entire tape can be read in 83% of the time (12.4 versus 15.2 min) it takes when the blocking factor is 7 records per block.

EXAMPLE 4: BUFFERING AND TAPE

Assume single buffering for the tape in the second space calculation example and a blocking factor of 24.

number of blocks = 33,881 blocks
time to read 1 block = 0.044 sec/block (44 ms/block)

If the processing time for one block is 25 ms, compute the total time necessary to input and process the entire file. Recall the equation for total time presented in Chapter 3.

total time = (input time/block + processing time/block)
$$\times \text{ number of blocks}$$
$$= (44 \text{ ms/block} + 25 \text{ ms/block}) \times 33{,}881 \text{ blocks}$$
$$= 2{,}337.79 \text{ sec}$$
$$= 38.96 \text{ min}$$

Assuming double buffering, rework the same problem to compute the total time to input and process the entire file. Since the time to input one block is longer than the time to process one block, the execution would be I/O-bound. Recall the equation for total time presented in Chapter 3.

total time = (input time × number of blocks) + processing time for 1 block
$$= (44 \text{ ms/block} \times 33{,}881 \text{ blocks}) + 25 \text{ ms}$$
$$= 1{,}490.79 \text{ sec}$$
$$= 24.85 \text{ min}$$

Double buffering allows the entire file to be input and processed in 24.85 min versus 38.96 min using single buffering. I/O-bound double buffering is 36.2% faster than single buffering for this particular file.

MAGNETIC DISKS

A **magnetic disk** is a direct-access storage device (DASD) that allows a particular record to be accessed directly, without reference to preceding records. A magnetic disk can store files that employ any of the organization schemes that Chapter 1 discussed (sequential, random, indexed sequential, and multikey). Records stored on disk may be accessed sequentially or randomly, depending on file organization. Two types of magnetic disks will be discussed: A **hard disk** is actually a collection of disks in a disk pack and is usually found on large computers; a **floppy disk** is the flexible disk that microcomputers usually use.

Hard Disks

A **disk pack** is a collection of aluminum platters that are attached to and rotate on a center spindle. The disk pack is constantly rotating on the center spindle at a high speed, typically 3,600 revolutions per sec. A disk pack is similar to a stack of phonograph records. The upper and lower surfaces of each platter are coated with a magnetic oxide which serves as the recording medium. Often the outermost surfaces of the top and bottom platters are not used for storing data because they may be more easily damaged. The data are stored serially around concentric circles or tracks as shown in Figure 4.7. The number of tracks on a surface varies from 200 tracks on a surface to as many as 400 or 800 tracks per surface; the number depends on the type of pack and the drive that employs it.

The capacity of each track must be the same regardless of the physical circumference of the tracks because the rotational velocity of the disk pack is constant. In order for all tracks to have the same storage capacity, the density of information on each track must be different. The storage capacity of a track is based on the maximum density allowed on the smallest track, which on a disk with 200 tracks is track 199. Different track densities allow data to pass under the read/write heads at the same rate regardless of the track being accessed. The uniform rate at which all tracks on the same disk pass under the read/write heads is called the **transfer rate**.

A disk pack may be **removable**, in that the pack may be mounted on a disk drive to access information and subsequently unmounted for storage. **Fixed** disk packs are permanently sealed in the disk drive.

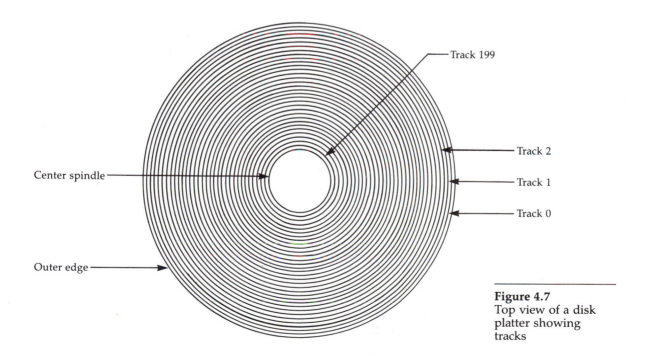

Figure 4.7
Top view of a disk platter showing tracks

Accessing Hard Disks   Each platter surface of a removable disk pack has one read/write head that reads from or writes to the disk. The read/write heads are mounted on an arm mechanism attached to the disk drive that suspends the heads a fraction of an inch from the surface of the disk as Figure 4.8 shows. Although Figure 4.8 shows 10 recording surfaces, disk packs with as many as 20 surfaces are not uncommon. The access arm mechanism moves the read/write heads along the tracks to access the data on the tracks. All read/write heads move as one unit, but only one read/write head transfers data at a time. Because the read/write heads must move to a particular track to transfer data, removable disks are also called **movable head disks**.

Accessing data stored on a removable disk pack involves four time factors: seek time, head activation time, latency, and transfer time. The time it takes the access arm to move the read/write heads to a particular track is **seek time**. Seek time is the most significant factor. **Head activation time** is the time necessary to electrically switch on the read/write head. Head activation time is negligible relative to the other time factors. **Latency** or **rota-**

Figure 4.8
Side view of a disk
pack

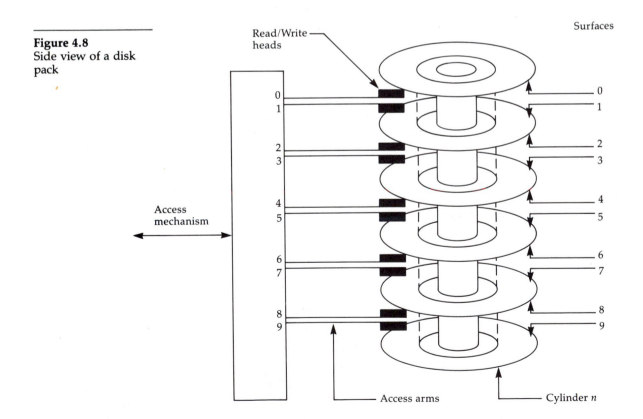

Read/Write heads

Surfaces

Access mechanism

Access arms   Cylinder n

tional delay is the time required for the beginning of the accessed block to rotate around to the read/write head. The time required for the entire block to pass under the read/write head constitutes the **transfer time**.

A disk pack with a **fixed head** is not removable; it is permanently sealed in the disk drive. Each track on every surface has a read/write head dedicated to that track. Data are stored in the same manner as with removable disks, but accessing data on a fixed-head disk is much faster than accessing data on a removable disk because the seek time is eliminated; a read/write head is already at each track. Fixed-head disks are often used in applications like airline reservation systems where several users access different parts of the disk at the same time. The access time on fixed-head disks includes head activation time, latency, and transfer time.

A variation of the fixed-head disk is the **Winchester disk**. Winchester disks contain the recording surfaces, the read/write heads, and the access mechanism in a sealed cartridge which may be removable or fixed in the disk drive. The densities of recorded data are much higher than the densities of other types of disks because the sealed cartridge allows the read/write heads to float much closer to the recording surface. Table 4.2 lists the characteristics of commercial disks that are current as of the writing of this book.

Table 4.2   Characteristics of current disk drives

Manufacturer and disk model	Transfer rate (bytes/sec)	Average seek time	Cylinders per unit	Tracks per cylinder	Sectors per track	Bytes per track
Removable Disks						
Burroughs B9484	425 K	30 ms	406	20	60	10,800
DEC RP07	1.5 M	23 ms	630	32	50	25,600
IBM 3330	806 K	30 ms	404	19	—	13,030
IBM 3380	3 M	16 ms	885	15	—	47,476
HP 3933	1.2 M	24 ms	1,321	13	92	23,552
Fixed Disks						
Burroughs B9370-2	300 K	—	100	2	100	10,000
DEC R503	250 K	—	64	1	64	4,096
IBM 2305	3 M	—	32	12	—	14,136
Winchester Disks						
Miniscribe 4020	500 K	120 ms	480	4	56	8,192
Maxtor XT1140	500 K	30 ms	918	15	56	8,192
Floppy Disks						
Shugart SA850 (8")	40 K	91 ms	77	2	26	6,656
TEAC FD-55F (5.25")	20 K	94 ms	80	2	16	4,096

EXAMPLE 5: ACCESS TIME AND HARD DISKS

The following computations require a grasp of some familiar terms and some new terms. A **kilobyte** is 1,024 bytes. **Minimum seek time** is the time needed to move the access arm to an adjacent track. **Maximum seek time** is the time it takes the access arm to move from the outermost or innermost track to the farthest track. Maximum seek time represents the longest possible seek time or the worst case. We use the **average seek time** (the average of the minimum and maximum times) when describing random access and when the relative positions of the access arm before and after the seek are unknown. **Rotational time** is the time needed for a disk pack to make one complete revolution. Consider rotational time in relation to rotational delay. The rotational delay lies between zero delay and the rotational time. The average rotational delay is the time needed to achieve one-half a rotation. For the computations that follow, use the average rotational delay, which is one-half the rotational time.

Assume a block size of 1,000 bytes and that the blocks are stored randomly. The disk drive has the following characteristics:

minimum seek time = 10 ms
maximum seek time = 50 ms
average seek time = 30 ms
rotational time = 16.67 ms
average rotational delay = 8.3 ms
transfer rate = 806 KB/sec
              = 1,024 bytes/K × 806 KB/sec
              = 825,344 bytes/sec

Compute the average access time per block and the percentage of the total access time for the seek and rotational delay.

$$\begin{aligned}
\text{average access time/block} &= \text{seek} + \text{latency} + \text{transfer} \\
&= 30 \text{ ms/block} + 8.3 \text{ ms/block} + \frac{1,000 \text{ bytes/block}}{825,344 \text{ bytes/sec}} \\
&= (30 \text{ ms} + 8.3 \text{ ms} + 1.21 \text{ ms})/\text{block} \\
&= 39.51 \text{ ms/block}
\end{aligned}$$

$$\begin{aligned}
\% (\text{seek} + \text{rotational delay}) &= \frac{\text{seek} + \text{rotational delay}}{\text{average access time}} \\
&= \frac{30 \text{ ms} + 8.3 \text{ ms}}{39.51 \text{ ms}} \\
&= 96.9\%
\end{aligned}$$

As discussed earlier, the seek time is the most significant factor of the access time and the transfer rate is the smallest factor—96.9 percent of the access time is seek time and rotational delay, and 3.1% is transfer time.

How would we figure access time if the disk were fixed? Fixed-head disks have one head per track; therefore, seek time does not apply to the access time calculation.

$$\text{average access time} = \text{latency} + \text{transfer}$$
$$= 8.3\,\text{ms} + 1.21\,\text{ms}$$
$$= 9.51\,\text{ms}$$

The access time for fixed-head disks (9.51 ms) is a great improvement over the access time for movable head disks (39.51 ms).

Addressing Hard Disks   Two addressing methods are commonly used for accessing data on a magnetic disk: the cylinder method and the sector method. In the cylinder method, data are stored on a disk using a cylinder number, a surface number, and a record number. When the access arm is positioned on a particular track, the tracks on all surfaces that are vertically aligned and have the same diameter are called a **cylinder**. A cylinder of data can be accessed each time the access arm is positioned. Cylinder n is pictured in Figure 4.8. If a disk pack contains 200 tracks per surface, then the disk pack has 200 cylinders. Cylinder 0 is the outermost cylinder and cylinder 199 is the innermost cylinder. The surface number indicates which surface within the cylinder contains the information. Each track is subdivided into blocks of logical records, and the length of each block may vary from one file to another or within a file. Since each track may hold several blocks, the record number indicates a particular physical record (block) from among those stored on a track.

On disks with the sector format, each track is subdivided into fixed-length **sectors**. Each sector can contain a fixed number of characters that is determined by the manufacturer. Sectoring is a simpler form of address calculation than the cylinder method because each sector on the disk pack has a unique sector number—there is no need for surface and record numbers. The physical records of data are stored in the sectors and, usually, no records cross sector boundaries. If the block length is larger than will fit with the boundaries of a single sector, the block is termed a **spanned record**. Sectoring may result in wasted space if the sector size is not a multiple of the record length. In addition, multiple sectors may be accessed if the physical record length is greater than the sector size.

EXAMPLE 6: CAPACITY OF A HARD DISK
_____

Consider the magnetic disk pack pictured in Figure 4.9. Suppose the disk is cylinder-addressable and has the following characteristics:

9 recording surfaces
surface inner diameter = 22 cm
surface outer diameter = 33 cm
maximum density = 1,600 bits/cm
minimum spacing between tracks = 0.25 mm
rotational speed = 3,600 revolutions per min

Calculate the maximum capacity of the entire disk pack in bits. First find the radius of the readable portion, or **readable radius**, of the surface. The readable radius is less than the actual radius since the outermost track cannot be on the very edge of the surface; neither can the innermost track be on the very edge. Thus the surface inner diameter and surface outer diameter delimit the readable portion of the surface.

$$\text{readable radius} = \frac{\text{outer diameter} - \text{inner diameter}}{2}$$

$$= \frac{33\,\text{cm} - 22\,\text{cm}}{2}$$

$$= 5.5\,\text{cm}$$

The number of tracks per surface depends on the minimum spacing allowable between tracks. Each surface containing n tracks will also contain $n - 1$ spaces between the n tracks. Dividing the radius of a surface by the minimum spacing allowed between tracks indicates the maximum number of spacings that fit on one surface ($n - 1$); the number of tracks is one more than the number of spacings: $(n - 1) + 1$.

$$\text{tracks/surface} = \frac{\text{readable radius}}{\text{spacing between tracks}} + 1$$

$$= \frac{5.5\,\text{cm}}{0.025\,\text{cm}} + 1$$

$$= 221\,\text{tracks/surface}$$

$$\text{bits/track} = \text{density} \times \text{circumference of smallest track}$$

$$= \text{density} \times \text{inner diameter} \times \text{pi}$$

$$= 1,600\,\text{bits/cm} \times 22\,\text{cm/track} \times 3.14159$$

$$= 110,580\,\text{bits/track}$$

$$\text{bits/pack} = \text{bits/track} \times \text{tracks/surface} \times \text{surfaces/pack}$$

$$= 110,580 \times 221 \times 9$$

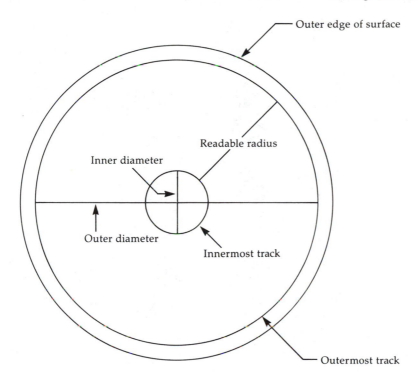

Figure 4.9
The readable radius
of a disk surface

$$= 219,943,620 \text{ bits/pack}$$

$$\sim 26.2 \text{ MB/pack}$$

The capacity of a disk pack is usually expressed in **megabytes** (MB) where *mega* is 2^{20} (1,048,576). The pack has a capacity of approximately 26.2 megabytes.

Now assume that each track in the example above is formatted into 24 sectors instead of cylinders (see Figure 4.10). Calculate the maximum capacity of the entire disk in bits.

$$\text{bits/sector} = \frac{\text{bits/track}}{\text{sectors/track}}$$

$$= \frac{110,580 \text{ bits/track}}{24 \text{ sectors/track}}$$

$$= 4,607 \text{ bits/sector [4,607.5 truncated]}$$

$$\text{bytes/sector} = \frac{\text{bits/sector}}{\text{bits/byte}}$$

$$= \frac{4,607 \text{ bits/sector}}{8 \text{ bits/byte}}$$

$$= 575 \text{ bytes/sector [575.875 truncated]}$$

Figure 4.10
A disk surface
divided into 24
sectors

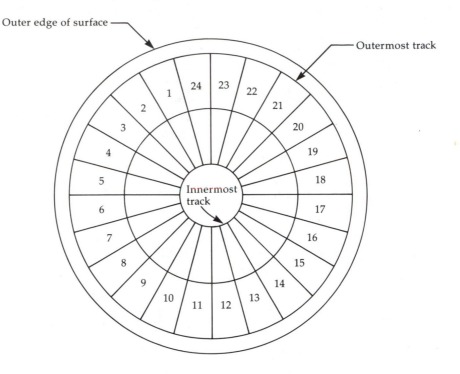

$$\text{bits/track (sectoring)} = \text{bits/bytes} \times \text{bytes/sector} \times \text{sectors/track}$$
$$= 8 \times 575 \times 24$$
$$= 110{,}400 \text{ bits/track with sectoring}$$
$$\text{bits/pack (sectoring)} = \text{bits/track} \times \text{tracks/surface} \times \text{surfaces/pack}$$
$$= 110{,}400 \times 221 \times 9$$
$$= 219{,}585{,}600 \text{ bits/pack}$$
$$\approx 26.17 \text{ MB/pack}$$

The capacity of a disk pack using sectoring is approximately 26.17 MB, which is 358,020 bits (or 43.7 KB). The sector-addressable disk has a smaller capacity than the cylinder-addressable disk.

Return to the cylinder-addressable disk. Calculate the data transfer rate in bytes per second (assume 8 bits per byte). Recall that the transfer rate is the speed at which information passes by the read/write head. Two factors affect the transfer rate: the number of bytes per track and the rotational speed of the disk in revolutions (rev) per sec. Since one revolution is required to read one track of information, the number of bytes per track is also the number of bytes to be accessed per revolution of the disk pack.

$$\text{bytes/track} = \frac{\text{bits/track}}{\text{bits/byte}}$$

$$= \frac{110,580 \text{ bits/track}}{8 \text{ bits/byte}}$$

$$= 13,822 \text{ bytes/track}$$

$$= 13,822 \text{ bytes/revolution}$$

$$\text{transfer rate} = \text{bytes/rev} \times \frac{\text{revolutions per min}}{60 \text{ sec/min}}$$

$$= 13,822 \text{ bytes/rev} \times \frac{3,600 \text{ rev/min}}{60 \text{ sec/min}}$$

$$= 13,822 \text{ bytes/rev} \times 60 \text{ rev/sec}$$

$$= 829,320 \text{ bytes/sec}$$

$$\sim 809.9 \text{ KB/sec}$$

EXAMPLE 7: SPACE CALCULATION FOR HARD DISKS

Consider a magnetic disk drive and disk pack with the following characteristics:

575 bytes/sector
24 sectors/track
200 tracks/surface
20 surfaces/pack
transfer rate = 806 KB/sec
average latency = 8.3 ms
average seek = 30 ms

Compute the highest blocking factor for 80-byte records. Assume no block is split across a sector boundary. The largest blocking factor must be no larger than the size of one sector.

$$\text{blocking factor} = \frac{\text{number of bytes/sector}}{\text{number of bytes/record}} = \text{records/sector}$$

$$= \frac{575 \text{ bytes/sector}}{80 \text{ bytes/record}}$$

$$= 7 \text{ records/block [7.1875 truncated]}$$

Now compute the number of cylinders needed for storing 33,881 blocks of seven 80-byte records.

$$\text{capacity of track} \quad = 1\,\text{block/sector} \times \text{sectors/track}$$

$$= 1\,\text{block/sector} \times 24\,\text{sectors/track}$$

$$= 24\,\text{blocks on 1 track}$$

$$\text{capacity of cylinder} = \text{blocks/track} \times \text{tracks/cylinder}$$

$$= 24\,\text{blocks/track} \times 20\,\text{tracks/cylinder}$$

$$= 480\,\text{blocks/cylinder}$$

$$\text{number of cylinders} = \frac{\text{number of blocks}}{\text{blocks/cylinder}}$$

$$= \frac{33{,}881\,\text{blocks}}{480\,\text{blocks/cylinder}}$$

$$= 71\,\text{cylinders [70.585 rounded]}$$

(We stored the same file on a 2,400-foot tape in the second space calculation Example earlier in the chapter.) Now investigate the time needed to input and process the entire file from disk using single and double buffering.

EXAMPLE 8: BUFFERING AND HARD DISKS

Compute the total time necessary to sequentially input the disk file in the previous example. Assume the following parameters:

    80 bytes/record
    7 records/block
    33,881 blocks in 71 cylinders
    24 sectors/track
    200 tracks/surface
    20 surfaces/pack
    transfer rate = 806 KB/sec
    average latency = 8.3 ms
    average seek = 30 ms

Once the heads seek a particular cylinder, each block in that cylinder can be input with only latency time and transfer time.

$$\text{input time for entire file} = ((\text{latency} + \text{transfer}) \times \text{number of blocks})$$

$$+ (\text{seek} \times \text{number of cylinders})$$

$$= ((8.3\,\text{ms} + \frac{560\,\text{bytes/block}}{825{,}344\,\text{bytes/sec}}) \times 33{,}881\,\text{blocks})$$

$$+ (30\,\text{ms/cylinder} \times 71\,\text{cylinders})$$

$$= (8.3\,\text{ms/block} + 0.679\,\text{ms/block}) \times 33{,}881\,\text{blocks} + (2{,}130\,\text{ms})$$

$= 304.21749 \, \text{sec} + 2.130 \, \text{sec}$

$= 306.35 \, \text{sec}$

$= 5.1 \, \text{min} \, (9.04 \, \text{ms/block average})$

Compute the total time necessary to input the same disk file randomly. Random input requires that a seek take place for each record input.

input time for entire file $=$ (seek $+$ latency $+$ transfer) $\times$ number of blocks

$= (30 \, \text{ms} + 8.3 \, \text{ms} + 0.679 \, \text{ms}) \times 33,881 \, \text{blocks}$

$= (38.979 \, \text{ms}) \times 33,881 \, \text{blocks}$

$= 1,320.65 \, \text{sec}$

$= 22 \, \text{min}$

Random input of the entire file takes 22 min in contrast to 5.1 min for sequential input. We will examine this difference later in terms of file design and manipulation.

Assuming single buffering for the disk file with the processing time for one block of 25 ms, compute the total time necessary to sequentially input and process the entire file. Recall the equation for total time from Chapter 3.

total time $=$ input time for entire file

$\quad\quad + $ (processing time/block $\times$ number of blocks)

$= 5.1 \, \text{min} + (25 \, \text{ms/blocks} \times 33,881 \, \text{blocks})$

$= 5.1 \, \text{min} + 14.12 \, \text{min}$

$= 19.22 \, \text{min}$

Assuming double buffering, rework the same problem to compute the total time to input and process the entire file. Since the time to process one block (25 ms) is longer than the time to input one block (9.04 ms on the average), the execution with be processor-bound; therefore, we apply the appropriate equation from Chapter 3.

total time $=$ input time for first block

$\quad\quad + $ (processing time/block $\times$ number of blocks)

$= $ (seek $+$ latency $+$ transfer) $+ (25 \, \text{ms/block} \times 33,881 \, \text{blocks})$

$= (30 \, \text{ms} + 8.3 \, \text{ms} + 0.679 \, \text{ms}) + (847,025 \, \text{ms})$

$= 847.064 \, \text{sec}$

$= 14.12 \, \text{min}$

Double buffering allows the entire file to be input and processed in 14.12 min; the single-buffered file takes 19.22 min. Processor-bound double buffering is 26.5 percent faster than single buffering for this particular file. Table 4.3 lists the processing times that apply to this example. Using single buff-

Table 4.3 Tape and disk access with single and double buffering

	Disk	Tape		Disk/tape ratio
33,881 blocks	71 cylinders	2400	feet	
Average time to read 1 block	9.04 ms	44	ms	
Single buffering	19.22 min	38.96 min		49.3%
Double buffering	14.12 min (processor-bound)	24.85 min (I/O-bound)		56.8%

ering, access to the disk is faster than to the tape—a fact that accounts for the smaller time for the disk file. Using double buffering, disk processing is processor-bound and limited by processor speed. Tape processing is I/O-bound and not limited by the processor speed.

Magnetic disk packs and drives cost more than tape reels and drives and are usually used for files with organizations that tape will not accommodate. The advantage of the disk pack is that it rotates constantly; therefore, disk packs allow shorter access time.

Floppy Disks

A floppy disk, or floppy, is a single plastic platter that resembles a 45-rpm phonograph record. Floppies are usually either 8, $5\frac{1}{4}$, or $3\frac{1}{2}$ inches in diameter and are used for secondary storage with microcomputers. A floppy disk rotates and records information in concentric circles, or tracks. If it contains tracks only on one side, it is a **single-sided** disk. If it contains tracks on both sides, it is a **double-sided** disk. There are 40 tracks on a side, which are numbered from 0 to 39 from outermost to innermost. The outside-to-inside track numbering continues from 40 to 79 on the second side of a double-sided disk.

The density of information on floppies is **single-density**, **double-density**, or **quad-density**. Double-density floppies can store twice as much data as single-density floppies; double density is typically 3,200 bpi. The floppy disk is usually sealed in a protective square jacket that has two access holes (see Figure 4.11). The oval access hole in the middle of the lower half of the disk allows reading from and writing to the disk. When the write/protect notch in the upper right side of the disk is covered with a label, a user cannot add data to the disk, so the information already there is safe from overwriting.

Accessing Floppy Disks Single-sided floppy disk drives have one read/ write head as Figure 4.12 shows. Figure 4.13 shows that double-sided floppy

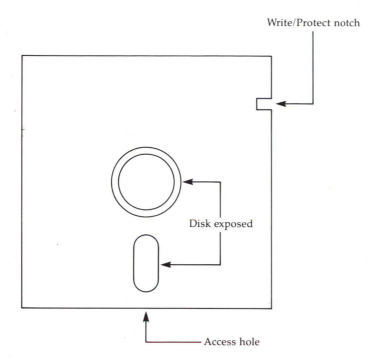

Figure 4.11
A floppy disk in its
protective jacket

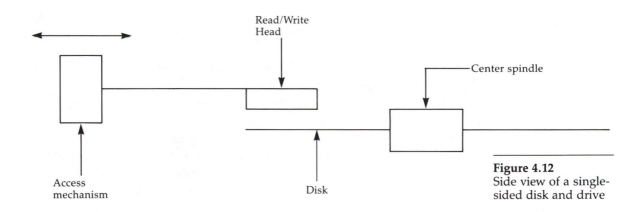

Figure 4.12
Side view of a single-
sided disk and drive

drives have two read/write heads to access both sides of a double-sided disk. Floppies are easy to remove from and load into the disk drive.

Each track is divided into several sectors that are uniquely numbered. Floppy disks have soft sectors or hard sectors. **Hard-sectored** floppies have 10, 16, or 32 hard sectors to a side with a ring of tiny index holes (one at each sector boundary) punched near the center of the disk. A beam of light senses the holes to determine the beginning of each sector. **Soft-sectored** floppies have one index hole that allows the read/write head to access the

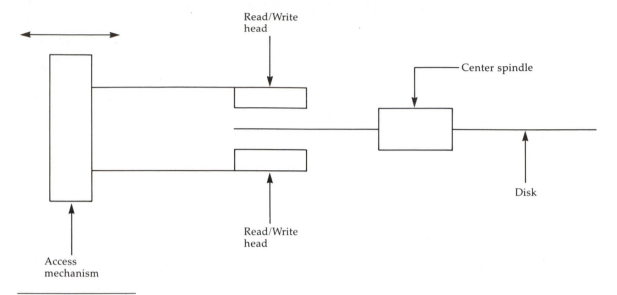

Figure 4.13
Side view of a dou-
ble-sided disk and
drive

disk through the jacket; computer software determines the boundaries
between sectors. The number of soft sectors per side ranges from 9 to 26.

Information on floppies is addressed by a sector number and the track
number within the sector. The track number indicates the side of a double-
sided floppy. Tracks 0 through 39 are on the first side and tracks 40 through
79 are on the second side.

The access time for floppy disks is composed of seek time, **head settle
time** (the time it takes for the read/write heads to settle onto the disk and
make contact), rotational delay, and the transfer rate.

Some microcomputers use a fixed disk (a hard disk with one platter).
These fixed disks are sometimes called Winchester disks after the Winchester disks used on larger computers. The fixed disk is nonremovable
and sealed within the disk drive. It offers higher densities, greater storage
capacities (10 to 30 megabytes), and faster access than floppy disks.

EXAMPLE 9: ACCESS TIME AND FLOPPY DISKS

Assume that the size of a block is 1,000 bytes and that blocks are stored
randomly on a floppy disk with the following characteristics:

tracks = 80
average seek time   =   154 ms
head settle time   =   25 ms
rotation time   =   166 ms/revolution
transfer rate   =   19.5 KB/sec (19,968 bytes/sec)

Compute the average access time per block.

average access time/block = seek + settle + latency + transfer

$$= 154\,ms + 25\,ms + 83\,ms + \frac{1{,}000\,bytes/blocks}{19{,}968\,bytes/sec}$$

$$= (154\,ms + 25\,ms + 83\,ms + 50\,ms)/block$$

$$= 312\,ms/block$$

As with hard disk packs, seek time is the most significant factor of disk access time.

EXAMPLE 10: CAPACITY OF A FLOPPY DISK
_____

Consider a floppy disk with the following characteristics:

tracks = 80
inner diameter   =   2.648 inches
track density   =   3,200 bits/inch

Compute the capacity of the entire disk in bits.

bits/track = density × circumference of innermost track
            = density × inner diameter × pi
            = 3,200 bits/inch × 2.648 inch × 3.14159
            = 26,620 bits/track

bits/disk = bits/track × tracks/side × sides/disk
           = 26,620 × 40 × 2
           = 2,129,600 bits/disk
           ≈ 260 KB/disk

The capacity of the floppy is 260 KB. The user-accessible capacity of a floppy varies from one operating system to another and depends on the amount of overhead to be stored on the floppy and the type of formatting (the number of sectors). A floppy disk with 80 tracks will have only 77 user-accessible tracks since the operating system uses three tracks.

SUMMARY

Magnetic tape is a sequential-access storage device that is compact, relatively inexpensive, and limited to sequential organization of data. Data are recorded serially along the length of the tape in various recording densities (usually 800; 1,600; or 6,250 bytes per inch). Physical records or blocks of data are separated on the tape by interblock gaps that facilitate the access of data. Several logical records can be grouped in a block to reduce the number of interblock gaps, use the tape space more efficiently, and improve access. A tape contains two physical markers (the load-point marker and the end-of-tape marker) and a number of labels (the volume label for the reel and the header and trailer labels for each file). Access time consists of the time it takes to start the tape moving, the time to transfer data, and the time to stop the tape.

A magnetic disk is a direct-access storage device that may have movable or fixed read/write heads. Magnetic disks allow direct and sequential organization of data. The magnetic disk pack is a collection of platters on which data are recorded serially along tracks (concentric circles) in the surface of each platter. Cylinders are vertically aligned tracks. Accessing information from disk involves seek time (for movable head disks only), head activation time (which is negligible), rotational delay, and transfer time. Magnetic disk packs are either sector-addressable (which means that each track is subdivided into sectors of fixed length) or cylinder-addressable (which means that each track is subdivided into blocks of fixed or variable length).

Floppy disks are flexible single-platter disks that are used for secondary storage with microcomputers. Floppy disks may be single- or double-sided; they may employ single-, double-, or quad-density; and they are soft- or hard-sectors. Access time for a floppy disk involves seek time, head settle time, rotational delay, and transfer time. Fixed (hard) disks are also available for microcomputers. These disks are sealed and are similar to the hard Winchester disks that large computers use.

Key Terms

ASCII	file trailer label
cylinder	fixed-head disks
disk pack	floppy disk
double-sided floppy	hard disk
EBCDIC	hard-sectored floppy
end-of-tape marker	head activation time
even parity	head settle time
file header label	interblock gap (IBG)

interrecord gap (IRG)	recording density
kilobyte	removable disk
latency	rotational delay
load-point marker	rotational time
magnetic disk	sector
magnetic tape	seek time
maximum seek time	single-sided floppy
megabyte	soft-sectored floppy
millisecond	spanned record
minimum seek time	start/stop time
movable-head disks	track
odd parity	transfer rate
parity bit	transfer time
physical record	volume label
readable radius	Winchester disk

Exercises

1. Why are interblock gaps (IBGs) necessary?

2. Explain how random access capabilities are achieved.

3. Which storage media provide random access and which provide sequential access?

4. What is meant by the density of a tape or disk?

5. What is the difference between a fixed-head disk and a movable-head disk with respect to data access time?

6. Which of the following activities accounts for the greatest amount of time when accessing a block of data on a movable-head disk?

    a. seek of a cylinder

    b. head activation

    c. rotational delay

7. Which of the following activities accounts for the greatest amount of time when accessing a block of data on a fixed-head disk?

    a. seek of a cylinder

    b. head activation

    c. rotational delay

8. What are the relative advantages and disadvantages of magnetic tape and magnetic disk?

9. What different types of data access exist, and what are the differences among these access methods?

10. How does file organization relate to the type of secondary storage device used?

11. Why are records blocked on magnetic tape? Consider transfer rate and tape capacity.

12. Why are records blocked on magnetic disk? Give examples in which blocked records are useful and in which blocked records are not useful.

13. Consider a section of tape containing the following binary digits:

track 1 : 1 1 1 1 1 1 1
           1 1 1 1 1 1 1
           0 0 0 0 0 1 1
           1 0 1 0 0 0 0
           0 0 1 1 0 0 1
           1 0 0 0 0 0 0
           1 0 0 0 0 1 0
track 8 : 1 1 1 1 1 1 0

What does track 9 contain if the data is recorded with even parity? With odd parity?

14. Consider a magnetic tape drive and reel with the following characteristics:
    length   = 2400 ft
    density = 1600 bpi
    IBG   = 0.5 inch

Compute the number of 120-byte records that can be stored on the tape reel with blocking factors of:

a. 5

b. 15

c. 25

15. Compute the time required to read the files in a, b, and c of exercise 14 if

transfer speed = 50 inches/sec
start or stop time = 10 ms (to traverse gap)

16. Distinguish between a volume and a file.

17. Consider a magnetic tape drive with:

density = 1,600 bpi
IBG = 0.5 inch

How many inches of tape are required to store 50,000 records of 120 bytes each with a blocking factor of 45?

18. Assume the following parameters

logical record length = 152 bytes
magnetic tape density = 1,600 bpi
IBG = 0.5 inch

Calculate the blocking factor necessary for 95% of the tape to hold all the data.

19. An I/O buffer of 1,000 bytes is available for a file of logical records. Each logical record is 92 bytes long. Choose a tape recording density of 800 or 1,600 bpi. Determine the blocking factor that yields the highest recording density. Which recording density and blocking factor yields the lowest recording density?

20. What is the cylinder size of a disk pack that has 10 platters? (Remember that the top and bottom platter surfaces are not used.) If a track stores 4,000 bytes, what is the disk capacity?

21. How many movements of the access mechanism (seeks) are required to read a sequential file stored on 21 cylinders of a disk?

22. Consider a disk with the following characteristics:

    512 bytes/sector
    20 sectors/track
    200 tracks/surface
    55 surfaces

    How many 120-byte logical records can be stored on 10 cylinders of this disk, assuming that no logical record is split across a sector boundary?

23. Consider a disk drive with the following characteristics:

    512 bytes/sector
    20 sectors/track
    200 tracks/surface
    5 surfaces

    a. What is the average latency in ms?
    b. How many sectors are there on each cylinder?

24. Explain why having one disk controller attached to three disk drives could make I/O operations too slow.

25. Distinguish between fixed-head disks and removable disks.

26. Consider a disk with the following characteristics:

    track = 10,000 bytes
    rotation = 10 ms

    and data in which:
    block = 1,000 bytes
    IBG = 100 bytes

    a. Compute the maximum transfer rate in bytes/sec.
    b. Compute the average transfer rate per track in bytes/sec.

PART II
SEQUENTIAL ACCESS

Chapter 5
Sequential File Organization

Chapter 6
External Sort/Merge Algorithms

Chapter 5

CHAPTER CONTENTS

Sequential File Organization

PREVIEW

THIS CHAPTER EXAMINES THE DESIGN and maintenance of sequential files that are stored on sequential- and random-access storage devices. Algorithms for the maintenance of sequential files stored on sequential-access devices are contrasted with algorithms for the maintenance of sequential files stored on random-access devices. All algorithms appear in Pascal-like pseudocode that employs the control structures Case, For, If, Repeat, and While. Indentation shows the nesting of control structures. (The indent scheme precludes the need for End statements, saves space, and keeps the algorithms compact.) A blank line follows the body of a control structure to enhance readability. The chapter shows how to apply the concepts of file implementation in an example involving a car-rental agency. The chapter also presents quantitative measures of access times.

PHYSICAL CHARACTERISTICS

Sequential file organization is the oldest type of file organization. It developed in the early 1950s as a result of an association with magnetic tapes, which were the first secondary storage devices available. Today, sequential files are also stored on mass-storage, direct-access devices—disks—which are characterized by greater storage capacity and faster access. The physical order of records in a sequential file is the same as the logical order. The records must be accessed sequentially from the beginning of the file to the end. The nth record of the file can be accessed only after the first $n - 1$ records have been accessed. The records in a sequential file may be stored **serially** (no order assumed) or in ascending or descending order by a **key**. (A KEY is a field in each record that contains a unique identifying value.)

MAINTENANCE

Updating a sequential master file involves adding new records, deleting existing records, and changing information in existing records. **Adding records** to serial nonkeyed files involves appending the new records at the end of the existing file—order is not important. Adding new records to keyed sequential files is more complex because the ascending or descending order of the keys must be maintained. Inserting the new records requires several steps: locating the point of insertion between two existing records, copying all the records prior to the insertion point to a new file, inserting the new record on the new file, then copying all remaining records after the insertion point to the new file.

    Deleting records from a keyed sequential file is as time-consuming as inserting new records into a keyed sequential file. Deletions require the same steps as insertions; all the records except the record to be deleted must be copied to a new file to maintain the physical sequence.

    Changes—changing information in existing records in a file—during a **sequential update** also require several steps: the records prior to the record to be changed are copied to a new file, the record is changed and written to the new file, and the copying continues. Some programming languages for use with direct-access storage devices allow a sequential file to be accessed randomly. These languages can change the information in a record and rewrite the changed record over the existing record on the file—time-consuming copying from one file to another is eliminated.

    Batch processing means that updates to the master file accumulate in a **transaction file** where they are sorted into the same key order as the master file and applied to the master file in a **maintenance run**. Each transaction contains the key value of the corresponding master record and an update code indicating the type of update: an insertion of a new record, a deletion of an existing record, or a change to one or more fields of an existing record. Transactions that indicate an insertion also contain all the fields contained on existing master records. The change transactions contain only fields that are to be changed on the master file.

Editing a transaction file before the maintenance run identifies invalid data. The master file may be created by a program other than the maintenance program or by processing each record as an add transaction against an empty master file. The time that elapses between maintenance runs depends on a number of factors: the rate of change of the data, the size of the master file, the need for current data in the master file, and the file activity (see Chapter 1).

As the time between updates becomes longer, the data on the master file becomes more outdated. The number of transactions becomes larger; therefore, the next maintenance run takes longer. If the master file is accessed between updates, the user should perform maintenance runs more often to keep the data current. Each maintenance run has a cost, however, and the cost must be weighed against the need for current data.

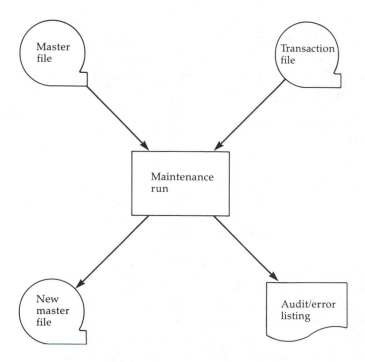

Figure 5.1
A representation of sequential file maintenance

During the updating process the master file (in ascending or descending order by a key field) is compared to the transaction file, which has been sorted in the same key order. When a specific key value appears in both files, the maintenance run changes or deletes the record as necessary. When the maintenance run encounters a transaction record whose key value does not match any key on the master file, the record must be new; it is added to the master file. The maintenance program must detect three common errors relative to the matching process: trying to insert a record with a key that exists on the master file, trying to delete a record whose key does not exist on the master file, and trying to change data on a record whose key does not exist on the master file. Different applications handle these errors differently.

An **audit/error listing** is output as part of the maintenance run. It lists transaction keys and update codes that summarize the additions, changes, and deletions that resulted from the maintenance run and any errors that occurred during the process. The user corrects the records that contain errors and stores the records in a new transaction file for the next update. The diagram in Figure 5.1 shows the input and output of a maintenance run.

TRADITIONAL ALGORITHMS FOR UPDATING SEQUENTIAL FILES

The algorithm required to update a master file with a batch of transactions is the same as the algorithm for merging two files. The keys in the transaction file are compared with the keys in the master file. When the keys are the same, changes are made to the master file records; when the keys are not the same, the records are merged into a new master file.

Changes

Consider first the case of a transaction file containing only changes to existing records (no additions or deletions) and only one transaction per master file record. The logic is given in pseudocode in Algorithm 5.1. Each iteration of the While loop processes the record with the smaller key value regardless of whether it is in the master record or the transaction record. The algorithm employs a While loop instead of a Repeat loop so that both files can be checked for an end of file condition at the first iteration. The algorithm terminates in case both files happen to be empty.

The primary function of the logic in Algorithm 5.1 is to compare the key of the master record with the key of the transaction record. There are three cases to consider. In the first case (lines 4 through 6) the master key is less than the transaction key; no transactions are applied to this master record,

Algorithm 5.1   Update_Master

```
                        {
                          change transactions;
                          one transaction per master record
                        }
1    Get_Next_Trans
2    Get_Next_Master
3    While Not (master_key = sentinel And trans_key = sentinel)
                    { until both end }
4        If master_key < trans_key
                        {
                          no trans for this master
                        }
5            output master record to new master
6            Get_Next_Master

7        Else
                        {
                          master key >= trans key
                        }
8            If master_key = trans_key
9                make change in master record
10               output master record to new master
11               Get_Next_Master
12               Get_Next_Trans
13           Else
                        {
                          master_key > trans_key
                        }
14               print 'no matching master record for trans key'
15               Get_Next_Trans

Algorithm Get_Next_Master

            If Eof (master)
                    master_key ← sentinel value
            Else
                    input master record

Algorithm Get_Next_Trans

            If Eof (trans)
                    trans_key ← sentinel value
            Else
                    input transaction record
```

so the master record is copied to the new master. The next master record must be input and matched with the current transaction key the next time through the loop. In the second case (lines 8 through 12) the master key and transaction key are the same. The specified change is made in the

Algorithm 5.2   Update_Master

```
                        {
                            change  transactions;
                            several  transactions  per  master  record
                        }
    1   Get_Next_Trans
    2   Get_Next_Master
    3   While  Not  (master_key  =  sentinel  And  trans_key  =  sentinel)
                        { until  both  end }
    4       If master_key  <  trans_key
                        {
                            no  transactions  for  this  master  or
                            changes  have  been  made
                        }
    5           output  master  record  to  new  master
    6           Get_Next_Master

    7       Else
                        {
                            master_key  >=  trans_key
                        }
    8           If master_key  =  trans_key
    9               make  change  in  master  record
   10               Get_Next_Trans
   11           Else
                        {
                            master_key  >  trans_key
                        }
   12               print 'no  matching  master  record  for  trans  key'
   13               Get_Next_Trans
```

master record, which is then copied to the new master. The next master record and the next transaction must be input for comparison the next time through the While loop. In the third case (lines 14 and 15) the master key is greater than the transaction key; no master record matches this transaction key, so an error message is printed and the next transaction record is input to compare with the current master record. If Eof is reached on the transaction file, a **sentinel value** (a value that is higher than any key occurring on either file) is moved to the transaction key. The remaining master file records are copied with no changes to the new master (according to the logic of lines 4 through 6). If Eof is reached on the master file, the same sentinel value is moved to the master key, and error messages are printed for the remaining transaction keys that did not match any master keys (lines 14 and 15).

A sentinel value in master_key and trans_key (rather than the standard functions, Eof(master) and Eof(trans)) stops the main While loop—the end of both of the files has been reached. The need to read another record from either file is determined by the algorithm; a read does not occur each time through the loop. Therefore, a sentinel loop is needed for reading and matching the two files. Algorithm 5.1 uses the standard function Eof after processing a transaction or master record, then moves the sentinel value to the key. Another approach is to add a sentinel value as the last record of the master and transaction files and to repeat until the sentinels are input.

Algorithm 5.1 is a simple form that assumes only one transaction per master record. This assumption is probably unrealistic because a transaction file may contain multiple changes to be applied to any given master record. The algorithm can be easily modified; by removing lines 10 and 11, the master record will not be written until the transaction key changes. The resulting algorithm, Algorithm 5.2, can handle multiple transactions.

Each iteration of the While loop processes one record. A record is the result of an unmatched master record, an unmatched transaction record, or a transaction with the same key as the master key. When the master key and the transaction key are the same (line 8), the specified change is made in the master record (line 9), but the master record is not output to the new master file because more transactions with the same key may follow. As soon as a transaction record with a different key is found, the master key is less than the transaction key (line 4). The changed master record is written to the new master file (line 5), and the next master record is input (line 6).

Additions

Consider next the case of a transaction file containing additions, changes, and multiple transactions per transaction key. The possibilities are:

1. one or more changes per transaction key
2. one addition per transaction key
3. several additions per transaction key
4. one addition and one or more changes per transaction key
5. several additions and one or more changes per transaction key

To keep track of the transactions that apply, the user must define a new field that specifies the updates. This field contains an **update code:** an A if the transaction is an addition to the master file or a C if the transaction is a change to an existing master record.

Algorithm 5.2 (lines 8 through 10) handles the first possibility, that the transaction file contains one or more changes per transaction key. The second possibility, in which there is one addition per transaction key, can be processed when the master key is greater than the transaction key and the update code is A. In this situation the transaction record will be output to the new master file as a new master record. The third possibility, that the transaction file contains several additions per transaction key, indicates an error in all but the first addition if all the master keys are to remain unique. In this case the first addition progresses as in number 2 in the list above, but each of the remaining additions for the same key cause an error message.

The need for one addition and one or more changes per transaction key arises if the time between updates is so long that changes have been identified since the addition transaction was entered. To process an addition and changes to the same key, the transaction file must record the date a transaction is entered. The transactions are sorted in ascending order by entry date within each transaction key. (The keys are also sorted in ascend-

Algorithm 5.3   Update_Master

```
                              {
                                  addition and change transactions;
                                  several transactions per master record
                              }
    1   Get_Next_Trans
    2   Get_Next_Master
    3   While Not (master_key = sentinel And trans_key = sentinel)
                          { until both end }
    4       If master_key < trans_key
                              {
                                  no transactions for this master or
                                  changes have been made
                              }
    5           output master record to new master
    6           Get_Next_Master

    7       Else
                              {
                                  master_key >= trans_key
                              }
    8           If master_key = trans_key
    9               Case update_code
    10                  'A' : print 'duplicate add'
    11                          Get_Next_Trans

    12                  'C' : make change in master record
    13                          Get_Next_Trans

    14                  Else : print 'invalid update code'
    15                          Get_Next_Trans
    16              Else
                              {
                                  master_key > trans_key
                              }
    17              Nomatch
```

Algorithm Nomatch

```
 1    Case update_code
 2       'A' : Build new record from trans record
 3            new_key ← trans_key
 4            Get_Next_Trans
 5            While trans_key <> sentinel
 6            And trans_key = new_key
 7                 Case update_code
 8                      'A' : print 'duplicate add'
 9                      'C' : make change in new record
10                      Else : print 'invalid update code'

11                 Get_Next_Trans

12            output new record to new master

13       'C' : print 'no matching master record for trans key'
14            Get_Next_Trans

15       Else : print 'invalid update code'
16            Get_Next_Trans
```

ing order.) A chronological sort ensures that transactions are processed in chronological order. Even though transactions are batched, the effect is the same as if the user performed each transaction as soon as the need arose.

The fifth possibility in the list above is a combination of number 3 and number 4. The first addition can be processed, all the following additions generate error messages, and the changes are processed. A transaction that contains invalid update codes (codes other than A and C) also causes an error message. Algorithm 5.3 processes all five possibilities discussed above, and it can also cue an error message if the file contains invalid update codes.

Two modifications are required to handle addition transactions that occur (1) when the master key equals the transaction key and (2) when the master key is greater than the transaction key. When the master and transaction keys are the same (line 8 of Algorithm 5.3) and the transaction is an addition (possibility number 2), the message duplicate add is printed (line 10 of Algorithm 5.3).

When the master key is greater than the transaction key (line 16), Algorithm 5.3 calls Algorithm Nomatch. If the transaction is a change, the error message no matching master record for trans key prints and Nomatch gets another transaction record (lines 13 and 14). If the transaction is an addition (possibility number 2), a new record is built using the data from the transaction record (line 2 of Nomatch). For any addition transaction that follows with the same key (possibilities 3 and 5), the message duplicate add prints (line 8 of Nomatch). For any change transactions that follow with the same key (possibilities 4 and 5), the specified changes are made in the new record (line 9 of Nomatch). When a different transaction key is input (line 6 of Nomatch), the new record is output to the new master (line 12 of Nomatch). Then the main algorithm continues to process the remaining master and transaction records.

Deletions

Consider finally the case of a transaction file containing additions, changes, deletions, and multiple transactions per transaction key. To accommodate deletion transactions, we employ Algorithm 5.4, a modification of Algorithm 5.3. Use Algorithm 5.4 in the following situations:

1. to perform one deletion per transaction key
2. to perform several deletions per transaction key
3. to perform an addition and a deletion per transaction key
4. to perform one or more changes and a deletion per transaction key
5. to perform an addition, one or more changes, and a deletion per transaction key

The update code may contain an A for addition, a C for changes, and a D for deletion of an existing master record. Any other update code is invalid. To implement Algorithm 5.4 which calls for three types of transactions, we sort the transactions in ascending order by entry date within each transaction key. Algorithm 5.4 will apply the transactions in the order in which they occurred in real time.

One deletion per transaction key (situation 1) can be processed when the master key and the transaction key are the same. The algorithm does not copy the master record to the new master file; rather, it causes the next master record to be input. Executing several deletions per transaction key (situation 2) is similar to executing several additions per transaction key: The first deletion per transaction key is processed, but the remaining deletions for the same key trigger an error message. The last three situations only occur if the time between updates is sufficient to allow changes and deletions to accumulate in the transaction file after additions to the same key.

The modified algorithm processes one addition and one deletion for the same key (situation 3) and one addition, changes, and one deletion for the same key (situation 5) as Algorithm 5.3 processes additions and changes for the same key. Assuming that an addition is entered before the deletion of the same key, the addition causes a new record to be built from the transaction record. The deletion that follows prevents the new record from being copied to the new master. Similarly, in situation 5 in the list above an addition causes a new record to be built from the transaction record. One or more changes to the new record follow, then a deletion prevents the new record from being copied to the new master.

In situation 4 multiple changes to an existing record usually precede a deletion of the same record. Multiple changes are processed by the algorithm as one change transaction per execution of the inner While loop. The need to perform a deletion for the same key is a situation similar to situation

Algorithm 5.4   Update_Master

```
                          {
                            addition, change, and deletion transactions;
                              several transactions per master record
                          }
1   Get_Next_Trans
2   Get_Next_Master
3   While Not (master_key = sentinel And trans_key = sentinel)
                          { until both end }
4       If master_key < trans_key
                          {
                            no transactions for this master or
                            changes have been made
                          }
5           output master record to new master
6           Get_Next_Master

7       Else
                          {
                            master_key >= trans_key
                          }
8           If master_key = trans_key
9               Case update_code
10                  'A' : print 'duplicate add'
11                         Get_Next_Trans

12                  'C' : make change in master record
13                         Get_Next_Trans

14                  'D' : Get_Next_Master
15                         Get_Next_Trans

16                  Else : print 'invalid update code'
17                         Get_Next_Trans

18          Else
                          {
                            master_key > trans_key
                          }
19              Nomatch
```

Algorithm Nomatch

```
1      Case  update_code
2        'A'  :  build  new  record  from  trans  record
3             new_key  ←  trans_key
4             delete_record  ←  FALSE
5             Get_Next_Trans

6             While  trans_key  <>  sentinel
7             And  trans_key  =  new_key
8             And  Not  delete_record
9                  Case  update_code
10                      'A'  :  print  'duplicate  add'
11                      'C'  :  make  change  in  new  record
12                      'D'  :  delete_record  ←  TRUE
13                      Else  :  print  'invalid  update  code'

14                  Get_Next_Trans

15             If  Not  delete_record
16                  output  new  record  to  new  master

17       'C',
18       'D'  :  print  'no  matching  master  record  for  trans  key'
19             Get_Next_Trans

20       Else  :  print  'invalid  update  code'
21             Get_Next_Trans
```

1: The master record, with changes, is not copied to the new master file; instead, the next master record is input.

To perform one deletion per transaction key (situation 1), the algorithm does not copy the master record to the next master file (line 14 of Algorithm 5.4). Instead it inputs the next master record. The transaction key of any deletion transactions that follow (situation 2) is lower than the remaining master record input (line 18 of Algorithm 5.4). The result is an error message (line 17 of Nomatch).

In situation 3, in which the transaction key of an addition is different than the pending master record (line 2 of Nomatch) and there is a deletion for the same transaction key, Nomatch sets the Boolean flag delete_record in line 12. The flag stops the While loop (line 6 of Nomatch) and prevents the newly built record from being copied to the new master file (lines 15 and 16 of Nomatch). In situation 4 (in which there are one or more changes and a deletion) and situation 5 (in which there are one addition, one deletion, and at least one change), the result is the same as in situation 3: The delete_record flag stops the While loop and prevents the new record from being written to the new master. In essence the algorithm ignores all transactions for this key value.

CASE STUDY 5.1

To demonstrate the effectiveness of Algorithm 5.4, consider an example involving a car-rental agency. Initially, assume the car-rental master file is empty. Table 5.1 shows Transaction File T1, which contains the data to be added to the master file. The id number is the primary key; notice that File T1 is arranged in the order of ascending id numbers. To compare Algorithm 5.4, a traditional algorithm, to the modern algorithm presented later, we will tally cases in which the operations in the traditional algorithm differ from the operations in the modern algorithm. These operations are usually Boolean operators and the assignment of values to flags. The operations in line 3 (two operations), line 4 (one operation), and line 8 (one operation) of the main algorithm and lines 3, 4, 6, 7, and 15 (one operation each) of Nomatch are the operations we will count. Upon execution of Algorithm 5.4, the following actions take place:

1. Get_Next_Trans inputs the first transaction.

2. Get_Next_Master finds the master file empty so, master_key is filled with the sentinel value that is higher than any transaction key.

3. In line 3 Not (master_key = sentinel And trans_key = sentinel) is TRUE. The operation count = 2.

4. Since master_key contains the sentinel value, line 4 is FALSE. In consequence we move to line 8. The operation count = 3.

5. The result of line 8 is FALSE since master_key contains the sentinel. We move to line 18. The operation count = 4.

Table 5.1 Transaction file T1, data for a car-rental agency

Code	Id no.	Make	Style	Model	Mileage	Color
A	C1	Dodge	2 DR	Omni	25,000	grey
A	C2	Dodge	2 DR	Aspen	7,000	tan
A	F1	Ford	2 DR HB	Escort	54,000	white
A	F2	Lincoln	4 DR	Continental	38,000	black
A	F3	Ford	2 DR	Thunderbird	35,000	blue
A	GM1	Cadillac	4 DR	Fleetwood	9,000	red
A	GM2	Oldsmobile	4 DR	Delta 88	28,050	blue
A	GM3	Chevrolet	2 DR	Camaro	33,000	silver
A	GM4	Cadillac	2 DR	Cimarron	63,000	maroon
A	GM5	Oldsmobile	4 DR	98	11,000	green
A	H1	Honda	4 DR	Accord	32,000	yellow
A	H2	Honda	2 DR HB	Accord	11,250	brown
A	T1	Toyota	2 DR HB	Celica	3,400	white

6. The main algorithm calls Nomatch.

7. Since update_code is A, a new record is filled with the information in the transaction record, the transaction key is saved in new_key, and delete_record is set to FALSE. The operation count = 6.

8. Get_Next_Trans inputs the next transaction record.

9. The Boolean expression in lines 6 through 8, trans_key = new_key is FALSE. We move to Nomatch line 15. The operation count = 9.

10. The variable delete_record is FALSE, so the new record is output to the new master file. The operation count = 10.

11. The body of While, which begins in line 3 of the main algorithm, executes the last transactions. Lines 3 through 19 are repeated for each transaction until Get_Next_Trans finds Eof (trans) is TRUE. Then trans_key is filled with the sentinel value. The operation count = 10 + (10 operations × 12 transactions) = 130.

12. The next pass through line 3 evaluates to FALSE, and the program terminates. The operation count = 131.

The While loop satisfactorily checks for Eof on both the master file and the transaction file. The loop terminates when both files have ended. In this case the master file was empty at the beginning of the algorithm, so all the addition transactions were written to the new master file. Table 5.2 shows the resulting master file.

Table 5.2   Car-rental agency master file

Id no.	Make	Style	Model	Mileage	Color
C1	Dodge	2 DR	Omni	25,000	grey
C2	Dodge	2 DR	Aspen	7,000	tan
F1	Ford	2 DR HB	Escort	54,000	white
F2	Lincoln	4 DR	Continental	38,000	black
F3	Ford	2 DR	Thunderbird	35,000	blue
GM1	Cadillac	4 DR	Fleetwood	9,000	red
GM2	Oldsmobile	4 DR	Delta 88	28,050	blue
GM3	Chevrolet	2 DR	Camaro	33,000	silver
GM4	Cadillac	2 DR	Cimarron	63,000	maroon
GM5	Oldsmobile	4 DR	98	11,000	green
H1	Honda	4 DR	Accord	32,000	yellow
H2	Honda	2 DR HB	Accord	11,250	brown
T1	Toyota	2 DR HB	Celica	3,400	white

Table 5.3 Transaction file T2

Code	Id no.	Make	Style	Model	Mileage	Color
A	GM6	Chevrolet	4 DR	Cimarron	11,250	brown

The transaction file T2 in Table 5.3 contains only one record, which is applied to the master file just created. The following is the trace of Algorithm 5.4:

1. Get_Next_Trans inputs the first transaction.
2. Get_Next_Master inputs the first master record.
3. Line 3 is TRUE. The operation count = 2.
4. Since master_key is C1 and trans_key is GM6, C1 is output to the new master file, and C2 is input (lines 4 through 6). The operation count = 3.
5. Line 3 is TRUE. The operation count = 5.
6. C2, master_key, is less than GM6, trans_key. As a result, C2 is output to the new master file, and F1 is input (lines 4 through 6). The operation count = 6.
7. Line 3 is TRUE. The operation count = 8.
8. F1, master_key, is less than GM6, trans_key. As a result, F1 is output to the new master file, and F2 is input (lines 4 through 6). The operation count = 9.
9. Line 3 is TRUE. The operation count = 11.
10. F2, master_key, is less than GM6, trans_key. As a result, F2 is output to the new master file, and F3 is input (lines 4 through 6). The operation count = 12.
11. Line 3 is TRUE. The operation count = 14.
12. F3, master_key, is less than GM6, trans_key. As a result, F3 is output to the new master file, and GM1 is input (lines 4 through 6). The operation count = 15.
13. Line 3 is TRUE. The operation count = 17.
14. GM1, master_key, is less than GM6, trans_key. As a result, GM1 is output to the new master file, and GM2 is input (lines 4 through 6). The operation count = 18.
15. Line 3 is TRUE. The operation count = 20.
16. GM2, master_key, is less than GM6, trans_key. As a result, GM2 is output to the new master file, and GM3 is input (lines 4 through 6). The operation count = 21.

17. Line 3 is TRUE. The operation count = 23.

18. GM3, master_key, is less than GM6, trans_key. As a result, GM3 is output to the new master file, and GM4 is input (lines 4 through 6). The operation count = 24.

19. Line 3 is TRUE. The operation count = 26.

20. GM4, master_key, is less than GM6, trans_key. As a result, GM4 is output to the new master file, and GM5 is input (lines 4 through 6). The operation count = 27.

21. Line 3 is TRUE. The operation count = 29.

22. GM5, master_key, is less than GM6, trans_key. As a result, GM5 is output to the new master file, and H1 is input (lines 4 through 6). The operation count = 30.

23. Line 3 is TRUE. The operation count = 32.

24. H1, master_key, is greater than GM6, trans_key. As a result, line 19 of the main algorithm calls Nomatch. The operation count = 34.

25. Since update_code is A, a new record is filled with the information in the transaction record GM6, the transaction key is saved in new_key, and delete_record is set to FALSE. The operation count = 36.

26. Get_Next_Trans finds Eof (trans) TRUE; therefore, trans_key is filled with the sentinel value.

27. The Boolean expression in lines 6 through 8 of Nomatch, trans_key = new_key, is FALSE. We move to line 15 of Nomatch. The operation count = 39.

28. The variable delete_record is FALSE, so the new record GM6 is output to the new master file. The operation count = 40.

29. The body of While, which begins in line 3 of the main algorithm, is TRUE. The operation count = 42.

30. H1, master_key, is less than trans_key (the sentinel), so H1 is output to the new master file and H2 is input (lines 4 through 6). The operation count = 43.

31. Line 3 is TRUE. The operation count = 45.

32. H2, master_key, is less than trans_key (the sentinel), so H2 is output to the new master file and the id T1 is input (lines 4 through 6). The operation count = 46.

33. Line 3 is TRUE. The operation count = 48.

34. T1, master_key, is less than the trans_key (the sentinel). As a result, the id T1 is output to the new master file and Get_Next_Master finds Eof (master) is TRUE; master_key is filled with the sentinel value (lines 4 through 6). The operation count = 49.

35. The next pass through line 3 evaluates to FALSE, and the algorithm terminates. The operation count = 51.

The While loop checks for Eof on both the master file and the transaction file, and the algorithm terminates when both files have ended. In this case the master records were copied to the new master file until the addition of transaction GM6, at which time the addition took place. The algorithm found no more transactions, so the rest of the master file was copied to the new master file. Table 5.4 shows the resulting master file.

The transaction file T3 in Table 5.5 illustrates a set of transactions that includes an addition, a change, a deletion, and a subsequent addition for the same key. GM7 is added to the fleet, the mileage is updated later, the car is subsequently wrecked and deleted from the fleet, and a navy Fiero is assigned the same key, GM7. (In this application deleted keys are reas-

Table 5.4 Master file after update with transaction file T2

Id no.	Make	Style	Model	Mileage	Color
C1	Dodge	2 DR	Omni	25,000	grey
C2	Dodge	2 DR	Aspen	7,000	tan
F1	Ford	2 DR HB	Escort	54,000	white
F2	Lincoln	4 DR	Continental	38,000	black
F3	Ford	2 DR	Thunderbird	35,000	blue
GM1	Cadillac	4 DR	Fleetwood	9,000	red
GM2	Oldsmobile	4 DR	Delta 88	28,050	blue
GM3	Chevrolet	2 DR	Camaro	33,000	silver
GM4	Cadillac	2 DR	Cimarron	63,000	maroon
GM5	Oldsmobile	4 DR	98	11,000	green
GM6	Chevrolet	4 DR	Cimarron	11,250	brown
H1	Honda	4 DR	Accord	32,000	yellow
H2	Honda	2 DR HB	Accord	11,250	brown
T1	Toyota	2 DR HB	Celica	3,400	white

Table 5.5 Transaction file T3

Code	Id no.	Make	Style	Model	Mileage	Color
D	F1					
A	GM7	Pontiac	2 DR	Fiero	1,250	orange
C	GM7				5,000	
D	GM7					
A	GM7	Pontiac	2 DR	Fiero	1,500	navy
D	H3					
C	T1				7,800	
D	T1					

signed when the cars are replaced by new ones.) The process of applying T3 to the master file is as follows:

1. Get_Next_Trans inputs the first transaction.

2. Get_Next_Master inputs the first master record.

3. Line 3 is TRUE. The operation count = 2.

4. Lines 3 through 6 are repeated for master records C1 through C2. The operation count = 6.

5. Line 3 is TRUE; master_key, F1, is the same as trans_key. The update_code is D, so Get_Next_Master inputs F2 and Get_Next_Trans inputs the code A and the id GM7. The operation count = 10.

6. Lines 3 through 6 are repeated for master records F2 through GM6, the point that master_key = H1 and trans_key = GM7. The operation count = 10 + (3 operations × 8 transactions) = 34.

7. Line 3 is TRUE; master_key, H1, is greater than trans_key, GM7. As a result, main algorithm line 19 calls Nomatch. The operation count = 38.

8. Since update_code is A, a new record is filled with the information in the transaction record GM7, the id number currently assigned to the orange Fiero. The transaction key is saved in new_key, and delete_record is set to FALSE. The operation count = 40.

9. Get_Next_Trans inputs the code C and the id GM7.

10. The Boolean expression in lines 6 through 8 of Nomatch is TRUE. As a result, the mileage change is made to GM7, and Get_Next_Trans inputs the code D and the id GM7. The operation count = 43.

11. Lines 6 through 8 of Nomatch evaluate to TRUE, so delete_record is set to TRUE and Get_Next_Trans inputs the code A and the id GM7. The operation count = 46.

12. Lines 6 through 8 of Nomatch evaluate to FALSE because Not delete_record is FALSE. We move to line 15. The operation count = 49.

13. The variable delete_record is TRUE, so we move to line 3 of the main algorithm. The operation count = 50.

14. Line 3 evaluates to TRUE. The operation count = 52.

15. H1, master_key, is greater than GM7, trans_key (the second A). As a result, main algorithm line 19 calls Nomatch. The operation count = 54.

16. The update_code is A, a new record is filled with data about the navy Fiero, GM7 is saved in a new key, and delete_record is set to FALSE. The operation count = 56.

17. Get_Next_Trans inputs code D and the transaction involving H3.

18. Lines 6 through 8 of Nomatch, trans_key = new_key, is FALSE, so we move to line 15. The operation count = 59.

19. The variable delete_record is FALSE, so the new record GM7, data about the navy Fiero, is output to the new master file. The operation count = 60.

20. Lines 3 through 6 of the master algorithm are repeated for master records H1 and H2. The operation count = 66.

21. In line 3, master_key = T1 and trans_key = H3; the line is TRUE, so the main algorithm calls Nomatch. The operation count = 70.

22. The update_code is D, so the error message no matching record for trans key is output.

23. Get_Next_Trans inputs the code C and the transaction involving T1.

24. In line 3 of the main algorithm, master_key = T1 and trans_key = T1. Because line 3 is TRUE, the algorithm changes the mileage. The operation count = 74.

25. Get_Next_Trans inputs the code D and the transaction involving T1.

26. Line 3 is TRUE; master_key and trans_key are the same (T1). Because the update_code is D, line 14 calls Get_Next_Master, which sets master_key to the sentinel value and calls Get_Next_Trans (line 15). Get_Next_Trans sets trans_key to the sentinel value. The operation count = 78.

27. Line 3 evaluates to FALSE, and the program terminates. The operation count = 80.

Table 5.6 shows the resulting master file. The only error message printed on the audit/error list refers to the code D and the id H3. The error in the transaction should be corrected and applied during the next maintenance run.

Table 5.6 Master file after update with transaction file T3

Id no.	Make	Style	Model	Mileage	Color
C1	Dodge	2 DR	Omni	25,000	grey
C2	Dodge	2 DR	Aspen	7,000	tan
F2	Lincoln	4 DR	Continental	38,000	black
F3	Ford	2 DR	Thunderbird	35,000	blue
GM1	Cadillac	4 DR	Fleetwood	9,000	red
GM2	Oldsmobile	4 DR	Delta 88	28,050	blue
GM3	Chevrolet	2 DR	Camaro	33,000	silver
GM4	Cadillac	2 DR	Cimarron	63,000	maroon
GM5	Oldsmobile	4 DR	98	11,000	green
GM6	Chevrolet	4 DR	Cimarron	11,250	brown
GM7	Pontiac	2 DR	Fiero	1,500	navy
H1	Honda	4 DR	Accord	32,000	yellow
H2	Honda	2 DR HB	Accord	11,250	brown

The control file for the maintenance run traced above contains the following totals:

Master records read	=	14
Valid additions	=	2
Invalid additions	=	0
Valid changes	=	2
Invalid changes	=	0
Valid deletions	=	3
Invalid deletions	=	1
Master records written	=	13

The following calculation allows the user to check the control totals to make sure the maintenance program performed correctly.

Master records read	14
+ Valid additions	2
− Valid deletions	3
Master records written	13

The master file in Table 5.6 does indeed contain 13 records.

Each execution of the body of the While loop in Algorithm 5.4 processes one matching transaction record or one unmatched master record, or it processes one group of unmatched transactions. If there are multiple matching transactions (changes or deletions to existing master records) or a key, the algorithm must make several passes through the body of the loop to process them.

Each pass for multiple matching transactions entails evaluation of three Boolean expressions in lines 3, 4, and 8:

```
3   While Not (master_key = sentinel And trans_key = sentinel)  : TRUE
4       If master_key < trans_key                               : FALSE
7       Else
8           If master_key = trans_key                           : TRUE
```

(The modern algorithm, which the next section examines, contains an improvement: A loop in line 8 processes all transactions of the same key, so each transaction can be applied with the evaluation of one Boolean expression (line 8) rather than three.)

When transaction keys do not match the master keys and the main algorithm calls Nomatch, three different updates (addition, change, and deletion) are allowed. A key cannot be added more than once; a key can be added and have several changes; a key can be added with 0 to n changes followed by only one deletion:

addition (change)$_n$ (deletion)

Once a key has been deleted, it may be assigned to another item. Algorithm Nomatch processes all additions and changes for a key that does not match, or it processes transactions through only the first deletion transaction. In some applications keys are unique and are not reassigned once deleted. Other applications, such as the car-rental agency example, allow keys to be deleted then reassigned to another entity. These applications are limited by the restriction Algorithm 5.4 places on the number of updates. If an addition follows a deletion for the same key (as in the application of transaction file T3 above), Algorithm Nomatch is called to process all transactions through the first deletion. The main algorithm continues executing the transaction, and Nomatch is called again with the second addition. Returning to the main program and reentering Nomatch to continue processing transactions for the same key is inefficient. The modern algorithm for a sequential file update uses a loop to process multiple matched transactions of the same key more efficiently and allows any number of addition, change, and deletion transactions for the same key in any order (although they are usually ordered by date of entry into the transaction file).

THE MODERN ALGORITHM FOR UPDATING SEQUENTIAL FILES

The traditional algorithms for sequential file update contain inefficiencies and put more emphasis on unmatched transactions and unmatched master records than on matched transactions—and attention to matched transactions is the purpose of the update. An algorithm that is more efficient than the traditional algorithms was invented by Feijen and discussed by Dwyer and Dijkstra (see Bibliography in Appendix). Those transactions that match records in the master file have primary importance, although the algorithm successfully handles unmatched transactions as well as master records that need no changes. Each iteration of the main loop processes all transactions for a given key by:

1. finding the master record that matches the transaction key
2. applying all transactions that are ordered by entry date
3. recording the updated master record

Step 2 applies the transactions if the master record for that key was found, it prints error messages if the transactions were changes or deletions and the master record was not found, or it processes additions if the master record was not found. The emphasis is on applying these transactions, whatever the resulting outcome.

The details of applying the transactions are hidden at a lower level of the program design so that they may vary depending on the type of secondary storage being used for storing the master file. The modern algorithm easily allows the sequential file to be stored on magnetic tape or disk. In the case of magnetic disk, the details of applying transactions may be conveniently modified to produce an algorithm that will update the master file randomly. In a random update the matching master record is located, the transactions are applied to the master record, and the updated master record is rewritten to the original location. (The capacity to rewrite to the original location is unique to random-access devices such as disks.) The savings that the random update realizes result from the fact that the entire master file need not be read and copied to another file; only the master records that matched transactions are read and written back to their original locations.

The next section presents the modern algorithm as a sequential update algorithm. We will then change the modern algorithm to perform random updates.

Sequential Update

Algorithm 5.5 presents the modern sequential update algorithm. The master_key and the trans_key are assigned a sentinel value upon reaching the end of the file. The sentinel value is higher than any value in the master file and the transaction file.

Algorithm 5.5 starts the sentinel loop by reading in the first transaction and the first master record (lines 1 and 2). Choose_Smaller_Key sets the current key to the smaller of trans_key and master_key. The smaller key is the next to be processed. The main While loop continues until the current key contains the sentinel value. (If the current key is the smaller of trans_key and master_key, and the current key contains the sentinel then both files

Algorithm 5.5   Modern_Sequential_Update

```
                        {
                            addition, change, and deletion transactions in
                            order (ordered by entry time); several
                            transactions per master record
                        }
   1   Get_Next_Trans   { same algorithm as for traditional algorithm }
   2   Get_Next_Master { same algorithm as for traditional algorithm }
   3   Choose_Smaller_Key { between trans_key and master_key }
   4   While current_key <> sentinel
   5        Check_Initial_Status_Of_Master { for current_key }
   6        While trans_key = current_key
   7             Process_One_Transaction
   8        Check_Final_Status_Of_Master { to see if record should be
                                                        output }
   9        Choose_Smaller_Key
```

Algorithm Choose_Smaller_Key

```
1   If trans_key < master_key
2       current_key ← trans_key { trans_key < master_key }
3   Else
4       current_key ← master_key { master_key <= trans_key }
```

Algorithm Check_Initial_Status_Of_Master { for current key }

```
1   If master_key = current_key
2       hold_master ← master record
3       master_allocated ← TRUE
4       Get_Next_Master
5   Else
6       master_allocated ← FALSE
```

Algorithm Check_Final_Status_Of_Master

```
1   If master_allocated
2       output hold_master to new master file
```

Algorithm Process_One_Transaction

```
1   If master_allocated
2       Case update_code
3           'A' : output 'duplicate add' error
4           'C' : change master record
5           'D' : master_allocated ← FALSE
                    {
                      so will not be output in
                      Check_Final_Status_Of_Master
                    }
6   Else
7       Case update_code
8           'A' : { build new master record from transaction }
9                     hold_master ← transaction record
10                    master_allocated ← TRUE

11          'C' : output 'no matching master record' error

12          'D' : output 'no matching master record' error

13  Get_Next_Trans
```

have been emptied.) The main While loop (lines 4 through 9) processes the record with the key of current_key whether the current key is a master record with no updates, a pair of matching master and transaction records, or an unmatched transaction.

Check_Initial_Status_Of_Master checks if a master record exists for the current key and sets the Boolean master_allocated accordingly. If the master record for the current key exists, the master record is saved in hold_master, and the next master record is read. Any matching transactions will use hold_master when making updates. The Boolean master_allocated is checked by Check_Final_Status_Of_Master after matching transactions are applied to determine if a record is to be written to the new master file.

If the master record for the current key exists but there are no matching transactions for the current key, Check_Initial_Status_Of_Master holds the master record and advances the master file, zero iterations of Process_One_Transaction occur, and Check_Final_Status_Of_Master copies the master record to the new master file. In this case the master key is the smaller key so the master record is processed, then the next master record is input.

When the master record for the current key exists and has a matching transaction, Process_One_Transaction is performed—it applies the transaction and inputs the next transaction for all matching transactions that follow. The Boolean master_allocated is used within Process_One_Transaction to indicate whether a matching master record exists. (TRUE means the matching record exists, FALSE means it does not.) For example, if master_allocated is FALSE, then an addition transaction is valid and causes master_allocated to be changed to TRUE as a new record is created. Any change transactions that followed are applied to the hold_master. A deletion transaction that followed sets master_allocated back to FALSE, which indicates that hold_master is inactive. There is no limit to the number or order of addition, change, and deletion transactions that may be applied for a single key. The final status of master_allocated indicates if anything is to be written to the new master file for the current key.

Comparison to Traditional Algorithms

The car-rental agency transaction files that were used to demonstrate the traditional algorithms can also demonstrate the efficiency of the modern sequential update algorithm. Operations in line 3 (two operations), line 4 (one operation), line 5 (two operations), lines 6 through 8 (one operation each), and line 9 (two operations) of the modern algorithm will be counted. Assume the car-rental master file is empty. Apply transaction file T1 (Table 5.1) to the empty master file. Upon execution of Algorithm 5.5, the following actions take place:

1. Get_Next_Trans inputs the first transaction.
2. Get_Next_Master finds the master file empty, so the master_key is filled with the sentinel value, which is higher than any transaction key.

3. Choose_Smaller_Key sets current_key to trans_key since master_key has the sentinel value. The operation count = 2.

4. In line 4 current_key <> sentinel is TRUE. The operation count = 3.

5. In line 5 Check_Initial_Status_Of_Master sets master_allocated to FALSE. The operation count = 5.

6. In line 6 trans_key = current_key is TRUE so Process_One_Transaction is called. The operation count = 6.

7. Since master_allocated is FALSE and the update_code is A, a new record is built in hold_master and master_allocated is set to TRUE. The operation count = 7.

8. Get_Next_Trans inputs the next transaction record, which is different than the last one input. We return to the main program.

9. Line 6 is FALSE so we move to line 8. The operation count = 8.

10. Check_Final_Status_Of_Master finds master_allocated TRUE, so the new record built is output to the new master file. The operation count = 9.

11. Choose_Smaller_Key sets current_key to trans_key. The operation count = 11.

12. The algorithm continues to the body of While, which begins in line 4. Lines 4 through 11 repeat for each transaction until in line 9 the current_key is assigned the trans_key, which is the sentinel value. The operation count = 11 + (9 operations × 12 transactions) = 119.

13. The next execution of line 4 evaluates to FALSE and the program terminates. The operation count = 120.

The While loop checks for the end of both the master file and the transaction file, and it terminates when both have ended. In this case the master file was empty at the beginning of the algorithm, so all the addition transactions were written to the new master file. The resulting master file is the same as for the traditional algorithms (Table 5.2).

The operation count for the modern algorithm when applying transaction file T1 is 120 operations; the operation count for the traditional algorithm is 131 operations. Transaction file T1 consists solely of additions, and the traditional algorithms check for master_key < trans_key first. If the condition is not met, it checks master_key = trans_key, and—failing again—it finally calls Nomatch to handle the additions. More operator evaluations take place in the traditional algorithms for each addition than in the modern algorithm. The modern algorithm emphasizes *processing* transactions; the traditional algorithms emphasize *copying master records* and *matching transactions* with master records during the copying process. The modern algorithm appears to be more efficient in creating the master file.

Transaction file T2 (Table 5.3) illustrates a transaction file with only one transaction. The trace of the execution of Algorithm 5.5 using the master file shown in Table 5.2 and transaction file T2 follows:

1. Get_Next_Trans inputs the first transaction.

2. Get_Next_Master inputs the first master record.

3. Choose_Smaller_Key sets current_key to master_key, which is C1. The operation count = 2.

4. In line 4 current key <> sentinel is TRUE. The operation count = 3.

5. In line 5 Check_Initial_Status_Of_Master stores master record C1 in hold_master, sets master_allocated to TRUE, and Get_Next_Master inputs the next master record. The operation count = 5.

6. In line 6 trans_key = current_key is FALSE, so we move to line 8. The operation count = 6.

7. Check_Final_Status_Of_Master finds master_allocated TRUE, so the record in hold_master is output to the new master file. The operation count = 7.

8. Choose_Smaller_Key will set current_key to master_key. The operation count = 9.

9. Lines 4 through 9 are repeated for master records C2 through GM5; Choose_Smaller_Key sets current_key to trans_key (GM6) rather than master_key (H1). The operation count = 9 + (7 operations × 9 transactions) = 72.

10. Line 4 is TRUE. The operation count = 73.

11. Check_Initial_Status_Of_Master will set master_allocated to FALSE for current_key (GM6). The operation count = 75.

12. In line 6 trans_key = current_key is TRUE, so Process_One_Transaction is called. The operation count = 76.

13. Since master_allocated is FALSE and the update_code is A, a new record is built in hold_master, and master_allocated is set to TRUE. The operation count = 77.

14. Get_Next_Trans will set trans_key to the sentinel.

15. Line 6 is FALSE, so we move to line 8. The operation count = 78.

16. Check_Final_Status_Of_Master finds master_allocated TRUE, so the record in hold_master is output to the new master file. The operation count = 79.

17. Choose_Smaller_Key will set current_key to master_key since trans_key has the sentinel. The operation count = 81.

18. The algorithm continues with the beginning of the body of the While in line 4. Lines 4 through 9 are repeated for each master record until in line 9 the current_key is assigned the trans_key, which is the sentinel value. The operation count = 81 + (7 operations × 3 transactions) = 102.

19. In the next pass of line 4 evaluates to FALSE, and the program terminates. The operation count = 103.

Algorithm 5.5 performs satisfactorily for a transaction file of only one transaction. The resulting master file is the same as the result of Algorithm 5.4 (Table 5.4). The operation count for the modern algorithm is 103 operations versus 51 operations for traditional Algorithm 5.4 when applying transaction file T2 (which contains only one transaction, an addition). Since the traditional algorithm emphasizes copying the master file and processing transactions during the copying process, only three operations are required for each master record copied, unchanged, to the new master file. The modern algorithm, on the other hand, emphasizes processing transactions; seven operations occur for each master record copied unchanged to the new master file.

The advantages of the modern algorithm over the traditional algorithm can be seen from applying transaction file T3, which contains a number of additions, changes, and deletions in multiples. The modern algorithm is especially useful when an addition follows a deletion and when there are multiple changes for an existing master record. The trace of applying T3 to the master file in Table 5.4 follows:

1. Get_Next_Trans inputs the first transaction.

2. Get_Next_Master inputs the first master record.

3. Choose_Smaller_Key sets current_key to master_key, which is C1. The operation count = 2.

4. In line 4 current key <> sentinel is TRUE. The operation count = 3.

5. In line 5 Check_Initial_Status_Of_Master stores master record C1 in hold_master, sets master_allocated to TRUE, and Get_Next_Master inputs the next master record. The operation count = 5.

6. In line 6 trans_key = current_key is FALSE, so we move to line 8. The operation count = 6.

7. Check_Final_Status_Of_Master finds master_allocated TRUE, so the record in hold_master is output to the new master file. The operation count = 7.

8. Choose_Smaller_Key sets current_key to master_key. The operation count = 9.

9. Lines 4 through 9 repeat for master record C2. Choose_Smaller_Key sets current_key to master_key (F1) since trans_key is not smaller. The operation count = 16.

10. Line 4 is TRUE. The operation count = 17.

11. Check_Initial_Status_Of_Master moves master record F1 to hold_master and sets master_allocated to TRUE. Get_Next_Master inputs F2. The operation count = 19.

12. In line 6 trans_key = current_key is TRUE so Process_One_Transaction is called. The operation count = 20.

13. The expression master_allocated is TRUE and the update_code is D, so master_allocated is changed to FALSE to prevent hold_master from being copied to the new master file. The operation count = 21.

14. Get_Next_Trans inputs the code A and the id GM7.

15. Line 6 is FALSE, so we move to line 8. The operation count = 22.

16. Check_Final_Status_Of_Master does nothing since master_allocated is FALSE. The operation count = 23.

17. Choose_Smaller_Key sets current_key to master_key (F1) since trans_key is GM7. The operation count = 25.

18. Lines 4 through 9 repeat for master records F2 through GM6. Choose_Smaller_Key sets current_key to trans_key (GM7), which is smaller than master_key (H1). The operation count = 25 + (7 operations × 8 transactions) = 81.

19. Line 4 is TRUE. The operation count = 82.

20. Check_Initial_Status_Of_Master sets master_allocated to FALSE for current_key (GM7). The operation count = 84.

21. In line 6 trans_key = current_key is TRUE, so Process_One_Transaction is called. The operation count = 85.

22. Since master_allocated is FALSE and the update_code is A, a new record is built in hold_master, and master_allocated is set to TRUE. The operation count = 86.

23. Get_Next_Trans inputs the code C and the id GM7.

24. In line 6 trans_key = current_key is TRUE, so Process_One_Transaction is called. The operation count = 87.

25. Since master_allocated is TRUE and the update_code is C, hold_master is changed. The operation count = 88.

26. Get_Next_Trans inputs the code D and the id GM7.

27. In line 6 trans_key = current_key is TRUE, so Process_One_Transaction is called. The operation count = 89.

28. Since master_allocated is TRUE and the update_code is a D, master_allocated is changed to FALSE. The operation count = 90.

29. Get_Next_Trans inputs the second code A and id GM7.

30. In line 6 trans_key = current_key is TRUE, so Process_One_Transaction is called. The operation count = 91.

31. Since master_allocated is FALSE and the update_code is A, a new record is built in hold_master, and master_allocated is set to TRUE. The operation count = 92.

32. Get_Next_Trans inputs the code D and the id H3.

33. Line 6 is FALSE, so we move to line 8. The operation count = 93.

34. Check_Final_Status_Of_Master finds master_allocated TRUE, so the record in hold_master (GM7) is output to the new master file. The operation count = 94.

35. Choose_Smaller_Key sets current_key to master_key (H1), which is smaller than trans_key (H3). The operation count = 96.

36. Lines 4 through 9 repeat for master records H1 through H2. Choose_Smaller_Key sets current_key to trans_key (H3), which is smaller than master_key (T1). The operation count = 96 + (7 operations × 2 transactions) = 110.

37. Line 4 is TRUE. The operation count = 111.

38. Check_Initial_Status_Of_Master sets master_allocated to FALSE for current_key (H3). The operation count = 113.

39. In line 6 trans_key = current_key is TRUE, so Process_One_Transaction is called. The operation count = 114.

40. Since master_allocated is FALSE and the update_code is D, the message no matching master record is output. The operation count = 115.

41. Get_Next_Trans inputs the code C and the id T1.

42. Line 6 is FALSE, so we move to line 8. The operation count = 116.

43. Check_Final_Status_Of_Master finds master_allocated FALSE, so nothing happens. The operation count = 117.

44. Choose_Smaller_Key sets current_key to master_key (T1) since trans_key (T1) is not smaller. The operation count = 119.

45. Line 4 is TRUE. The operation count = 120.

46. Check_Initial_Status_Of_Master moves master record T1 to hold_master and sets master_allocated to TRUE. Get_Next_Master sets master_key to the sentinel. The operation count = 122.

47. In line 6 trans_key = current_key is TRUE, so Process_One_Transaction is called. The operation count = 123.

48. Since master_allocated is TRUE and the update_code is a C, hold_master is changed. The operation count = 124.

49. Get_Next_Trans inputs the code D and the id T1.

50. In line 6 trans_key = current_key is TRUE, so Process_One_Transaction is called. The operation count = 125.

51. Since master_allocated is TRUE and the update_code is a D, master_allocated is changed to FALSE. The operation count = 126.

52. Get_Next_Trans sets trans_key to the sentinel.

53. Line 6 is FALSE, so we move to line 8. The operation count = 127.

54. Check_Final_Status_Of_Master finds master_allocated FALSE, so nothing happens. The operation count = 128.

55. Choose_Smaller_Key sets current_key to master_key (sentinel) since trans_key (sentinel) is not smaller. The operation count = 130.

56. Line 4 is FALSE, so the program terminates. The operation count = 131.

Transaction file T3 contains a variety of transactions: the deletion of an existing master record (F1), an addition, a change, the deletion and subsequent addition of a new key (GM7), the deletion of a nonexistent master record (H3), and finally the change and deletion of an existing master record (T1). The resulting master file is the same as the result of the traditional algorithm 5.4 (Table 5.6).

Each execution of the main While loop (lines 4 through 9) processes all records for a single key value. For multiple matching transactions, there are three Boolean expressions evaluated in the main While loop when the first transaction is processed:

```
4    While current_key <> sentinel : TRUE
5        If master_key = current_key : TRUE
6        While trans_key = current_key : TRUE
```

For each transaction that follows with the same key, there is only one Boolean expression evaluated in the main While loop:

```
6        While trans_key = current_key : TRUE
```

The modern algorithm performs seven operations when processing the transactions for an existing master record (T1); the traditional Algorithm 5.4 performs eight operations. Only two transactions were processed here, but the savings are greater for a larger number of transactions for a single key. The modern sequential update algorithm is more efficient than the traditional Algorithm 5.4 for multiple transactions for the same key because it contains fewer Boolean expressions to evaluate.

When the transactions do not match, any number of additions, changes, and deletions may be applied in any order. The flag master_allocated is checked after all transactions have been applied to determine the final status of the applications (whether a record is to be output to the new master file, for example). Three Boolean expressions are evaluated for the first of unmatched transactions:

```
4    While current_key <> sentinel : TRUE
5        If master_key = current_key : FALSE
6        While trans_key = current_key : TRUE
```

For each transaction that follows with the same key, there is only one Boolean expression evaluated in the main While loop:

```
6        While trans_key = current_key : TRUE
```

For processing the transactions for GM7, the traditional Algorithm 5.4 performed 22 operations, but the modern algorithm processed only 15 operations. The number of Boolean expressions evaluated for unmatched transactions is fewer in the modern algorithm than in the traditional Algorithm 5.4. Why? Because Algorithm Nomatch of the traditional Algorithm 5.4 returns to the main program when each deletion is encountered. The modern algorithm handles multiple transactions more easily. It is more efficient and simpler than the traditional Algorithm 5.4 when performing maintenance on a master file with high activity or high volatility, and it is also shorter in terms of the number of lines in the algorithm. Table 5.7 summarizes the operation counts for both algorithms that result from the application of all three transaction files.

Table 5.7 Operation counts for modern and traditional algorithms

Transaction file	Modern algorithm	Traditional algorithm
T1	120	131
T2	103	51
T3	131	80

Random Update

Algorithm 5.6 presents the modern random update algorithm. The changes needed to convert Algorithm 5.5, a sequential update, to a random update are few. Algorithm 5.6 inputs the first transaction but not the first master. In the random update the transaction file is the primary force behind the main While loop. Notice in line 2 that current_key is set to the trans_key. The main While loop is the same as the loop in the sequential update. Only Check Initial_Status_Of_Master and Check_Final_Status_Of_Master differ.

Check_Initial_Status_Of_Master retrieves a master record from the master file that matches current_key, if one exists. The process of retrieving a matching master record differs from one application to another; it involves either a sequential read or a direct random access (see Chapter 7). If a matching master record is retrieved, the master record is stored in hold_master, and master_allocated is set to TRUE. In a similar fashion Check_Final_Status_Of_Master checks the status of the Boolean master_allocated. It either writes the record in hold_master as a new record in the current master file or as a replacement for the existing record in the original location from which it was read.

A random update requires that random access is available, and random access is available only on magnetic disk. A random update is more efficient since only the master records that have matching transactions are input and updated within the current master file; it does not copy all master records to a new master file.

The number of input/output operations for the random update is greatly reduced from that of the sequential update. The number of input/output operations for the sequential update using transaction file T3 is:

Master records read	=	14
Master records written	=	13
Transaction records read	=	8
Total I/O operations	=	35

Only the changed master records or additions need to be output to the master file for the random update:

Reads attempted to master file	=	4 (F1, GM7, H3, T1)
Master records written	=	3 (D F1, A GM7, D T1)
Transaction records read	=	8
Total I/O operations	=	15

The algorithm makes four attempts to input a record from the master file. Only two of those four attempts are successful (F1, and T1). Both records

Algorithm 5.6   Modern_Random_Update

```
                              {
                                  addition, change, and deletion transactions in
                                  order (ordered by entry time); several
                                  transactions per master record
                              }
  1   Get_Next_Trans   { same algorithm as for traditional algorithm }
  2   current_key ← trans_key { rather than Choose_Smaller_Key }
  3   While current_key <> sentinel
                          { same as for Modern Sequential Update }
  4       Check_Initial_Status_Of_Master { for current_key }
  5       While trans_key = current_key
  6           Process_One_Transaction
  7       Check_Final_Status_Of_Master { to see if record should be
                                                  output }
  8       current_key ← trans_key { rather than Choose_Smaller_Key }
```

Algorithm Check_Initial_Status_Of_Master { for current key }

```
  1   If current_key exists in master file
  2       input master record with current_key into hold_master
  3       master_allocated ← TRUE
  4   Else
  5       master_allocated ← FALSE
```

Algorithm Check_Final_Status_Of_Master

```
  1   If master_allocated
  2       output hold_master to new master file
                      { either a new record or replaces old record }
```

are subsequently "deleted"; they are written over rather than actually being
physically deleted. The third output operation to the master file adds GM7.
The random update has a total of 15 input/output operations; the sequential
update compared has 35 input/output operations. Since each input or output operation may take 30 to 40 milliseconds, the random update represents
quite a savings in access time (provided that random access is available).

SUMMARY

Sequential organization of data files is the oldest type of file organization.
Updating a sequential file involves the addition of new records, the changing of information on existing records, and the deletion of existing records.
Additions and deletions involve inserting records into or deleting records
from a file in such a way that the order of keyed records within the file is

maintained. Without direct-access storage devices, the updating of a sequential file requires the copying of the existing file to another file.

A master file may be created by a special creation program or by applying each transaction to an empty file as an addition in the maintenance program. A batch maintenance run requires that transactions be sorted in the same order (by ascending entry date within ascending transaction key) as the master file. The length of time between maintenance runs depends on the rate of change of data, the size of the master file, the need for current data on the master file, and the file activity.

During the maintenance run the keys of the master records are matched with the keys of the transaction records to produce a new master file and an audit/error report. When transaction records have keys that match master record keys one of three actions occur: (1) addition transactions cause error messages, (2) change transactions modify the master record, and (3) deletion transactions prevent the copying of the master record to the new master file. When transaction records have keys that do not match keys on the master file: (1) additions cause new records to be built for the new master file, (2) changes with keys matching previous additions cause changes to the new record, (3) deletions with keys matching previous additions prevent the new record from being output to the new master file, and (4) changes and deletions with keys that do not match previous additions generate error messages. The chapter presented several algorithms: the traditional algorithms, which are used when sequential storage devices (magnetic tapes) are available, and a modern algorithm, which is easily modified for either sequential or random update when using direct-access storage devices (magnetic disks).

Key Terms

adding records	random update
audit/error listing	sequential file organization
batch processing	sequential update
deleting records	sentinel value
editing	serially
key	transaction file
maintenance run	update code

Exercises

1. An installation has two tape drives and one disk drive. An application program requires access to three sequential files: an old master file, a transaction file, and an updated master file. Each file should be on a different device. Which file should be stored on the disk?

2. Consider a master file of 10 records and the following batch of transactions:

TRANSACTIONS FILE		MASTER FILE
Code	Key	Key
C	0196	0195
A	0196	0196
D	0196	2000
D	2111	2111
A	2111	2150
D	2111	2473
C	3342	2732
A	4000	3340
C	4000	3342
		4000

What is the file activity ratio?

3. Consider a master file of 10 records and the following batch of transactions:

TRANSACTION FILE		MASTER FILE
Code	Key	Key
C	0196	0195
A	0196	0196
D	0196	2000
D	2111	2111
A	3310	2150
D	3310	2473
C	3342	2732
A	4200	3340
C	4200	3342
		4000

What is the file activity ratio? What is the file volatility ratio?

4. Suppose the transaction file in exercise 3 were in the following order:

Code	Key
D	2111
D	0196
A	0196
A	4200
C	0196
C	3342
C	4200
A	3310
D	3310

If the master file is stored on tape, would it be possible to update the master file with the transaction file in this order? If the master file is stored on disk, would it be possible?

5. What factors should be considered in determining how frequently a sequential master file should be updated?

6. Discuss the limitations of sequential files.

7. What is the major disadvantage of batch processing?

8. A sequential file is to be created containing records describing potential new acquisitions for a library. The author's surname will be the key to accessing information concerning a new book. Are there any advantages to ordering the file by the surname assuming that

   a. search requests are not batched?

   b. search requests are batched?

9. How can updating a master file stored on magnetic disk differ from updating a master file stored on magnetic tape?

10. How does a file update differ from a file merge?

Programming Problems

1. Write a program to create a sequential payroll file where each record contains the following information:

   employee number (the key)
   employee name
   employee salary
   social security number
   tax exemption amount
   insurance premium
   parking fee
   association dues

2. Write a program to print or display the contents of the sequential payroll file created in problem 1.

3. Write a program that updates the sequential payroll file created in problem 1 and creates a new version of the file. Accommodate record additions, changes, and deletions by employing the following:

UPDATE CODE	INFORMATION
A (addition)	all the information listed in problem 1.
C (change)	employee number
	one or more field identifiers and changes:
	N and new name
	S and new salary
	X and new tax exemption
	I and new insurance premium
	P and new parking fees
	D and new association dues
D (deletion)	employee number

Assume that there will be a maximum of one transaction applied to a master file record.

4. Repeat problem 3 with the assumption that there may be up to five transactions per master record. Process the transactions in the order in which they are received.

5. Write a program to update an input sequential master file that contains data about an inventory of parts with input transaction records. (The input transaction file has been sorted.) You will produce an updated sequential master file on disk and print an audit/error list.

Input the master file in which the key field is a part number. The file is a non-text file and contains the following in each record:

part number (10 characters)
part description (26 characters)
part price (real)

Input the transaction file in which the major key field is a part number and the minor key field is the entry date. A text file of update information contains several different formats:

a. additions:
    update code (A)
    part number (10 characters)
    part description (26 characters)
    part price (real)

b. changes:
    description
        update code (C)
        part number (10 characters)
        change id (D)
        new description (26 characters)
    price
        update code (C)
        part number (10 characters)
        change id (P)
        new price (real)

c. deletions:
    update code (D)
    part number (10 characters)

    Output an updated master file and an audit/error list with the following information for each transaction:

    updated code
    part number
    error message (if any)

The program should perform the following operations:

a. Without using INPUT validate each transaction record to ensure that it contains one of the following update codes:

A for add
C for change
D for delete

b. Create a master record for each valid add transaction.

c. Change the appropriate master field for each valid change transaction.

d. Delete the master record for each valid delete transaction.

e. Identify the following error conditions:

ERROR CONDITION	ERROR MESSAGE
Add a transaction that is already on master file	INVALID ADD-ALREADY ON MASTER
Change a transaction that is not on master file	INVALID CHANGE-NOT ON MASTER
Delete a transaction that is not on master file	INVALID DELETE-NOT ON MASTER
Invalid update code	INVALID UPDATE CODE

f. Indicate on the audit/error list what field was changed (price or description), and print the new field. For additions, print the price and description of each record added.

g. Tally the master- and transaction-record counts, and print the tally after the audit/error list.

h. Input the new master file and print the audit/error list to make sure the information is right.

i. Count the number of lines output on the page and reprint headings at the top of each new page. Do not print across the page perforations. Also print page numbers at the top of each page.

6. Write a program to update an input sequential master file that describes various vendors by inputting vendor transaction records. The input transaction file has been sorted in a prior program step. You will output an updated sequential vendor master file on disk and print an audit/error list.

Input the master file in which the major key field is a vendor number and the minor key is the date the product is due. The file is a non-text file and contains the following in each record:

vendor number (8 characters)
vendor date due (yymmdd)

vendor name (20 characters)
vendor amount due (real)

Input a transaction file in which the major key field is a vendor number, the intermediate key field is the date due, and the minor key field is the entry date. A text file of update information contains several different formats:

a. additions:
    update code (A)
    vendor number (8 characters)
    vendor date due (yymmdd)
    vendor name (20 characters)
    vendor amount due (real)

b. changes:
    name
        update code (C)
        vendor number (8 characters)
        vendor date due (yymmdd)
        change id (N)
        new name (20 characters)
    amount due
        update code (C)
        vendor number (8 characters)
        vendor date due (yymmdd)
        change id (A)
        new amount due (real)

c. deletions:
    update code (D)
    vendor number (8 characters)
    vendor date due (yymmdd)

Output an updated vendor master file and print an audit/error list with the following information for each transaction:

update code
vendor number
vendor date due
error message (if any)

Repeat each of the program operations you completed in problem 5 using the data about vendors.

Chapter 6

CHAPTER CONTENTS

External Sort/Merge
Algorithms

PREVIEW

THIS CHAPTER EXAMINES SEVERAL external sort/merge algorithms used for sorting large data files that exceed the main memory of a computer. Algorithms are presented for the two-way sort/merge, the balanced two-way sort/merge, the balanced *k*-way sort/merge, and the polyphase sort/merge. An algorithm is also presented for the Fibonacci distribution that is used in the polyphase sort/merge only. The sort/merge routines discussed are compared for efficiency in numerous examples.

TWO-WAY SORT/MERGE

One of the requirements of the sequential file maintenance algorithms presented in Chapter 5 is that the transaction file of updates be sorted by the key into the same order (ascending or descending) as the master file. Often a transaction file is so large that the whole file will not fit into main memory; in these cases an internal sort is inappropriate. Sorting is common not only for sequential file maintenance but for other types of file organization. Sorting transactions to match the key order of the master file can reduce the time it takes to locate a matching master record, regardless of the type of organization. Many reports generated from files require that the file be sorted by certain fields other than the key. External sort/merge algorithms are the most common method for sorting data files that are larger than main memory.

A simple sort/merge algorithm involves two phases:

1. The records on the file to be sorted are divided into several groups. Each group is called a **run**, and each run fits into main memory. An internal sort is applied to each run, and the resulting sorted runs are distributed to two external files.

2. One run from each of the external files created in phase 1 merge at one time into larger runs of sorted records. The result is stored in a third external file. The data is distributed from the third file back into the first two files, and merging continues until all records are in one large run.

The external storage devices used for storing the three files of the sort/ merge algorithm may be either magnetic tape or magnetic disk, but each file needs to be on a separate device to allow easy access during the merge phase.

EXAMPLE 6.1

Suppose a file of records to be sorted contains the following keys in this order:

50 110 95 10 100 36 153 40 120 60 70 130 22 140 80

The size of a run is three records; that is, main memory can only hold three records at a time. In phase 1 groups of three records are read into main memory, sorted by an internal sort, and alternately written to one of two external files. Figure 6.1 shows the results after each step of the merge. After phase 1 (Figure 6.1(a)) file 1 contains run 1 (keys 50 110 95 in sorted order), run 3 (keys 153 40 120 in sorted order), and run 5 (keys 22 140 80 in

File 1 | 50 95 110 | 40 120 153 | 22 80 140

File 2 | 10 36 100 | 60 70 130

(a) Results of Phase 1 sort

Figure 6.1
Two-way sort/
merge—Example 6.1

File 1 Empty

File 2 Empty

File 3 | 10 36 50 95 100 110 | 40 60 70 120 130 153 | 22 80 140

(b) Result of merge 1

File 1 | 10 36 50 95 100 110 | 22 80 140

File 2 | 40 60 70 120 130 153

File 3 Empty

(c) Results of redistribution after merge 1

File 3 | 10 36 40 50 60 70 95 100 110 120 130 153 | 22 80 140

(d) Results of merge 2

File 1 | 10 36 40 50 60 70 95 100 110 120 130 153

File 2 | 22 80 140

(e) Results of redistribution after merge 2

File 3 | 10 22 36 40 50 60 70 80 95 100 110 120 130 140 153

(f) Results of merge 3

sorted order). File 2 contains run 2 (keys 10 100 36 in sorted order), and run 4 (keys 60 70 130 in sorted order). Consecutive runs are alternately stored in files 1 and 2 so the two files contain the same number of runs for the merge phase. (At worst, one of the files may have one more run than the other.)

In phase 2 the first run in file 1 is merged with the first run in file 2 to produce a sorted run containing six records in file 3. The second run in file 1 is merged with the second run in file 2 to produce a second sorted run of six records in file 3. This merging is continued until files 1 and 2 are empty (Figure 6.1(b)). The runs in file 3 are now redistributed alternately to files 1 and 2. After the redistribution file 3 is empty, and files 1 and 2 contain the records (Figure 6.1(c)); we are ready to start merge 2. The merging phase is repeated until all records are in one run. The second merge stores two runs in file 3 as shown in Figure 6.1(d). Redistributing the two runs to files 1 and 2 (Figure 6.1(e)) and merging a third time leaves all records in one run (Figure 6.1(f)).

EXAMPLE 6.2

Suppose the initial file to be sorted is

   50 110 95 10 100 36 153 40 120 60 70 130

The number of runs is even (12 records ÷ 3 runs = 4 runs on 2 files). After the sorting phase files 1 and 2 contain the same number of runs (Figure

Figure 6.2
Two-way sort/
merge—Example 6.2

File 1 | 50   95   110 | 40   120   153 |

File 2 | 10   36   100 | 60   70   130 |

(a) Results of phase 1 sort

File 1 Empty

File 2 Empty

File 3 | 10   36   50   95   100   110 | 40   60   70   120   130   153 |

(b) Results of merge 1

File 1 | 10   36   50   95   100   110 |

File 2 | 40   60   70   120   130   153 |

(c) Results of redistribution after merge 1

File 1 Empty

File 2 Empty

File 3 | 10   36   40   50   60   70   95   100   110   120   130   153 |

(d) Results of merge 2

6.2(a)). The first execution of the merge phase merges the first run of both files and produces a sorted run in file 3 then merges the second run of both files and produces a second sorted run in file 3 as shown in Figure 6.2(b). Now since both input files are empty, the runs from file 3 are redistributed to files 1 and 2 (Figure 6.2(c)) in order to merge again. The resulting file contents from the second execution of the merge phase are shown in Figure 6.2(d).

Phase 1 (the **sort phase**) of the sort/merge sorts the records into runs of a specified length and distributes the runs alternatively to two external files. Once phase 1 is complete, phase 2 (the **merge phase**) merges runs into larger runs, redistributing and merging runs until all records are in one run.

A variety of merge algorithms are available. Example 6.2 is an example of a two-way sort/merge that merges runs from two input files into one output file. The algorithm for the **two-way sort/merge** is presented in pseudocode in Algorithm 6.1.

Each pass of the two-way sort/merge doubles the size of each run, thus cutting the number of runs in half. Two runs of one record each merge into

Algorithm 6.1   Two-Way Sort/Merge

```
                            { Sort Phase }
        initial  distribution
                            { Merge Phase }
        Repeat
              runs ← 0
              Repeat
                            {
                                merge next runs from 2 input files
                            }
                     input first record from file 1
                     input first record from file 2
                     Repeat
                            {
                                output record with smaller key to file 3
                            }
                        file_k ← Smallest_key
                        output record from file_k to file 3
                        input next record from file_k
                     Until End_Of_Run_On_Both_Files

                     increment runs by 1
              Until End_Of_Both_Files

              If runs > 1
                     Distribute

        Until runs = 1
```

Algorithm Smallest_Key

```
If End_Of_Run_On_File (file 1)
Or Eof (file 1)
    Smallest_Key ← file 2
Else
    If End_Of_Run_On_File (file 2)
    Or Eof (file 2)
        Smallest_Key ← file 1
    Else
        If key 1 < key 2
            Smallest_Key ← file 1
        Else
            Smallest_Key ← file 2
```

Algorithm End_Of_Run_On_Both_Files

```
    test_end ← TRUE
    For i ← 1 To 2
        test_end ← test_end And End_Of_Run_On_File (file i)

    End_Of_Run_On_Both_Files ← test_end
```

Algorithm End_Of_Both_Files

```
    test_end ← TRUE
    For i ← 1 To 2
        test_end ← test_end And Eof (file i)

    End_Of_Both_Files ← test_end
```

Algorithm Distribute

```
    j ← 0
    For i ← 1 To runs
        Repeat
            input record from run i of file 3
            output record to file (1 + j)
        Until End_Of_Run_On_File (file 3)

        j ← 1 − j
```

one run in one pass. Three runs of one record each merge into two runs (two records in the first run and one record in the second run) during the first pass, then into one run in the second pass. Four runs of one record each merge into two runs of two records each in the first pass, then one run of four records in the second pass. The total number of passes through the two-way sort/merge (Algorithm 6.1) is $\lceil \lg NR \rceil$, if $NR > 1$ and NR is the number of runs produced during the initial sorting phase. (The notation $\lg$

NR means the *logarithm to the base 2 of NR*, and the symbol $\lceil x \rceil$ means the ceiling of x.)

For example, two runs take $\lceil \lg 2 \rceil = 1$ pass. Three runs take $\lceil \lg 3 \rceil = 2$ passes. Four runs take $\lceil \lg 4 \rceil = 2$ passes. Each pass of the two-way sort/ merge transmits each record to the output file during the merging portion, then transmits each output record back to one of the original input files during the distribution procedure. Therefore, each pass except for the last pass of the merge phase of Algorithm 6.1 transmits each record twice. As a result, the number of passes through the file of records is $2\lceil \lg NR \rceil - 1$ for the merge phase plus one for the sort phase—a total of $2\lceil \lg NR \rceil$ passes.

BALANCED TWO-WAY SORT/MERGE

An improvement of the two-way sort/merge algorithm increases the number of files available for the merge. Instead of merging two input files into one output file, the **balanced two-way sort/merge** algorithm merges two input files and stores the merged runs alternately on two output files. Increasing the number of output files to the same number of input files eliminates the need to redistribute the runs to the two input files before the merge can be repeated. The I/O time it takes to simply read and copy runs in order to distribute them into two files is a needless waste that the balanced algorithm avoids. The balanced two-way sort/merge algorithm merges runs from files 1 and 2 and stores the merged runs into files 3 and 4. Then it inputs files 3 and 4, merges the runs, and stores the merged runs in output files 1 and 2. The algorithm continues until all records are merged into one run.

EXAMPLE 6.3
_____

Consider the file of records used in Example 6.1.

   50 110 95 10 100 36 153 40 120 60 70 130 22 140 80

In the first execution of the merge phase of the balanced two-way sort/ merge, runs from file 1 and 2 (Figure 6.3(a)) merge to yield the file contents shown in Figure 6.3(b). Files 3 and 4 are input files for the next execution of the merge phase that stores the merged runs in output files 1 and 2 (Figure 6.3(c)). One more merge cycle is necessary to merge all records in one run (Figure 6.3(d)).

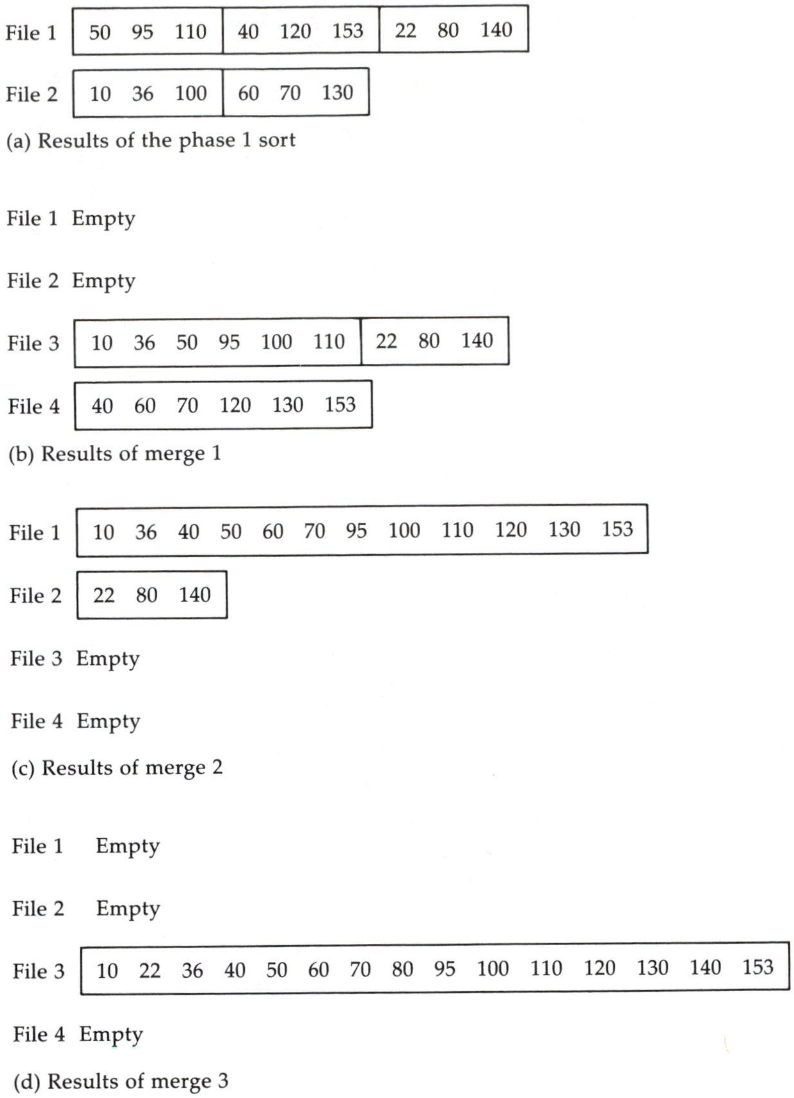

Figure 6.3
Balanced two-way
sort/merge—Example
6.3

File 1 | 50   95   110 | 40   120   153 | 22   80   140

File 2 | 10   36   100 | 60   70   130

(a) Results of the phase 1 sort

File 1 Empty

File 2 Empty

File 3 | 10   36   50   95   100   110 | 22   80   140

File 4 | 40   60   70   120   130   153

(b) Results of merge 1

File 1 | 10   36   40   50   60   70   95   100   110   120   130   153

File 2 | 22   80   140

File 3 Empty

File 4 Empty

(c) Results of merge 2

File 1   Empty

File 2   Empty

File 3 | 10   22   36   40   50   60   70   80   95   100   110   120   130   140   153

File 4 Empty

(d) Results of merge 3

EXAMPLE 6.4

In this example the initial file is the same as Example 6.2:

50 110 95 10 100 36 153 40 120 60 70 130

In contrast to Example 6.3, the number of runs on each file after the sort phase is even. After the sorting phase file 1 and 2 contain the same number of runs (Figure 6.4(a)). The first execution of the merge phase merges runs from files 1 and 2 and stores the merged runs alternately into files 3 or 4 with the results shown in Figure 6.4(b). Files 3 and 4 are input files for the

File 1 | 50   95   110 | 40   120   153

File 2 | 10   36   100 | 60   70   130

(a) Results of phase 1 sort

File 1 Empty

File 2 Empty

File 3 | 10   36   50   95   100   110

File 4 | 40   60   70   120   130   153

(b) Results of merge 2

File 1 | 10   36   40   50   60   70   95   100   110   120   130   153

File 2 Empty

File 3 Empty

File 4 Empty

(c) Results of merge 2

Figure 6.4
Balanced two-way
sort/merge—Example
6.4

next execution of the balanced merge phase, which alternately stores the merged runs in output files 1 or 2. The results of the second execution of the balanced merge phase are shown in Figure 6.4(c).

The two-way sort/merge performs a merge of two input files to one output file, distributes the runs back to the two input files, and repeats until all records are in one run. The balanced two-way sort/merge performs a merge of runs from files 1 and 2 to files 3 and 4, merges runs from files 3 and 4 back to files 1 and 2, and repeats until all records are in one run. The savings in execution time provided by the balanced two-way sort/merge are due to the elimination of the redistribution of runs between merges.

Algorithm 6.2 presents the balanced two-way sort/merge algorithm that applies to cases in which the number of output files is the same as the number of input files.

Each pass of the merge phase of the balanced two-way sort/merge cuts the number of runs in half, so the number of passes of the merge phase required is $\lceil \lg NR \rceil$. (NR is the number of runs produced during the initial sorting phase.) The number of passes through the merge phase of the balanced two-way sort/merge is the same as the number through the two-way sort/merge. The difference is that each pass of the merge phase of the balanced two-way sort/merge transmits each record of the file once. Each pass except the last pass of the merge phase of the two-way sort/merge transmits each record of the file twice. The number of passes through the file for the balanced two-way sort/merge is roughly half ($\lceil \lg NR \rceil + 1$) that of the two-way sort/merge ($2\lceil \lg NR \rceil$).

Algorithm 6.2　Balanced Two-Way Sort/Merge

```
                        { Sort Phase }
initial  distribution
                        { Merge Phase }
number_of_output_files ← 2
in_file [1] ← 1
in_file [2] ← 2
out_file [1] ← 3
out_file [2] ← 4
Repeat
     runs ← 0
     Repeat
                        {
                            perform 2-way merge on files (in_file [1])
                            and (in_file [2]) evenly distributing output
                            to files (out_file [1]) and (out_file [2])
                        }
            input  first  record  from  each  input  file
            runs ← runs + 1
                        {
                            The remainder of runs / number_of_output_files will
                            be 0 or 1 for 2 output files.  So the remainder
                            + 1 will select output file 1 or 2 alternately.
                        }
            outfile ←   Mod (runs / number_of_output_files)  + 1
            Repeat
                        {
                            output  record  with  smaller  key
                        }
               file_k ← Smallest_Key
               output record from file_k to out_file [outfile]
               input next record from  in_file [file_k]
            Until  End_Of_Run_On_Both_Files

       Until  End_Of_Both_Files

       If Total_Runs > 1 Then
            For i ← 1 To 2
                 hold ← in_file [i]
                 in_file [i] ← out_file [i]
                 out_file [i] ← hold

Until Total_Runs = 1
```

Algorithm Total_Runs

```
    total ← 0
    For j ← out_file [1] To out_file [2]
        total ← total + runs (file j)

    Total_Runs ← total
```

Algorithm Smallest_Key

```
If End_Of_Run_On_File (in_file [1])
Or Eof (in_file [1])
    Smallest_Key ← in_file [2]
Else
    If End_Of_Run_On_File (in_file [2])
    Or Eof (in_file [2])
        Smallest_Key ← in_file [1]
    Else
        If key (in_file [1]) < key (in_file [2])
            Smallest_Key ← in_file [1]
        Else
            Smallest_Key ← in_file [2]
```

Algorithm End_Of_Run_On_Both_Files

```
    test_end ← TRUE
    For i ← in_file [1] To in_file [2]
        test_end ← test_end And End_Of_Run_On_File (i)

    End_Of_Run_On_Both_Files ← test_end
```

Algorithm End_Of_Both_Files

```
    test_end ← TRUE
    For i ← in_file [1] To in_file [2]
        test_end ← test_end And Eof (file i)

    End_Of_Both_Files ← test_end
```

BALANCED *k*-WAY SORT/MERGE

The balanced two-way sort/merge algorithm improved on the two-way sort/merge by increasing the number of output files to match the number of input files. The result is the elimination of the redistribution of merged runs back to two files. By merging runs from two input files and storing merged runs on two output files, the next merge pass reverses the use of the input and output files; the two nonempty files merge to the two empty files. An obvious improvement is to increase the number of files available for the sort/merge to *k* input files and *k* output files. By increasing the number of input and output files, each file contains fewer runs with the result that

fewer merges have to be performed. The merging process is more complicated with k input files because a k-way merge needs to distribute merged
runs into k output files.

EXAMPLE 6.5
_____

Consider the initial file used in Examples 6.1 and 6.3:

   50 110 95 10 100 36 153 40 120 60 70 130 22 140 80

Assume that there are three input files and three output files. The sort
phase produces the result illustrated in Figure 6.5(a). The merge phase now
performs a three-way merge of files 1, 2, and 3, then stores merged runs

Figure 6.5
Balanced k-way sort/
merge—Example 6.5

File 1	50 95 110	60 70 130

File 2	10 30 100	22 80 140

File 3	40 120 153

(a) Results of phase 1 sort

File 1 Empty

File 2 Empty

File 3 Empty

File 4	10 36 40 50 95 100 110 120 153

File 5	22 60 70 80 130 140

File 6 Empty

(b) Results of merge 1

File 1	10 22 36 40 50 60 70 80 95 100 110 120 130 140

File 2 Empty

File 3 Empty

File 4 Empty

File 5 Empty

File 6 Empty

(c) Results of merge 2

alternately in files 4, 5, and 6. The file contents in Figure 6.5(b) result. (File 6 is empty because of the small number of runs originally in files 1, 2, and 3.) The second execution of the merging operation merges files 4, 5, and 6 (if 6 is not empty) and stores merged runs in files 1, 2, and 3. The process is repeated until all runs are in one file. (In this case, the second merge is all that is necessary.) The resulting file contents are pictured in Figure 6.5(c).

For this file of data the balanced two-way sort/merge performed the merge phase three times to merge all the runs into one run in one file. Using the balanced three-way sort/merge, the same file of data could be merged into one run with only two passes through the merge phase. Ideally, if each sorted run from the sort phase (phase 1) were stored in a separate file (each requiring a separate external device), then one merge cycle could merge all runs into one run; only a total of $k + 1$ files would be needed— that is, k input files and 1 output file.

EXAMPLE 6.6

_____

Use the same data:

   50 110 95 10 100 36 153 40 120 60 70 130 22 140 80

Allocating each sorted run from the sort phase to a separate file results in the file contents in Figure 6.6(a). Now the merge phase performs a five-

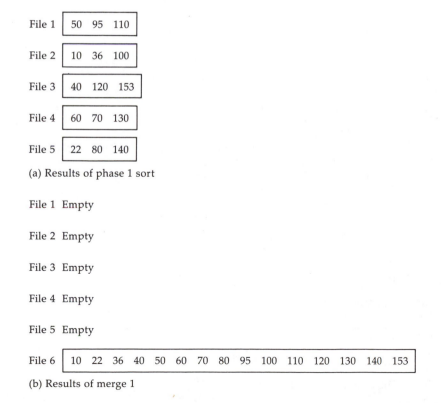

File 1 | 50 95 110

File 2 | 10 36 100

File 3 | 40 120 153

File 4 | 60 70 130

File 5 | 22 80 140

(a) Results of phase 1 sort

File 1 Empty

File 2 Empty

File 3 Empty

File 4 Empty

File 5 Empty

File 6 | 10 22 36 40 50 60 70 80 95 100 110 120 130 140 153

(b) Results of merge 1

Figure 6.6
Balanced *k*-way sort/
merge—Example 6.6

way merge; it merges runs from files 1, 2, 3, 4, and 5 and stores merged runs in file 6 (Figure 6.6(b)).

The realistic sort/merge situation is somewhere between the balanced two-way merge, which merges two input files into two output files, and the idealistic balanced k-way sort/merge, which uses k input files for k runs and merges to one output file. The **balanced k-way sort/merge** algorithm presented in Algorithm 6.3 uses k input files and k output files to perform an extended version of the balanced two-way sort/merge presented in Algorithm 6.2.

Algorithm 6.3   Balanced k-Way Sort/Merge

```
                    { Sort Phase }
initial  distribution
                    { Merge Phase }
number_of_output_files ← k
i ← 0
Repeat
    runs ← 0
    Repeat
        j ← 1 − i
                {
                    perform k-way merge on file (i * k + 1) thru
                    file (i * k + k) evenly distributing output to
                    file (j * k + 1) thru file (j * k + k)
                }
        input first record from each input file
        runs ← runs + 1
        outfile ←  Mod (runs / number_of_output_files) + 1
        Repeat
                {
                    output record with smaller key
                }
            file_k ← Smallest_Key
            output record from file_k to file (j * k + outfile)
            input next record from file_k
        Until End_Of_Run_On_All_Files

    Until End_Of_All_Files

    If Total_Runs > 1
        i ← 1 − i

Until Total_Runs = 1

Algorithm Total_Runs

    total ← 0
    For lcv ← 1 To k
        total ← total + runs (file (i * k + lcv) )

    Total_Runs ← total
```

Algorithm Smallest_Key

    lcv ← 1
    first_file ← Find_Nonempty_File
    small ← first_file
    While first_file <> 0
        second_file ← Find_Nonempty_File
        If second_file <> 0
            If key (first_file) > key (second_file)
                small ← second_file

        first_file ← second_file

    Smallest_Key ← small

Algorithm Find_Nonempty_File

    nonempty ← 0
    While nonempty = 0
    And lcv <= k
        If Not End_Of_Run_On_File (i * k + lcv)
        And Not Eof (file (i * k + lcv)
            nonempty ← i * k + lcv

        lcv ← lcv + 1

    Find_Nonempty_File ← nonempty

Algorithm End_Of_Run_On_All_Files

    test_end ← TRUE
    For lcv ← 1 To k
        test_end ← test_end And End_Of_Run_On_File (i * k + lcv)

    End_Of_Run_On_All_Files ← test_end

Algorithm End_Of_All_Files

    test_end ← TRUE
    For lcv ← 1 To k
        test_end ← test_end And Eof (file (i * k + lcv))

    End_Of_All_Files ← test_end

Each pass of the merge phase of a two-way sort/merge cuts the number of runs to one-half the number of runs at the start of that phase. Each pass of the merge phase of a three-way sort/merge cuts the number of runs to one-third the number of runs at the start of that phase—that is, the number is reduced by a factor of three. Each pass of the merge phase of a four-way sort/merge cuts the number of runs to one-fourth the number of runs at the start of that phase; the number is reduced by a factor of four. So, in general, the number of passes for the merge phase of a *k*-way sort/merge is $\lceil \log_k NR \rceil + 1$. The variable k is the number of files to be merged and the number of output files, and NR is the number of runs produced during the initial sorting phase.

For example, when $NR = 36$, a three-way sort/merge requires $\lceil \log_3 36 \rceil$ = 4 passes of the merge phase. A four-way sort/merge requires $\lceil \log_4 36 \rceil$ = 3 passes of the merge phase. Since each pass of the merge phase transmits each record of the file once, the number of passes through a file to be sorted is one pass for the sort phase plus the number of passes through the merge phase.

POLYPHASE SORT/MERGE

Close examination of the balanced two-way sort/merge algorithm indicates the need for two improvements: the reduction of copying when the number of runs is not a multiple of the number of files being merged and the reduction of the number of output files required. Example 6.7 explains how an algorithm with these improvements, the polyphase sort/merge, works.

EXAMPLE 6.7

Consider the records to be sorted:

50 110 95 10 100 36 153 40 120 60 70 130 22 140 80

The number of runs in file 1 after the sort phase is greater than the number of runs in file 2 (Figure 6.7(a)). After the first two pairs of runs are merged from files 1 and 2, file 2 is empty, but file 1 still has one unprocessed run (Figure 6.7(b)). The balanced two-way sort/merge algorithm and the balanced k-way sort/merge algorithm simply copy the last run from file 1 into the output file.

An improved algorithm reduces the copying of runs at the end of a file in this manner: When an input file becomes empty, file 1 still has an unprocessed run, while the output file 3 has two merged runs. To maximize the merging phase, files 1 and 3 merge into file 2 (which is empty). Figure 6.7(c) shows the resulting file contents. Now file 1 is empty, file 2 (the output file) has one run, and file 3 still has one run. Files 2 and 3 merge into empty file 1 to produce one run that contains all the records (Figure 6.7(d)). In effect the improved algorithm performs a two-way sort/merge until one of the input files becomes empty—the end of a merge pass. The empty file is

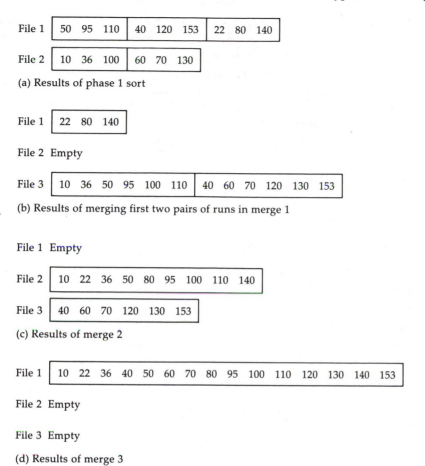

Figure 6.7
Polyphase sort/
merge—Example 6.7

the one output file to receive runs merged from the other two files. Table 6.1 summarizes the number of runs on each file after the sort phase and after each pass of the merge phase.

The process uses only three files ($k + 1$), where the balanced two-way sort/merge algorithm used four files ($2k$), but it performs a k-way merge only until one input file is empty. Then it merges k input files into one

Table 6.1 Summary of polyphase sort/merge using Example 6.1 data

	No. of runs on		
	File 1	**File 2**	**File 3**
Sort phase	3	2	0
Merge pass 1	1	0	2
Merge pass 2	0	1	1
Merge pass 3	1	0	0

output file until all records are in one run. The merge process discussed here is the polyphase sort/merge algorithm. The sort phase distributes sorted runs into *k* files, then the merge phase merges *k* input files into one output file. The first input file emptied in each merge phase becomes the output file for the next phase. The improvement realized is that a *k*-way merge is performed that requires a total of $k + 1$ files. (The balanced *k*-way sort/ merge algorithm requires 2*k* files.) The improved algorithm, the **polyphase sort/merge** algorithm, is presented in Algorithm 6.4.

Algorithm 6.4 Polyphase Sort/Merge

```
                        { Sort Phase }
        initial distribution
                        { Merge Phase }
        outfile ← k + 1
        Repeat
             runs ← 0
             Repeat
                        {
                            perform k-way merge on k input files
                            with output to outfile
                        }
                    input first record from each input file
                    runs ← runs + 1
                    Repeat
                        {
                            output record with smaller key
                        }
                    file_k ← Smallest_Key
                    output record from file_k to outfile
                    input next record from file_k
                Until End_Of_Run_On_All_Files

            Until End_Of_A_File (empty_file)

            rewind outfile
            outfile ← empty_file
        Until Total_Runs = 1

        Algorithm Total_Runs

            total ← 0
            For lcv ← 1 To k + 1
                total ← total + runs (file (lcv) )

            Total_Runs ← total
```

Algorithm Smallest_Key

```
lcv ← 1
first_file ← Find_Nonempty_File
small ← first_file
While first_file <> 0
    second_file ← Find_Nonempty_File
    If second_file <> 0
        If key (first_file) > key (second_file)
            small ← second_file

    first_file ← second_file

Smallest_Key ← small
```

Algorithm Find_Nonempty_File

```
nonempty ← 0
While nonempty = 0
And lcv <= k + 1
    If lcv <> outfile
        If Not End_Of_Run_On_File (lcv)
        And Not Eof (file (lcv)
            nonempty ← lcv

    lcv ← lcv + 1

Find_Nonempty_File ← nonempty
```

Algorithm End_Of_Run_On_All_Files

```
test_end ← TRUE
For lcv ← 1 To k + 1
    If lcv <> outfile
        test_end ← test_end And End_Of_Run_On_File (lcv)

End_Of_Run_On_All_Files ← test_end
```

Algorithm End_Of_A_File

```
lcv ← 1
test_end ← FALSE
While lcv <= k + 1
And Not test_end
    If lcv <> outfile
        test_end ← test_end Or Eof (file (lcv) )

    lcv ← lcv + 1

empty_file ← lcv
End_Of_A_File ← test_end
```

Table 6.2   Analysis of polyphase sort/merge

P	No. of Passes	
2	$1.504 \ln NR + 0.992$	$(= 1.040 \lg NR + 0.99)$
3	$1.015 \ln NR + 0.965$	$(= 0.703 \lg NR + 0.96)$
4	$0.863 \ln NR + 0.921$	
5	$0.795 \ln NR + 0.864$	
6	$0.762 \ln NR + 0.767$	
7	$0.744 \ln NR + 0.723$	
8	$0.734 \ln NR + 0.646$	
9	$0.728 \ln NR + 0.568$	
19	$0.721 \ln NR - 0.030$	

An extensive analysis of the polyphase sort/merge found in Knuth (1973) is summarized in Table 6.2. The polyphase sort/merge that uses a perfect Fibonacci distribution with $p = 2$ (a two-way merge) requires approximately $1.04 \lg NR + 0.99$ pass through the data. (NR is the number of initial runs after the sort phase.) This characteristic makes it competitive with the balanced two-way sort/merge ($\lceil \lg NR \rceil + 1$ pass), and the polyphase sort/merge needs only three files instead of four.

For a three-way merge, the polyphase sort/merge makes $0.703 \lg NR + 0.96$ pass through the data. For a file of 36 initial runs ($NR = 36$), the balanced three-way makes four passes over the data and requires six files; the polyphase sort/merge makes 5.178 passes over the data but requires only four files. An additional pass over the data is a small price to pay to reduce the number of files required by one-third (from six files to four files). Note that the number of passes through the data decreases as the number of files increases. (The variable p indicates the number of files to be merged.) The balanced k-way sort/merge makes $\lceil \lg NR \rceil + 1$ pass through the data. The number of passes for the polyphase sort/merge is $1/NR$ times the total number of initial runs processed during the initial distribution and merge phases. The polyphase sort/merge becomes more efficient at the point that the number of files being merged (p) is greater than three.

Fibonacci Distribution

The basic principle behind the efficiency of the polyphase sort/merge algorithm is the unbalanced distribution of initial runs from the sort phase. Unbalanced distribution ensures that one file will end before any of the other files, so fewer passes over the data are required. R. L. Gilstad, who developed the polyphase sort/merge in 1960, found that an unbalanced distribution of initial runs, using the **perfect Fibonacci distribution**, provided a much improved performance over a balanced distribution (see Knuth, 1973).

The perfect Fibonacci distribution maximizes the merge phase by reducing the copying of runs, thus reducing the number of merge cycles. The **pth-order Fibonacci series** is used to distribute runs to each file. The variable p indicates both the number of files to be merged and the order of the Fibonacci series to be used. The runs are distributed to p files and merged p-way into one output file.

The pth-order Fibonacci series for the nth-level perfect distribution is defined as:

$$F_n^{(p)} = F_{n-1}^{(p)} + F_{n-2}^{(p)} + \ldots + F_{n-p}^{(p)} \text{ for } n \geq p$$

$$F_n^{(p)} = 0 \text{ for } 0 \leq n \leq p - 2$$

$$F_{p-1}^{(p)} = 1$$

When $p = 2$, $F_0^{(2)} = 0$, and $F_1^{(2)} = 1$, this is the usual Fibonacci sequence:

$$F_{n+1}^{(2)} = F_n^{(2)} + F_{n-1}^{(2)}$$

Each next item in the series is the sum of the previous two items in the series. For $p = 3$ the pth-order Fibonacci series computes each item in the series as the sum of the previous three items in the series.

Consider the case where $p = 3$. Three files are used for the initial distribution, a three-way merge is performed, and a total of four files are required. If 17 runs are sorted, the perfect Fibonacci distribution is seven runs on file 1, six runs on file 2, and four runs on file 3. Table 6.3 illustrates the number of runs on each file after the sort and merge phases of the polyphase sort/merge for 17 runs. Merge pass 1 merges four runs from files 1, 2, and 3. File 3 becomes empty, leaving three runs on file 1, two runs on file 2, and four merged runs on file 4. Merge pass 2 merges two runs from each of three files when file 2 becomes empty.

A file of 17 runs requires four passes of the merge phase, and the number of runs merged is never less than three. This approach is more efficient

Table 6.3 Summary of polyphase sort/merge on 17 runs.

	No. of runs on			
	File 1	File 2	File 3	File 4
Sort phase	7	6	4	0
Merge pass 1	3	2	0	4
Merge pass 2	1	0	2	2
Merge pass 3	0	1	1	1
Merge pass 4	1	0	0	0

Table 6.4 Summary of balanced two-way sort/merge on 17 runs

	No. of Runs on					
	File 1	File 2	File 3	File 5	File 5	File 6
Sort phase	6	6	5	0	0	0
Merge pass 1	0	0	0	2	2	2
Merge pass 2	1	1	0	0	0	0
Merge pass 3	0	0	0	1	0	0

than the balanced three-way sort/merge. (Table 6.4 shows the results of the balanced three-way sort/merge on 17 runs.) Since the number of runs is not a multiple of three, the last merged run produced by each merge phase of the balanced three-way sort/merge is a merge of two runs (the only two runs left). The polyphase algorithm maximizes the merging process by stopping the merge pass when a file empties.

The distribution of runs among the nonempty files after each merge pass is a perfect **nth-level distribution**; one file always ends before all the other files, and the last merge pass merges one run from the nonempty files into the empty file. A perfect Fibonacci distribution ensures that the polyphase sort/merge always has one run on each of k files to be merged during the last pass of the merge phase.

Look from the bottom up at Table 6.3, the distribution of runs on the files—the zeroth-level distribution for $p = 3$. The table reads 1, 0, 0, 0, which indicates that the sort/merge is finished. The first-level distribution of runs on the nonempty files is 1, 1, 1; the level indicates that one pass of the merge phase is required to merge the runs into one run. The second-level distribution is 1, 2, 2, which indicates that two merge passes are required to merge all runs into one run. The third-level distribution is 3, 2, 4, which means that three merge passes are required to merge all runs into one run.

Where $p = 3$ files to be merged, the third-order Fibonacci series is used for initial distribution of runs from the sort phase. The nth-level indicates the number of merge passes that are required to merge all runs into one run. The first six terms of the third-order Fibonacci series are computed as:

$$0 \leqslant n \leqslant p - 2 : 0 \leqslant n \leqslant \quad 1 \quad : n = 0; \ F_n^{(3)} = F_0^{(3)} = 0$$

$$n = 1; \ F_1^{(3)} = 0$$

$$n = p - 1: \quad n = \quad 2 \quad : n = 2; \ F_2^{(3)} = 1$$

$$n \geqslant p: \quad n \geqslant \quad 3 \quad : n = 3; \ F_3^{(3)} = F_2^{(3)} + F_1^{(3)} + F_0^{(3)}$$

$$= 1 + 0 + 0$$

$$= 1$$

$$n = 4; \quad F_4^{(3)} = F_3^{(3)} + F_2^{(3)} + F_1^{(3)}$$
$$= 1 + 1 + 0$$
$$= 2$$
$$n = 5; \quad F_5^{(3)} = F_4^{(3)} + F_3^{(3)} + F_2^{(3)}$$
$$= 2 + 1 + 1$$
$$= 4$$

The third-order Fibonacci series is computed by summing the three previous terms. The result is

0, 0, 1, 1, 2, 4, 7, 13, 24, 44, 81, . . .

In the nth-level distribution, the number of initial runs that the kth file contains, is

$$F_{n+p-2}^{(p)} + F_{n+p-3}^{(p)} + \ldots + F_{n+k-2}^{(p)}$$

The subscripts indicate which consecutive Fibonacci terms must be summed to determine the number of runs on the kth file, where the subscripts never become negative. The first subscript is the first term to be summed, and the last subscript is the last in a series of consecutive Fibonacci terms to be summed.

For $n = 1$, file 1 ($k = 1$) contains:

$$F_{n+p-2}^{(3)} + F_{n+p-3}^{(3)} + \ldots + F_{n+k-2}^{(3)}$$
$$= F_{1+3-2}^{(3)} + F_{1+3-3}^{(3)} + \ldots + F_{1+1-2}^{(3)}$$
$$= F_2^{(3)} \quad\quad + F_1^{(3)} \quad\quad + \ldots + F_0^{(3)}$$
$$= F_2^{(3)} \quad\quad + F_1^{(3)} \quad\quad + F_0^{(3)}$$
$$= 1 \quad\quad\quad + 0 \quad\quad\quad + 0 \quad = 1 \text{ run}$$

File 2 contains:

$$F_{n+p-2}^{(3)} + \ldots + F_{n+k-2}^{(3)}$$
$$= F_{1+3-2}^{(3)} + \ldots + F_{1+2-2}^{(3)}$$
$$= F_2^{(3)} \quad\quad + \ldots + F_1^{(3)}$$
$$= 1 + 0 = 1 \text{ run}$$

For file 3 the first term—$n + p - 2$—is:

$$F_2^{(3)}$$

The last term is—$n + k - 2$—is:

$$F_2^{(3)}$$

File 3 contains one run. For $n = 2$, file 1 ($k = 1$) contains:

$$F^{(3)}_{n+p-2} + \ldots + F^{(3)}_{n+k-2}$$
$$= F^{(3)}_{2+3-2} + \ldots + F^{(3)}_{2+1-2}$$
$$= F^{(3)}_3 \qquad + \ldots + F^{(3)}_1$$
$$= 1 + 1 + 0 = 2 \, \text{runs}$$

File 2 contains:

$$F^{(3)}_{n+p-2} + \ldots + F^{(3)}_{n+k-2}$$
$$= F^{(3)}_{2+3-2} + \ldots + F^{(3)}_{2+2-2}$$
$$= F^{(3)}_3 \qquad + \ldots + F^{(3)}_2$$
$$= 1 + 1 = 2 \, \text{runs}$$

File 3 contains:

$$F^{(3)}_{n+p-2} + \ldots + F^{(3)}_{n+k-2}$$
$$= F^{(3)}_{2+3-2} + \ldots + F^{(3)}_{2+3-2}$$
$$= F^{(3)}_3$$
$$= 1 \, \text{run}$$

For $n = 3$ file 1 contains:

$$F^{(3)}_{n+p-2} + \ldots + F^{(3)}_{n+k-2}$$
$$= F^{(3)}_{3+3-2} + \ldots + F^{(3)}_{3+1-2}$$
$$= F^{(3)}_4 \qquad + \ldots + F^{(3)}_2$$
$$= 2 + 1 + 1 = 4 \, \text{runs}$$

File 2 contains:

$$F^{(3)}_{n+p-2} + \ldots + F^{(3)}_{n+k-2}$$
$$= F^{(3)}_{3+3-2} + \ldots + F^{(3)}_{3+2-2}$$
$$= F^{(3)}_4 \qquad + \ldots + F^{(3)}_3$$
$$= 2 + 1 = 3 \, \text{runs}$$

File 3 contains:

$$F^{(3)}_{n+p-2} + \ldots + F^{(3)}_{n+k-2}$$
$$= F^{(3)}_{3+3-2} + \ldots + F^{(3)}_{3+3-2}$$
$$= F^{(3)}_4$$
$$= 2 \, \text{runs}$$

For $n = 4$ file 1 contains:

$$F_{n+p-2}^{(3)} + \ldots + F_{n+k-2}^{(3)}$$
$$= F_{4+3-2}^{(3)} + \ldots + F_{4+1-2}^{(3)}$$
$$= F_5^{(3)} \quad + \ldots + F_3^{(3)}$$
$$= 4 + 2 + 1 = 7 \text{ runs}$$

File 2 contains:

$$F_{n+p-2}^{(3)} + \ldots + F_{n+k-2}^{(3)}$$
$$= F_{4+3-2}^{(3)} + \ldots + F_{4+2-2}^{(3)}$$
$$= F_5^{(3)} \quad + \ldots + F_4^{(3)}$$
$$= 4 + 2 = 6 \text{ runs}$$

File 3 contains:

$$F_{n+p-2}^{(3)} + \ldots + F_{n+k-2}^{(3)}$$
$$= F_{4+3-2}^{(3)} + \ldots + F_{4+3-2}^{(3)}$$
$$= F_5^{(3)}$$
$$= 4 \text{ runs}$$

Table 6.5 presents the nth-level perfect Fibonacci numbers for three files ($p = 3$, which signifies a three-way merge into one file). The table indicates the distribution of runs on the three nonempty files that is "perfect" at the nth level, where n indicates the number of passes of the merge phase that are required to merge all runs into one run. For 17 runs where $p = 3$, the initial perfect Fibonacci distribution is seven runs, six runs, and four runs on three files as computed earlier. After the first merge pass, the number of runs is nine distributed as four runs, three runs, and two runs. After the second merge pass, the number of runs is five distributed as two, two, and one. The next merge pass leaves three runs with one on each file, so the final merge pass merges the three remaining runs into one run to complete the polyphase sort/merge.

Consider the data in Example 6.1 that produced five sorted runs for the merging phase. The polyphase merge algorithm distributes the runs "per-

Table 6.5 nth-level perfect Fibonacci numbers for $p = 3$.

Level n	File 1	File 2	3	Total No. of runs
0	1	0	0	1
1	1	1	1	3
2	2	2	1	5
3	4	3	2	9
4	7	6	4	17
5	13	11	7	31
6	24	20	13	57
7	44	37	24	105
8	81	68	44	193
n	a_n	b_n	c_n	t_n
$n+1$	$a_n + b_n$	$a_n + c_n$	a_n	$t_n + 2a_n$

fectly" with one run on file 1, two runs on file 2, and two runs on file 3 as shown in Figure 6.8(a). The first execution of the merging phase merges files 1, 2, and 3 into output file 4; file 1 is emptied (Figure 6.8(b)). File 1 now becomes the output file for the next merge pass, in which the remaining runs on files 2 and 3 merge with the run on file 4. As a result all records are in one run on one file (Figure 6.8(c)).

For this file of data, the balanced two-way sort/merge performed the merge phase three times to put all the records in one run, and the process required three files. The balanced three-way sort/merge executed the merge phase twice and required six files. The polyphase sort/merge, using a perfect Fibonacci distribution, performed the merge phase twice and required only four files. The efficiency of the balanced k-way merge is achieved, and the number of files is reduced from $2k$ to $k + 1$.

To develop an algorithm for initially distributing runs using the Fibonacci series, assume three files store sorted runs from the sort phase. The first cycle of the distribution algorithm distributes runs in a "perfect" fash-

Figure 6.8
Polyphase sort/merge
of Example 6.1 data

File 1 | 50 95 110 |

File 2 | 10 36 100 | 40 120 153 |

File 3 | 60 70 130 | 22 80 140 |

(a) Results of phase 1 sort on Example 6.1 data

File 1 Empty

File 2 | 40 120 153 |

File 3 | 22 80 140 |

File 4 | 10 36 50 60 70 95 100 110 130 |

(b) Results of merge 1

File 1 | 10 22 36 40 50 60 70 80 95 100 110 120 130 140 153 |

File 2 Empty

File 3 Empty

File 4 Empty

(c) Results of merge 2

ion for level one—namely, one run on the first file. Assuming that the number of runs on files 1 through k are $a_n, b_n, c_n, \ldots$, respectively, at the nth-level of distribution (Table 6.5), where $a_n >= b_n >= c_n >= \ldots$, the distribution at the $n + 1$st level can easily be computed using the number of runs in the nth level:

level $= n + 1$

file 1 $= a_n + b_n$ runs

file 2 $= a_n + c_n$ runs

file 3 $= a_n$ runs

total runs $(t_{n+1}) = t_n + 2a_n$ runs

The Fibonacci distribution used in the sort phase to distribute sorted runs to the files is presented in Algorithm 6.5.

For example, assume nine runs are distributed using Algorithm 6.5. The first pass through the While loop loads run 1 (R1) on file 1 as shown by Table 6.6. The second pass through the While loop stores run 2 (R2) on file 2 and stores run 3 (R3) on file 3. The result is a perfect distribution—1, 1, and 1—at level 1. The third pass through of the While loop loads run 4 (R4) to file 1 and loads run 5 (R5) to file 2. The result is a perfect second-level distribution—2, 2, and 1. The fourth pass through the While loop continues

Algorithm 6.5 Fibonacci Distribution Sort

```
number_of_files ← 3
For i ← 1 To number_of_files
      fib [i] ← 0
      runs [i] ← 0

fib [1] ← 1

level ← 1
While more runs
      For file_k ← 1 To number_of_files
            If runs [file_k] < fib [file_k]
                  write a sorted run on file_k
                  runs [file_k] ← runs [file_k] + 1

            { compute n + 1st-level distribution }

      an ← fib [1]
      For file_k ← 1 To number_of_files − 1
            fib [file_k] ← an + fib [file_k + 1]

      fib [number_of_files] ← an
```

Table 6.6   Distribution of runs produced by Algorithm 6.5

| | Contents of | | |
	File 1	**File 2**	**File 3**
Pass 1 of Wh i l e loop adds	R1		
Pass 2 of Wh i l e loop adds		R2	R3
Pass 3 of Wh i l e loop adds	R4	R5	
Pass 4 of Wh i l e loop adds	R6	R7	R8
	R9		
Total runs of each file	4	3	2

through the file to put run 6 (R6) on file 1, run 7 (R7) on file 2, run 8 (R8) on file 3, and run 9 (R9) on file 1. The result is a perfect fourth-level distribution—four, three, and two runs.

EXAMPLE 6.8
_____

The polyphase merge performs most efficiently if the number of runs of records to be sorted coincides exactly with a perfect Fibonacci distribution. When the number of runs does not agree, the polyphase merge can still be used, although the merge will be somewhat less efficient. By adding **dummy runs** (also called null runs and empty runs), we can obtain the required number of runs on each file.

Suppose seven runs are distributed instead of the nine runs distributed above. The distribution is four runs (file 1), two runs (file 2), and 1 run (file 3)—not a perfect Fibonacci distribution. Two dummy runs (D1 and D2) are loaded to files 2 and 3 in place of the missing runs (R8 and R9). The dummy runs make the files have the correct number of runs even though some files are empty. This ensures that only one file will end before the rest of the files and that the one empty file at the end of each merge pass will subsequently be the output file of the next merge pass.

Table 6.7 shows the contents of each file after each merge pass. The initial distribution is four, three, and two runs. After merge pass 1, the distribution is two, two, and one. After merge pass 2, the distribution is one, one, and one, and merge pass 4 merges all runs into one run on file 2.

Algorithm 6.5 must be modified to write dummy runs to the files with less than the perfect number of runs. The modified Algorithm 6.5 is presented in Algorithm 6.6 with the modified lines beginning with a plus sign. The dummy runs are equalized on all files as much as possible. Since the number of records to be sorted is not known in advance, the dummy runs are written to the end of all files that do not contain a perfect number of runs. Algorithm 6.6 does not produce the optimal distribution of dummy

Table 6.7 Summary of file contents of polyphase sort/merge with dummy runs

| | **No. of runs on** | | | |
	File 1	**File 2**	**File 3**	**File 4**
Sort phase	R1	R2	R3	empty
	R4	R5	D2	
	R6	D1		
	R7			
Merge pass 1	R6	D1	empty	R1 + R2 + R3
	R7			R4 + R5 + D2
Merge pass 2	R7	empty	R1 + R2 + R3 + R6 + D1	R4 + R5 + D2
Merge pass 3	empty	all runs	empty	empty

runs, but Tremblay and Sorenson (1984) have found that this distribution allows the polyphase sort to perform only 2 percent to 3 percent below the optimum. (Knuth [1973] presented the optimal distribution, in which dummy runs are artificially inserted at the beginning of all files—a procedure that is more complex.)

Algorithm 6.6 Modified Fibonacci Distribution Sort

```
            number_of_files ← 3
            For i ← 1 To number_of_files
                fib [i] ← 0
                runs [i] ← 0

        fib [1] ← 1

        level ← 1
        While more runs
            For file_k ← 1 To number_of_files
                If runs [file_k] < fib [file_k]
                    write a sorted run on file_k
                    runs [file_k] ← runs [file_k] + 1

                    { compute n + 1-level distribution }

            an ← fib [1]
            For file_k ← 1 To number_of_files − 1
                fib [file_k] ← an + fib [file_k + 1]

            fib [number_of_files] ← an

†                   { add dummy runs if necessary }
†       For file_k ← 1 To number_of_files
†           While runs [file_k] < fib [file_k]
†               output dummy run {end_of_run_marker} to file_k
†               runs [file_k] ← runs [file_k] + 1
```

PHYSICAL ASPECTS OF SORTING

The number of passes through the data is not the only means of measuring the time necessary to perform an external sort/merge. The physical characteristics of the external storage device used for storing the sort files during the merge phase also have a significant impact on the sort time.

If the files used for the sort/merge are stored on magnetic tape, which can be accessed only sequentially, each file needs to be on a separate reel. A balanced three-way sort/merge requires six tape reels and—for maximum efficiency—six tape drives. If there are fewer than six tape drives, the six tape reels have to be switched a number of times.

Another factor in the total sorting time is the time needed to rewind the tape when the end of a file has been reached. In all the sort/merges discussed, when all the runs from a file have been input, the tape must be rewound to the beginning of the file to serve as an output file for the next cycle of the merge phase. (Some tape drives have a high-speed rewind that reduces the rewind time.)

Data may be in multireel files (files that require more storage space than a single tape can provide). In this case the sort proceeds one reel at a time. Then all sorted reels merge onto reel 1 until it is full, then they merge onto reel 2, and so on, until all the sorted reels have been merged.

The fact that magnetic disks can be accessed randomly makes it possible to store all the files used in a sort/merge on one disk. (The deciding factor is the size of the files.) To perform the balanced three-way sort/merge, six files stored on one disk require only one disk drive. The reduction in the number of physical devices (one disk drive rather than six tape drives) is not without additional cost, however. The disk input/output operations necessary to access an individual run for a particular file are characterized by more overhead (seek time + latency time) than tape input/output operations (start time + stop time). As a counter to this additional cost in time, the data transfer rate is much faster for disk than for tape.

The access overhead of seek and latency can be reduced by distributing the files to more than one disk so the input/output operations of different disks overlap. (Each disk must have a separate disk controller.) Several disks serviced by one device controller yield the same results as storing all files on one disk—that is, the controller can access only one device at a time. With a separate controller for each disk drive, input/output requests are directed to a file on each disk in parallel and the buffers fill in parallel. As with the tape reels, one file per disk is the arrangement that yields optimal sort time, but this arrangement is possible only as long as the resources are available. The discussion here assumes that only one user is applying the sort/merge at a time. In a multiuser environment each user is competing with other users for disk access.

SUMMARY

External sort/merge algorithms are necessary for sorting large data files that exceed the main memory of a computer. The external sort/merge algorithm consists of two phases: a sort phase and a merge phase. The sort phase inputs a portion of the file to be sorted into main memory, it sorts these records with an internal sort algorithm, and it distributes the sorted runs on one or more output files. The output files from the sort phase are input to the merge phase, in which runs from the input files are merged into larger runs and stored in one or more output files.

The two-way sort/merge algorithm merges two input files into one output file, then redistributes the runs from the output file back to the two input files. The merge continues until all records are in one file. The balanced two-way sort/merge algorithm merges two input files by alternately storing merged runs in one of two output files. The advantage of the balanced two-way sort/merge over the two-way sort/merge is that the redistribution of runs from the output file back to the two input files is eliminated. When one merge cycle is completed, the two output files become input files, and records are merged and stored in the two empty files.

The balanced k-way sort/merge algorithm allocates $2k$ files for the merge phase to reduce the number of cycles of the merge phase. The k input files are merged with the merged runs stored in k output files. At the end of one cycle, the output files become the input files for the next cycle, and the input files become the output files for the next cycle. The polyphase sort/merge algorithm requires that the sort phase distribute runs on k files using a perfect Fibonacci distribution so the number of runs on the k files are unbalanced (unlike the balanced k-way sort/merge). The polyphase sort/merge algorithm then merges k input files and stores merged runs on only one output file until one of the input files becomes empty. The empty input file becomes the output file for the next merge cycle. The merge algorithm continues merging the unprocessed runs on the k nonempty files and stores merged runs into the empty file.

For further information, the reader can consult the following sources:

Knuth, Donald E. *The Art of Computer Programming. Vol. 3, Sorting And Searching.* Reading, MA: Addison-Wesley, 1973.

Lum, V. Y., et al. "Key-to-address transform techniques," *Communications of the ACM,* 14(4):228–229, 1971.

Lum, V. Y., and Yuen, P. S. T. "Additional results on key-to-address transform techniques," *Communications of the ACM,* 15(11):996–997, 1972.

Lum, V. Y. "General performance analysis of key-to-address transformation methods using an abstract file concept," *Communications of the ACM,* 16(10):603–612, 1973.

Tremblay, Jean-Paul, and Sorenson, Paul G. *An Introduction to Data Structures With Applications.* New York: McGraw-Hill, 1984.

Key Terms

balanced k-way sort/merge

balanced two-way sort/merge

dummy runs

merge phase

nth-level distribution

perfect Fibonacci distribution

polyphase sort/merge

pth order Fibonacci series

run

sort phase

two-way sort/merge

Exercises

1. Show the distribution of 33 runs to five files using Algorithm 6.6. Remember to add dummy runs to provide a "perfect" distribution.

2. Create a table similar to tables 6.3 and 6.4 that shows the number of runs on each file after the sort and after each merge phase of the distribution in exercise 1 and the polyphase sort/merge ($p = 5$).

3. Create a table similar to tables 6.3 and 6.4 that shows the number of runs on each file after the sort and after each merge phase for sorting 31 runs using the:

   a. two-way sort/merge with two input files

   b. balanced two-way sort/merge with two input files

   c. balanced k-way sort/merge ($k = 3$)

   d. polyphase sort/merge ($p = 3$).

4. Compute the number of passes through the data for each of the four sort/merge algorithms in exercise 3.

5. Given that each time a disk access is made the seek time is 50 ms, the latency time is 20 ms, and the transfer time is 1 ms/record, compute the total time to input and output the records being sorted in exercise 3.

6. Compute the Fibonacci distribution of 25 runs into four files.

7. Repeat exercise 3 but show the number of runs per file for sorting 25 runs. Use $k = 4$ for part c and $p = 4$ for part d.

8. Compute the number of passes through the data for each of the four sort/merge algorithms in exercise 7.

9. Why are external sort/merge algorithms analyzed in terms of the number of passes through the data rather than the number of comparisons made?

10. Contrast the two-way sort/merge and the balanced two-way sort/merge.

11. Contrast the balanced k-way sort/merge and the polyphase sort/merge.

12. Consider the following record keys:

6 29 1 10 23 48 17 13 16 12 11 7 2 3

Show the file contents after the sort phase and after each merge phase of each of the following algorithms. Assume that the initial runs contain only one record.

a. two-way sort/merge

b. balanced two-way sort/merge

c. balanced k-way sort/merge ($k = 3$)

d. polyphase sort/merge ($p = 3$).

Programming Problems

1. Write a Pascal program to perform the sort phase used by the two-way and balanced k-way sort/merge algorithms in the chapter. Use a run size and internal sort of your choice.

2. Write a Pascal program to implement the two-way sort/merge in Algorithm 6.1. Use the program in problem 1 as the sort phase.

3. Write a Pascal program to implement the balanced two-way sort/merge in Algorithm 6.2. Use the program in problem 1 as the sort phase.

4. Write a Pascal program to implement the balanced k-way sort/merge in Algorithm 6.3. Use the program in problem 1 as the sort phase.

5. Vary the value of k in the program in problem 4 and measure the time it takes to sort a file of data.

6. Write a Pascal program to implement the modified Fibonacci distribution sort in Algorithm 6.6.

7. Write a Pascal program to implement the polyphase sort/merge in Algorithm 6.4. Use the Fibonacci distribution sort routine of problem 6 as the sort phase.

8. Vary the value of k in the program in problem 7 and measure the time it takes to sort a file of data.

9. Use a variety of values for k in the programs in problems 4 and 7. Measure and compare the time it takes to sort the same file of data with the two sort/merges.

PART III

RANDOM ACCESS

Chapter 7
Relative File Organization

Chapter 7

CHAPTER CONTENTS

Relative File Organization

PREVIEW

THIS CHAPTER BEGINS WITH A DISCUSSION of the basic structures of random-access files. Random-access file organization is an indexing technique that allows a user to locate a record in a file with as few accesses as possible (ideally, only one). As a result, random-access files provide faster access than sequential files. A random-access file has two components: an indexing scheme used to locate a record in the data file and a physical organization of the data records. (The organized records are called the data file.) The indexing scheme allows the user to determine the location in the data file of the record to be accessed, then the user interrogates the location. Chapter 5 already explored one physical organization: sequential organization. Another physical organization presented in this chapter is relative file organization. The remaining chapters explore several indexing techniques: direct addressing (absolute addressing and relative addressing), hashing, binary search trees, B-trees, and multiple-key indexing. (These indexing techniques usually employ relative file organization. Relative file organization is the physical organization upon which all indexing techniques discussed in Chapters 7, 8, 9, and 10 are based.) Direct addressing and a variety of randomizing (hashing) schemes for obtaining random access to data files (including prime-number division, digit extraction, folding, radix conversion, and perfect hashing) are presented in Chapter 7.

All the nonperfect hashing schemes presented cause collisions. The chapter contains several examples that illustrate methods for handling hashing collisions (linear probing, separate overflow area, double hashing, synonym chaining, bucket addressing, and dynamic hashing). Algorithms for creating and maintaining random-access files in versions of Pascal with the random-access files extension are included. The car-rental agency data used in Chapter 5 are stored in a random-access file, and quantitative measures of access times are computed for comparison of the random and sequential access.

DIRECT ADDRESSING

Sequential file organization limits the user to sequential access to the records in the file. Maintenance of sequential files most often consists of batching transactions to be applied periodically to the master file. During the maintenance run all the records in the master file must be read—whether a change is in order or not—and copied to a new master file.

With **direct file organization** there exists a predictable relationship between the key used to identify an individual record and that record's **absolute address** on an external file. Direct file organization allows direct access to a record by the key of the record; the position of the record in the overall key sequence is not a consideration. The logical ordering of the records need not have any relationship to the physical sequence of the records on the file, so the file is sometimes characterized as providing random access. The absolute address of the record is a machine-dependent address consisting of cylinder-number, surface-number, and record-number if cylinder addressing is used (Figure 7.1). If sector addressing is used the absolute address consists of sector-number and record-number (Figure 7.2). Absolute addressing is device-dependent and requires that the user know exactly how the data are to be stored physically. Relocation of the direct file to another part of the disk requires changing the absolute addresses.

Relative file organization is a common implementation of direct file organization using relative addressing (Figure 7.3). Once a key-position relationship is established, the position of the record in the file is specified as a record number relative to the beginning of the file, where the first record is record number 0. A relative file with space for N records contains positions with relative record numbers 0, 1, 2, . . ., $N - 1$ where the ith record has the relative record number $i - 1$. Relative file organization is a machine-independent implementation of direct file organization that is supported in several high-level programming languages: COBOL, FORTRAN, PL/1, VAX-11 Pascal, OMSI Pascal, TURBO Pascal and UCSD Pascal. Maintenance of a relative file involves processing one transaction at a time rather than batching transactions to be applied to the master file. The record in the relative file to be modified is accessed randomly, the change made to the record, and the modified record written back to the relative file in the same position from which it was read. Only those records in the relative file that have matching transaction records need be input and modified—a definite advantage over sequential organization.

The key-position relationship must be a predictable relationship so that direct access to the record is possible once it is stored in the relative file. The relationship is a mapping function from the key values to the addresses in the external file, and it is designated when the relative file is established. One of the simplest mapping functions is one in which the key value for

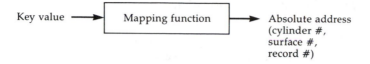

Figure 7.1
Key-position relation-
ship with direct
organization on cylin-
der-addressable
devices

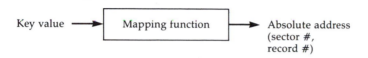

Figure 7.2
Key-position relation-
ship with direct
organization on sec-
tor-addressable
devices

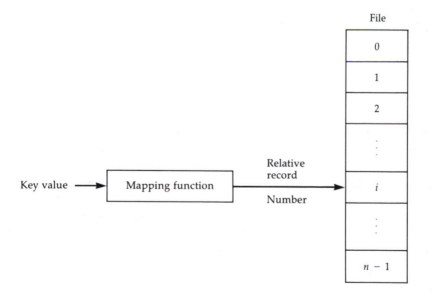

Figure 7.3
Key-position relation-
ship with relative
organization

the record is the same as the record's relative address or position in the external file. For a file of N records, the key values supplied by the user are in the range of 1 to N. The primary advantage to this approach is that there is no processing time needed to determine the record's relative address in the file when the record is to be accessed. For example, for a relative file that contains 5,000 part numbers in the range of 1 to 5000 (called **dense**

keys because the values of consecutive keys differ by only one), a relative file of 5,001 record locations (0 through 5000) is established, and part number 2534 is stored in the position in the file with a relative record number 2534. Accessing the record later is as easy as specifying the part number.

For a range of key values that do not start with 1 or 0, such as 5,000 numbers of parts in inventory in the range of 10001 to 15000 (dense keys), the address could be the part number less a constant (in this case, 10,000). A part number in the range of 10001 to 15000 is stored in relative record positions 1 through 5000.

For data with a large range of key values that are not dense, such as employee data with social security numbers as the key values, the programmer may have to allocate a large relative file in order to use the key as the relative record number. As a result, a high percentage of the file space may be wasted, or empty. For example, the use of social security numbers as the key and the relative record number requires the allocation of a file with 999,999,999 records. If the lowest social security number is 100-00-0000, the data are stored in record 100000000; the positions with relative record numbers 0 to 099999999 are never used—they are wasted. If the file contains data for 10,000 employees with keys (social security numbers) in the nondense range of 0 to 999999999, only 10,000 locations, or 0.001 percent of the file, are used; 99.999 percent of the file is empty. The employee data is easy to access since the key is the relative record number, but a great deal of space is wasted.

A common solution to the problem of waste in random addressing is to map the large range of nondense key values into a smaller range of record positions in the file. With the use of a mapping scheme, the key is no longer the address of the record position in the file where the record with this key is found. Table 7.1 illustrates the need for an indexing technique for determining the address of a record if the key is given. A number of mapping schemes have been applied to a set of five-digit keys. Notice that the keys are listed in key order in the table, but the corresponding record positions where each key will be stored is definitely not in order. Therefore, several indexing techniques have been used to recall the key and the corresponding record position address for each record in the file. These indexing techniques include hashing, binary search trees, B-trees, index tables, inverted files, and multilist files. Hashing, which provides random access or sequential access according to physical order of records, will be discussed in this chapter. B-trees, which provide sequential access of records by key order as well as random access, will be discussed in Chapter 8; index tables, which provide random access or sequential access by key order, will be presented in Chapter 9; and inverted files and multilist files, which provide access by more than one key per record, will be investigated in Chapter 10.

Table 7.1 Five hashing functions applied to file positions 0 through 99

Key values	Hashing functions				
	1	2	3	4	5
24964	35	49	13	56	16
25936	37	69	95	50	49
32179	72	91	0	25	89
38652	46	26	38	58	25
40851	14	18	59	57	25
53455	8	54	89	5	25
53758	20	87	95	0	25
54603	89	36	49	59	0
63388	47	83	21	36	44
81347	61	73	60	3	56
Number of synonyms	0	0	1	0	3

Hashing function legend

1 = Prime-number division remainder (divisor = 97)
2 = Digit extractions (third and fifth positions)
3 = Folding (123 + 45)
4 = Radix conversion (base = 12)
5 = Mid-square (234 squared)

HASHING

A common approach to establishing a key-position relationship that does not waste space is to perform a calculation on the key value that results in a relative record number. **Hashing** is the application of a function to the key value that results in mapping the range of possible key values into a smaller range of relative addresses. For the data that uses the social security numbers of 10,000 employees as keys, the hash function needs to map the range of key values (1 to 999999999) into 10,000 relative positions (0 to 9999). The hash function must map a large range of values, where not all values in the range will be used (the values are not dense), into a smaller range of relative addresses. The hashing function is also referred to as a **randomizing scheme** since the function randomly selects a relative address for a specific key value without regard to the physical sequence of records in the file. Random access to the records in the file—not sequencing records in the file—is the intent.

Many times a key value contains characters that make it difficult to manipulate the key to compute an address. A nonnumeric key value can be converted to a numeric value by using the numerically coded internal representation of each character in the key. For example, the numeric ASCII or EBCDIC representation of each letter can be used in place of each character to provide a numeric key. The ASCII representation of the key **C1** is **6749** (67 is the ASCII code for **C**, and 49 is the ASCII code for **1**). A hashing function is applied to the numeric key **6749** rather than to the nonnumeric key **C1**.

The primary problem with most hashing functions is that the function does not always produce unique relative addresses. When the hashing function for two keys that are not the same results in the same relative address, a **collision** occurs; only one record can be stored in a single relative address. The two keys are said to have hashed to the same relative address and are considered **synonyms**.

Most hashing functions can be improved by allocating more file space than the number needed to store the keys. The relationship between file space and the number of keys is described by three terms that mean the same thing: **load factor**, packing factor, and packing density. The load factor is the ratio of the number of key values to be stored versus the number of file positions:

$$\text{load factor} = \frac{\text{number of key values}}{\text{number of file positions}}$$

Twenty percent of a file with a load factor of 80 percent is empty. Such an arrangement reduces the number of collisions over a file with a load factor of 100 percent since the range of key values is mapped into a larger file space. The number of file locations needed for a load factor of 80 percent is

$$0.80 \times \text{number of file positions} = \text{number of key values}$$

or

$$\text{number of file positions} = \frac{\text{number of key values}}{0.80}$$

or

$$\text{number of file positions} = 1.25 \times \text{number of key values}$$

The smaller the load factor, the less dense the file is, and the less chance of collisions. The disadvantage of a low load factor (less than 50 percent) is the great amount of file space that is wasted by being empty. A balance must be achieved between the number of collisions and the amount of file space wasted. Descriptions of a number of more common hashing functions follow.

Prime-Number Division Remainder

A number of randomizing schemes are available for transforming the key value into a relative record number. The most common randomizing scheme is called the **prime-number division remainder method**. If the key value is divided by a number (N), the remainder of the division yields a number in the range of 0 to $N - 1$. If the divisor (N) is the number of relative positions in the file, this method can be used to map the keys into N record locations; the remainder is the relative address of the record with the key. Since a large range of key values is being mapped into a smaller range of record positions, collisions may occur between keys that yield the same remainder. The divisor should also be chosen to attempt to reduce the number of collisions. Buchholz (1963) showed that an even divisor is a poor choice and that a prime divisor is better than an even divisor. Lum (1971 to 1973) found that any divisor performs sufficiently as long as it does not contain prime factors less than 20. Researchers generally find that choosing a prime number that is close to the number of record locations in the file results in relative addresses that are less prone to collision. The prime-number division remainder method preserves the uniformity of the key set. Keys that are close are mapped to close but unique positions. Collisions occur when keys divided by the number of file positions yield the same remainder, but choosing a prime number close to the number of file positions reduces collisions.

Another factor that affects the probability of collisions is the load factor of the file. As the load factor increases, the probability of collisions rises drastically. A load factor of 70 percent to 80 percent is generally considered the maximum for reasonable performance. If space is available for a smaller load factor, the probability of collisions is reduced. The prime-number division remainder scheme is generally preferred if the distribution of key values is unknown.

Digit Extraction

Another randomizing scheme is **digit extraction**. The distribution of this hashing function is dependent on the distribution of the key values. The key values are analyzed to determine which digit positions of the key are more evenly distributed. The more evenly distributed digit positions are assigned from right to left. The digit values in the chosen digit positions are extracted, and the resulting integer is used as the relative address. If none of the digit positions has a uniform distribution, more collisions occur.

Suppose, for example, that analysis of nine-digit key values reveals that the four more evenly distributed digits are in the ninth, seventh, fifth and second positions. For a key value of 546032178, the relative address is 8134.

The digit extraction scheme maps key values into a range of 0 to 9999. This capability makes it a viable approach for storing the employee data that uses social security numbers as keys. The scheme requires that the key values be known in order to determine the digit positions for extraction.

Folding

Another randomizing scheme involves **folding**. To form the relative address, the key value is split into two or more parts and then summed, or subjected to And or Xor, as if each part were an integer. If the resulting address contains more digits than the highest address in the file, the excess high-order digits are truncated. Suppose an eight-digit key is mapped into a relative file with addresses in the range of 0 to 9999. For the key value 25936715, folding in half (splitting the key into two parts and summing) yields 2593 + 6715 or 9308 as the relative address; folding in thirds (splitting the key into three parts and summing) yields 259 + 36 + 715 or 1010 as the relative address; folding alternate digits (digits in the odd positions form one part and digits in the even positions form the other part) yields 2961 + 5375 or 8336 as the relative address.

Folding is useful for converting keys with a large number of digits (larger than can be stored in a word of memory) to a smaller number of digits so the address fits into a word of memory (for faster access). Folding is easier to compute than some of the other hashing schemes, but it can produce erratic results.

Radix Conversion

Radix conversion is another randomizing scheme. The key value is interpreted as having a different base or radix and is converted to a decimal number. (Excess high-order digits are truncated.) Consider a five-digit key and a relative file with an address range of 0 to 9999. The decimal key value 38652 is considered a value in base 11 and is converted to a decimal and yields the following relative address:

$$3 \times 11^4 + 8 \times 11^3 + 6 \times 11^2 + 5 \times 11^1 + 2 \times 11^0 = 55354$$

Since the result of the conversion from base 11 to a decimal is a five-digit integer, truncate the high-order 5 to yield 5354, which is a four-digit integer in the range of addresses in the relative file.

Mid-Square

Another randomizing scheme is the **mid-square**. The middle n digits are extracted from the key value and squared to form a relative address. The value of n (the number of middle digits to extract) depends on the required size of the resulting address. Excess high-order digits of the squared result are truncated. Consider a relative file with an address range of 0 to 9999 and a nine-digit key. Suppose the middle three digits are extracted from the key and squared. For the key value 29615834, the middle three digits are 158, and the square of 158 is 24964. Truncating the high-order 2 yields a relative address of 4964. The mid-square hashing function works well if the keys do not have several leading or trailing zeros, and if low load factors are used.

This chapter has presented just a few of the many possible hashing schemes. For thorough performance analysis of many hashing functions with various load factors, see the list of sources at the end of the summary of this chapter.

EXAMPLE 7.1

Table 7.1 includes a list of key values that have been used with the five hashing functions that have been discussed. The table reports the number of synonyms generated for the 10 key values by each hashing function. The prime-number division remainder uses a prime divisor of 97. Analysis of the digit extraction reveals that positions 3 and 5 were the more evenly distributed. The folding scheme summed the first three digits as one integer and the last two digits as another integer and truncated the sum to two digits. The base for radix conversion was base 12. The mid-square used digit positions 2, 3, and 4 as the integer to be squared, then truncated to two digits.

The prime-number division remainder scheme, digit extraction, and radix conversion yielded the fewest synonyms (none) for this small set of 10 keys. Folding yielded one synonym. (The distribution and combination of digits in the third and fifth positions produced the last digit of the address.) The mid-square yielded three synonyms that were a result of several keys having the same digit in position 4, the rightmost digit of the integer squared. (The digit 5 occurred in position 4 a total of three times.)

Table 7.2 illustrates the occupied file positions (in ascending order) for each of the five hashing functions listed in Table 7.1. The prime-number division remainder scheme yields the most uniform distribution, with digit extraction close behind. The folding hashing function produced a synonym at position 95, and it tends to have three of the 10 records clustered around positions 89 through 95.

The radix conversion scheme clusters one-half of the records in positions 50 through 59, which leaves empty positions for synonyms in positions 60

Table 7.2   Occupied file positions for Table 7.1

Hashing functions

1	2	3	4	5
8	18	0	0	0
14	26	13	3	16
20	36	21	5	25
35	49	38	25	25
37	54	49	36	25
46	69	59	50	25
47	73	60	56	25
61	83	89	57	44
72	87	95	58	49
89	91	95	59	89

Hashing function legend

1 = Prime-number division remainder (divisor = 97)
2 = Digit extraction (third and fifth positions)
3 = Folding (123 + 45)
4 = Radix conversion (base = 12)
5 = Mid-square (234 squared)

through 99. The key values were not uniformly distributed throughout the file, so the empty positions are not uniformly distributed.

The mid-square produced four synonyms for location 25 with 90 percent of the keys in locations 0 through 56. Again, like the radix conversion, most of the empty positions tend to be in the back half of the file.

Conduct an analysis such as this on a sample of key values (if available) to determine the best hashing function for this particular application. If a sample of key values is not available, the prime-number division remainder method is usually the best scheme for uniform distribution with a load factor less than 100 percent.

Perfect Hashing

A hashing function that provides one-to-one mapping from a key into a position is termed a **perfect hashing function** since no collisions occur. A perfect hashing function requires the knowledge of the set of key values in order to generate a perfectly uniform distribution of addresses. Perfect hashing functions could be applied to a table lookup for reserved words in compilers, filtering high-frequency words in natural-language processing, and a table lookup for month abbreviations used in dates. Several perfect hashing functions will be reviewed here. For algorithms and analysis of each of the perfect hashing schemes discussed, see the sources listed at the end of the summary of this chapter.

Quotient Reduction   The perfect hashing function known as **quotient reduction** was introduced by Sprugnoli (1977) and is defined by the formula:

hash $(w) = (w + s)/N$

The variable w is the key value being hashed, and s and N are constants in the same set. This method assumes the set of keys are in ascending order, so that:

hash (first key) $= 0$

The constants s and N are used to adjust the other key values to different intervals based on the differences between key values in the ascending set. For example, for the set of key values {1, 3, 8, 14, 17, 23}, the quotient-reduction algorithm produces the hashing function:

hash $(w) = (w + 3)/5$

The respective hashed addresses generated are {0, 1, 2, 3, 4, 5}. The hashing function is unique to the static set of keys, and it hashes the key values to a minimal range of addresses. The quotient-reduction method works well when the set of key values is uniformly distributed.

Remainder Reduction   Sprugnoli also introduced the perfect hashing function known as **remainder reduction**. Remainder reduction is similar to the quotient-reduction method except that the set of key values does not have to be uniformly distributed; they are scrambled using modular arithmetic before the quotient-reduction algorithm is applied. The formula for the remainder reduction method is

hash $(w) = ((d + wq) \bmod M)/N$

As with the quotient-reduction method, the constants d, q, N, and M must be chosen via an extensive algorithm for this particular key set.

Associated Value Hashing   Cichelli presented a hash function known as **associated value hashing** that works well for characters. The formula for the hash function has the form:

hash (key) = key length +
        associated value of the key's first character +
        associated value of the key's last character

Cichelli's hashing function involves extensive searching of the words in the set of keys in order to assign an associated value to each letter that is either the first character or the last character of a key. The associated value is based on the frequency of use of each letter in either the first or last position of the word. Once the associated values for all possible letters have been computed, the hashed address for each key in the set is simple to compute.

Cichelli's hashing function, since it assumes the key values are characters, is an application to reserved word lookup in compilers, for month abbreviations, or for frequently occurring English words in natural-language processing.

Reciprocal Hashing   Introduced by Jaeschke (1981), **reciprocal hashing**, involves finding constants, c, d, and e. The hashing function is

$$\text{hash } (w) = c/(d \times w + e) \text{ Mod } n$$

The variable n is the number of keys in the set. The constants c, d, and e must be determined with special algorithms, as with quotient reduction and remainder reduction. The constant c is determined so that (c/w) Mod n is different for each key (w) in the set of keys. The constants d and e are determined so that $d \times (w) + e$ are pairwise relatively prime for all keys (w) in the set of key values. The constants d and e are used to transform the set of key values into a set of keys that are relatively prime to each other. Then the relatively prime keys are mapped into unique addresses.

The ordered minimal perfect hashing scheme devised by Chang (1984) is a modification of reciprocal hashing:

$$\text{hash } (w) = c \text{ Mod } p(w)$$

The constant c is the same as the constant computed in reciprocal hashing, and $p(w)$ is a prime-number function. The keys in the static key set can be stored in ascending order by ordering the keys, then applying Chang's hashing method to each key.

Most perfect hashing functions require extensive manipulations of the key sets and apply to static key sets only. In most file processing environments where data files are not static but updated to keep current, perfect hashing functions are not applicable.

TECHNIQUES FOR HANDLING COLLISIONS

Even with a load factor less than 100 percent, collisions occur. Several techniques are available for handling collisions and synonyms. Two classes of collision-handling techniques exist: open addressing and chaining. Both classes will be described along with several variations of each class. For all the techniques examined, n positions are allocated in the file (numbered 0,

1, . . ., $n - 1$) where each position contains a flag, which is initialized as empty. The flag indicates that nothing has yet been stored in that position. Once information has been stored in a particular position in the file, the flag is occupied.

Linear Probing

One of the simplest techniques for resolving collisions is **linear probing**, in which the file is scanned sequentially as a circular file, and the synonym is stored in the nearest available space to the hashed address. Locating a record involves hashing the key, accessing the hashed address (i) to determine that the data in the hashed address is or is not the record being sought. If it is not, a sequential search through positions $i + 1, i + 2, . . ., n, 0, 1, 2, . . ., i - 1$ of the file is in order.

The file is searched as a circular file to use as many empty positions as possible. In a search of a noncircular file, a key hashes to position i, which is occupied, and positions $i + 1, . . ., n - 1$ are searched for an empty position. The back portion of the file tends to fill up, leaving more empty positions at the front portion of the file. In a search of a circular file, the entire file is searched, starting at position $i + 1$, and the synonyms are distributed throughout the file, not clustered at the back portion. Storing the synonym in the nearest available position is simple, but accessing the synonym later may require a sequential search of the entire file.

Position	Data
0	
1	A
2	
3	
4	
5	
6	
7	IN
8	
9	OF
10	
11	AND
12	
13	
14	
15	
16	
17	
18	
19	
20	
21	
22	
23	
24	
25	THE
26	
27	TO
28	
29	
30	
31	
32	
33	
34	
35	
36	
37	
38	
39	
40	

EXAMPLE 7.2

Suppose that a set of words are to be stored in a relative file using the hash function formed by the exclusive or (Xor) of the bit strings of the decimal position of each letter of the word as it appears in the alphabet. An A is in position 1 of the alphabet or the bit string 1; B is in position 2 of the alphabet or the bit string 10; and so on to Z, which is in position 26 of the alphabet or bit string 11010. A string of 5 bits is needed to assign unique representations to all 26 letters of the alphabet. The Xor of the bit strings of each letter of the word results in a string of five bits representing 32 different binary values (0 through 31). So the file size is 32 positions. This hashing function, when applied to THE results in the following address computation:

$$\text{hash (THE)} = 10100_2 \text{ Xor } 01000_2 \text{ Xor } 00101_2 = 11001_2 = 25_{10}$$

Linear probing is used to resolve collisions. The set of words and the hashed values for each word are presented in Table 7.3. The relative file after the first six additions is presented in Figure 7.4. THE, OF, AND, TO, A, and

Figure 7.4
Relative file with the first six additions

Table 7.3 Set of words with hashed positions

WORD	hash (WORD)	WORD	hash (WORD)
THE	25	AT	21
OF	9	BY	27
AND	11	I	9
TO	27	THIS	6
A	1	HAD	13
IN	7	NOT	21
THAT	9	NO	1
IS	26	TON	21
WAS	5	SAYS	24
HE	13	ARE	22
FOR	27	BUT	3
IT	29	FROM	22
WITH	2	OR	29
AS	18	HAVE	26
HIS	18	AN	15
ON	1	THEY	0
BE	7		

IN have been added to the file, and the next word added, THAT, causes a collision with position 9. Since THAT collides with OF, which is already in position 9, THAT will be stored in the nearest available location, position 10. Then IS, WAS, and HE are added before a collision occurs again (as a result of attempting to add FOR in position 27). Figure 7.5 illustrates the relative file just before the second collision occurs.

FOR is stored in the next location, position 28. IT, WITH, and AS are added to the relative file, (Figure 7.6) but HIS collides with AS in position 18. HIS is stored in the nearest location, position 19 (Figure 7.7).

The next word to be added, ON, collides with A in position 1. Position 2 is occupied with the word WITH, so ON has a secondary collision with the word WITH in attempting to store ON in the nearest available position. A sequential search of the file from position 2 to position 3 continues until an available position is found. Since position 3 is available, ON is stored in position 3, two positions away from the hashed address (position 1). Accessing ON later means searching from position 1 to position 3 to find the word.

BE collides with IN in position 7 so must be stored in position 8. The word AT is stored in position 21 without any collisions (Figure 7.8). BY hashes to position 27 but collides with TO in position 27, FOR in position 28, and IT in position 29, so it must be stored in position 30. I collides with OF in position 9, THAT in position 10, AND in position 11 so the nearest

Position	Data		Position	Data		Position	Data	
0			0			0		
1	A		1	A		1	A	
2			2	WITH		2	WITH	
3			3			3		
4			4			4		
5	WAS		5	WAS		5	WAS	
6			6			6		
7	IN		7	IN		7	IN	
8			8			8		
9	OF		9	OF		9	OF	
10	THAT	Synonym of 9	10	THAT	Synonym of 9	10	THAT	Synonym of 9
11	AND		11	AND		11	AND	
12			12			12		
13	HE		13	HE		13	HE	
14			14			14		
15			15			15		
16			16			16		
17			17			17		
18			18	AS		18	AS	
19			19			19	HIS	Synonym of 18
20			20			20		
21			21			21		
22			22			22		
23			23			23		
24			24			24		
25	THE		25	THE		25	THE	
26	IS		26	IS		26	IS	
27	TO		27	TO		27	TO	
28			28	FOR	Synonym of 27	28	FOR	Synonym of 27
29			29	IT		29	IT	
30			30			30		
31			31			31		
32			32			32		
33			33			33		
34			34			34		
35			35			35		
36			36			36		
37			37			37		
38			38			38		
39			39			39		
40			40			40		

Figure 7.5
Relative file just
before the second col-
lision occurs

Figure 7.6
Relative file when
third collision occurs

Figure 7.7
Relative file with HIS

available location is position 12. THIS is stored in position 6 with no collisions (Figure 7.9).

HAD collides with HE in position 13 so is stored in position 14. NOT
collides with AT in position 21 so is stored in position 22. NO hashes to
position 1 but is stored in the nearest location which is position 4. TON
collides with AT in position 21 and NOT in position 22 so must be stored
in position 23. SAYS hashes and is stored in position 24 (Figure 7.10).

Position	Data	
0		
1	A	
2	WITH	
3	ON	Synonym of 1
4		
5	WAS	
6		
7	IN	
8	BE	Synonym of 7
9	OF	
10	THAT	Synonym of 9
11	AND	
12		
13	HE	
14		
15		
16		
17		
18	AS	
19	HIS	Synonym of 18
20		
21	AT	
22		
23		
24		
25	THE	
26	IS	
27	TO	
28	FOR	Synonym of 27
29	IT	
30		
31		
32		
33		
34		
35		
36		
37		
38		
39		
40		

Figure 7.8
Relative file with ON, BE, and AT

Position	Data	
0		
1	A	
2	WITH	
3	ON	Synonym of 1
4		
5	WAS	
6	THIS	
7	IN	
8	BE	Synonym of 7
9	OF	
10	THAT	Synonym of 9
11	AND	
12	I	Synonym of 9
13	HE	
14		
15		
16		
17		
18	AS	
19	HIS	Synonym of 18
20		
21	AT	
22		
23		
24		
25	THE	
26	IS	
27	TO	
28	FOR	Synonym of 27
29	IT	
30	BY	Synonym of 27
31		
32		
33		
34		
35		
36		
37		
38		
39		
40		

Figure 7.9
Relative file with BY, FOR, IT, I, and THIS

Position	Data	
0		
1	A	
2	WITH	
3	ON	Synonym of 1
4	NO	Synonym of 1
5	WAS	
6	THIS	
7	IN	
8	BE	Synonym of 7
9	OF	
10	THAT	Synonym of 9
11	AND	
12	I	Synonym of 9
13	HE	
14	HAD	Synonym of 13
15		
16		
17		
18	AS	
19	HIS	Synonym of 18
20		
21	AT	
22	NOT	Synonym of 21
23	TON	Synonym of 21
24	SAYS	
25	THE	
26	IS	
27	TO	
28	FOR	Synonym of 27
29	IT	
30	BY	Synonym of 27
31		
32		
33		
34		
35		
36		
37		
38		
39		
40		

Figure 7.10
Relative file with HAD, NOT, NO, TON, and SAYS

The next word to be added is ARE, which hashes to position 22. Location 22 holds NOT, however, which hashed to position 21 and collided with AT. The situation presented here represents one of the major disadvantages of linear probing: **displacement**. ARE is displaced from position 22 by a word that hashed to another address, but because linear probing is used, position 22 was available. A linear search finally finds that position 31 is the nearest available to position 22 for storing ARE.

BUT collides with ON in position 3 and collides with words in positions 4 through 14. BUT is finally stored in position 15. FROM collides with NOT in position 22 and collides with words in positions 23 through 31; FROM is stored in position 32. OR collides with IT in position 29. After a linear search OR is placed in position 33 (Figure 7.11).

HAVE hashes to position 26, which is occupied by IS. A linear search through positions 27, 28, 29, 30, 31, 32, . . . reveals that the nearest available position is 34, nine positions away from the hashed address. AN hashes to position 15 and is displaced by BUT, so AN is stored in position 16. THEY hashes to position 0. Figure 7.12 presents the relative file with all the words added.

One of the problems with linear probing is the number of positions that must be searched (or probed) before a synonym is located. The word HAVE hashed to position 26, but the first available position nearest the hashed address was position 34. The look up for accessing HAVE involved three steps:

1. The hash: hash (HAVE) = 26

2. Accessing the hashed position − 26

3. HAVE was not in position 26, so the algorithm sequentially searched the file until HAVE was located or until the entire file was searched.

HAVE was located after searching positions 26 through 34—a total of nine probes. If a word is stored in its hashed position, the number of probes is one.

The second problem with linear probing is the number of probes necessary to discover that a word is not present. Searching for a word that is not present in the file involves:

1. Hash (WORD) = 15

2. Access hashed position 15; the word is not found.

3. Serially search positions 16 through 40 and 0 through 14.

Knuth (1973) states that the formula for the average number of probes for an unsuccessful search is

$$\frac{1}{2}\left(1 + \frac{1}{(1-a)^2}\right)$$

The variable a is the load factor. For a load factor of 80 percent, the average number of probes for an unsuccessful search is 13 probes. The formula for the average number of probes for a successful search is

$$\frac{1}{2}\left(1 + \frac{1}{1-a}\right)$$

Position	Data	
0		
1	A	
2	WITH	
3	ON	Synonym of 1
4	NO	Synonym of 1
5	WAS	
6	THIS	
7	IN	
8	BE	Synonym of 7
9	OF	
10	THAT	Synonym of 9
11	AND	
12	I	Synonym of 9
13	HE	
14	HAD	Synonym of 13
15	BUT	Hashes to 3
16		
17		
18	AS	
19	HIS	Synonym of 18
20		
21	AT	
22	NOT	Synonym of 21
23	TON	Synonym of 21
24	SAYS	
25	THE	
26	IS	
27	TO	
28	FOR	Synonym of 27
29	IT	
30	BY	Synonym of 27
31	ARE	Hashes to 22
32	FROM	Synonym of 22
33	OR	Synonym of 29
34		
35		
36		
37		
38		
39		
40		

Figure 7.11
Relative file with
ARE, BUT, FROM,
and OR

Position	Data	
0	THEY	
1	A	
2	WITH	
3	ON	Synonym of 1
4	NO	Synonym of 1
5	WAS	
6	THIS	
7	IN	
8	BE	Synonym of 7
9	OF	
10	THAT	Synonym of 9
11	AND	
12	I	Synonym of 9
13	HE	
14	HAD	Synonym of 13
15	BUT	Hashes to 3
16	AN	Hashes to 15
17		
18	AS	
19	HIS	Synonym of 18
20		
21	AT	
22	NOT	Synonym of 21
23	TON	Synonym of 21
24	SAYS	
25	THE	
26	IS	
27	TO	
28	FOR	Synonym of 27
29	IT	
30	BY	Synonym of 27
31	ARE	Hashes to 22
32	FROM	Synonym of 22
33	OR	Synonym of 29
34	HAVE	Synonym of 26
35		
36		
37		
38		
39		
40		

Figure 7.12
Relative file storing
the entire set of
words

For a load factor of 80 percent, the average number of probes for a successful search is three probes. Table 7.4 lists the average number of probes for successful and unsuccessful searches through a file using linear probing for a variety of load factors.

Another problem with linear probing is the fact that storing the synonym in the nearest available location (*i*) may displace another record added later

Table 7.4   Number of probes for linear probing

Load factor	Average no. of successful probes	Average no. of unsuccessful probes
.10	1.056	1.118
.20	1.125	1.281
.30	1.214	1.520
.40	1.333	1.889
.50	1.500	2.500
.60	1.750	3.625
.70	2.167	6.060
.80	3.000	13.000
.90	5.500	50.500
.95	10.500	200.500

that hashes to position i but is not a synonym of the record in position i. The displacement of records from the hashed address causes more records to be stored away from the hashed address and leads to more extensive linear probing later.

Two-Pass File Creation with Hashing

The displacement problem of linear probing usually occurs when the relative file is initially created with a one-pass algorithm. A one-pass algorithm hashes the key of each record to be loaded to the relative file. It stores a record in the hashed address, if empty, and stores synonyms in the first available position nearest the hashed address. A two-pass algorithm reduces the displacement problem by loading hashed positions in the first pass and loading synonyms in the available positions in the second pass. The first pass of the two-pass algorithm hashes the key of each record to be loaded to the relative file and stores the record in the hashed address, if empty. The synonyms are stored in an output file that will be used during the second pass. The second pass inputs the synonyms separated by the first pass, hashes the key of each record, and stores the synonym in the first available position nearest the hashed address. The two-pass algorithm allows more records to be stored in the positions to which they were hashed, thereby reducing the amount of linear probing that must be done later to access any record without synonyms. The two-pass algorithm works well if the set of key values is known before the file is created. Any additions to the file after the initial loading may produce displacement problems similar to those produced by the one-pass algorithm. Table 7.5 indicates that three words were displaced by synonyms of other words. The two-pass algorithm

Table 7.5   Hashed positions for a two-pass algorithm

First pass		Second pass		
WORD	**hash (WORD)**	**WORD**	**hash (WORD)**	
THE	25			
OF	9			
AND	11			
TO	27			
A	1			
IN	7			
		THAT	9	(synonym)
IS	26			
WAS	5			
HE	13			
		FOR	27	(synonym)
IT	29			
WITH	2			
AS	18			
		HIS	18	(synonym)
		ON	1	(synonym)
		BE	7	(synonym)
AT	21			
		BY	27	(synonym)
		I	9	(synonym)
THIS	6			
		HAD	13	(synonym)
		NOT	21	(synonym)
		NO	1	(synonym)
		TON	21	(synonym)
SAYS	24			
ARE	22 *			
BUT	3 *			
		FROM	22	(synonym)
		OR	29	(synonym)
		HAVE	26	(synonym)
AN	15 *			
THEY	0			

*Would have been displaced by a nonsynonym in the one-pass algorithm

eliminates the displacement of records from their hashed addresses. The words that are synonyms are separated to the right column for the second pass.

Figure 7.13 shows the relative file contents after the first pass. The second pass adds the synonyms that were skipped during the first pass with the resulting file contents shown in Figure 7.14. The three words displaced

Position	Data
0	THEY
1	A
2	WITH
3	BUT
4	
5	WAS
6	THIS
7	IN
8	
9	OF
10	
11	AND
12	
13	HE
14	
15	AN
16	
17	
18	AS
19	
20	
21	AT
22	ARE
23	
24	SAYS
25	THE
26	IS
27	TO
28	
29	IT
30	
31	
32	
33	
34	
35	
36	
37	
38	
39	
40	

Figure 7.13
Relative file of words
in Table 7.3 after the
first pass

Position	Data	
0	THEY	
1	A	
2	WITH	
3	BUT	Synonym of 1
4	ON	
5	WAS	
6	THIS	
7	IN	
8	BE	Synonym of 7
9	OF	
10	THAT	Synonym of 9
11	AND	
12	I	Synonym of 9
13	HE	
14	HAD	Synonym of 13
15	AN	
16	NO	Synonym of 1
17		
18	AS	
19	HIS	Synonym of 18
20		
21	AT	
22	ARE	
23	NOT	Synonym of 21
24	SAYS	
25	THE	
26	IS	
27	TO	
28	FOR	Synonym of 27
29	IT	
30	BY	Synonym of 27
31	TON	Synonym of 21
32	FROM	Synonym of 22
33	OR	Synonym of 29
34	HAVE	Synonym of 26
35		
36		
37		
38		
39		
40		

Figure 7.14
Relative file after the
second pass

during the one-pass loading algorithm in the previous example (ARE, BUT, and AN) are stored in their respective hashed addresses; access to these records will be direct. Linear probing is used only for those records that hashed to a position that was already occupied.

Table 7.6 lists the hashed position for each word in the discussion of the one-pass and two-pass algorithms as well as the actual position in which each word was stored during the algorithms. The table compares the algorithms by including the number of probes necessary to locate each word in

226

Chapter 7 / Relative File Organization

Table 7.6 Comparison of one-pass and two-pass algorithms

WORD	hash (WORD)	One-pass location	No. of probes	Two-pass location	No. of probes
THE	25	25	1	25	1
OF	9	9	1	9	1
AND	11	11	1	11	1
TO	27	27	1	27	1
A	1	1	1	1	1
IN	7	7	1	7	1
THAT	9	10	2	10	2
IS	26	26	1	26	1
WAS	5	5	1	5	1
HE	13	13	1	13	1
FOR	27	28	2	28	2
IT	29	29	1	29	1
WITH	2	2	1	2	1
AS	18	18	1	18	1
HIS	18	19	2	19	2
ON	1	3	3	4	5 (+2)
BE	7	8	2	8	2
AT	21	21	1	21	1
BY	27	30	4	30	4
I	9	12	4	12	4
THIS	6	6	1	6	1
HAD	13	14	2	14	2
NOT	21	22	2	23	3 (+1)
NO	1	4	4	16	13 (+9)
TON	21	23	3	31	11 (+8)
ARE *	22	31	10	22	1 (−9)
BUT *	3	15	13	3	1 (−12)
FROM	22	32	11	32	11
OR	29	33	5	33	5
HAVE	26	34	9	34	9
AN *	15	16	2	15	1 (−1)
THEY	0	0	1	0	1
Average number of probes			2.97		2.91

*Displaced during the one-pass algorithm

the file. The one-pass algorithm displaces two words (ARE and BUT) several positions away from their hashed positions; it takes several probes to locate them (10 and 13 probes, respectively). Displacement does not occur with the two-pass algorithm. The result is a faster access on the average. Some of the synonyms are farther away from their hashed positions as a result of eliminating displacements, but in the two-pass algorithm the average number of probes for all words in the file is less (2.91 probes) than the number for the one-pass algorithm (2.97). Words added after the file is created with the two-pass algorithm could result in displacement.

Separate Overflow Area

Another alternative to the the two-pass algorithm for loading the relative file initially is storing synonyms sequentially in a **separate overflow area**. Using a separate overflow area eliminates the displacement problem altogether and allows use of the one-pass loading algorithm. Accessing synonyms entails sequentially searching all the records in the overflow area, which is probably not as large as the hashed positions of the relative file. Depending on the size of the overflow area, the searching time for locating synonyms could be lengthy. For the set of words in Table 7.3, the first-pass loading algorithm results in the storage presented in Figure 7.13. The synonyms are stored sequentially in an overflow area as indicated in Figure 7.15. Accessing a record that is not in the hashed address involves sequentially searching the overflow area for the record.

The average number of probes for a file with synonyms stored in a separate overflow area depends on the number of synonyms. Table 7.7 lists the

Figure 7.15
Overflow area for relative file in Figure 7.13

Position	Overflow Data
0	THAT
1	FOR
2	HIS
3	ON
4	BE
5	BY
6	I
7	HAD
8	NOT
9	NO
10	TON
11	FROM
12	OR
13	HAVE
14	
15	
16	
17	
18	
19	
20	
21	
22	
23	
24	
25	
26	
27	
28	
29	
30	

Table 7.7 Separate overflow area reduces probes for words in Table 7.3

WORD	No. of probes	WORD	No. of probes
THE	1	BE	6
OF	1	AT	1
AND	1	BY	7
TO	1	I	8
A	1	THIS	1
IN	1	HAD	9
THAT	2	NOT	10
IS	1	NO	11
WAS	1	TON	12
HE	1	ARE	1
FOR	3	BUT	1
IT	1	FROM	13
WITH	1	OR	14
AS	1	HAVE	15
HIS	4	AN	1
ON	5	THEY	1

Average number of probes 9.91

number of probes for the file of words in Figure 7.15. The average number of probes for this file is 9.91—considerably worse than either the one-pass or two-pass algorithms, which do not employ a separate overflow area.

Double Hashing

When a separate overflow area is established for synonyms, the synonym is stored in the next available overflow position. Rather than searching sequentially for the next available overflow position or searching sequentially for the synonym later, the synonym is often hashed to an overflow record position. Hashing synonyms to an overflow area using a second hash function is **double hashing**. The record is initially hashed to a relative file position. If the hashed address is not available, a second hash function is applied and added to the first hashed value, and the synonym is hashed to the overflow area. If the hashed overflow area is not available, a **secondary collision** occurs; then linear probing is used. The access to synonyms is more direct than searching the overflow area sequentially. The synonyms involved in secondary collisions are the only records that have to be accessed sequentially.

Reconsider the set of words in the Example 7.2. Suppose the synonyms are hashed to an overflow area using a second hash function, which is defined as the remainder of the division of the bit string of the letters in the word by the constant 31. Therefore,

$$\text{hash2 (THE)} = 1010000100000101_2 \text{ Mod } 31 = 20741_{10} \text{ Mod } 31 = 2$$

The resulting value of the second hash function is an integer in the range of 0 through 30. The hashed position for storing the synonym in the overflow area is the sum of the results of the two hash functions. If the sum is greater than 30 (the largest numbered location in the file), the remainder of the division of the sum by 31 is the position number in the range of 0 through 30. The second hash function values for the synonyms are presented in the Table 7.8.

The relative file can be loaded with a one-pass algorithm by hashing a record to a position in the prime or home area of the file as before. If the hashed address is occupied, the synonym is hashed using the second hash function value added to the first hash function value as shown in the table. If the resulting double hashed address in the overflow area is not occupied, the synonym is stored in the double hashed overflow address. If the double hashed address is occupied, then linear probing of the overflow area is applied as before.

The words THAT, FOR, HIS, ON, and BE are stored in their respective double-hashed addresses as shown in Figure 7.16. The next word to be added that is a synonym of a home address is BY, which double hashes to

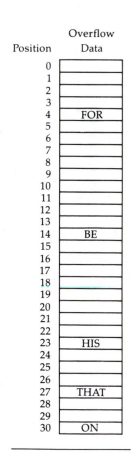

Position	Overflow Data
0	
1	
2	
3	
4	FOR
5	
6	
7	
8	
9	
10	
11	
12	
13	
14	BE
15	
16	
17	
18	
19	
20	
21	
22	
23	HIS
24	
25	
26	
27	THAT
28	
29	
30	ON

Figure 7.16
Overflow area for file in Figure 7.13 after double hashing

Table 7.8   Using double hashing to organize words from Example 7.2

WORD	hash1 (WORD)	hash2 (WORD)
THE	25	
OF	9	
AND	11	
TO	27	
A	1	
IN	7	
THAT	9	(synonym) + 18 = 27
IS	26	
WAS	5	
HE	13	
FOR	27	(synonym) + 8 = 35 Mod 31 = 4
IT	29	
WITH	2	
AS	18	
HIS	18	(synonym) + 5 = 23
ON	1	(synonym) + 29 = 30
BE	7	(synonym) + 7 = 14
AT	21	
BY	27	(synonym) + 27 = 54 Mod 31 = 23 (synonym)
I	9	(synonym) + 9 = 18
THIS	6	
HAD	13	(synonym) + 13 = 26
NOT	21	(synonym) + 18 = 39 Mod 31 = 8
NO	1	(synonym) + 29 = 30 (synonym)
TON	21	(synonym) + 18 = 39 Mod 31 = 8 (synonym)
SAYS	24	
ARE	22	
BUT	3	
FROM	22	(synonym) + 21 = 43 Mod 31 = 12
OR	29	(synonym) + 2 = 31 Mod 31 = 0
HAVE	26	(synonym) + 5 = 31 Mod 31 = 0 (synonym)
AN	15	
THEY	0	

overflow position 23. Position 23 is occupied by HIS. Linear probing is applied to store BY in the nearest available position, namely overflow position 24. The words I, HAD, and NOT are added to file in their respective overflow positions. A secondary collision occurs when NO double hashes to overflow position 30, which is occupied by ON. A circular search of the file ensues from position 30 to position 0 and finally to position 1 before an empty position is found. TON also collides with NOT in position 8 and is

Figure 7.17
Overflow area after
seven additions

Position	Overflow Data
0	OR
1	NO
2	
3	
4	FOR
5	
6	
7	
8	NOT
9	TON
10	
11	
12	FROM
13	
14	BE
15	
16	
17	
18	I
19	
20	
21	
22	
23	HIS
24	BY
25	
26	HAD
27	THAT
28	
29	
30	ON

stored in position 9. FROM and OR are double hashed to their respective overflow positions (Figure 7.17).

The last word to be added that is a synonym of a home address, HAVE, collides with OR in position 0 and NO in position 1. HAVE must be stored in overflow position 2. The prime or home area is as in the previous example. The relative file overflow area is shown in Figure 7.18.

Table 7.9 lists the number of probes for each of the words stored in a separate overflow area using double hashing. The average number of probes for a successful search of this file is 1.63 where the load factor is 50 percent—an average that is comparable to linear probing at the same load factor.

The formula for determining the average number of probes using double hashing for a successful search is

$$\left(-\frac{1}{a} \ln (1 - a) \right)$$

The formula for determining the average number of probes using double hashing for an unsuccessful search is

$$\left(\frac{1}{1 - a} \right)$$

Table 7.9 Probes of separate overflow area using double hashing

Word	No. of Probes	Word	No. of Probes
THE	1	BE	2
OF	1	AT	1
AND	1	BY	3
TO	1	I	2
A	1	THIS	1
IN	1	HAD	2
THAT	2	NOT	2
IS	1	NO	4
WAS	1	TON	3
HE	1	ARE	1
FOR	2	BUT	1
IT	1	FROM	2
WITH	1	OR	2
AS	1	HAVE	4
HIS	2	AN	1
ON	2	THEY	1

Average number of probes 1.63

Table 7.10 Number of probes for double hashing

Load factor	Average no. of successful probes	Average no. of unsuccessful probes
.10	1.054	1.111
.20	1.116	1.250
.30	1.189	1.429
.40	1.277	1.667
.50	1.386	2.000
.60	1.527	2.500
.70	1.720	3.333
.80	2.012	5.000
.90	2.558	10.000
.95	3.153	20.000

Table 7.10 summarizes the average number of probes for a variety of load factors. For a load factor of 80 percent, the average number of probes for a linear probe is 3.000 (see Table 7.4), but it is 2.012 for double hashing. For a load factor of 95 percent, the double hashing method is more efficient for successful searches (3.153 probes) than the linear probing method (10.5 probes) and even more efficient for unsuccessful searches (20.0 probes for double hashing versus 200.5 probes for linear probing).

Synonym Chaining

Synonym chaining is a technique used with and without a separate overflow area to reduce the number of records examined when searching for a synonym. The initial creation of a relative file that uses synonym chaining involves hashing the key of the record to be loaded and retrieving the record in the hashed address. If the hashed address is occupied, then the synonym is stored using one of the techniques discussed above. The record in the initial hashed address contains a link to the position containing the synonym. If several synonyms hash to one address, all the synonyms are linked together even though the synonyms are not physically stored in contiguous positions in the file. Access to any synonym involves searching only the linked synonyms rather than searching the whole file (if linear probing is used) or the whole overflow area (if a separate overflow area is used). Each record is enlarged to include a link field, but the access of a synonym record is more direct than any of the techniques discussed.

Given the set of words used in Example 7.2, synonym chaining could reduce collisions. The use of a separate overflow area for storing synonyms eliminates the displacement problem found in the linear probing example.

Position	Overflow Data
0	OR
1	NO
2	HAVE
3	
4	FOR
5	
6	
7	
8	NOT
9	TON
10	
11	
12	FROM
13	
14	BE
15	
16	
17	
18	I
19	
20	
21	
22	
23	HIS
24	BY
25	
26	HAD
27	THAT
28	
29	
30	ON

Figure 7.18 Complete overflow area

Each position in the home and overflow areas in the relative file contains a link field in addition to the other information that will contain the address of the next synonym in overflow. The relative file must be allocated with the number of necessary positions, an empty value must be recorded in each position, and a null value (-1, for example) must be recorded in the link field of each record. Each record that hashes to an occupied home address is stored in the next available position in the overflow area (allocating the next available position sequentially), and a link field is maintained from the home address to the synonym in overflow. Each later record that is a synonym of a home address is stored in the next available position in overflow and included in the linked list of all synonyms that hashed to this particular home address.

The relative file in Figure 7.19 shows the words THE, OF, AND, TO, A, and IN stored in their respective positions with THAT being the first synonym encountered. THAT hashes to home position 9, which is occupied by OF, so THAT is stored in the first overflow position. Home position 9 retains a link (in the form of the relative position number of overflow) to overflow position 1.

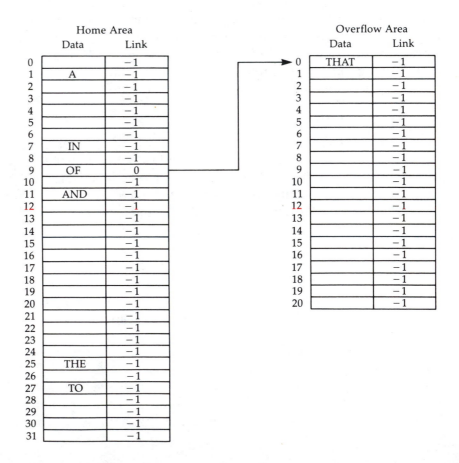

Figure 7.19
Relative file using synonym chaining

The words IS, WAS, and HE are added to the home area, but FOR is a synonym for home position 27, so it is stored in overflow position 1. Home position 27 is linked to overflow position 1. IT, WITH, and AS reside in home positions, HIS is a synonym for home position 18, ON is a synonym for home position 1, and BE is a synonym for home position 7. The file contents are shown in Figure 7.20.

Then AT is stored in home position 21. BY is a synonym for home position 27, which is linked to overflow position 1 (which holds FOR). BY is stored in the next available overflow position, the content of the link field of home position 27 (1) is recorded in the link field of BY. BY links with the synonym FOR, so the address of BY (5) is stored in the link field of the home position. As a result, home area 27 (TO) has the address of the last synonym added (BY in overflow position 5), and BY has the address of the previous synonym (FOR in overflow position 1).

Similarly, I hashes to home position 9, which is linked to overflow position 0. I is added in overflow position 6, so overflow position 6 now has a link to overflow position 0, and home position 9 has the address of I (6)

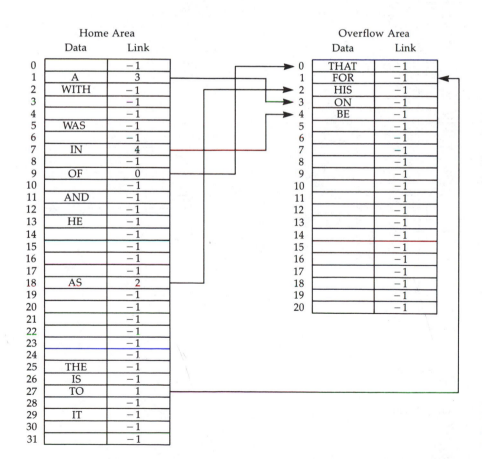

Figure 7.20
Synonym chaining
after 13 additions

(Figure 7.21). The rest of the words in the set are added in a similar manner to result in the relative file contents presented in Figure 7.22.

Table 7.11 lists the number of probes for each of the words in the file of words stored in the overflow area of Figure 7.22. The average number of probes for a successful search of this file is 1.563 where the load factor is 60 percent—a number comparable with the average for double hashing at the same load factor.

The formula for determining the average number of probes in a successful search using synonym chaining into a separate overflow area is

$$\left(1 + \frac{a}{2}\right)$$

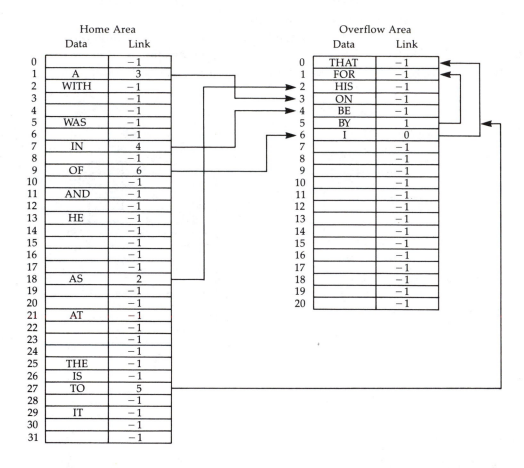

Figure 7.21
Relative file from Figure 7.20 with three additions

Table 7.11 Probes for words in overflow area of Figure 7.22

WORD	No. of Probes	WORD	No. of Probes
THE	1	BE	2
OF	1	AT	1
AND	1	BY	2
TO	1	I	2
A	1	THIS	1
IN	1	HAD	2
THAT	3	NOT	3
IS	1	NO	2
WAS	1	TON	2
HE	1	ARE	1
FOR	3	BUT	1
IT	1	FROM	2
WITH	1	OR	2
AS	1	HAVE	2
HIS	2	AN	1
ON	3	THEY	1

Average number of successful probes 1.563

The formula for determining the average number of probes in an unsuccessful search of the same kind is

$$(a + e^{-a})$$

Table 7.12 summarizes the average number of probes for a variety of load factors. For a load factor of 80 percent, the average number of probes for linear probing is 3.000 (see Table 7.4), for double hashing is 2.012 (see Table 7.10), and for synonym chaining is 1.400. For a load factor of 95 percent, the average numbers of probes for a successful search are

linear probing = 10.500 probes,
double hashing = 3.153 probes,
synonym chaining = 1.475 probes,

With the same load factor, the average numbers of probes for unsuccessful searches are

linear probing = 200.500 probes,
double hashing = 20.000 probes,
synonym chaining = 1.337 probes

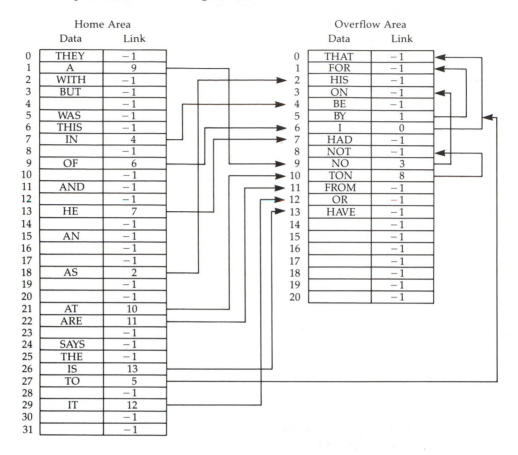

Figure 7.22
Synonym chaining
after all additions

Table 7.12 Number of probes for synonym chaining

Load factor	Average no. of successful probes	Average no. of unsuccessful probes
.10	1.050	1.005
.20	1.100	1.019
.30	1.150	1.041
.40	1.200	1.070
.50	1.250	1.107
.60	1.300	1.149
.70	1.350	1.197
.80	1.400	1.249
.90	1.450	1.307
.95	1.475	1.337

The average number of probes for a successful search is not much improved by synonym chaining, but a great reduction in the number of probes can be realized by using chaining during an unsuccessful search.

Bucket Addressing

Bucket addressing involves allocating a group of record positions, termed a **bucket**, to be associated with a particular hash address. The primary idea behind bucket addressing is to allocate the bucket size of each hash address so it is as large as the maximum number of synonyms for any hash address. All the synonyms for a particular hash address are then stored sequentially in the bucket for the particular hash address. Accessing a record in a relative file that uses bucket addressing involves hashing the key, then sequentially searching the bucket of records at the hashed address. The number of records that must be examined to find a record is limited by the bucket size; the algorithm does not have to search the whole file or the whole overflow area.

The major problem with bucket addressing as a technique for resolving hashing collisions is the amount of space wasted if the number of synonyms for any one hashed address varies greatly. Since the bucket size is determined by the maximum number of synonyms for any hashed address (each hashed address has the same size bucket), those hashed addresses having a lower number of synonyms also have buckets with unused space—space that is wasted. A secondary problem in using bucket addressing is determining the bucket size. Suppose data in a relative file were unavailable for analysis prior to the creation of the file, and the bucket size is smaller than the maximum number of synonyms as a result. All the synonyms that hash to a bucket address cannot be stored in the bucket, so hashing collisions must be resolved by using one of the techniques discussed above. To prevent the problem, the programmer could set a very large bucket size, but this solution is at the expense of wasted space.

For the set of words used in Example 7.2, the maximum number of synonyms for any one hashed address is three, so the bucket size is 3. (In other words each hashed address holds three records.) All the synonyms will be stored in the bucket in the hashed address. Accessing a record involves sequentially searching the bucket in the hashed address. The relative file with a bucket size of 3 for the set of words of Table 7.3 has the contents shown in Figure 7.23.

One solution to hashing collisions in bucket addresses is **consecutive spill addressing**. If a hashing collision occurs with bucket addressing, the nearest bucket with available space is used to store the synonym. The term *spill addressing* is derived from the fact that when a bucket becomes full, the full bucket spills over into the next bucket. Searching for the synonym later

Position   Bucket size of 3

THEY		
A	ON	NO
WITH		
BUT		
WAS		
THIS		
IN	BE	
OF	THAT	I
AND		
HE	HAD	
AN		
AS	HIS	
AT	NOT	TON
ARE	FROM	
SAYS		
THE		
IS	HAVE	
TO	FOR	BY
IT	OR	

Figure 7.23
Words in Table 7.3 in
a relative file with a
bucket size of 3

Position   Bucket size of 2

Pos		
0 THEY		
1 A	ON	
2 WITH	**NO**	
3 BUT		
4		
5 WAS		
6 THIS		
7 IN	BE	
8		
9 OF	THAT	
10 **I**		
11 AND		
12		
13 HE	HAD	
14		
15 AN		
16		
17		
18 AS	HIS	
19		
20		
21 AT	NOT	
22 **TON**	ARE	
23 **FROM**		displaced from 22 by TON
24 SAYS		
25 THE		
26 IS	HAVE	
27 TO	FOR	
28 **BY**		
29 IT	OR	
30		
31		

Figure 7.24
Relative file with a
bucket size of 2 using
consecutive spill
addressing

involves the same problems encountered with linear probing: The synonym is not located in the hashed addresses, so a sequential search of consecutive buckets must take place. Figure 7.24 illustrates the use of the bucket size of 2 and consecutive spill addressing. The third synonym that hashes to a bucket is stored in the next bucket with available space. For example, TON is stored in the next bucket (bucket 22) displacing FROM, which hashes to 22. The words that are not stored in their hashed positions are in bold type in the figure (NO, I, TON, and BY).

Maintaining a directory of free space for the file aids in locating the next bucket with available space. The directory improves spill addressing greatly. It identifies all the buckets containing available space, so the bucket with available space nearest the hashed address can be determined by probing the directory.

Another solution to hashing collisions in bucket addressing is **bucket chaining**. If a hashing collision occurs, an overflow bucket is allocated to store the synonym, and the primary bucket is chained to the new overflow bucket. If the overflow bucket fills, another overflow bucket is allocated and chained to the other buckets with synonyms. With bucket chaining the file can be expanded without rehashing all the records into a larger file. The overflow bucket usually holds only one key rather than being the same size as the home bucket.

Figure 7.25 illustrates the relative file of words with a bucket size of 2 for both the home area and the overflow area. When a word hashes to a full bucket, the word is stored in the next available overflow area (allocated sequentially as needed); the home bucket has the address of the overflow bucket. Should the overflow bucket fill, it spills into another overflow bucket and they are linked. The chaining of buckets reduces the number of probes it takes to locate all the synonyms of an address.

The primary disadvantage to bucket chaining is the number of buckets that must be accessed to locate a record. All the buckets chained to a hashed

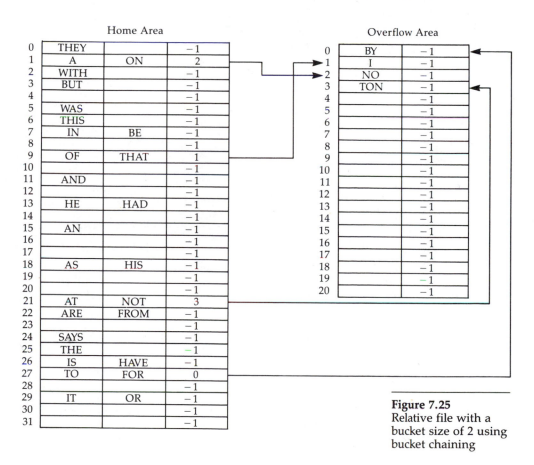

Figure 7.25
Relative file with a bucket size of 2 using bucket chaining

address may have to be searched to find a record. Fewer probes are required if the bucket size is large enough to hold all synonyms.

Table 7.13 lists the number of probes for each of the words stored using bucket addressing with home buckets chained to overflow buckets. The

Table 7.13 Probes for words in Table 7.3 in separate overflow area using bucket chaining

WORD	No. of Probes	WORD	No. of Probes
THE	1	BE	1
OF	1	AT	1
AND	1	BY	2
TO	1	I	2
A	1	THIS	1
IN	1	HAD	1
THAT	1	NOT	1
IS	1	NO	2
WAS	1	TON	2
HE	1	ARE	1
FOR	1	BUT	1
IT	1	FROM	1
WITH	1	OR	1
AS	1	HAVE	1
HIS	1	AN	1
ON	1	THEY	1

Average number of probes 1.125

Table 7.14 Number of probes for bucket chaining

Load factor	Bucket size of 2		Bucket size of 50	
	Average no. of successful probes	Average no. of unsuccessful probes	Average no. of successful probes	Average no. of unsuccessful probes
.10	1.006	1.001	1.000	1.000
.20	1.024	1.009	1.000	1.000
.30	1.052	1.027	1.000	1.000
.40	1.088	1.058	1.000	1.000
.50	1.132	1.104	1.000	1.000
.60	1.182	1.164	1.000	1.001
.70	1.238	1.238	1.001	1.018
.80	1.299	1.327	1.015	1.182
.90	1.364	1.428	1.083	1.920
.95	1.400	1.500	1.200	2.700

average number of probes for a successful search of this file is 1.125 where the load factor is 60 percent—bucket chaining is an improvement over synonym chaining (a special case in which the bucket size is 1).

Table 7.14 summarizes the average numbers of probes for a variety of load factors for bucket sizes of 2 and 50. For a load factor of 80 percent, the average number of probes for a successful search is lower for bucket addressing using buckets of size 2 (1.299) than for any of the other methods discussed in this chapter. Unsuccessful searches using bucket addressing and chaining to a separate overflow area actually require fewer probes than successful searches up to a load factor of 70 percent. For a bucket size of 50, the number of probes for successful and unsuccessful searches is close to 1 up to a load factor of 95 percent.

DYNAMIC HASHING

One of the problems with conventional hashing is that the number of records to be stored in the file must be known before the file is created. Each

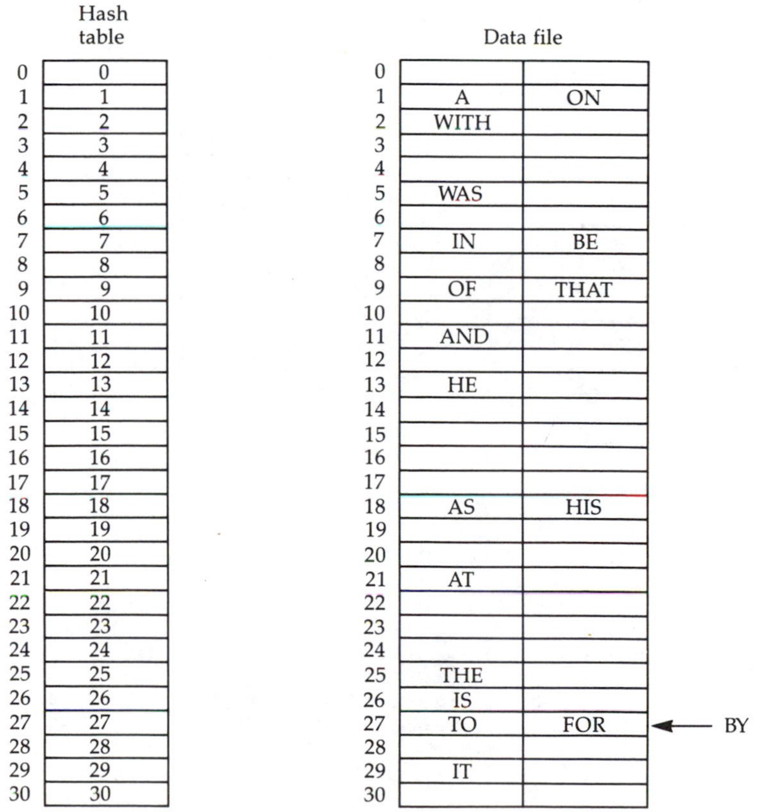

Figure 7.26
Dynamic hashing with bucket size of 2 when the first bucket overflows

time the file becomes full, the entire file can be rehashed by using a different hashing function into a larger file. **Dynamic hashing** is a technique used to dynamically change the hashing function to access a hashed file that increases in size as records are added. A hash table is created as an index to the hashed file. Suppose the words in Table 7.3 are stored in a file with a bucket size of 2. Figure 7.26 shows the file when the first collision occurs. When an overflow occurs with bucket addressing (BY is added, hashing to position 27), a new hashing function is applied to all records within the bucket and to the synonym being added to split the records between the addressed bucket and a new overflow bucket. At the same time the entry in the hash table for bucket 27 becomes a binary tree that chains to the two buckets as a result of the split. If the binary representation of the key used by the hashing function is available, all keys with a zero bit in the first position stay in the primary bucket, and all keys with a one bit in the first position are moved to a new overflow bucket. In this case the key is character data, so any randomizing function can be applied to the first character of the key to randomly split the records between the two buckets.

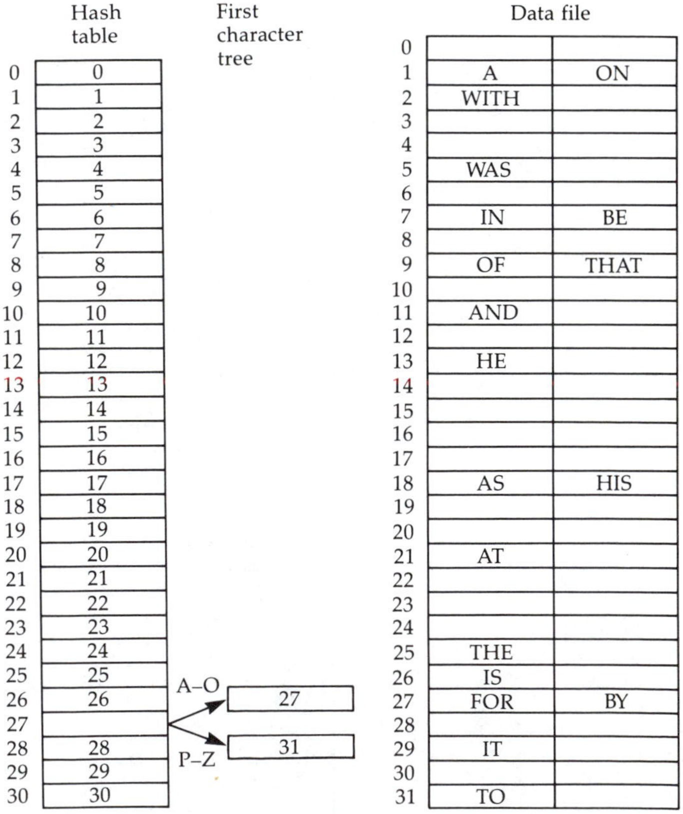

Figure 7.27
Dynamic hashing after the first split

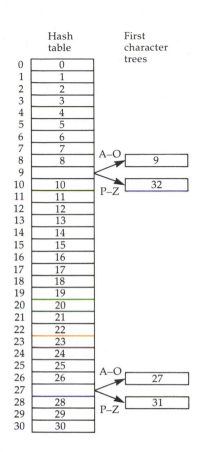

Hash table / First character trees

Data file		
0	THEY	
1	A	ON
2	WITH	
3	BUT	
4		
5	WAS	
6	THIS	
7	IN	BE
8		
9	OF	I
10		
11	AND	
12		
13	HE	HAD
14	AN	
15		
16		
17		
18	AS	HIS
19		
20		
21	AT	NOT
22	ARE	FROM
23		
24		
25	THE	
26	IS	HAVE
27	FOR	BY
28		
29	IT	OR
30		
31	TO	
32	THAT	

Figure 7.28
Complete dynamic hashing file

In this example all keys starting with *A* through *O* stay, but all keys starting with *P* through *Z* move to a new overflow bucket. The primary bucket is chained to the new overflow bucket. The entry in the hash table for position 27 becomes the root of a binary tree containing the two bucket addresses as a result of the split bucket. Figure 7.27 presents the file and hash table after the split. Figure 7.28 shows the file and hash table after all the words have been added.

Suppose the word TAN (hashing to position 27) is added to the file. Entry 27 in the hash table has the address of bucket 27 for those words with the first letter less than or equal to *O* and the address of bucket 31 for all other synonyms. TAN starts with *T*, so bucket 31 is searched for an available slot in which to store TAN. Since bucket 31 only contains one word, TAN is added (Figure 7.29). When LOX is added and it hashes to position 27, the hash table indicates that bucket 27 should be searched. An overflow occurs in bucket 27, and the contents are split according to the second letter of the words (since this is the second split for synonyms of bucket 27). The node in the binary tree pointing to bucket 27 becomes the root of a subtree that indicates bucket 27 has words with the first two letters in the range of 'AA' through 'OO', and bucket 34 has words with the first two letters in the range of 'AP' through 'OZ'. Figure 7.30 shows the resulting file contents and hash table.

A better distribution for splitting words between buckets is to use the *i*th letter (depending on the level in the hashing tree) and perform a hashing function in that letter. Simply using the letter to split the bucket may leave the words in a bucket that is not large enough to hold them all.

As long as the hashing tree is held in main memory, all words can be accessed with one file access. If any part of the hashing tree is accessed from external storage, the number of file accesses for a successful probe will increase.

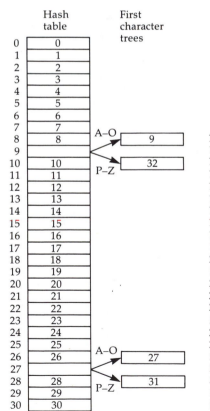

Figure 7.29
Dynamic hashing file after TAN is added

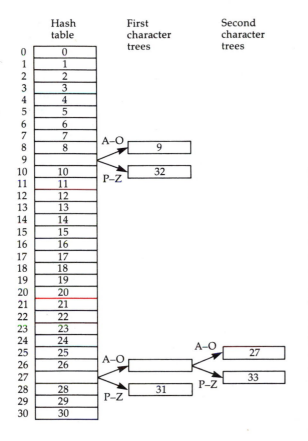

Hash table	First character trees	Second character trees	Data file	
0 — 0			0 — THEY	
1 — 1			1 — A	ON
2 — 2			2 — WITH	
3 — 3			3 — BUT	
4 — 4			4	
5 — 5			5 — WAS	
6 — 6			6 — THIS	
7 — 7	A–O → 9		7 — IN	BE
8 — 8			8	
9 —	P–Z → 32		9 — OF	I
10 — 10			10	
11 — 11			11 — AND	
12 — 12			12	
13 — 13			13 — HE	HAD
14 — 14			14 — AN	
15 — 15			15	
16 — 16			16	
17 — 17			17	
18 — 18			18 — AS	HIS
19 — 19			19	
20 — 20			20	
21 — 21			21 — AT	NOT
22 — 22			22 — ARE	FROM
23 — 23			23	
24 — 24		A–O → 27	24	
25 — 25	A–O →		25 — THE	
26 — 26		P–Z → 33	26 — IS	HAVE
27 —			27 — FOR	**LOX**
28 — 28	P–Z → 31		28	
29 — 29			29 — IT	OR
30 — 30			30	
			31 — TO	TAN
			32 — THAT	
			33 — BY	

Figure 7.30
Dynamic hashing file after LOX is added

RELATIVE FILES IN PASCAL

Sequential file organization is the only type of file organization defined in Standard Pascal as defined by Jensen and Wirth. **Relative files** are supported in UCSD Pascal, which is available on many microcomputers. UCSD Pascal is the basis of the programs in this and later chapters that involve relative files. Relative files can be easily simulated with an array of records to represent the file and allow random access. Relative files may also be simulated by using sequential files and scanning through the first n records to simulate random access to the nth record in the file.

One of the procedures in UCSD Pascal that is required to directly access record positions in a relative file is the **seek procedure**. The format for the procedure call is

```
Seek (filename, record_number)
```

In this case filename is the internal identifier for the relative file, and record_number is the **relative record number** for a record position in the relative file. The procedure Seek moves the file pointer to the record position in the file filename whose relative record number is record_number. The expression record_number must be an integer in the range of relative record addresses for the file (0 through N − 1). To randomly access a relative file, the Seek procedure call must precede a Get or a Put to the file. Seek positions the file pointer to a particular record location, Get inputs that record into the file buffer, and Put outputs the file buffer contents to that record position. Given the following declarations

```
TYPE
     Record_type = Record
                         .
                         .
                         .
                       End;
VAR
     record_number    : Integer;
     relative_file    : File of Record_type;
     relative_record  : Record_type;
```

the sequence of Pascal code to input data from a relative file is

```
Seek (relative_file, record_number);
Get (relative_file);
relative_record := relative_file^
```

The sequence of Pascal code to output data to a relative file in address record_number is

```
relative_file^ := relative_record;
Seek (relative_file, record_number);
Put (relative_file)
```

In this situation Seek positions the file pointer to the record address indicated by record_number, Get causes the specified record to be input into the file buffer, and Put causes the contents of the file buffer to be output to the file in the specified address.

A relative file may be created using sequential access or random access. When using sequential access the records of data are written to the relative file in sequential order; the first record is stored in position 0, the second record is stored in position 1, the third record is stored in position 2, and so on. This scheme for creating the file is often used when a directory is to accompany it to provide indirect access.

When creating the relative file using random access, the key of the record is hashed to a random position; therefore, the relative file must first be skeletonized with dummy records in a sequential fashion. Then records can be inserted in random order. The skeletonization of the relative file with dummy records involves initializing the record with dummy information. For example, character fields might be filled with spaces, and numeric fields and link fields for chaining synonyms might be filled with zeros. The dummy record is written to each record position in the file of n record positions. Once the file has been skeletonized, records can be stored randomly into the file. The skeletonization also ensures that empty record positions can be easily recognized because the fields in the record have spaces and zeros.

Algorithm 7.1 creates a relative file by using random access. It is a one-pass algorithm that uses a separate overflow area for storing synonyms. Algorithm 7.1 also uses the chaining method to link all synonyms—including the record in the hashed location and all synonyms in the overflow area. To facilitate locating the next available position in overflow, an overflow pointer that indicates the position is saved in position 0 of the relative file. Data is assigned to positions 1 through n.

Once the relative file is created, it can be accessed sequentially to list the contents by using a counter that takes on the values 0 through n. Listing the contents of the relative file after the creation is an excellent test to make sure the program performed properly. Algorithm 7.2 is the pseudocode for listing the file contents.

Retrieving a record from the file entails checking the hashed address, and if the record in the hashed address is not the one being sought, a search of the linked list of synonyms is in order. The algorithm for finding a record in the relative file created previously (in Algorithm 7.1) is presented in Algorithm 7.3. The call to the procedure Findrecord is

```
previous ← 0
relative_record_number ← Hash (key)
Findrecord (key, relative_record, relative_record_number,
          previous, error)
```

In this procedure key is the key of the record being sought, and if the key is found, the contents of the file location is returned by the procedure in relative_record. The variable relative_record_number is the address of the home position. The variable previous is returned by the procedure as the address of the record that is the predecessor of the record being sought (it aids in maintaining the file; previous facilitates deleting records, for example.) The variable error returns TRUE if the record being sought is not on file; otherwise, error returns FALSE.

Updating a relative file with additions, changes, and deletions is simpler than updating a sequential file in that the relative file can be accessed directly. Each transaction key is hashed, a call to Findrecord is made, and if error returns TRUE, the record is not on file. In this case the addition

Algorithm 7.1   Relative File Creation

```
                    {
                         skeletonize  the  relative  file
                    }
       Rewrite  (relativefile)
       Initialize  dummy_record  to  spaces  and  zeros
       set  number_of_records  in  relativefile
       For  i  ←  0  To  number_of_records
            relativefile^  ←  dummy_record
            Put  (relativefile)

       Close  (relativefile)
                    {
                         set  next  to  keep  next  available  position  in
                         the  overflow  area
                    }
       next  ←  start_of_overflow_area
       Reset  (relativefile)
       Reset  (inputfile)
       While  Not  Eof  (inputfile)
                    {
                         input  each  record  from  inputfile,  hash  the  key
                         and  store  in  the  relativefile
                    }
            Get_a_record_from_inputfile
            relative_record_number  ←  Hash  (key_from_inputfile_record)
            Seek  (relativefile,  relative_record_number)
            Get  (relativefile)
            relative_record  ←  relativefile^;
                    {
                         if  the  relative_record  is  a  dummy  record
                         the  hashed  position  is  empty  and  the
                         inputfile_record  can  be  put  into  this  empty
                         position
                    }
            If  relative_record  =  dummy_record
                    {
                         Seek  the  record  position  and  place  the  file
                         pointer  to  the  beginning  of  the  position
                    }
                    inputfile_record.synonym  ←  −1
                    Seek  (relativefile,  relative_record_number)
                    relativefile^  ←  inputfile_record
                    Put  (relativefile)
```

Else
  {
        the hashed position is full so call
        procedure Overflow to store the synonym in
        the next available position in the overflow
        area and link the record with all other
        synonyms of this hashed address
  }
Overflow

  {
        store next in the link field (synonym) of
        record zero for future reference
  }

Initialize dummy_record to spaces and zeros
dummy_record.synonym ← next
Seek (relativefile, 0)
relativefile^ ← dummy_record
Put (relativefile)
Close (relativefile)

Algorithm Overflow

If next > number_of_records
    print error ('overflow area full')
Else
    inputfile_record.synonym ← relative_record.synonym
    relative_record.synonym ← next
            {
                store relative_record back to hashed address
                with link changed to include new record
            }
    Seek (relativefile, relative_record_number)
    relativefile^ ← relative_record
    Put (relativefile)
            {
                store the inputfile_record (new record) in
                position next and increment next
            }
    Seek (relativefile, next)
    relativefile^ ← inputfile_record
    Put (relativefile)
    next ← next + 1

transaction may be processed while change and deletion transactions cannot be processed. On the other hand, if error returns FALSE, change and deletion transactions can be processed because the record has been found; addition transactions cannot be processed because the record exists already.

   Deletion transactions require that the master record to be deleted is
"marked" as inactive. (The master file is not copied during the maintenance
run as it is in sequential files, so the record cannot actually be deleted.) The
easiest way to mark a record for deletion is by returning that position back
to a dummy record as initially skeletonized. Some methods of collision
resolution may require an additional field in every record that is a delete
flag, which indicates whether the record is active or marked as deleted. If
a record contains a delete flag, the search procedure skips the record.
   The transaction file and the relative master file do not have to be matched
sequentially as they must be in sequential files. In relative files transactions

Algorithm 7.2   Listing

```
reset (relative file)
relative_record_number ← 0
relative_record ← relativefile^
While Not Eof (relativefile)
    If relative_record <> spaces and zeros
            {
                skip dummy records
            }
        print fields of relative_record

    relative_record_number ← relative_record_number + 1
    Get (relativefile)
    relative_record ← relativefile^
close (relative file)
```

Algorithm 7.3   Findrecord

```
error ← false
Seek (relativefile, relative_record_number)
Get (relativefile)
relative_record ← relativefile^
If relative_record.key = key
    return
Else
    If relative_record.synonym = −1
        error ← TRUE
        return
    Else
        previous ← relative_record_number
        relative_record_number ← relative_record.synonym
        Findrecord (key, relative_record,
                    relative_record_number,
                        previous, error)
```

for one transaction key are processed independently. If several transactions have the same transaction key, the transactions need to be sorted according to the entry date of the transaction. Algorithm 7.4 updates the relative master file.

Algorithm 7.4   Relative File Update

```
                    {
                        input the next available overflow address
                    }
        Reset (relativefile)
        Seek (relativefile, 0)
        Get (relativefile)
        relative_record ← relativefile^
        next ← relative_record.synonym
        While Not Eof (transactionfile)
            Get_next_trans
            position ← Hash (trans_key)
            home ← position
            previous ← 0
            Findrecord (trans_key, trans_record, position, previous, error)
            Case update_code
                'A' : If error
                            Add_new_record
                      Else
                            print 'duplicate add'

                'C' : If error
                            print ' not on file'
                      Else
                            Change_record

                'D' : If error
                            print 'not on file'
                      Else
                            Delete_record

                Else : print 'invalid update code'

  Algorithm Add_New_Record

        Seek (relativefile, home)
        Get (relativefile)
        relative_record ← relativefile^
        If relative_record.key = spaces
            Seek (relativefile, home)
            relativefile^ ← relative_record
            Put (relativefile)
        Else
            Overflow
```

Algorithm Overflow

```
If next > MAXIMUM_OVERFLOW_LOCATIONS
    print 'overflow full'
Else
    trans_record.synonym ← relative_record.synonym
    relative_record.synonym ← next
            {
                store home record back with link field changed
            }
    Seek (relativefile, home)
    relativefile^ ← relative_record
    Put (relativefile)
            {
                store trans_record into position next
            }
    Seek (relativefile, next)
    relativefile^ ← trans_record
    Put (relativefile)
    next ← next + 1
```

Algorithm Change-Record

```
make transaction change in relative_record
Seek (relativefile, position)
relativefile^ ← relative_record
Put (relativefile)
```

Algorithm Delete-Record

```
If position = home
    If relative_record.synonym = −1
            {
                delete home position with no synonyms
            }
        Seek (relativefile, home)
        relativefile^ ← dummy { with spaces and zeros}
        Put (relativefile)
    Else
            {
                delete home position that has synonyms
                by moving first synonym from overflow
                to the home position
            }
        Seek (relativefile, relative_record.synonym)
        Get (relativefile)
        Seek (relativefile, home)
        Put (relativefile)
```

```
            Else
                        {
                            delete  a  synonym  that  is  in  overflow
                        }
                Seek  (relativefile,  previous)
                Get  (relativefile)
                relativefileˆ.synonym  ←  relative_record.synonym
                Seek  (relativefile,  previous)
                Put  (relativefile)
                relativefileˆ  ←  dummy
                Seek  (relativefile,  position)
                Put  (relativefile)
```

CASE STUDY 7.1: THE CAR-RENTAL AGENCY

The data from the car-rental agency case study examined in Chapter 5 will be used to create a relative master file using Algorithm 7.1, which stores synonyms in a separate overflow area and chains them together. The data to be stored in the master file initially is listed in Table 5.1. Since the key (id number) is character data, the first letter and the last digit will form the numeric key to be hashed, and the ASCII decimal representation will be substituted for the first letter.

Thirteen records are to be initially loaded to the file, and some additions will be made later, so 18 positions will be allocated—17 for the home area plus one position for the indicator of the next available overflow position. The positions will bear the numbers 0 through 17. The prime-number division remainder method will be used, and the divisor will be 17 (the largest prime number close to the number of positions). The hashing function

hash (key) = (numeric key Mod 17) + 1

will hash the records into positions 1 through 17. Synonyms will be stored in the overflow area, (positions 18 through 21 of the file), and the load factor will be 80 percent.

Table 7.15 lists the keys and the hashed addresses of the records to be loaded to the master file initially. Notice that there are three synonyms for position 9—they will be linked together. The first step is to skeletonize the relative file with dummy records as in Figure 7.31. Dummy records include blanks in all fields except the link fields, which are initialized to -1 to indicate that the record has no other synonyms.

The result of creating the master file with linked synonyms is shown in Figure 7.32. Notice that the records are not stored in order by the key as they were in the sequential file. The order of records in the file is dependent

Table 7.15 Car-rental agency data:
Keys with hashed positions

Key	Numeric Key	hash (key)
C1	671	9
C2	672	10
F1	701	5
F2	702	6
F3	703	7
GM1	711	15
GM2	712	16
GM3	713	17
GM4	714	1
GM5	715	2
H1	721	8
H2	722	9
T1	841	9

Figure 7.31
Skeletonized relative
master file

Car-Rental Agency Relative Master File

	Id no.	Make	Style	Model	Mileage	Color	Link
0							18
1							−1
2							−1
3							−1
4							−1
5							−1
6							−1
7							−1
8							−1
9							−1
10							−1
11							−1
12							−1
13							−1
14							−1
15							−1
16							−1
17							−1
18							−1
19							−1
20							−1
21							−1
							−1

on the hashing function. Each transaction record is input, the key is hashed, and the hashed position is input. If the hashed position contains a dummy record, the transaction record is stored in the hashed location. Each transaction record—with the exception of the two synonyms that are not stored in the hashed position—causes one input access and one output access to

Car-Rental Agency Relative Master File

	Id no.	Make	Style	Model	Mileage	Color	Link
0							20
1	GM4	Cadillac	2 DR	Cimarron	63,000	maroon	−1
2	GM5	Oldsmobile	4 DR	98	11,000	green	−1
3							−1
4							−1
5	F1	Ford	2 DR HB	Escort	54,000	white	−1
6	F2	Lincoln	4 DR	Continental	38,000	black	−1
7	F3	Ford	2 DR	Thunderbird	35,000	blue	−1
8	H1	Honda	4 DR	Accord	32,000	yellow	−1
9	C1	Dodge	2 DR	Omni	25,000	grey	19
10	C2	Dodge	2 DR	Aspen	7,000	tan	−1
11							−1
12							−1
13							−1
14							−1
15	GM1	Cadillac	4 DR	Fleetwood	9,000	red	−1
16	GM2	Oldsmobile	4 DR	Delta 88	28,050	blue	−1
17	GM3	Chevrolet	2 DR	Camaro	33,000	silver	−1
18	H2	Honda	2 DR HB	Accord	11,250	brown	−1
19	T1	Toyota	2 DR HB	Celica	3,400	white	18
20							−1
21							−1
							−1

Figure 7.32
Car-rental agency relative master file after creation

the relative master file. H2, the first synonym, causes the following I/O accesses:

1. Hashed position 9 is input and is found to be occupied.
2. Position 0 is input to determine the next available position (18).
3. The link field of position 9 (−1) is stored in the link field of H2, which is written to position 18.
4. The link field of the home position (9) is changed to 18 and written back to the file.
5. The overflow pointer in position 0 is changed to 19 and written back to position 0.

Similarly, T1 causes the following I/O accesses:

1. Hashed position 9 is input and is found to be occupied.
2. Position 0 is input to determine the next available position (19).
3. The link field of position 9 (18) is stored in the link field of H2, which is written to position 19.
4. The link field of the home position (9) is changed to 19 and written back to the file.
5. The overflow pointer in position 0 is changed to 20 and written back to position 0.

Creating the car-rental relative master file takes two accesses for each of the 11 nonsynonyms and five accesses for each of the two synonyms. Therefore, the total number of input/output accesses to the master file is 32. To create a sequential file in Chapter 5 required 13 input/output operations. If each access requires 35 ms, the total time to access the relative car-rental master file during creation is 1.120 seconds; it takes 0.455 seconds total access time to create a sequential master file.

Transaction file T2 in Table 5.3 contains only one transaction, an addition of key GM6. The key GM6 hashes to position 3. The relative master update algorithm performs the following I/O operations to process the transaction:

1. Position 3 is input and found to be empty.
2. Transaction GM6 is written to position 3.

These two operations each take 35 ms or a total of 70 ms total access time to add one record to the relative car-rental agency master file. The sequential file update requires 29 operations and a total access time of 1.015 seconds (1015 ms). In cases with a low volatility ratio, relative files with random access require less access time to make additions or deletions than sequential files. Figure 7.33 shows the relative car-rental master file after applying transaction file T2. The added record is shown in bold.

Transaction file T3 in Table 5.5 contains a number of transactions, including a group for one key. The deletion transaction F1 requires that the hashed

Car-Rental Agency Relative Master File

	Id no.	Make	Style	Model	Mileage	Color	Link
0							
1	GM4	Cadillac	2 DR	Cimarron	63,000	maroon	20
2	GM5	Oldsmobile	4 DR	98	11,000	green	−1
3	**M6**	**Chevrolet**	**4 DR**	**Cimarron**	**11,250**	**brown**	**−1**
4							−1
5	F1	Ford	2 DR HB	Escort	54,000	white	−1
6	F2	Lincoln	4 DR	Continental	38,000	black	−1
7	F3	Ford	2 DR	Thunderbird	35,000	blue	−1
8	H1	Honda	4 DR	Accord	32,000	yellow	−1
9	C1	Dodge	2 DR	Omni	25,000	grey	19
10	C2	Dodge	2 DR	Aspen	7,000	tan	−1
11							−1
12							−1
13							−1
14							−1
15	GM1	Cadillac	4 DR	Fleetwood	9,000	red	−1
16	GM2	Oldsmobile	4 DR	Delta 88	28,050	blue	−1
17	GM3	Chevrolet	2 DR	Camaro	33,000	silver	−1
18	H2	Honda	2 DR HB	Accord	11,250	brown	−1
19	T1	Toyota	2 DR HB	Celica	3,400	white	18
20							−1
21							−1
							−1

Figure 7.33
Relative master file after applying T2

position 5 be input, that the key field be replaced with a dummy key (blanks), and the record written back to the file (two accesses).

The first addition, A GM7, inputs the hashed position (hash (GM7) = 4). The hashed position contains a dummy key, so transaction GM7 is stored in position 4 (two accesses). The transaction C GM7 causes position 4 to be input to change the mileage and subsequently write the changed record back to position 4 (two accesses). The transaction D GM7 inputs position 4, replaces the key field with blanks, and writes the record back to position 4 (two accesses). The second A GM7 transaction performs as the first (two accesses). Processing a group of transactions for the same key turns out to be the same as processing independent transactions. Each transaction causes the input of one or more records and the output of at least one record. Each transaction is independent of the preceding or succeeding transactions.

The transaction D H3 is hashed to position 10, position 10 is input to find key C2. Since H3 is not found in the hashed position, the link field of position 10 indicates where synonyms are located. The link field of position 10 is −1, which indicates that there are no synonyms for this position in the file. An error message is output, indicating that H3 was not found. An invalid deletion causes one access to the master file.

The final two transactions, C T1 and D T1, cause two accesses each to change record T1 then replace the key with a dummy key. Figure 7.34 shows the file contents after applying transaction file T3. The modifications made to the master file are highlighted in bold.

Car-Rental Agency Relative Master File

	Id no.	Make	Style	Model	Mileage	Color	Link
0							20
1	GM4	Cadillac	2 DR	Cimarron	63,000	maroon	−1
2	GM5	Oldsmobile	4 DR	98	11,000	green	−1
3	**GM6**	**Chevrolet**	**4 DR**	**Cimarron**	**11,250**	**brown**	−1
4	**GM7**	**Pontiac**	**2 DR**	**Fiero**	**1,500**	**navy**	−1
5		**Ford**	**2 DR HB**	**Escort**	**54,000**	**white**	−1
6	F2	Lincoln	4 DR	Continental	38,000	black	−1
7	F3	Ford	2 DR	Thunderbird	35,000	blue	−1
8	H1	Honda	4 DR	Accord	32,000	yellow	−1
9	C1	Dodge	2 DR	Omni	25,000	grey	19
10	C2	Dodge	2 DR	Aspen	7,000	tan	−1
11							−1
12							−1
13							−1
14							−1
15	GM1	Cadillac	4 DR	Fleetwood	9,000	red	−1
16	GM2	Oldsmobile	4 DR	Delta 88	28,050	blue	−1
17	GM3	Chevrolet	2 DR	Camaro	33,000	silver	−1
18	H2	Honda	2 DR HB	Accord	11,250	brown	−1
19		**Toyota**	**2 DR HB**	**Celica**	**3,400**	**white**	**18**
20							−1
21							−1

Figure 7.34
Car-rental agency relative master file after applying transaction file T3

The total number of accesses to the relative master file is 15. Each access requires 35 ms, so the total access time to apply transaction file T3 is 525 ms. To perform 27 accesses in the sequential file update takes 945 ms (almost double the relative update access time). For a low activity ratio (42 percent), the relative file with random access requires much less time than the sequential file with sequential access.

SUMMARY

Direct file organization exhibits a predictable relationship between the key used to identify an individual record and that record's absolute address on an external file. Relative file organization is a common implementation of direct file organization that uses relative addressing. Relative addressing refers to the address of a record in the file that is in the form of an integer record number relative to the beginning of the file. The first record in the file is usually numbered 0 or 1.

Relative file organization is a machine-independent implementation of direct file organization that is supported in several high-level programming languages : COBOL, FORTRAN, PL/1, VAX-11 Pascal, OMSI Pascal, TURBO Pascal, and UCSD Pascal. Maintaining a relative file is simpler than maintaining a sequential file in that each transaction is processed independently; the transactions are not applied to the master file in batches.

Direct addressing is the most direct way of locating a record in a file since the key is the address of the record's position in the file. When the range of key values is larger than the range of record positions in the file, indexing techniques such as hashing, trees, index tables, inverted files, and multilist files determine the record's position given the key of the record.

Hashing is an indexing technique that allows sequential access by physical ordering of records (not key order). A hashing function is applied to the key value of the record to map the range of possible key values into a smaller range of relative addresses. A number of hashing techniques were discussed: prime-number division remainder, digit extraction, folding, radix conversion, mid-square, and perfect hashing.

The primary problem with all hashing functions is that the function does not always produce unique relative addresses. Hashing collisions are the result of this limitation. A number of techniques resolve hashing collisions: linear probing, establishing a separate overflow area for synonyms, double hashing into a separate overflow area, synonym chaining, bucket addressing, consecutive spill addressing, and bucket chaining into a separate overflow area.

Dynamic hashing is a technique that dynamically changes the hashing function so the file can be enlarged more easily. Each entry of the hash table containing bucket addresses is modified into a binary tree that contains the two bucket addresses when a bucket is split.

Relative files in UCSD Pascal use a seek procedure to move the file pointer to the record indicated by the record number parameter. The procedure is followed by a call to `Get`, which inputs the record into the file buffer. The procedure may be followed by a call to `Put`, which stores the file buffer contents into the record location in the file referenced by the file pointer. To create a relative file in random fashion, the file must first be skeletonized with dummy records (records that contain spaces and zeros in all fields) in each record location of the file. When the file has been created, a call to `Close` keeps the file on the disk. The algorithm for updating the file involves hashing the key of the transaction record, retrieving the record from the relative file (if the record exists), making a change to the record, and storing the changed record back to the same position from which it was retrieved. The car-rental agency data used in Chapter 5 was stored in a relative file and quantitative measures of random-access times were compared to access times of a sequential file with sequential access.

For further information and thorough performance analysis of hashing functions, the reader should consult the following sources:

Buchholz, W. "File organization and addressing," *IBM Systems Journal*, 2: 86–91, June 1963.

Chang, C. C. "The study of an ordered minimal perfect hashing scheme," *Communications of the ACM*, 27(4):384–387, April 1984.

Cichelli, R. J. "Minimal perfect hash functions made simple," *Communications of the ACM*, 23(1):17–19, January 1980.

Cook, C. R. "A letter oriented minimal perfect hashing function," *Sigplan Notices*, 17(9):18–27, September 1982.

Fagin, R. et al. "Extendable hashing: A fast access method for dynamic files," *ACM Transactions on Database Systems*, 4(3):315–344, September 1979.

Ghosh, S. P. and V. Y. Lum. *An analysis of collisions when hashing by division*, IBM Research Report RJ1218, May 1973.

Guibas, L. U. "The analysis of hashing techniques that exhibit k-ary clustering," *Journal of ACM*, 25(4):544–555, October 1978.

Jaeschke, G. G. and G. Osterburg. "On Cichelli's minimal perfect hash functions method," *Communications of the ACM*, 23(12):728–729, December 1980.

Jaeschke, G. "Reciprocal hashing: a method for generating minimal perfect hashing functions," *Communications of the ACM*, 24(12):829–833, December 1981.

Jensen, Kathleen and Nicklaus Wirth. *Pascal User Manual and Report*. Third Edition. Revised by Andrew B. Mickel and James F. Miner. New York: Springer-Verlag, 1985.

Knott, G. D. "Hashing functions," *Computer Journal*, 18(3):265–278, August 1975.

Knuth, Donald E. *The Act of Computer Programming. Vol. 3, Sort and Searching.* Reading, MA: Addison-Wesley, 1973.

Litwin, W. "Virtual hashing: a dynamically changing hashing," *Proceedings of the Fourth Conference on Very Large Databases*, West Berlin, September 1978, pp. 517–523.

Lum, V. Y. "General performance analysis of key-to-address transformation methods using an abstract file concept," *Communications of the ACM*, 16(10):603–612, October 1973.

Lum, V. Y., P. S. T. Yuan, and M. Dodd, "Key-to-address transform techniques," *Communications of the ACM*, 14(4):228–229, April 1971.

Lum, V. Y., and P. S. T. Yuan. "Additional results on key-to-address transform techniques," *Communications of the ACM*, 15(11):996–997, November 1972.

Maurer, W. D., and T. G. Lewis. "Hash table methods," *ACM Computing Surveys*, 7(1):5–20, March 1975.

Scholl, M. "New file organization based on dynamic hashing," *ACM Transactions on Database Systems*, 6(1):194–211, March 1981.

Sprugnoli, R. "Perfect hashing functions: a single probe retrieving method for static sets," *Communication of the ACM*, 11(10):841–850, November 1977.

Key Terms

absolute address
associated value hashing
bucket addressing
bucket chaining
collision
consecutive spill addressing
dense keys
digit extraction
direct file organization
displacement
double hashing
dynamic hashing
folding
hashing
linear probing
load factor
mid-square

packing density
packing factor
perfect hashing function
prime-number division remainder method
quotient reduction
radix conversion
randomizing scheme
reciprocal hashing
relative files
relative record number
remainder reduction
secondary collision
seek procedure
separate overflow area
synonyms
synonym chaining

Exercises

1. Using the prime-number division remainder method of hashing with $N = 101$ and assuming an EBCDIC representation, compute the hash addresses for the following set of keys:

   PAY

   AGE

   RATE

   NUMBER

2. Repeat exercise 1 using an ASCII representation of the keys.

3. Use an open addressing method of collision resolution with linear probing to obtain the file contents for the following set of keys:

   PAY and RATE mapped into 1

   TAX mapped into 2

   PENSION mapped into 4

   DEDUCT, STATUS, DEPENDENTS, SEX, SALARIED mapped into 8

   Apply the prime-number division remainder method of hashing with $N = 11$, and assume that the insertions are performed in the following order: PAY, RATE, TAX, PENSION, DEDUCT, STATUS, DEPENDENTS, SEX, SALARIED

4. Describe the problems of linear probing.

5. Describe the problems of bucket addressing with consecutive spill addressing.

6. Compare the relative advantages and disadvantages of absolute addressing and relative addressing.

7. Discuss the advantages and disadvantages of using a directory lookup table in memory to locate data in a relative file.

8. What factors affect the performance of a hashing function?

9. How is the performance of a hash function evaluated?

10. Compare the complexity of the nonperfect hashing functions presented in the chapter.

11. If information about a set of key values is not available, which type of hashing function performs the best?

12. What is the maximum optimum load factor?

13. Why does synonym chaining into a separate overflow area prevent displacement?

14. Describe the primary purpose of each of the following
    a. hashing function
    b. linear probing
    c. double hashing
    d. synonym chaining
    e. bucket addressing

15. Explain two methods of collision resolution for bucket addressing.

16. Can a bucket size greater than 1 allow for variable-length records? Explain.

Programming Problems

1. Write a program that creates a relative master file using the prime-number division remainder hashing function and linear probing.

2. Write a program to update the master file created in problem 1. Count the number of accesses it takes to update the file.

3. Write a program that creates a relative master file using the prime-number division remainder hashing function, linear probing, and synonym chaining (without a separate overflow area). Use the data in problem 1.

4. Write a program to update the master file created in problem 3 using the transaction file in problem 2. Count the number of accesses it takes to update the file.

5. Compare the number of accesses computed in problems 2 and 4. Which storage method resulted in the fewest number of accesses to update the master file?

6. Create a directly accessed relative master file that describes an inventory of parts from a nontext sequential master file. The sequential master file has the following characteristics:

key field = part number
a nontext file of part data containing the following in each record:

    part number (10 characters)
    part description (26 characters)
    part price (real)

The relative master file should have these characteristics:

key field = part number
record positions 1 through 59 should be allocated for the prime data area of home addresses
record positions 60 through 100 should be allocated for the overflow data area

record position 0 should contain the record address of the next available (empty) position in overflow (initially, position 60).

Your program should perform the following operations:

a. Apply prime-number division as a randomizing (hashing) routine in creating the relative master file. Use the formula (key Mod 59) + 1 = range of 1, . . ., 59)

b. Use a linked list to link all synonyms, storing the first synonym in the home address and all other synonyms in the next available position in overflow. (Record 0 indicates the next available position.) The link field contains the record number of the position of the next synonym or 0 if there is no next synonym.

c. Before attempting to write any information to the file, initialize the entire file of 101 record positions to a file of dummy records. Use blanks for part number and description and zeros for price and link field.

Use the following Pascal declarations:

```
TYPE
    Part_record = Record
                    part_number : Packed Array[1..10] of Char;
                    part_description : Packed Array[1..26] of Char;
                    part_price : Real;
                    synonym : Integer
                  End;
```

Here are some hints to help you achieve exemplary program style and clarity:

Output the new relative master file on a printer to make sure the information is right. Be sure to skip over dummy records and not print them!

Print headings and page numbers at the top of each new page. Do not print across the page perforations.

Tally the number of records input from the sequential master file and output to the relative master file.

7. In problem 7, you will randomly update the relative master file you created for problem 6 with input transaction records. Use a synonym link (integer). The input transaction file has already been sorted. Produce an updated relative master file (on disk) and an audit/error list (on the printer).

The transaction file consists of:

a. key fields = part number (major)
                 update code (minor)

   b. a text file of update information containing several different formats:

       additions
          update code (A)
          part number (10 characters)
          part description (26 characters)
          part price (real)
       changes
          description
             update code (C)
             part number (10 characters)
             change id (D)
             new description (26 characters)
      price
         update code (C)
         part number (10 characters)
         change id (P)
         new price (real)
       deletions
          update code (D)
          part number (10 characters)

The output files should consist of:

a. relative master file (updated)

b. audit/error list with the following information for each transaction:
update code
part number
error message (if any)

Your program should perform the following operations:

a. Input the synonym field of record 0 into a variable Next.

b. Read each input transaction record (without using Input). Validate each transaction to ensure that it contains one of the three update codes.

c. Create a master record for each valid add transaction.

d. Change the appropriate master field for each valid change transaction.

e. Delete the master record for each valid delete transaction.

f. Identify the following error conditions.

Error condition	Error message
Add a transaction that is already on master file	INVALID ADD-ALREADY ON MASTER
Change a transaction that is not on master file	INVALID CHANGE-NOT ON MASTER
Delete a transaction that is not on master file	INVALID DELETE-NOT ON MASTER
Invalid update code	INVALID UPDATE CODE

g. When all transactions have been processed, put the value of `Next` back out to record 0.

Here are some hints to help you achieve exemplary program style and clarity:

Tally master and transaction record counts and print them after the audit/error list.

Print the updated relative master file to make sure the information is right.

Print headings and page numbers at the top of each new page.

Do not print across the page perforations.

8. You will create a directly accessed relative master file from a nontext sequential part master file. The sequential master file has the following components:

key field = part number

a nontext file of part information containing the following in each record:
  part number (10 characters)
  part description (26 characters)
  part price (real)

The relative master file has the same components as the master file in problem 6.

Follow the hints listed in problem 7 and use the following Pascal declarations:

```
TYPE
    Part_record =
        Record
            part_number : Packed Array [1..10] of Char;
            part_description : Packed Array [1..26] of Char;
            part_price : Real;
            synonym : Integer
        End;
    Hash_table_entry =
        Record
            part_number : Packed Array [1..10] of Char;
            synonym : Integer
        End;
    Hash_table = Array [1..100] of Hash_table_entry;
```

Your program should include the following operations:

a. Apply prime-number division as a randomizing (hashing) routine in creating the relative master file. Use the formula (key MOD 59) + 1 = range of 1, . . ., 59)

b. Use a linked list to link all synonyms, storing the first synonym in the home address and all other synonyms in the next available position in overflow. (Record 0 indicates the next available position.) The link field contains the record number of the position of the next synonym or 0 if there is no next synonym.

c. Before attempting to write any information to the file, initialize the entire file of 101 record positions to a file of dummy records. (Use blanks for part number and description and zeros for price and link field.)

d. As the relative file is created, create an internal hash table that contains part number and synonym from each record position in the file. As records are linked, also record the part number and synonym fields in the hash table to correspond to the relative file. The hash table will allow faster access to the record being sought and will use only one Get. The subscript for an entry in the hash table is the same as the record number where the part number can be found.

9. In problem 9, you will randomly update a relative master file with input transaction records. The input transaction file has already been sorted. Produce an updated relative master file (on disk) and an audit/error list (on the printer). Use the relative master file, the transaction file, and the output files that you created for problem 8. Follow the hints listed in problem 8.

Your program should include the following operations:

a. Input the synonym field of record 0 into a variable NEXT.

b. Sequentially read the entire relative file and store the part number and synonym from each record in the corresponding position of a hash table as used in program 8. The hash table will be used to chase links to locate a record to allow only one Get.

c. Read each input transaction record (without using INPUT). Validate each transaction to ensure that it contains one of the three update codes.

d. Create a master record for each valid add transaction.

e. Change the appropriate master field for each valid change transaction.

f. Delete the master record for each valid delete transaction.

g. Identify the error conditions listed in the table in problem 7.

h. When all transactions have been processed, put the value of NEXT back out to record 0.

PART IV

TREE-STRUCTURED FILE ORGANIZATION

Chapter 8
B-Trees

Chapter 9
Indexed Sequential File Organization

Chapter 8

CHAPTER CONTENTS

Search Trees

PREVIEW

MOST HASHING FUNCTIONS RANDOMIZE KEYS to a file in a random (nonsequential) fashion, so sequentially accessing a random file from record 0 to record $n - 1$ does not indicate any ordering of keys. This chapter provides a description of several types of tree structures that are useful in sequentially accessing random-access (hashed) files. Binary search trees, AVL trees, m-way search trees, B-trees, B^+-trees, and B^*-trees will be discussed. The most important tree structure is the B-tree (and varieties thereof) since a B-tree is an external tree structure. This chapter discusses the representation and manipulation of B-trees along with algorithms that describe the manipulation. The application of trees that allow sequential and random access to the hashed car-rental agency file created in Chapter 7 is presented.

BINARY SEARCH TREES

A **binary search tree** provides the flexibility of a linked list and allows quicker access to any node than a linked list. With a linked list each node contains one pointer to another node that follows as illustrated in Figure 8.1. With a binary search tree each node contains two pointers to two other nodes: the left pointer to a subtree containing values less than the current node and a right pointer to a subtree containing values greater than the current node (Figure 8.2). A search through the binary tree in Figure 8.2 could be as efficient as a binary search through an array in terms of the number of nodes that are visited.

Since values are ordered in the tree from the left subtree to the right subtree, we can reference the immediate predecessor and immediate successor of a node. The **immediate predecessor** of a node is the largest value

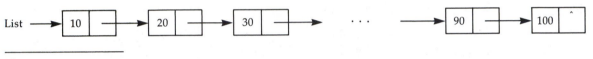

Figure 8.1
A linked list

Figure 8.2
Binary Tree

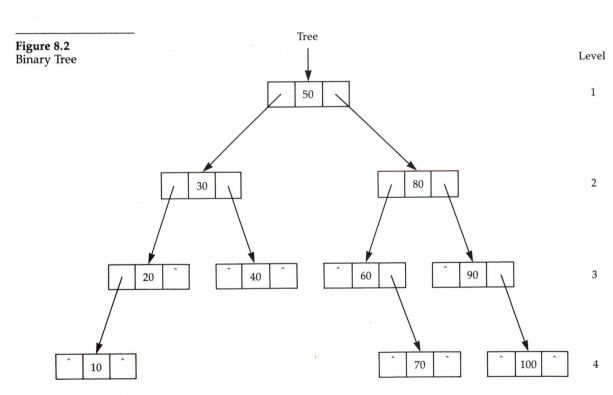

in the left subtree. The immediate predecessor is located by choosing the left pointer and chasing right pointers until a node is reached with a nil right pointer. For example, the immediate predecessor of node 50 can be found by choosing the left pointer to 30, then chasing right pointers until a node contains a nil right pointer. The value 40 is the largest value in the left subtree and thus the immediate predecessor of 50.

The **immediate successor** of a node is the reverse of the predecessor. The immediate successor is the smallest value in the right subtree. Locate it by choosing the right pointer of a node, then chase left pointers until a node is reached with a nil left pointer. Using this method, 60 is the immediate successor of node 50. If the tree is traversed **inorder**, we visit the left subtree, visit the root, then visit the right subtree; 40 immediately precedes 50 and 60 immediately succeeds 50.

The **root** of a tree is the top node that is pointed to by no other node except an external pointer. TREE is the external pointer in the tree in Figure 8.2—it points to the root node 50. The root node 50 is the **parent** of node 30 and node 80; similarly, any node in the tree is the parent of all nodes pointed to by the node. Node 80 is the parent of node 60 and node 90. Nodes that point to no other node are **leaf nodes** or **terminal nodes**. Nodes 10, 40, 70, and 100 are leaf or terminal nodes. Nodes 20 and 40 are **sibling nodes** since both have the same parent (both are pointed to by the same node). Node 50 is an **ancestor** of all other nodes in the tree. Node 20 is a **descendant** of node 50. A node that is neither a root nor a terminal node is the **root of a subtree**—it contains all descendants and is at the same time the **child** of its parent node. For example, node 30 is the root of the subtree containing nodes 30, 20, 40, and 10 and is at the same time the left child of node 50.

The **level** on which any node resides is the distance the node is from the root of the tree. The root of a tree is on level 1. The children of the root of a tree are on level 2 of the tree. Nodes 30 and 80 in the tree in Figure 8.2 are on level 2, and nodes 20, 40, 60, and 90 are on level 3. (The distance is three levels down when starting at the root.) The maximum number of nodes for a tree of level h is $2^h - 1$. The **height** (h) of a tree is the number of levels of nodes contained in the tree. The height of the tree in Figure 8.2 is 4, and the height of the subtree whose root is 30 is 3.

The **degree of a node** is the number of subtrees pointed to by the node. The degree of a nonterminal node of a binary tree may be a maximum of 2 since the node may contain pointers to at most two other nodes. The degree of a terminal node of a binary tree is 0 since the node contains null pointers. The degree of node 80 is 2 while the degree of node 60 is 1. The **degree of a tree** is the maximum degree of the nodes in the tree. The degree of a binary tree is 2, which is the maximum number of pointers a node may contain.

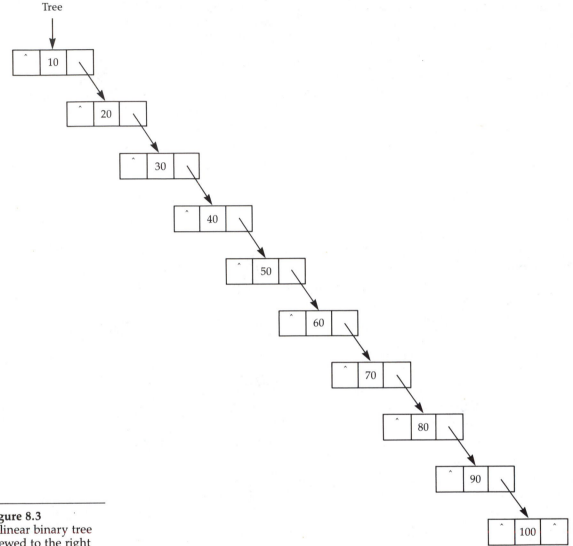

Figure 8.3
A linear binary tree
skewed to the right

The height of a tree is the most important characteristic since the height indicates the maximum number of nodes that must be visited (or compared) to locate a value in a tree. The height of a binary tree may vary depending on the order in which values are added to a tree. If the values from the binary tree in Figure 8.2 are inserted in ascending order, the resulting tree (Figure 8.3) is **skewed** to the right of the root. The height of the tree in Figure 8.3 is 10; the height of the tree in Figure 8.2 is 4. When searching for a value of 10, only four nodes need to be visited in the balanced tree in Figure 8.2; all ten nodes need to be visited in the skewed tree in Figure 8.3.

The number of nodes, N, in the trees is related to the height as presented earlier:

$$N = 2^h - 1$$

Balancing a binary tree minimizes the height of the tree, making the tree more efficient to search. The minimum height, h, of a binary tree may be computed for a given number of nodes, N, by solving the equation above for h:

$$N \leq 2^h - 1$$
$$N + 1 \leq 2^h$$
$$h \leq \lceil \lg (N + 1) \rceil$$

A **balanced tree** is one in which the height is a minimum for the number of nodes. Maintaining a balanced tree for dynamic insertions and deletions is complex and costly. On the other hand, balanced binary trees work well for a static set of values in which the balanced tree is initially built, where no insertions or deletions are made, and search times are of the order $\lg (N)$. A variation of the balanced binary search tree that prevents the shape of the tree from becoming too far out of balance and which provides an access time only slightly less than that of a balanced binary search tree is a height-balanced binary tree.

HEIGHT-BALANCED BINARY SEARCH TREES

A binary tree structure that is balanced with respect to the heights of subtrees is a **height-balanced binary tree**, which was introduced by Adelson-Velskii and Landis in 1962 (see Knuth (1973)). This type of tree is usually termed an **AVL tree** for the authors' initials. The purpose of the AVL tree is to monitor the shape of the search tree and keep it close to a perfectly balanced tree (to provide a more efficient search time) without rebalancing the entire tree. If an insertion or deletion causes the tree to become too far out of balance, the tree is rebalanced. The definition of an AVL tree follows.

A nonempty binary tree T is height balanced when:

1. T_L is the root of the left subtree (left child) of T
2. T_R is the root of the right subtree of T
3. T_L and T_R are height balanced
4. h_L is the height of T_L
5. h_R is the height of T_R
6. $|h_L - h_R| <= 1$

An AVL tree is simply a tree in which the heights of the subtrees of each node never differ by more than one level. Consider the tree in Figure 8.2: Node 50 is the root, node 30 is the root of the left subtree (T_L), and node 80 is the root of the right subtree (T_R). The height of the left subtree whose root is 30 ($h_L(30)$) is 2. In addition:

1. The subtrees with roots 10, 70, and 100 are height balanced since the left and right subtrees are empty.

2. $h_L(20) = 1$; $h_R(20) = 0$ and $|h_L(20) - h_R(20)| = 1$, so the subtree with root 20 is height balanced

3. $h_L(40) = 0$; $h_R(40) = 0$ and $|h_L(40) - h_R(40)| = 0$, so the subtree with root 40 is height balanced

4. $h_L(60) = 0$; $h_R(60) = 1$ and $|h_L(60) - h_R(60)| = 1$, so the subtree with root 60 is height balanced

5. $h_L(90) = 0$; $h_R(90) = 1$ and $|h_L(90) - h_R(90)| = 1$, so the subtree with root 90 is height balanced

6. $h_L(30) = 2$; $h_R(30) = 1$ and $|h_L(30) - h_R(30)| = 1$, so the subtree with root 30 is height balanced

7. $h_L(80) = 2$; $h_R(80) = 2$ and $|h_L(80) - h_R(80)| = 0$, so the subtree with root 80 is height balanced

8. $h_L(50) = 3$; $h_R(50) = 3$ and $|h_L(50) - h_R(50)| = 0$, so the tree with root 50 is height balanced

Since the AVL trees are height balanced, random retrievals can be performed in O[lg (N)] time (the time is on the Order of [lg(N)]) if the tree has N nodes. A new node can be inserted into or deleted from the tree in time O[lg (N)], and the tree remains height balanced. To see the rebalancing that must take place after an insertion to keep a tree height-balanced, consider the tree with one node in Figure 8.4. If the value 20 is inserted, the tree still meets the requirements of an AVL tree (Figure 8.5).

The insertion of the value 30 leaves the tree skewed to the right (Figure 8.6). The height of the left subtree of the root is 0 and the height of the right subtree of the root is 2; the tree is no longer height balanced. A simple rotation makes the tree height balanced again. The rotation is termed an **RR rotation** since the insertion has been made in the **R**ight subtree of the **R**ight subtree of the root causing the height to become too large.

Node a in Figure 8.6 represents the node nearest the insertion point where subtree heights differ by more than one level. Node b represents the child of node a in the direction of the insertion, and node f (which is nil in this case, and not shown in the figure, since a is the root of the tree) is the parent of node a. Using these definitions, an RR rotation may be defined as:

Tree

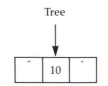

Figure 8.4
AVL tree with one node

```
aˆ.rightchild ← bˆ.leftchild        { rightchild of 10 is ˆ }
bˆ.leftchild ← a                    { leftchild of 20 is 10 }
If f = nil
      b is the new root of the tree  { 20 is new root }
Else
      fˆ.rightchild ← b
```

The tree at the bottom of Figure 8.6 is the result of the RR rotation. Node b is the new root, and the tree is height balanced.

The insertion of the value 40 in Figure 8.7 leaves the tree height balanced even though the subtrees have different heights. The insertion of the value

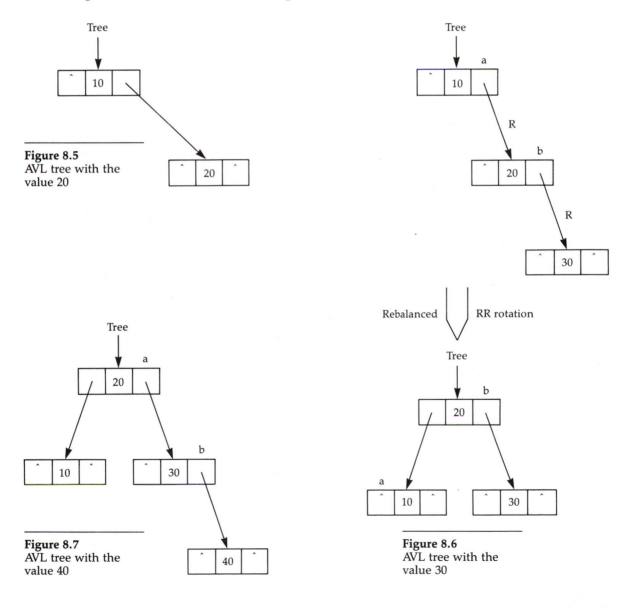

Figure 8.5
AVL tree with the value 20

Figure 8.7
AVL tree with the value 40

Figure 8.6
AVL tree with the value 30

50 (Figure 8.8) leaves the tree skewed to the right, so an RR rotation is applied to the subtree that is not height balanced (the subtree with the root 30). The resulting AVL tree is shown at the bottom of Figure 8.8.

The insertion of the value 70 (Figure 8.9) again leaves the tree skewed to the right with labels a and b having the same definitions as before. Even

Figure 8.8
AVL tree with the value 50

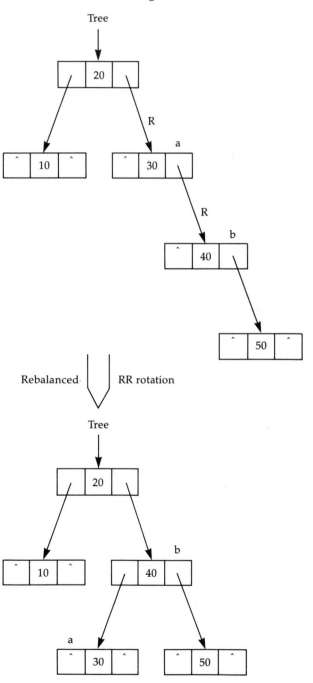

Figure 8.9
AVL tree with the
value 70

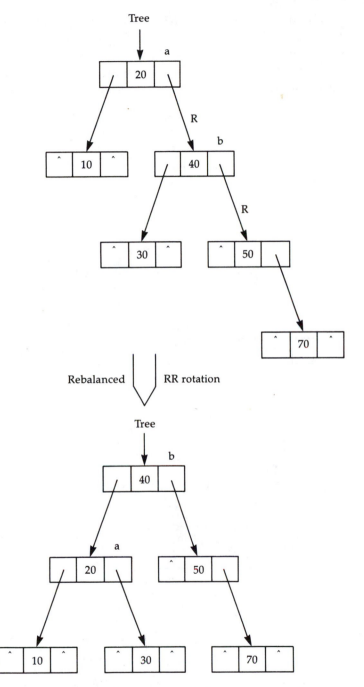

though the tree after the RR rotation looks more complex than the RR rotations in previous figures, the same steps are involved. The immediate successor of node a becomes the right child of a, and node a becomes the left child of node b to move two nodes to the left subtree of the root; the tree is height balanced.

A more complex rotation is the **RL rotation**, in which the insertion is made in the **L**eft subtree of a node that is the **R**ight child of its parent (Figure 8.10). The insertion of the value 60 leaves the subtree with root 50 no longer height balanced. The nodes in the subtree with root 50 are rotated using the more complex RL rotation. The RL rotation requires that node b be the

Figure 8.10
AVL tree with the value 60

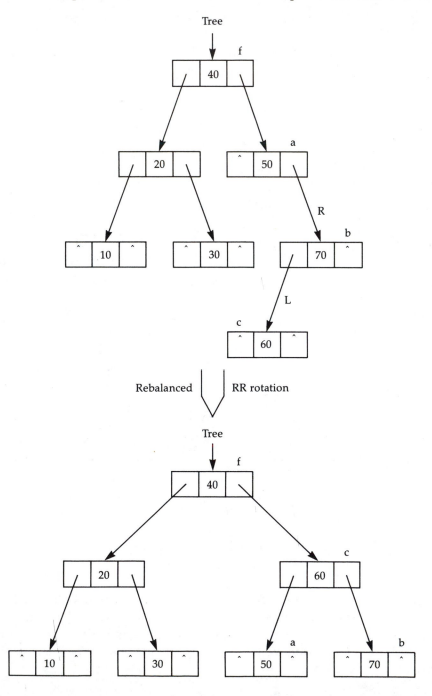

right child of node a (the R in RL) and that node c be the left child of node b (the L in RL). The steps of the RL rotation are

```
b^.leftchild ← c^.rightchild       { leftchild of 70 is ^ }
a^.rightchild ← c^.leftchild       { rightchild of 50 is ^ }
c^.rightchild ← b                  { 70 is successor of 60 }
c^.leftchild ← a                   { 50 is predecessor of 60 }
If f = nil
     c is the new root of the tree
Else
     f^.rightchild ← c             { rightchild of 40 is 60 }
```

All insertions that leave the tree skewed to the right may be rebalanced using either the RR or RL rotation.

An insertion that leaves the tree skewed to the left requires rotations symmetric to the RR and RL rotations. The left rotations are LL and LR. Beginning with an AVL tree with two nodes (Figure 8.11), the insertion of the value 2 leaves the tree skewed to the left (Figure 8.12). An LL rotation

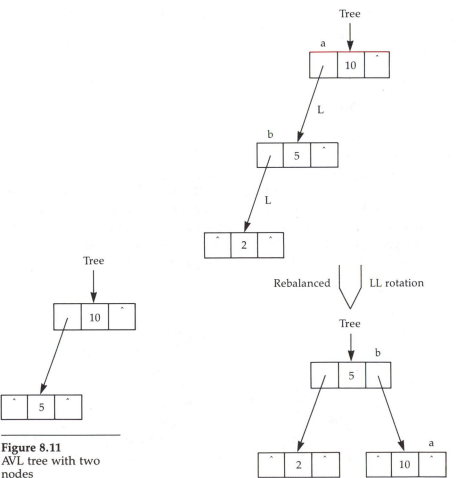

Figure 8.12
AVL tree with the value 2

Figure 8.11
AVL tree with two nodes

makes 50 the new root, leaving the tree height balanced. The steps of an **LL rotation** are symmetric to the RR rotation and are defined as:

```
aˆ.leftchild ← bˆ.rightchild          { leftchild of 10 is ˆ }
bˆ.rightchild ← a                     { rightchild of 5 is 10}
If f = nil
      b is the new root of the tree   { 5 is new root }
Else
      fˆ.leftchild ← b
```

Adding the value 4 to the AVL tree in Figure 8.12 results in the tree remaining height balanced as shown in Figure 8.13. The further addition of the value 3 leaves the tree skewed to the left (Figure 8.14). The path is the **Right** child of the **Left** child of the root **(LR rotation)**. The LR rotation is more complex than but is symmetric to the RL rotation. The LR rotation is defined as:

```
bˆ.rightchild ← cˆ.leftchild          { rightchild of 2 is 3 }
aˆ.leftchild ← cˆ.rightchild          { leftchild of 5 is ˆ }
cˆ.leftchild ← b                      { 2 is predecessor of 4 }
cˆ.rightchild ← a                     { 5 is successor of 4 }
If f = nil
      c is the new root of the tree   { 4 is new root }
Else
      fˆ.leftchild ← c
```

The four rotations presented rebalance the subtree containing the newly inserted value to keep the entire tree height balanced after each insertion. The same rotations are used for rebalancing the tree after deletions that leave the tree no longer height balanced. The tree is prevented from becoming too far out of balance to keep the access time to a minimum. Adelson-Velskii and Landis proved that a height-balanced tree is never more than 45 percent higher than a perfectly balanced tree with the same number of nodes. The height of the AVL tree has been proved to be

$$h \le 1.4404 \ [\lg (N + 2)] - 0.328$$

or $O(1.4 \ [\lg (N)])$. By rebalancing a subtree after each insertion or deletion, the number of nodes accessed to locate a value (height) is slightly less than the number accessed in a perfectly balanced tree ($O[\lg (N)]$)—all without the expense of rebalancing the entire tree.

The AVL trees that have been presented in this chapter are internal structures (that is, they reside in main memory). If the AVL tree is used to store keys of a random file, the tree must be built in main memory from the random file before $\lg (N)$ accesses could be realized. Building the tree each time the random file needs to be accessed could become expensive.

An alternative is to store the AVL tree on disk. Then each node accessed from the tree is a retrieval from disk, and the maximum number of disk accesses for an AVL tree of N nodes is the maximum height of an AVL-tree with N nodes ($\lceil 1.4 \lceil lg (N) \rceil \rceil$). If an AVL tree contains a million nodes that

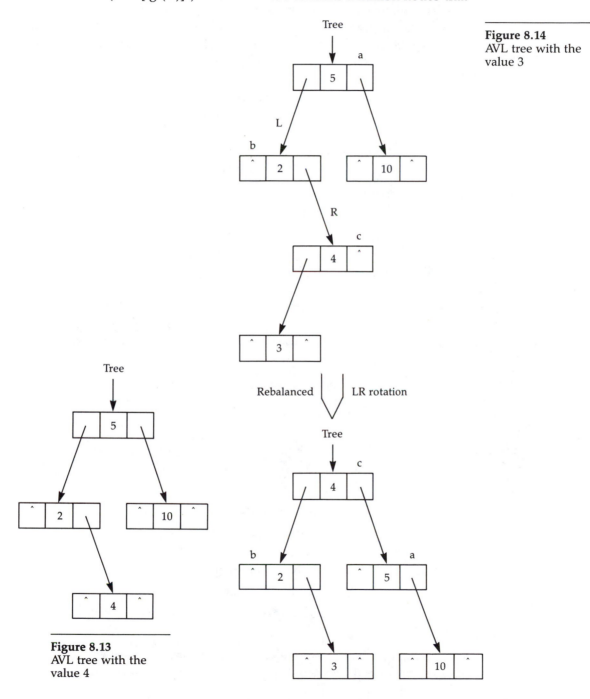

Figure 8.14
AVL tree with the value 3

Figure 8.13
AVL tree with the value 4

represent a million key values in the random file, the maximum number of node accesses (disk accesses) is 23. This small number of disk access is a lot better than sequentially searching the random file for a key value—the worst case of the sequential search is a million accesses to the random file!

Main memory is not always large enough to build a tree. Some structures contain a large number of key values, such as the tree in the previous example with one million. A special class of tree structures, called *m*-**way search trees**, addresses the class of trees that are too large to build in main memory or take too long to build in order to access a file. When a tree is stored externally, the number of disk accesses (the number of nodes visited) must be kept to a minimum or the access time becomes intolerable. Reduction in the number of disk accesses to tree structures stored externally can be realized with the use of a balanced *m*-way search tree instead of a height-balanced binary search tree (an AVL tree).

m-WAY SEARCH TREES

A balanced search tree in which all nodes are of degree *m* or less is an *m*-way search tree. Thus each node in an *m*-way search tree contains 0 to *m* pointers to other nodes. An *m*-way search tree T has the following characteristics:

1. Each node in the tree T contains the following information:

    $n,$
    $S_0,$
    $(K_1, A_1, S_1), \ldots, (K_n, A_n, S_n)$

2. n is the number of key values, $1 \leq n < m$.
3. K_i $(1 \leq i \leq n)$ is a key value, where $K_i < K_{i+1}$ for $1 \leq i < n-1$.
4. S_0 is a pointer to a subtree containing key values less than K_1.
5. S_i $(1 \leq i \leq n)$ is the pointer to a subtree containing key values between K_i and K_{i+1}.
6. S_n is a pointer to a subtree containing key values greater than K_n.
7. S_i $(0 \leq i \leq n)$, is a pointer to an *m*-way search tree.
8. A_i $(1 \leq i \leq n)$ is the address in the file of the record with key K_i.

Figure 8.15 is an example of a three-way search tree with both the diagram form and the format of each node. To locate any key value, search_ value, in the tree, the root node a is first examined for the value of *i* so that

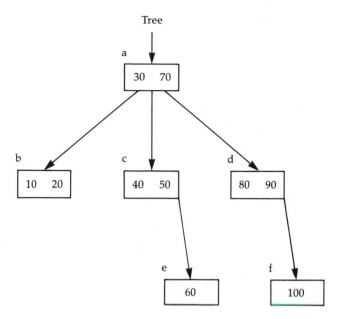

(a) Diagram form of a three-way search tree

Node	Format
a	2, b, (30, addr[30], c), (70, addr[70], d)
b	2, 0, (10, addr[10], 0), (20, addr[20], 0)
c	2, 0, (40, addr[40], 0), (50, addr[50], e)
d	2, 0, (80, addr[80], 0), (90, addr[90], f)
e	1, 0, (60, addr[60], 0)
f	1, 0, (100, addr[100], 0)

(b) Format of each node in (a)

Figure 8.15
Diagram of and format of nodes in a three-way search tree

K [i] <= search_value < K [i + 1]. In this case K [0] is a constant smaller than all legal keys (0 in this case), and K [n + 1] is a value larger than all legal keys (999 in this case). If search_value = K [i], then the address of the record containing K [i] is returned (A [i]). If search_value ≠ K [i], then the subtree S [i] needs to be searched for the value search_value. For example, if search_value = 60, the root node a is examined to find 30 < 60 < 70. search_value is not equal to 30, so subtree c, S [1], is searched for the value search_value. The node c is examined to find search_value larger than the largest key value, K [2], in the node: 50 < search_value < 99, so the subtree e, S [2], is searched next. In examining node e, 60 is found to be the only key value, so the search is complete. The address of the record in the file containing the key value 60, A [1], is returned.

Algorithm 8.1 searches *m*-way search tree p for key value search_value using the scheme discussed above.

Algorithm 8.1   Search

```
If p = 0 {tree is empty}
    Return (0)
Else
    i ← 1
    While (i <= p^.n)
        If search_value < p^.K [i]
            kindex ← i
            sindex ← i − 1
            parent_node ← p
            p ← p^.S [i − 1]
            Search { subtree pointed to by S [i − 1] }
            Return
        Else
            If search_value = p^.K [i]
                Return (p^.A [i])
            Else { search_value > p^.K [i] }
                i ← i + 1

    kindex ← n
    sindex ← n
    parent_node_ ← p
    p ← p^.S [n]
    Search { subtree pointed to by S [n] }
```

The algorithm to search an *m*-way search tree is called with the following calling routine:

```
parent_node ← 0
p ← root of m-way search tree to be examined
search_value ← the key value to be located
Search
```

The value returned by the algorithm Search is either (1) the address of the record in the file (A [*i*]) that contains the key value located or (2) 0 if the key value is not found in the tree. If the returned value is 0, p = 0, but parent_node is a pointer to the node last examined when it was determined that the key value did not exist in the tree. When the key value does not exist, an insertion can be made into position i of parent_node.

The search for 60 reveals that p = node e, i = position 1 (K [1]), and parent_node = node c. The search for 45 reveals p = 0 (45 is not found), parent_node = node c, and i = 2 (45 < K [2]). Since 45 was not found in the tree, 45 can be added (node g) as a child of parent_node (node c), with

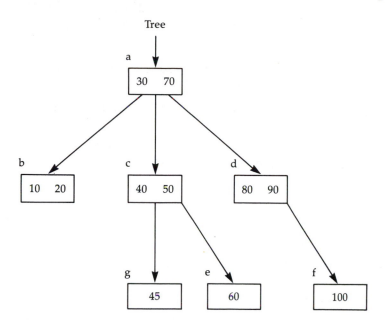

Figure 8.16
Diagram of three-way
search tree with the
value 45

the address of node g being S [i − 1] or S [1]. Node c now contains the following information:

   2, 0, (40, addr[40], g), (50, addr[50], e)

Node g contains the following information:

   1, 0, (45, addr[45], 0)

The tree with 45 added is presented in diagram form in Figure 8.16.

In analyzing the *m*-way search tree, the maximum number of disk accesses is equal to the height (*h*) of the tree. So the size of *m* needs to be increased to keep the height as small as possible. The maximum number of key values in an *m*-way search tree of height *h* is $m^h − 1$. The maximum number of key values in a three-way search tree of height 3 is $27 − 1$ or 26 values. For a 200-way search tree with a height of 3, the maximum number of key values is $8 \times 10^6 − 1$. For a large *m* and small *h*, each access of a node from the tree requires the buffer for the file to be large enough to hold all the data in one node. For a 200-way search tree, the buffer must be large enough to hold *n*, S_0, and 199 tuples (a **tuple** contains the 3 values of [K_i, A_i, S_i]).

B-TREES

To give the best performance, an *m*-way search tree should be balanced. One type of balanced *m*-way search tree is a **B-tree** (named for one of its authors, Bayer, from Bayer and McCreight (1972)), which has the following characteristics:

1. A B-tree is an *m*-way search tree that is either empty or has a height $>= 1$.

2. The root node has at least two children; therefore, it has at least one value.

3. All nonterminal nodes other than the root node (with $S_i \neq 0$), have at least $\lceil m/2 \rceil$ children; therefore, they have at least $\lceil m/2 \rceil - 1$ values. ($\lceil x \rceil$ is the ceiling of x.)

4. All terminal nodes (with $S_i = 0$), are at the same level.

A B-tree of order 3 (degree of 3) must have a height of at least 1, a root node with at least two children, and all nonterminal nodes (without any 0 subtree addresses) must have at least $\lceil m/2 \rceil$ or at least two children and as many as three children. The three-way search tree of Figure 8.16 is not a B-tree since nodes with $S_i = 0$ occur on levels 2 and 3. This violates the definition above. A B-tree of order 3 containing the data in Figure 8.16 is shown in Figure 8.17. The B-tree of Figure 8.17 has one more node than the three-way search tree of Figure 8.16, but the height of both trees is 3, which indicates that the most number of disk accesses for either tree is three. The B-tree is balanced with all 0 subtree addresses (S_i) on the same level. The three-way search tree has only two nodes with less than the maximum number of keys, but the B-tree has four nodes with less than two

Figure 8.17
Diagram of B-tree of order 3

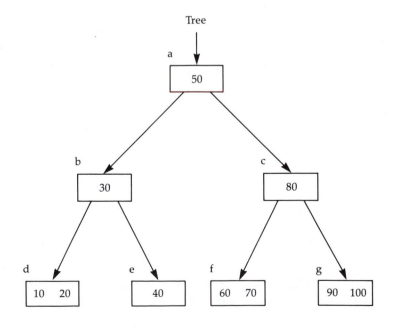

keys. These four nodes with less than the maximum number of keys allow for easy insertion of new key values without increasing the height of the B-tree.

The B-tree is maintained in a balanced fashion so that after inserting and deleting key values, the B-tree always adheres to the properties listed in the definition. The B-tree is always the most efficient form for use as an indexing structure for a file where the m-way search tree could be unbalanced after several insertions.

The utilization of storage is an important advantage offered by the externally stored B-tree. Each node is at least half-full of key values. At worst a B-tree containing a total of N keys with between n and $2n$ key values in each node requires $\log_n(N + 1)$ node accesses. If each node requires a disk access, the worst case is $\log_n(N + 1)$ disk accesses—a number of accesses comparable to a perfectly balanced tree. These advantages allow for simple search, insertion, and deletion algorithms.

Insertions

Inserting 75 into the tree in Figure 8.17 calls for an attempt to add 75 into node f, which is already full. If 75 were added to node f, the information in the node would be

3, 0, (60, addr[60], 0), (70, addr[70], 0), (75, addr[75], 0)

Each node can hold only two tuples, however, so the node is split into two nodes of at least $\lceil m/2 \rceil$ key values. The $m + 1 = 3$ key values are equally distributed (split) between the current node and the new node. Since one node is split in two, an additional key needs to be inserted into the parent node to adhere with the requirements of the B-tree (two key values in node c for three child nodes). The middle key of the $m + 1$ keys is extracted and added to the parent node, and the two nodes after the split become children. The three keys in node f are split so that the keys lower than the middle key stay in node f:

1, 0, (60, addr[60], 0)

The keys higher than the middle key are split into node h:

1, 0, (75, addr[75], 0)

Nodes f and h become the children of node c. Then the tuple

(70, addr[70], h)

which is the middle key, is added into the parent of f or into node c. Since node c has only one tuple (80), the tuple (70, addr[70], h) can be added into node c as shown in Figure 8.18.

Inserting 55 into the tree in Figure 8.18 entails simply adding a tuple with (55, addr[55], 0) into node f, which has only one tuple (60, addr[60], 0). Figure 8.19 shows the tree after 55 has been added.

Inserting 57 into the tree in Figure 8.19 calls for 57 to be inserted into node f between 55 and 60. Node f contains the following data:

3, 0, (55, addr[55], 0), (57, addr[57], 0), (60, addr[60], 0)

In this case node f contains three tuples instead of two. Therefore, node f is split as before:

3, 0, (55, addr[55], 0), (57, addr[57], 0), (60, addr[60], 0)
+ + + + + + + + +   ************************

New node f contains the tuples 1 through $\lceil m/2 \rceil - 1$ (underlined with +s):

1, 0, (55, addr[55], 0)

A new node i with tuples $\lceil m/2 \rceil + 1$ through n (underlined with *) above:

1, 0, (60, addr[60], 0)

and the tuple (57, addr[57], i) is inserted into the parent of f (node c).

Node c already contains the two tuples

3, f, (57, addr[57], i), (70, addr[70], h), (80, addr[80], g)
+ + + + + + + + +   ************************

Inserting (57, addr[57], i) causes node c to be split into a new node j. Node c contains the data underlined with +:

1, f, (57, addr[57], i)

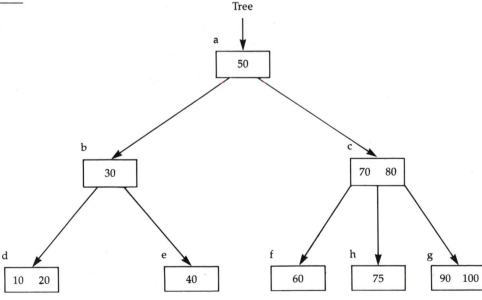

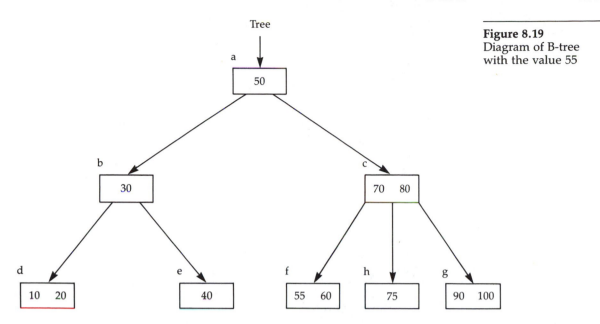

Figure 8.19
Diagram of B-tree
with the value 55

The new node j contains the data underlined with *:

   1, h, (80, addr[80], g)

The two new nodes c and j are children of node a, and the tuple (70, addr[70], j) is added to the parent node a. Since node a contains only one tuple

   1, a, (50, addr[50], c)

the node a will now contain

   2, a, (50, addr[50], c), (70, addr[70], j)

The resulting tree with the addition of the value 57 is shown in Figure 8.20.

    The last type of change that results from an insertion is the growth of the height of the tree. Consider the insertion of 95, 85, and 87, in that order. The insertion of 95 into the B-tree in Figure 8.20 results in node g being split, 90 in node g, 100 in new node k, and the middle value, 95, promoted to the parent node j as shown in Figure 8.21. The insertion of 85 into the B-tree (Figure 8.22) fills node g with 85 and 90. Finally, the insertion of 87 into the B-tree causes the splitting of node g, with 85 remaining in node g, 90 being moved to a new node l, and the middle value, 87, being promoted to the parent node j (Figure 8.23). Node j has three values, which is more than the maximum number of two, so node j is split: The value 80 remains in node j, 95 moves to new node m, and 87 moves up to the parent node

Figure 8.20
Diagram of B-tree
with the value 57

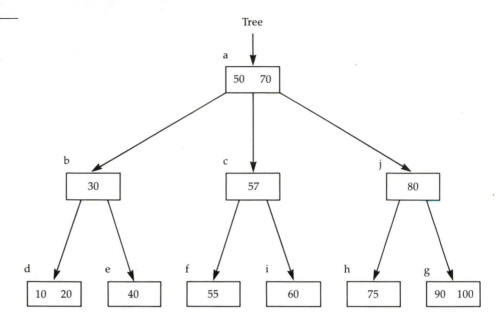

Figure 8.21
Diagram of B-tree
with the value 95

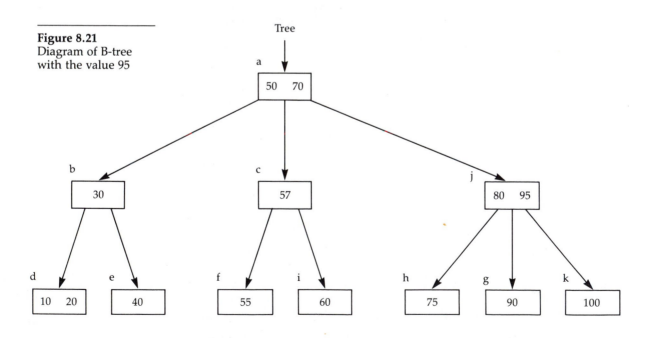

Tree

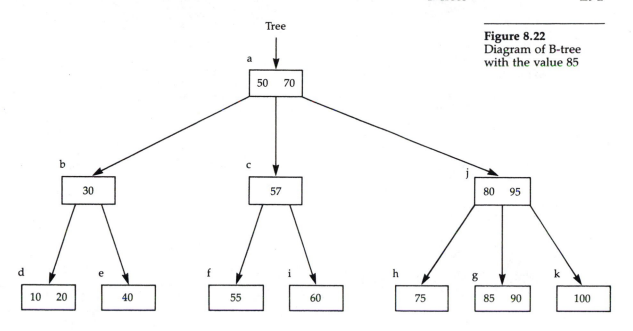

Figure 8.22
Diagram of B-tree
with the value 85

Tree

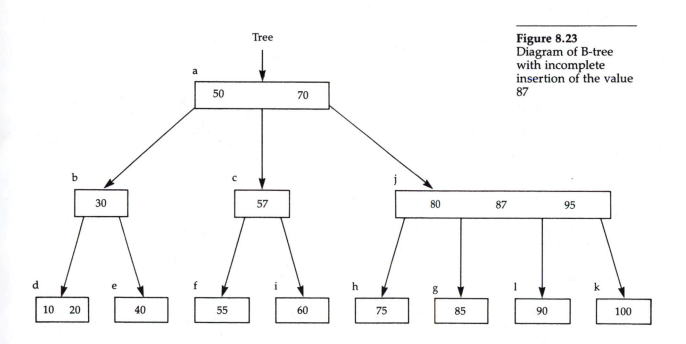

Figure 8.23
Diagram of B-tree
with incomplete
insertion of the value
87

Figure 8.24
Diagram of B-tree
with the value 87
promoted to the root
node

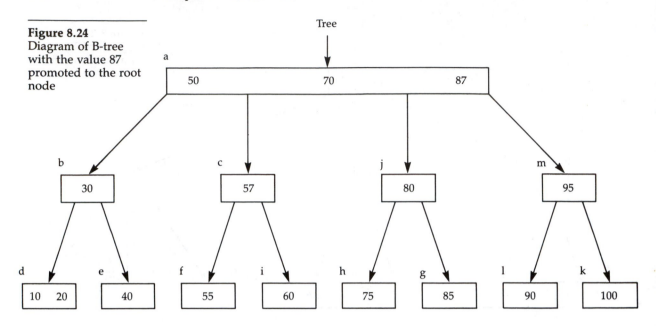

Figure 8.25
Diagram of B-tree
with complete inser-
tion of the value 87

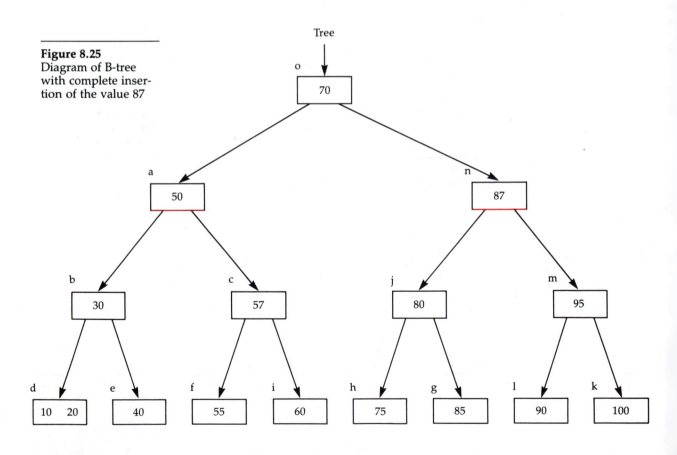

a (Figure 8.24). Node a is now above the maximum capacity, so the root node a is split: 50 remains in node a, 87 is moves to new node n, and the middle value (70) is promoted (Figure 8.25). Since node a has no parent (node a is the root), a new root is formed with 70 as the root. The new node n is the right child of the new root, and the old root is the left child of the new root. The tree has grown to a height of 4.

Algorithm 8.2 inserts a tuple Key, addr into B-tree p using the scheme described above. As a node is split, the middle tuple key value is withdrawn with the address of the new tuple containing the second half of the split node. It is inserted into the parent of the node that was split. To access the parent of the split node, Algorithm Search is called recursively.

Algorithm 8.2   Insertion

```
root ← 0
Rewrite (B_Tree_File)
Output (B_Tree_File, root of zero in location zero)
Close (B_Tree_File)
Reset (B_Tree_File)
next ← 0   { next available location in B_Tree_File }
While Not Eof (hashed_file)
    Input (hashed_file, key, addr)
    hold_tuple ← (key, addr, 0)
    Search (hold_tuple, root, insert_required)
    If insert_required
            {
                new root contains hold_tuple with old root as
                s0
            }
        next ← next + 1
        newnode.n ← 1
        newnode.s0 ← root
        newnode.tuple [1] ← hold_tuple
        Output (B_Tree_File, newnode, next)
        root ← next
        Output (B_Tree_File, root, zero)

Algorithm Search (VAR hold_Tuple; p; VAR insert_required)

    If p = 0
        insert_required ← TRUE
    Else
        Input (B_Tree_File, node, p) { node ← contents of p }
        If hold_tuple.key > node.tuple[node.n].key
            i ← node.n + 1
            Search (hold_tuple, node.tuple[node.n].s, insert_required)
            If insert_required
                Insert { hold_tuple into position i of node }
```

```
                    Else
                        i ← 1
                        found ← FALSE
                        done ← FALSE
                        While Not done And Not found
                            If hold_tuple.key < node.tuple[i].key
                                done ← TRUE
                            Else
                                If hold_tuple.key = node.tuple[i].key
                                    found ← TRUE
                                Else { > }
                                    i ← i + 1

                        If found
                            Output ('duplicate entry')
                        Else { done }
                            If i = 1
                                Search (hold_tuple, node.s0, insert_required)
                            Else
                                Search (hold_tuple, node.tuple[i − 1].s, insert_required)

                            If insert_required
                                Insert { hold_tuple into position i of node }


Algorithm Insert { internal to Search }

        If node.n < M − 1 { resulting node is large enough for addition }
            insert_required ← FALSE
            For count ← node.n DownTo i
                node.tuple [count + 1] ← node.tuple [count]

            node.n ← node.n + 1
            node.tuple [i] ← hold_tuple
            Output (B_Tree_File, node, p)
        Else
            { node is full so addition will cause a split }
            Split


Algorithm Split { internal to Index }

        big_node ← node
        For count ← node.n DownTo i
            big_node.tuple [count + 1] ← big_node.tuple [count]

        big_node.tuple [i] ← hold_tuple
        big_node.n ← node.n + 1

        middle ← (M − 1) / 2 + 1

                        { split lower values into node }
```

```
For count ← 1 To middle − 1
    node.tuple[count] ← big_node.tuple[count]
node.n ← middle − 1

                { move middle tuple into hold_tuple }
hold_tuple ← node.tuple [middle]
next ← next + 1
hold_tuple.s ← next

                { split higher values into new_node }
new_node.s0 ←   big_node.tuple[middle].s
i ← 0
For count ← middle + 1 To big_node.n
    i ← i + 1
    new_node.tuple [i] ← big_node.tuple [count]
new_node.n ← i
Output (B_Tree_File, newnode, next)

node.n ← middle − 1
Output (B_Tree_File, node, p)
{ insert_required remains TRUE upon return }
```

Deletions

Deletions of values from the B-tree may involve merging values from two nodes into one node rather than splitting values into two nodes to ensure that the tree maintains the characteristics of a B-tree. Deleting a value from a leaf node simply involves removing the tuple with that value from the node. Given the B-tree of order 5 in Figure 8.26, deleting 250 from node k, which contains more than the minimum number of tuples, is the simplest deletion (Figure 8.27). Note that node e stores data in format form:

2, 0, (40, addr[40], 0), (50, addr[50], 0)

Deleting 50 from the B-tree leaves node e with only one value:

1, 0, (40, addr[40], 0)

Node e now contains fewer than the minimum number of tuples ($\lceil m/2 \rceil$ − 1). The algorithm for deletion in this situation requires that the nearest right sibling with $> \lceil m/2 \rceil$ tuples be located. Node f is the nearest right sibling of node e with more than the minimum number of tuples. The parent node b

2, d, (30, addr[30], e), (60, addr[60], f)

of node e has a value $K[i] = 60$ (the immediate successor of 50), and $S[i − 1] = e$. The relationship of the value to be deleted (50), to the value $K[i]$ in the parent node (60), to $K[1]$ of the nearest right sibling (70) is $50 < 60 < 70$. Since node f contains more than the minimum tuples for a

Figure 8.26
Diagram form of B-
tree of order 5

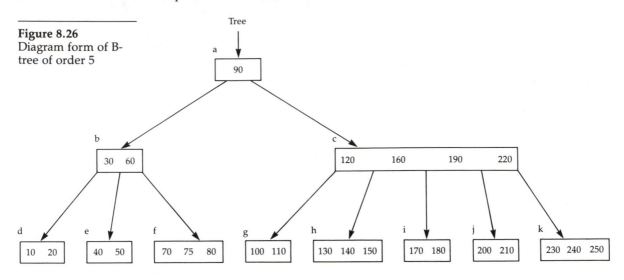

Figure 8.27
Diagram of B-tree
after deleting the
value 250

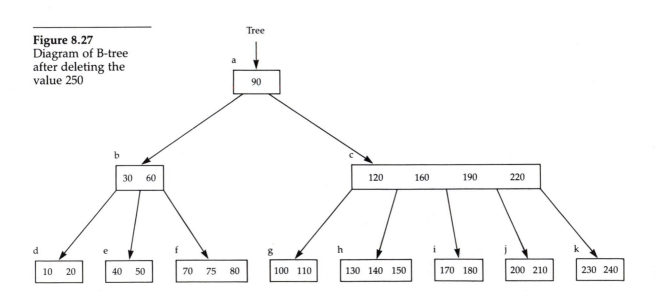

node, rotation of these three values takes place so that the immediate successor of 50 (K [i] = 60, underlined in the following with +) in the parent node and S [0] (underlined in the following with *) from the right sibling node f are moved into node e:

2, 0, (40, addr[40], 0), (60, addr[60], 0)
                        + + + + + +   *

The value K[1], which is underlined in the following with +s, is moved from node f into node b:

2, d, (30, addr[30], e), (70, addr[70], f)
                        + + + + + + +

The resulting B-tree with the value 50 deleted is illustrated in Figure 8.28.

If the nearest right sibling had not had more than the minimum of tuples in the node, the nearest left sibling and the immediate predecessor in the parent node (the Key K [i]) could have been used as well. The next deletion illustrates the algorithm if both the nearest siblings have exactly the minimum number of tuples.

Deletion of the value 20 from the B-tree in Figure 8.28 causes a merger of values from three nodes since the nearest right sibling (node e) contains the minimum of two tuples (40 and 60), and node d has no left sibling. The immediate successor of 20 is K [i] = 30 with S [i − 1] = d from node b:

2, d, (30, addr[30], e), (70, addr[70], f)

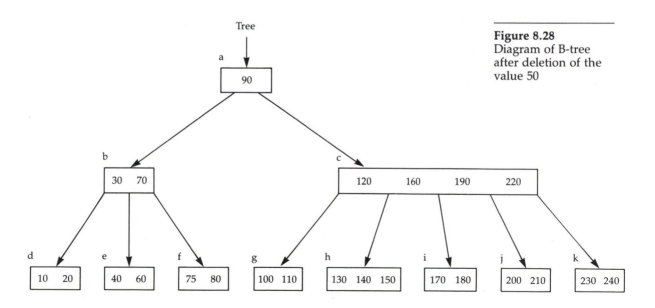

Figure 8.28
Diagram of B-tree after deletion of the value 50

The nearest right sibling node e contains K [1] = 40. Deleting the value 20 from node d leaves it with less than the minimum number of tuples:

1, (10, addr[10], 0)

The remaining values in node d, the immediate successor K [i] = 30, and the nearest right sibling node e (underlined by +) are merged into node d:

4, 0, (10,addr[10],0), (30,addr[30],0), (40,addr[40],0), (60,addr[60],0)

+ + + + + + + + + + + + + +

Node b is left with only one tuple:

1, d, (70, addr[70], f)

Node e is discarded because it has been emptied of all information. The B-tree of Figure 8.29 is the resulting tree.

Node b has only one tuple (the minimum number of tuples is two), so the process is repeated. The successor value merges from the parent node b (90) and the first subtree pointer of the nearest right sibling (the pointer to g) into node b:

2, d, (70, addr[70], f), (90, addr[90], g)

The K [1] from node c moves into the node vacated by the value 90 (node a). The B-tree after complete deletion of the value 20 is shown in Figure 8.30.

Deletion of values from nonleaf nodes requires that an immediate successor (or predecessor) be located and moved into the place left by the

Figure 8.29
Diagram of B-tree with incomplete deletion of the value 20

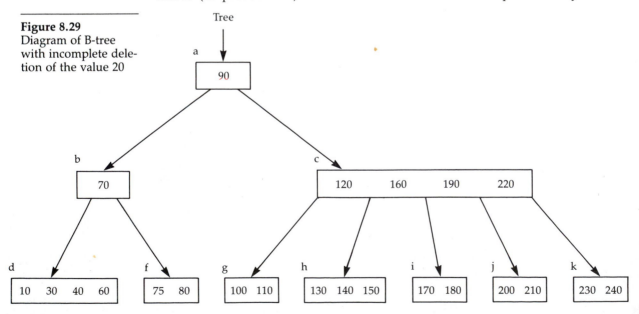

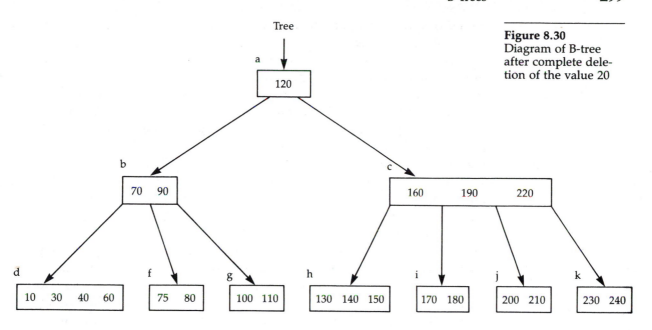

Figure 8.30
Diagram of B-tree
after complete dele-
tion of the value 20

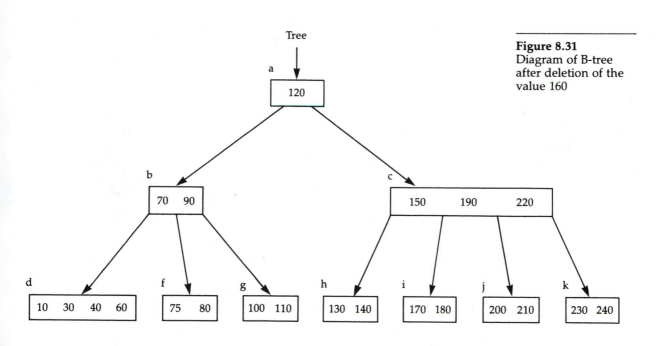

Figure 8.31
Diagram of B-tree
after deletion of the
value 160

deleted value. To illustrate, suppose the value 160 is deleted from the B-tree in Figure 8.30. The deletion of 160 causes a rotation from the predecessor node h, which has more than the minimum number of tuples. The immediate predecessor of 160 is 150, so 150 moves into the spot left by the deletion of 160 (Figure 8.31).

The deletion of 90 from the B-tree in Figure 8.31 causes the immediate predecessor 80 to move up to the parent node b (Figure 8.32), leaving node f with less than the minimum number of tuples. The nearest right sibling of node f (node g) has only the minimum contents, but the left sibling of node f has more than the minimum contents, so the value 70 of the parent node is moved into node f (the immediate successor of 75), and 60 (from the nearest left sibling, node d) moves into node b, (Figure 8.33).

The two last deletion examples involve deletion of the one tuple in the root node and the deletion of a tuple in a node with minimum contents, which causes the height to decrease because all the children, siblings, and parent nodes are also in a minimum state. The deletion of the only tuple in the root node, 120, brings the immediate predecessor, 110, up into the spot vacated by the tuple 120 (Figure 8.34). Moving 110 to the root node leaves node g with a subminimum number of tuples. Node g has no right siblings, and its left sibling, node f, has only the minimum number of tuples. The contents of node g and the immediate predecessor in the parent node b (80) merge into the left sibling, node f (Figure 8.35). Node b is left with less than the minimum number of tuples. As a result, the successor value from the parent node of node b (110) and S[0] (the pointer to node h) from node b's sibling node c are merged into node b. K [1] (150) moves to node a into the tuple position vacated by the value 110 (Figure 8.36).

Figure 8.32
Diagram of B-tree after incomplete deletion of the value 90

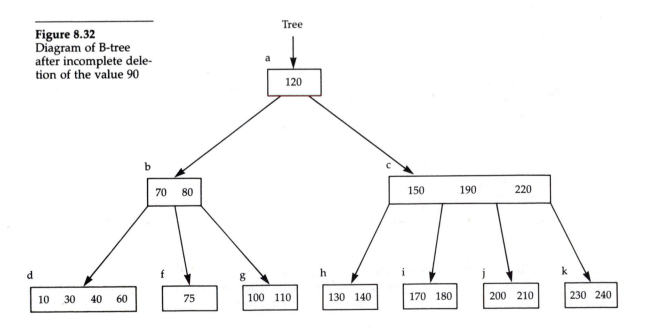

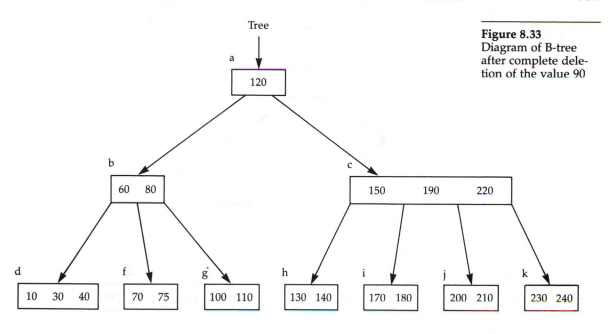

Figure 8.33
Diagram of B-tree after complete deletion of the value 90

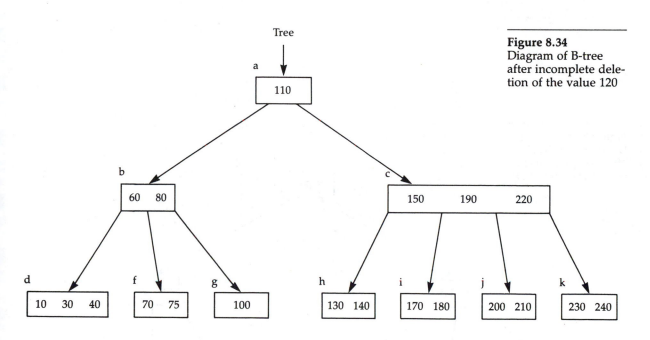

Figure 8.34
Diagram of B-tree after incomplete deletion of the value 120

The B-tree in Figure 8.36 now has nodes in the right subtree of the root that have minimum contents. If a value is deleted from the right subtree of the root, the tree attempts to rotate a value from a sibling. A deletion from

Figure 8.35
Diagram of B-tree
showing incomplete
deletion of the value
120

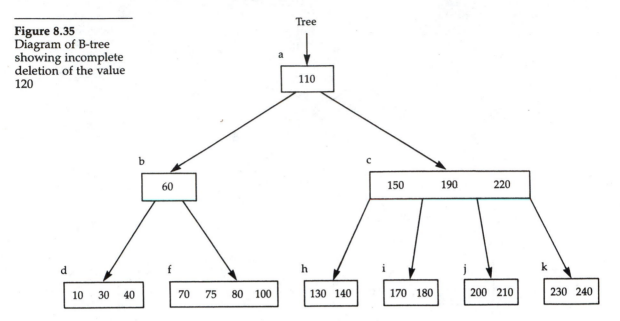

Figure 8.36
Diagram of B-tree
after complete dele-
tion of the value 120

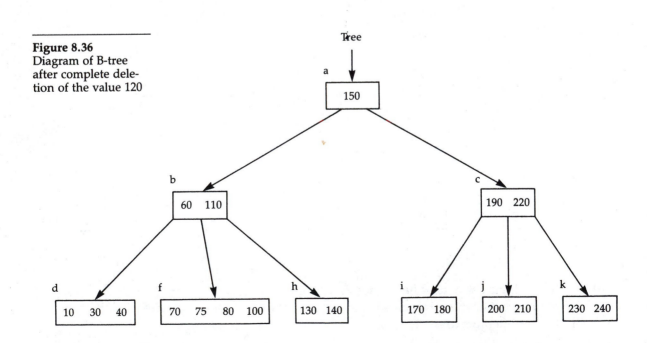

nodes i, j, or k causes a merging of nodes, which results in the reduction in the height of the tree. Similarly, the deletion of a value from node c causes a reduction in height since the left (and only) sibling of node c as well as the parent (root) node have only minimum contents.

For example, the deletion of the value 190 from the B-tree in Figure 8.36 first causes a rotation of the predecessor to replace 190; 180 is moved from node i into the spot vacated by 190 in node c (Figure 8.37). Now node i has less than the minimum number of tuples, so the parent value 180 and the right sibling, node j, are merged into node i, which deletes node j (Figure 8.38). This leaves node c with less than the minimum contents. Node c has no right sibling. Its parent node, a, has the minimum contents for a root node, and its left sibling has only the minimum contents. Therefore, a merge takes place: The subminimum node c and the parent value, node a, merge into the left sibling, node b (Figure 8.39). Node c is deleted entirely and so is node a, which is empty. Node b becomes the new root of the B-tree, which now has a height of only 2. The number of tuple values has decreased to the point that a B-tree of order 5 and height 3 cannot have all nodes filled to the minimum, so the height is reduced. The number of nodes in the tree has reduced from nine nodes in Figure 8.36 to only six nodes in Figure 8.39.

Algorithm 8.3 deletes a tuple (delete_value) from B-tree p using the scheme discussed above. Deletion from a nonleaf node is performed first so that after the predecessor is moved up in the tree, the deletion of the predecessor from a leaf node follows.

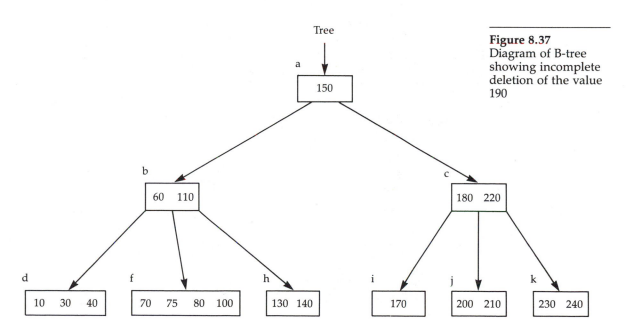

Figure 8.37
Diagram of B-tree showing incomplete deletion of the value 190

Figure 8.38
Diagram of B-tree
after deletion of
node j

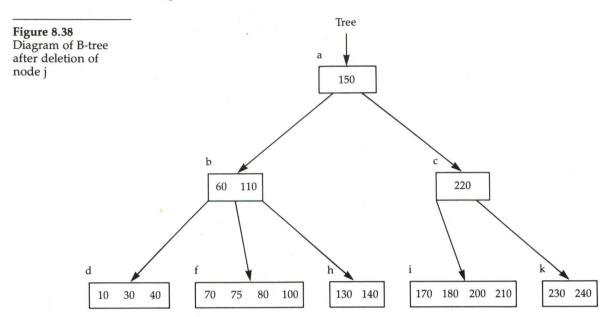

Figure 8.39
Diagram of B-tree
after complete dele-
tion of the value 190

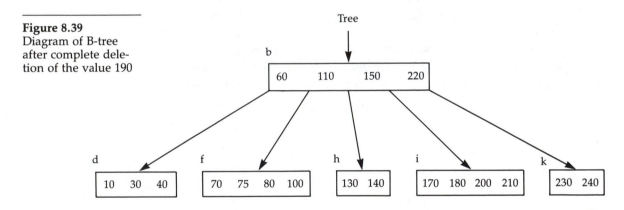

Algorithm 8.3   Deletion

```
minimum ← [M / 2] - 1
maximum ← M - 1
Reset (B_tree_file)
Input (B_tree_File, root, 0)
Input (B_tree_File, root_node, root)
While Not Eof
    Input (delete_value)
    Delete (delete_value, root, node_undersized)
    If node_undersized
        If root_node.n = 0
            root ← root_node. s0
            Output (B_tree_file, root, 0)
```

```
Algorithm Delete (delete_value, p; VAR node_undersized)
                { search node with address p for key }
    If p = 0
        node_undersized ← FALSE
    Else
        Input (B_tree_file, node, p) { node ← contents of p }
        If delete_value > node.tuple [node.n].key
            i ← node.n
            child ← node.tuple[node.n].s
            Delete (delete_value, child, node_undersized)
            If node_undersized
                Under_Flow (node, child, i, node_undersized)
        Else
            i ← 1
            found ← FALSE
            done ← FALSE
            While Not done And Not found
                If delete_value < node.tuple [i].key
                    done ← TRUE
                Else
                    If delete_value = node.tuple [i].key
                        found ← TRUE
                    Else
                        i ← i + 1

            If found
                If i = 1
                    child ← node.s0
                Else
                    child ← node.tuple[i − 1].s

                If child = 0
                    { delete key[i] from leaf node }
                    node.n ← node.n − 1
                    node_undersized ← node.n < minimum
                    For j ← i To node.n
                        node.tuple[j] ← node.tuple[j + 1]
                    Output (B_tree_file, node, p)

                Else { delete key[i] from nonterminal node; find
                        predecessor to replace key[i] }
                    Find_Predecessor (child, node_undersized)
                    If node_undersized
                        Under_Flow (p, child, i − 1, node_undersized)

            Else { done }
                child ← node.tuple[i − 1].s
                Delete (delete_value, child, node_undersized)
                If node_undersized
                    Under_Flow (p, child, i − 1, node_undersized)
```

```
Algorithm Find_Predecessor (descendant; VAR node_undersized)
                    { global references made to node, i }
Input (B_tree_file, descendant_node, descendant)
q ← descendant_node.tuple[descendant_node.n].s
If q = 0 { leaf node }
    descendant_node.tuple[descendant_node.n].s ← node.tuple[i].s
    node.tuple[i] ← descendant_node.tuple[descendant_node.n]
    descendant_node.n ← descendant_node.n − 1
    node_undersized ← descendant_node.n < minimum
    Output (B_tree_file, node, p)
    Output (B_tree_file, descendant_node, descendant)

Else { look deeper in tree for predecessor }
    Find_Predecessor (q, node_undersized)
    If node_undersized
        Under_Flow (descendant, q, descendant_node.n, node_undersized)

Algorithm Under_Flow (VAR parent, child; si; VAR node_undersized)
                    { child_node contents below minimum }
Input (B_tree_file, child_node, child)
                    { child_node ← contents of child }
Input (B_tree_file, parent_node, parent)
                    { parent_node ← contents of parent }
If si < parent_node.n
                    { a right sibling exists }
    si ← si + 1
    right ← parent_node.tuple[si].s
    Input (B_tree_file, right_node, right)
                    { right_node ← contents of right }
    right_extras ← (right_node.n − minimum + 1) DIV 2
                    { right_extras = number of tuples over the minimum
                      that can be balanced between child_node
                      and right_node
                    }
    child_node.n ← child_node.n + 1
    child_node.tuple[child_node.n] ← parent_node.tuple[si + 1]
    child_node.tuple[child_node.n].s ← right_node.s0
                    { replace predecessor of node to original
                      location
                    }
    If right_extras > 0  { move extras number of tuples from right_node
                          to child_node }
        Balance_From_Right
    Else      { check to see if left sibling exists and has right_extras }
        If si <> 0 { left sibling exists}
            Choose_Left_Sibling
            If left_extras > 0
                Balance_From_Left
            Else { left sibling has no extras so merge child_node
                  and right_node into child_node }
                Merge_With_Right
```

```
                    Else { left sibling does not exist so merge child_node and
                            right_node into child_node }
                         Merge_With_Right
            Else
                          { no right sibling exists; choose left sibling }
                 Choose_Left_Sibling
                 If left_extras > 0
                     Balance_From_Left
                 Else
                     Merge_With_Left


Algorithm Choose_Left_Sibling

    If si = 1
        left ← parent_node.s0
    Else
        left ← parent_node.tuple[si − 1].s

    Input (B_tree_file, left_node, left)
                   { left_node ← contents of left}
    left_extras ← (left_node.n − minimum + 1) DIV 2


Algorithm Balance_From_Right

    For j ← 1 To right_extras − 1
        child_node.tuple[child_node.n + j] ← right_node.tuple [j]

    parent_node.tuple[si] ← right_node.tuple[right_extras]
    parent_node.tuple[si].s ← right

    right_node.s0 ← right_node.tuple[right_extras].s
    right_node.n ← right_node.n − right_extras

    For j ← 1 To right_node.n
        right_node.tuple[j] ← right_node.tuple[right_extras + j]

    child_node.n ← minimum + right_extras − 1
    node_undersized ← FALSE

    Output (B_tree_file, child_node, child)
    Output (B_tree_file, right_node, right)
    Output (B_tree_file, parent_node, parent)


Algorithm Merge_With_Right

    For j ← 1 To minimum
        child_node.tuple[minimum + j] ← right_node.tuple[j]

    For j ← si To parent_node.n − 1
        parent_node.tuple[j] ← parent_node.tuple[j + 1]
```

```
          child_node.n ← maximum
          parent_node.n ← parent_node.n − 1
          node_undersized ← parent_node.n < minimum

          Output (B_tree_file, child_node, child)
          Output (B_tree_file, parent_node, parent)
          { Dispose (right) }
```

Algorithm Balance_From_Left

```
     For j ← minimum − 1 DownTo 1 { move tuples over "left_extras" places
                                       to make room for tuples at lower
                                       end
                                    }
          child_node.tuple[j + left_extras] ← child_node.tuple[j]

     child_node.tuple[left_extras] ← parent_node.tuple[si]
     child_node.tuple[left_extras].s ← child_node.s0

     left_node.n ← left_node.n − minimum + 1

     For j ← left_extras − 1  DownTo  1
          child_node.tuple[j] ← left_node.tuple[left_node.n + j]

     child_node.s0 ← left_node.tuple[left_node.n].s

     parent_node.tuple[si] ← left_node.tuple[left_node.n]
     parent_node.tuple[si].s ← child

     left_node.n ← left_node.n − 1
     child_node.n ← minimum − 1 + left_extras
     node_undersized ← FALSE
     Output (B_tree_file, child_node, child)
     Output (B_tree_file, left_node, left)
     Output (B_tree_file, parent_node, parent)
```

Algorithm Merge_With_Left

```
     left_node.n ← left_node.n + 1
     left_node.tuple [left_node.n] ← parent_node.tuple[si]
     left_node.tuple[left_node.n].s ← child_node.s0

     For j ← 1 To child_node.n − 1
          left_node.tuple[left_node.n + j] ← child_node.tuple[j]

     left_node.n ← maximum
     parent_node.n ← parent_node.n − 1
     node.undersized ← parent_node.n < minimum

     Output (B_tree_file, left_node, left)
     Output (B_tree_file, parent_node, parent)
     { Dispose (child_node) }
```

B*-TREES

Bayer and McCreight (1972) applied a modification to the B-tree known as the **overflow technique**, which improves the insertion algorithm by using local rotation to cause keys to overflow from a full node into a sibling node that is less than full. The net effect is that every node is at least two-thirds full rather than half-full as in B-trees. Keeping the nodes two-thirds full uses the available space more efficiently and also reduces the number of nodes necessary to hold a fixed number of keys. The search time is improved over that for the B-tree. The tree that employs the overflow technique is the **B*-tree**, and it has the following characteristics:

1. It is an m-way search tree that is either empty or has a height $>= 1$.

2. The root node has at least two children (therefore at least one value) and a maximum of $2\lfloor(2m - 2)/3\rfloor + 1$. ($\lfloor x\rfloor$ is the floor of x.)

3. All nonterminal nodes (with $S_i \neq 0$) other than the root node have at least $\lceil(2m - 1)/3\rceil$ children (and therefore at least $\lceil(2m - 1)/3\rceil - 1$ values. ($\lceil x\rceil$ is the ceiling of x.)

4. All terminal nodes (with $S_i = 0$) are at the same level.

5. All nonterminal nodes with k S_is have $k-1$ keys.

The primary difference between the B-tree and the B*-tree is that the interior nodes of a B-tree are at least half-full of tuples, and the B-*tree is at least two-thirds full of tuples. Fewer nodes are necessary with the B*-trees to store the same number of keys.

For example, consider trees of order 7. The minimum and maximum number of children and keys for a B-tree of order 7 is ($m = 7$):

```
root node       –       (2, m)  = 2 <= children <= 7
                                = 1 <= keys     <= 6
interior nodes  –   (⌈m/2⌉, m)  = 4 <= children <= 7
                                = 3 <= keys     <= 6
```

The minimum and maximum number of children and keys for the B*-tree of order 7 is

```
root node       –   (2, 2⌊(2m – 2)/3⌋ + 1)  = 2 <= children <= 9
                                            = 1 <= keys     <= 8
interior nodes  –   (⌈(2m – 1)/3⌉, m)       = 5 <= children <= 7
                                            = 4 <= keys     <= 6
```

Notice that interior nodes (nonterminal nodes except the root) of a B-tree of order 7 are half-full, which translates to a minimum of three keys. The maximum number of keys in the root node is twice the minimum number of keys for the interior node, so when an insertion into a full root ($m - 1$ keys) occurs, a split occurs, leaving a minimum number ($\lceil m/2\rceil$ keys) in each of two nodes that are children of the root node. The root node now has

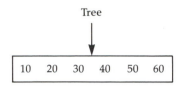

(a) Diagram of B-tree of order 7 with full root node

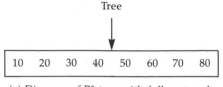

(a) Diagram of B*-tree with full root node

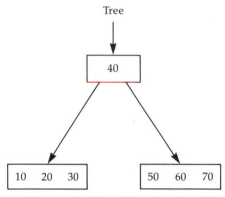

(b) Diagram of B-tree of order 7 when the value 70
is inserted

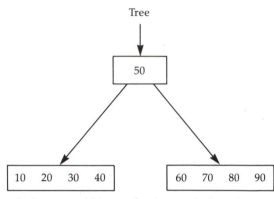
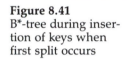

(b) Diagram of B*-tree of order 7 with the value 90

Figure 8.40
B-tree during inser-
tion of keys at first
split

Figure 8.41
B*-tree during inser-
tion of keys when
first split occurs

only one key. For example, Figure 8.40(a) shows a B-tree of order 7 after six keys have been inserted. The root node is full with $m - 1$ or six keys. If the key 70 is inserted, the root node is split, leaving the middle key in the root node and $\lceil m/2 \rceil$ or three keys in each of the children (Figure 8.40(b)).

The interior nodes of a B*-tree of order 7 are two-thirds full so the minimum number of keys is four. For the same situation to occur with B*-trees, the root node has to have enough keys to allow a split that leaves each of the two children two-thirds full. The root node for a B*-tree has to allow a maximum of twice the minimum number of keys in an interior node $(2\lfloor (2m - 2)/3 \rfloor)$. When an insertion causes a split of the root node, the root node has the middle key, and the two children are two-thirds full $(\lceil (2m - 1)/3 \rceil - 1)$.

Figure 8.41 illustrates a B*-tree with a full root node. When the key 70 is inserted, the root node retains the middle key, 50, and each of the children have the minimum number of keys (Figure 8.41(b)). As the keys 100 and 110 are inserted into the B*-tree in Figure 8.41, and the right child of the root fills, the insertion of key 120 causes a split in a B-tree node. In a B*-tree insertions into a full node cause a local rotation to a sibling that is not full. Figure 8.42(b) presents the B*-tree after insertions of keys 100, 110,

Figure 8.42
B-tree and B*-tree
with insertions

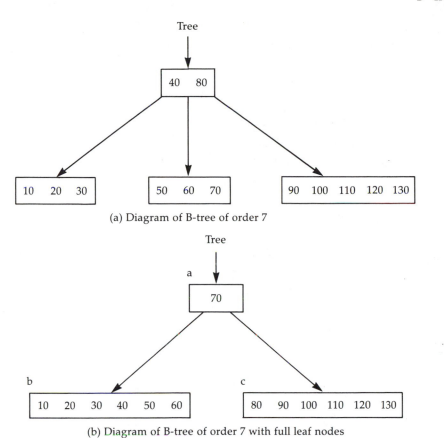

(a) Diagram of B-tree of order 7

(b) Diagram of B-tree of order 7 with full leaf nodes

120, and 130. A local rotation with the left sibling involves moving the parent value to the left sibling node and moving the first key in the full node to the parent node to make room for insertion of a key into a full node. The B*-tree has two leaf nodes that are full with a total of 13 keys in the tree of three nodes (Figure 8.42(b)). The same 13 keys inserted in order into a B-tree (Figure 8.42(a)) requires a total of four nodes; the B-tree uses more space.

The insertion into a full node of a B*-tree with full sibling nodes causes a split of the keys in the two sibling nodes into three sibling nodes. For example, the insertion of the key 140 into the B*-tree in Figure 8.42(b) causes a split of node c—a rotation cannot be done because node b is also full. However, moving the middle key (110) to the parent node and splitting the remaining keys into two nodes leaves only three keys in each of the split nodes—a number below the minimum of two-thirds. A split for a node in a B*-tree must involve splitting the keys from the full node that requires the insertion (node c, with m keys after the insertion) and a full sibling (node b, with $m - 1$ keys) into three nodes, each of which are at least two-thirds full with ($\lfloor(2m - 2)/3\rfloor$, $\lfloor(2m - 1)/3\rfloor$, and $\lfloor 2m/3\rfloor$ keys respectively.

Where key $_{\text{parent}}$ is the key in the parent node that separates the two siblings the equations for determining the number of keys to be stored in each node are as follows:

1. node b has lowest $\lfloor(2m - 2)/3\rfloor$ keys or

    $\text{key}_1 \ldots \text{key}_{\lfloor(2m - 2)/3\rfloor}$ from original node b

    $= \text{key}_1 \ldots \text{key}_4$ from original node b

2. parent node of b has $\text{key}_{\lfloor(2m - 2)/3\rfloor + 1} = \text{key}_{\lfloor(2m + 1)/3\rfloor}$ or

    $= \text{key}_5$ from original node b

3. node c has next $\lfloor(2m - 1)/3\rfloor$ keys or

    $= \text{key}_{\lfloor(2m - 2)/3\rfloor + 2} \ldots \text{key}_{m - 1}$ from original node b, $\text{key}_{\text{parent}}$ and

    $\text{key}_1 \ldots \text{key}_{\lfloor(m - 1)/3\rfloor}$ from original node c

    $= \text{key}_6$ from original node b, 70, and

    $\text{key}_1 \ldots \text{key}_2$ from original node c

4. parent node of c has $\text{key}_{\lfloor(m - 1)/3\rfloor + 1}$ from original node c

    $= \text{key}_3$ from original node c

Figure 8.43
B-tree and B*-tree after the addition of the value 140

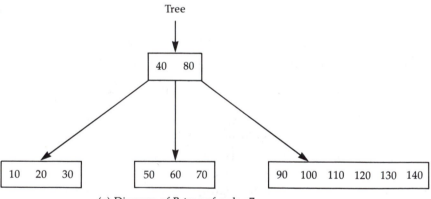

(a) Diagram of B-tree of order 7

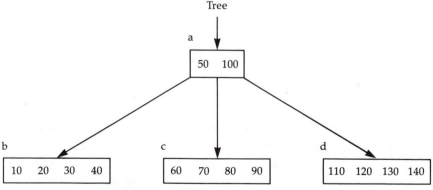

(b) Diagram of B*-tree of order 7, split from two into three nodes

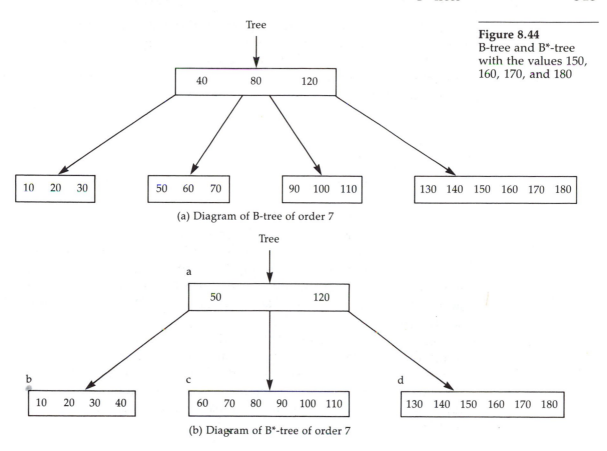

Figure 8.44
B-tree and B*-tree
with the values 150,
160, 170, and 180

(a) Diagram of B-tree of order 7

(b) Diagram of B*-tree of order 7

5. node d has last $\lfloor 2m/3 \rfloor$ keys or

$$\text{key}_{(\lfloor m-1)/3 \rfloor + 2} \ldots \text{key}_m \text{ from original node c}$$
$$= \text{key}_4 \ldots \text{key}_7 \text{ from original node c}$$

If the original node has no left sibling, the right sibling can be used in the same way. Figure 8.43(b) illustrates the B*-tree after nodes b and c have been split into nodes b, c, and d. A B-tree with the same keys is shown in Figure 8.43(a). Notice that both trees now have the same number of nodes; the B-tree has two leaf nodes at a minimum level and one leaf node at a maximum level, and the B*-tree has all leaf nodes at a minimum level. Insertions of keys larger than 140 cause a split in the B-tree but not in the B*-tree.

Figure 8.44 shows both trees after the insertion of keys 150, 160, 170 and 180. The rotation of keys from node d into sibling node c allows the insertions without splitting. The B*-tree still has four nodes after the insertions. The same cannot be said for the B-tree (Figure 8.44(a)), which now has five nodes.

The important characteristic of B*-trees is that each node except the root is at least two-thirds full rather than half full. This improves the search time so that a B*-tree with N keys and between $(\lceil (2m - 1)/3 \rceil - 1)$ and $(m - 1)$ keys in each node requires at worst $\log_{\lceil (2m - 1)/3 \rceil - 1} (N + 1)$ node accesses (disk accesses).

B^+-TREES

A **B^+-tree** is similar to a B-tree with each node at least half-full, except that interior nodes have only keys (no addresses to the records in the data file) and subtree pointers to other nodes. The leaf nodes of a B^+-tree are the only nodes that contain addresses of records in the data file, and all keys appear in the leaf nodes. In addition the leaf nodes are linked in key sequence to facilitate rapid sequential accessing. The nonterminal nodes can contain more keys in the same amount of space than B-trees, so that the height decreases for a large number of keys—a characteristic that leads to shorter search times (fewer disk accesses).

Figure 8.45 shows a B-tree of order 3. The dashed lines indicate addresses of records in the data file. Each tuple contains a key (K), an address of the record in the file with that key (A), and a subtree pointer (S). If the As are deleted from each tuple, each nonterminal node could easily hold one more tuple. The terminal nodes still hold a maximum of two tuples, with the format:

$$S_0, (K_1, A_1, S_1), (K_2, A_2, S_2)$$

The nonterminal nodes contain three tuples of the form:

$$S_0, (K_1, S_1), (K_2, S_2), (K_3, S_3)$$

S_{i-1} points to a subtree with keys less than or equal to K_i, and S_n points to a subtree with keys greater than K_n. Each K_i in the nonterminal nodes indicates the largest key value in the child node addressed by S_{i-1}. A B^+-tree in the format described above with the same key values as the B-tree in Figure 8.45 is shown in Figure 8.46. Notice that node b contains two keys and two subtree pointers, and node c contains two keys and three subtree pointers. This is a unique characteristic of B^+-trees that does not occur with B-trees. Since the nonterminal nodes can contain three tuples instead of two, the height of the B^+-tree does not increase as fast as the height of the B-tree as keys are inserted.

The disadvantage of the B^+-tree is that each search must continue to a terminal level before locating a key. The search of the B-tree locates the key value 50, for example, in the root node; the search of the B^+-tree has to visit a node on all levels to locate 50. The countering advantage is that the B^+-tree usually contains fewer levels than a B-tree.

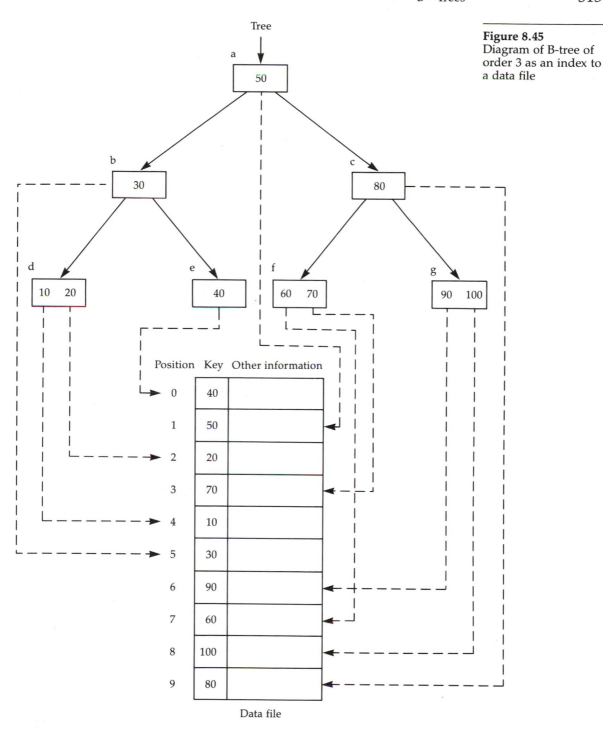

Tree

a

50

b
30

c
80

d
10   20

e
40

f
60   70

g
90   100

Position	Key	Other information
0	40	
1	50	
2	20	
3	70	
4	10	
5	30	
6	90	
7	60	
8	100	
9	80	

Data file

Figure 8.45
Diagram of B-tree of order 3 as an index to a data file

The B⁺-tree structure is a common structure for storing an index to a data file where each terminal node is a block of records in a data file, and the nonterminal nodes constitute the index for the data file. The nonter-

Figure 8.46
Diagram of B*-tree of
order 3 as an index to
a data file

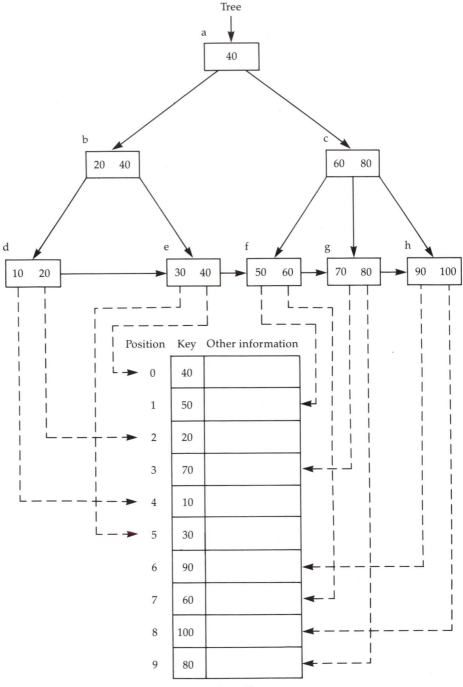

Data file

minal nodes are usually stored in an index file separate from the data file.
Examples of the use of the B$^+$-tree for indexing a data file are IS files used
on CDC machines and VSAM files used on IBM machines. Both examples
will be described in detail in Chapter 9.

CASE STUDY 8.1: THE CAR-RENTAL AGENCY

The car-rental agency relative master file created in Chapter 7 allowed rapid access to individual records by hashing the key value to determine the position of the record in the file. One major disadvantage of the relative file organization is that the records are no longer stored physically in key order; the hashing function randomly distributes the records throughout the file space. Sequential listings of the file in key order are no longer possible. Sequential access to keys was sacrificed to provide rapid access to individual records.

A B-tree structure of the key values could provide a sequential index to the records in the car-rental agency relative master file created and updated in Chapter 7. A B-tree of order 5 requires that interior nodes have a minimum of three children or two keys. Table 5.1 in Chapter 5 is a listing of the transaction file T1 used to create the car-rental agency relative master file shown in Figure 7.32 in Chapter 7. The B-tree structure of order 5 that provides sequential access to the records consists of the key values, which are inserted into the B-tree as each record is inserted into the relative master file. The resulting B-tree is illustrated in diagram form in Figure 8.47, and the file containing the nodes of the B-tree with subtree pointers (subtree pointer S) is listed in Table 8.1.

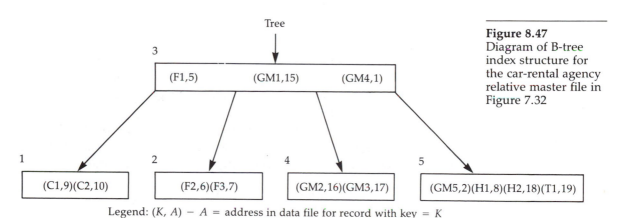

Figure 8.47
Diagram of B-tree index structure for the car-rental agency relative master file in Figure 7.32

Legend: $(K, A) - A$ = address in data file for record with key = K

Table 8.1 B-tree file of nodes for B-tree in Figure 8.47

	n	S_0	K_1	A_1	S_1	K_2	A_2	S_2	K_3	A_3	S_3	K_4	A_4	S_4
0	3													
1	2	0	C1	9	0	C2	10	0						
2	2	0	F2	6	0	F3	7	0						
3	3	1	F1	5	2	GM1	15	4	GM4	1	5			
4	2	0	GM2	16	0	GM3	17	0						
5	4	0	GM5	2	0	H1	8	0	H2	18	0	T1	19	0

The address of the root node is stored in the first integer field of record 0 in the file (3 indicates that the root is in record 3). The root node (record 3) points to subtree nodes in positions 1, 2, 4, and 5. The B-tree is stored externally in the B-tree file, and the nodes accessed as needed. An inorder traversal of the nodes in the B-tree file provides a sequential listing of the records in the file in order by key values:

```
Algorithm Inorder_Traversal (record_number)

Input (B_tree_file, node, record_number)
p ← node.s0
If p <> 0
     Inorder_traversal (p)

For i ← 1 To node.n
     Output (node.tuple[i].key)
     If node.tuple[i].s <> 0
          Inorder_traversal (node.tuple[i].s)
```

In this case the traversal is called initially with the root as the parameter:

```
Input (B_tree_file, head_node, 0)
root ← head_node.n
Inorder_traversal (root)
```

Transaction file T2 (Figure 5.3) is applied next to the car-rental agency relative master file, resulting in the data file in Figure 7.33. As GM6 is added to the relative master file, it is also added to the B-tree file resulting in the B-tree structure shown in Figure 8.48 and corresponding file contents in Table 8.2. The key value GM6 is added into node 5, which causes a split into node 6, adding key H1 into the parent node 3. The B-tree file must keep current with the contents and location of keys in the relative master file so that the data file may be listed sequentially after each update run.

Figure 8.48
Diagram of B-tree index structure for the car-rental agency relative master file in Figure 7.33

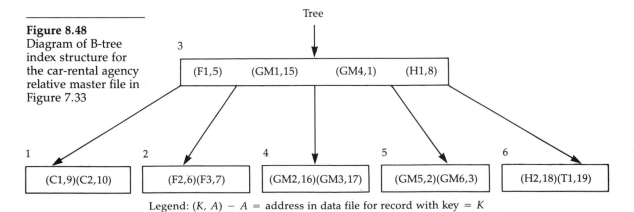

Legend: $(K, A) - A$ = address in data file for record with key = K

The last transaction file T3 (Table 5.5) is applied to the relative master file resulting in additions and deletions shown in Figure 7.34. As the additions and deletions are made to the relative master file, they must also be made to the B-tree file. Figure 8.49 and Table 8.3 represent the B-tree after deleting F1, adding GM7, and deleting T1. The deletion of F1 with two child nodes—at a minimum—causes nodes 1 and 2 to be merged into node

Table 8.2 B-tree file of nodes for B-tree in Figure 8.47

	n	S_0	K_1	A_1	S_1	K_2	A_2	S_2	K_3	A_3	S_3	K_4	A_4	S_4
0	3													
1	2	0	C1	9	0	C2	10	0						
2	2	0	F2	6	0	F3	7	0						
3	3	1	F1	5	2	GM1	15	4	GM4	1	5	H1	8	6
4	2	0	GM2	16	0	GM3	17	0						
5	4	0	GM5	2	0	GM6	3	0						
6	2	0	H2	18	0	T1	19	0						

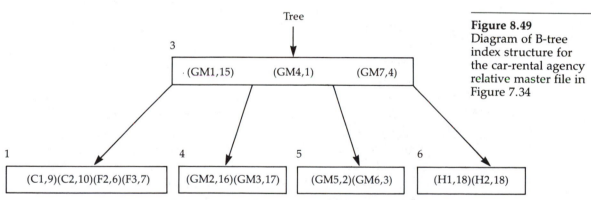

Legend: $(K, A) - A$ = address in data file for record with key $= K$

Figure 8.49
Diagram of B-tree index structure for the car-rental agency relative master file in Figure 7.34

Table 8.3 B-tree file of nodes for B-tree in Figure 8.48

	n	S_0	K_1	A_1	S_1	K_2	A_2	S_2	K_3	A_3	S_3	K_4	A_4	S_4
0	3													
1	2	0	C1	9	0	C2	10	0	F2	6	0	F3	7	0
2														
3	3	1	GM1	15	4	GM4	1	5	GM7	4	6			
4	2	0	GM2	16	0	GM3	17	0						
5	4	0	GM5	2	0	GM6	3	0						
6	2	0	H1	8	6	H2	18	0						

1, leaving node 2 empty. The addition of GM7 causes the tuple with GM7 to be added to node 5, but the subsequent deletion of T1 leaves node 6 with less than the minimum number of keys. As a result, the parent value, H1, is moved into node 6, and the key, GM7, is moved to the parent node. The update routine for the relative master file takes a little longer to execute since changes are made to both the relative master file and the B-tree file. The benefit of the longer execution is that the relative master file may be accessed randomly by hashing or by searching the B-tree as well as sequentially by traversing the B-tree inorder.

SUMMARY

A binary search tree provides the flexibility of a linked list for inserting and deleting nodes and allows access to any node in the tree almost as quickly as a binary search through an array (allowing for disk accesses for each node visited). AVL trees are height-balanced binary trees with random retrievals occurring in $O[\lg(n)]$ time for a tree of n nodes. Further reduction in the number of accesses can be realized with the use of an m-way search tree, which is an m-way (instead of binary) AVL tree. The chapter also discusses a B-tree structure that is a balanced m-way search tree that guarantees that each node is at least half-full of key values. Improvements to the B-tree structure known as B*-trees (which keep each node at least two-thirds full) and B^+-trees (which store only key values and subtree pointers in nonterminal nodes) are discussed. The B^+-tree structure is the common structure for providing indexing to data files (for example, with SIS and VSAM files) that allow both random and sequential access. Algorithms (originally designed by Wirth) for searching an m-way search tree, inserting nodes into a B-tree, and deleting nodes from a B-tree were presented in the chapter. A B-tree external file was built for the car-rental agency case study, and modified as the master file was updated.

For further reading on B-trees see:

Bayer, R. and McCreight, E. "Organization and Maintenance of Large Ordered Indexes," *Acta Informatica*, 1(3):173–189, 1972.

Knuth, Donald E. *The Art of Computer Programming. Vol. 3, Sorting And Searching*. Reading, MA: Addison-Wesley, 1973.

Key Terms

ancestor	B*-tree
AVL tree	B^+-tree
B-tree	balanced tree

binary search tree	LL rotation
child	LR rotation
degree of a node	*m*-way search trees
degree of a tree	overflow technique
descendant	parent
height	RL rotation
height-balanced binary tree	root
immediate predecessor	root of a subtree
immediate successor	RR rotation
inorder	sibling nodes
leaf nodes	skewed
level	terminal nodes

Exercises

1. Describe the difference between a binary search tree and an *m*-way search tree.

2. If an AVL tree is a balanced binary search tree, what is a balanced *m*-way search tree?

3. A 16-way search tree contains how many keys and how many subtree pointers?

4. For a B-tree of order 9, what are the minimum and maximum number of key values in the root node?

5. For a B-tree of order 9, what are the minimum and maximum number of key values in the nonterminal nodes?

6. What is the maximum number of nodes in a B-tree of order 5 with a height of 3? What is the maximum number of keys?

7. How many nodes need to be visited in the worst case to find a key in a B-tree of order 4 with 243 keys?

8. Draw the B-tree of order 6 after each insertion of the following keys: 25, 26, 24, 39, 32.

9. Insert the following keys into the B-tree in exercise 8: 9, 28, 45, 13. Show the tree structure after each insertion.

10. Continue by inserting the following keys into the B-tree in exercise 9: 41, 5, 23, 19, 27, 6, 14, 34, 21, 31, 11, 28. Draw the tree after each insertion.

11. Using the B-tree in exercise 10, draw the tree after deletion of each of the following keys: 26, 21, 11, 9, 45, 13, 39, 6, 14.

12. Repeat exercises 8 through 11 for a B*-tree of order 6.

13. Describe the difference between a B-tree, a B*-tree, and a B$^+$-tree.

14. Write an algorithm to perform the overflow technique used by B*-trees when a node becomes full and has a sibling node that is not full.

15. Write the algorithm to perform the three-way split of key values from two full nodes of a B*-tree into three nodes. The node with m keys has a full left sibling node.

16. Describe which keys are split into which nodes for the three-way splitting technique explained in the chapter where the node with m keys (more than maximum) has a right sibling node that is full. (In the chapter the node with m keys had a left sibling node that was full.) The process is symmetric to the one described in the chapter.

17. Repeat exercise 15 for the symmetric process described in exercise 16.

Programming Problems

1. Write a program that builds a B-tree of order 3 (stored externally) for a sequence of key values.

2. Write a program that lists the key values in the B-tree built in problem 1 in sequential order.

3. Write a program that searches the B-tree built in problem 1.

4. Write a program that performs insertions and deletions to the B-tree built in problem 1.

5. Write a program to implement the overflow algorithm written in exercise 14.

6. Write a program to implement the three-way splitting technique for B*-trees written in exercise 15.

7. Write a program to input the hashed file created in programming problems 6 or 8 from Chapter 7 (input in sequential order by relative record number) and build the three-way B-tree to be used in listing the part numbers in sequence. Each node of the B-tree should have the following contents:

n = the number of key values

S0 = the record number of the subtree with values less than K1

Two tuples of the form (Ki, Ai, Si) where i = 1, . . .,n
   Ki = a part number
   Ai = the relative record number within the hashed file where part number Ki can be found
   Si = the record number of the subtree with values greater than Ki

M = 3, so the maximum value of n is M − 1 or 2, so each node may have as many as two key values (Ki) and three subtrees (Si)

8. Input the three-way B-tree created in problem 7, then output it, listing the contents of the file.

9. Use the B-tree to print an inorder traversal that results in a sequential listing of the relative file.

10. Apply the instructions in problems 7 through 9 to a B-tree of order 7.

Chapter 9

Indexed Sequential File Organization

PREVIEW

SEQUENTIAL FILE OPERATION is limited to sequential access of the records in the file. Sequential files do not provide direct access to individual records in the file. Relative file organization provides rapid access to individual records in the file by establishing a predictable relationship between the key used to identify an individual record and that record's relative address on the file. Sequential access of a relative file may or may not be meaningful, depending on the physical ordering of the records in the file. Hashing is usually used to randomly access records on a relative file, resulting in no relationship between the logical ordering and physical ordering of records in the file. The B-tree structure for a hashed file provides indexed random files whereby the key is hashed to randomly access the record, or the B-tree is accessed as the index for the hashed file to access the file sequentially. The chapters that follow will look at several ways of providing both sequential and random access to a data file.

This chapter contains a comprehensive description of common implementations of indexed sequential organization, in which records are stored sequentially in data blocks and an index is used to access the data blocks either randomly or sequentially. Included in the discussion are implementations that use a tree structure, such as the B^+-tree, for storing the indexes. Those implementations studied include: SIS files (used on CDC computers) that use a B^+-tree with no minimum restrictions for the index, ISAM file organization (used on IBM computers) that uses a static structure for the index, and VSAM file organization (more commonly found on IBM computers today) that uses a B^+-tree for the indexes.

STRUCTURING INDEXED SEQUENTIAL FILES

Indexed sequential file organization for a collection of records in a file provides sequential access to the records by one primary key field as well as random access to an individual record by the same primary key field. An indexed sequential file provides the sequential access available with sequential files by storing the records physically in order by a primary key. They make random access available in relative files by including an index of pointers to the sequential data file.

Two common methods exist for structuring indexed sequential files: (1) the index-and-data-blocks method and (2) the cylinder-and-surface indexing method. The index-and-data-blocks method is used on CDC (Control Data Corporation) computers and in VSAM on IBM (International Business Machines) computers; the cylinder-and-surface indexing method is used in ISAM on IBM computers.

INDEX-AND-DATA-BLOCKS METHOD

The **index-and-data-blocks method** used on CDC computers is known as Scope Indexed Sequential **(SIS) file organization**. An SIS file is a collection of data blocks and index blocks. Each data block or index block is transferred by a single I/O instruction. The data blocks are a fixed size and contain a header for the block, a number of logical records, and a number of keys corresponding to the logical records in the data block. The information is arranged as shown in Figure 9.1, where each Ri is a logical record of the file, and each key i is the primary key value for each corresponding record Ri.

The logical records are stored in contiguous positions at one end of the data block and physically ordered by key values to provide sequential access to the data. The keys corresponding to the logical records in the data block are stored in contiguous positions at the other end of the data block. The data block is, therefore, filled from the two ends toward the middle of the block. This allows all unused space (padding) within the block to be in one area. As deletions are made to the data block, records and keys are moved to maintain the records in contiguous positions at one end, keys in contiguous positions at the other end, and unused space in the middle. For example, consider the data block containing three logical records and three keys in Figure 9.2. The deletion of record 2 (104 John Smith) causes record 3 and key 3 to move to respective ends of the data block, so all unused space is in the middle (Figure 9.3). The number of entries in the header is changed from three to two records.

Each record may be fixed or variable in length because each record is preceded by a header word (not shown in previous diagrams) that defines the record length in bytes. The size of the keys is fixed and is stored in the header for the block along with the number of entries (record-key pairs) in the data block.

SIS files contain one or more index blocks to provide rapid access to the data blocks. The index blocks are all of a fixed size and contain a header and pairs of keys and addresses corresponding to the data blocks. Each index block in an SIS file has the format shown in Figure 9.4. The data blocks and index blocks are organized in a B^+-tree.

Each key i is the lowest key value in data block i, each address i is the pointer to data block i, and

$$\text{key } 1 < \text{key } 2 < \ldots < \text{key } i < \ldots < \text{key } n$$

In this case there are n entries in the index block. The number of entries (key, address pairs) in the index block is stored in the header for the index block. The key-address pairs are maintained in ascending order by key values to provide rapid searching during random access. The data blocks

Header	R1	R2	R3	. . . Padding . . .	Key 3	Key 2	Key 1

Figure 9.1
Format of a data block on CDC computers

3	101 Jane Doe	104 John Smith	106 Sally Adams		106	104	101

Figure 9.2
Data block containing three records and keys

2	101 Jane Doe	106 Sally Adams		106	101

Figure 9.3
Data block after deletion of one record

Header (no. of entries)	
Key 1	Address 1
Key 2	Address 2
Key 3	Address 3
⋮	⋮
Key i	Address i
⋮	⋮
Key n	Address n
padding	

Figure 9.4
Format of an index block on CDC computers

are linked in sequential order to provide fast sequential access. Figure 9.5 is an example of an SIS file with three data blocks and one level 0 index block.

To access a record randomly with key k, the entries in the level 0 index block are scanned until the first key in the index block larger than the key k is located. The previous entry points to the data block that should contain the record with key k. The data block pointed to by the entry in the level 0 index block is accessed, and the logical records are scanned for the record with key k. To access the SIS file sequentially, the data blocks are accessed in order of the key-address entries in the level 0 index blocks from key-address 1 to key-address n. As each data block is accessed, the logical records within are accessed in physical order.

Suppose the record with key 109 in the SIS file below is to be accessed. The level 0 index block is scanned starting with key 101. The first key value in the level 0 index block larger than key 109 is 111. The key previous to 111 is 107, which points to the second data block and should contain the record with key 109 if it is present. The second data block is accessed, and the keys of the data block are searched to locate key 109. Key 109 is found to be the second key, so the second record is the record being sought, namely: 109 Pete Lama.

When updating the SIS files, logical records are maintained in sequence by ascending key values within the data blocks, and entries are maintained in sequence by ascending key values within the level 0 data block. Additions of logical records to the SIS file may cause a data block to fill by using all the padding space in the middle of the data block. When attempting an addition to a full data block, the data block is split into two data blocks to allow for the expansion.

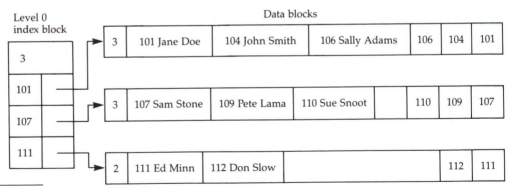

Figure 9.5
SIS file with three data blocks and one level 0 index block

During a **data block split**, roughly one-half of the original logical records in the data block remain along with the corresponding keys, and the number of entries recorded in the data block header is changed. The other remaining logical records from the original data block are written to a new data block with the number of entries being recorded in the header for the new data block. The lowest key value in the new data block and a pointer to the new data block form a new entry that is inserted into the level 0 index block in sequence by the keys. The data blocks do not necessarily have to be in contiguous positions; the level 0 index block stores the keys and pointers of the data blocks in sequence to allow either random or sequential access to the data blocks.

The number of logical records that remain in the data blocks is described above as roughly one-half because the decision concerning where the data block is to be split is actually based on where the new record should be inserted in sequence. For the SIS file in Figure 9.5, suppose a record with the data

```
105 Hal Hacker
```

is added to the file. To decide into which data block the new record should be added, the searching routine used to locate an existing record is performed. If the record with key value 105 is present, it resides in the first data block with the lowest key of 101. The new record should then be added to the same data block since the lowest value of the next data block is larger than 105 (107). Data block 1 is accessed, found to be full, and split into two data blocks to allow for the addition of record 105 in key sequence. The record with keys 101 and 104 remain in the original data block but the last record has a key higher than 105 (106). Record 105 is inserted at the beginning of a new data block, then record 106 is moved from the original data block and stored in the contiguous location following record 105. No shifting of records within a block is necessary to store the records in key sequence. A new key-address entry for the new data block must be added into the index block. The resulting SIS file is shown in Figure 9.6.

By making the split at the insertion location rather than splitting half the records to a new data block, then moving to allow an addition of a new record, the movement of records is minimized. By inserting the record 105 in a new data block instead of following 104, free space is available in both blocks for further additions.

If enough new data blocks are added to the SIS file to fill up the space in the level 0 index block, the level 0 index block is split in much the same manner. Part of the original entries remain in the level 0 index block, and the other entries move to a new level 0 (sibling) index block. The location of the split actually depends on where the new entry should be inserted in

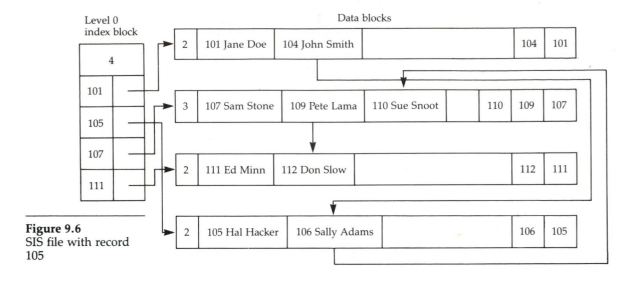

Figure 9.6
SIS file with record
105

the key sequence. Since there are now two level 0 index blocks, a new and higher level 1 index block is added, which contains an entry for each level 0 index block. The first entry is the lowest key value in the original level 0 index block and a pointer to the index block. The second entry is the lowest key value in the new level 0 index block and a pointer to the index block. When the level 1 index block fills, the split of the level 1 index block occurs, causing the addition of a level 2 index block.

Suppose a record with the following data

```
108 Larry Loper
```

is added to the SIS file in Figure 9.6. A search of the level 0 index block yields a pointer to the data block beginning with key 107 because it is the block for inserting record 108. Since the data block is full, it must be split with record 107 remaining in the data block and record 108 being inserted into a new data block. Records 109 and 110 are copied to the new data block. The data blocks now contain data as shown in Figure 9.7.

An entry for the new data block with 108 as the lowest key should be added to the level 0 index block. If the level 0 index block is full, it is split at the first key entry larger than 108, entry 108 is moved to a new level 0 index block, and entry 111 is moved to follow 108. Figure 9.8 presents the new SIS file with two level 0 index blocks and a level 1 index block. Since two level 0 index blocks exist, a level 1 index block is created with the same format as the level 0 index block of key-address pairs, except the address in each entry is a pointer to a level 0 index block with the corresponding key. In the level 1 index block in Figure 9.8, the first entry is key value 101 with a pointer to the level 0 index block, which contains the lowest key value 101. The second entry is key value 108 with a pointer to the level 0

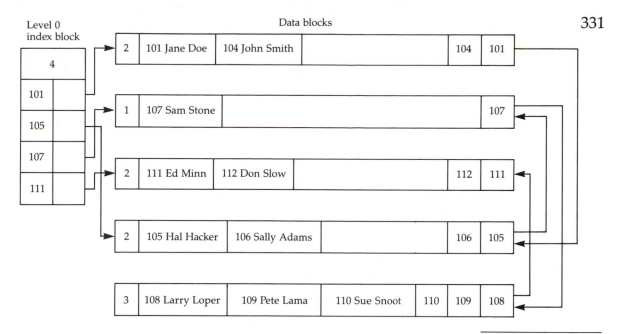

Figure 9.7
SIS file with record 108

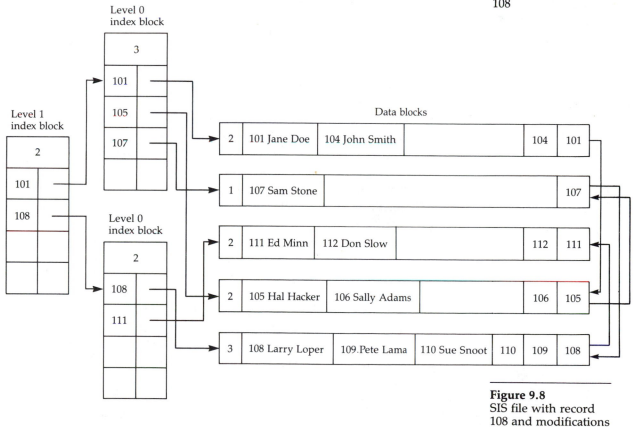

Figure 9.8
SIS file with record 108 and modifications to index blocks

index block with the lowest key value 108. (We assume, in this case, that each of the level 0 index blocks can point to as many as four data blocks as illustrated in Figures 9.7 and 9.8.)

The SIS method of indexed file organization allows for dynamic additions and deletions to the file without much reorganization since the data blocks and index blocks are not necessarily in contiguous positions. The time it takes to retrieve data from the data blocks is not affected by the splitting of index blocks as long as the primary level of index blocks (where the level 0 index blocks are at the lowest level) remains only one index block.

To access an SIS file with several levels of index blocks, the primary level is searched to find a pointer to the level $n - 1$ index block. The level $n - 1$ index block is scanned to locate a pointer to the level $n - 2$ index block. The process continues until the level 0 index block (found by chasing pointers) is scanned to locate a pointer to the one data block that should contain the desired data.

Deletions of logical records from a data block may empty the data block of all logical records and keys, in which case the data block is freed (or chained to other free data blocks for use later). The entry for this data block in the level 0 index block is removed. Should this entry be the first entry in the level 0 index block, a modification to the level 1 index block is in order.

To illustrate the changes necessary as a result of deletions from the file, suppose the record with key 107 is deleted from the SIS file in Figure 9.8. Since 107 is the only record in the data block, the number of entries in the header for the data block becomes 0, the data block is freed, and the key-address entry for 107 in the level 0 index block is removed. If there were key-address entries in the level 0 index block below entry 107, they would be moved up so all the empty space were in contiguous locations. The number of entries in the header of the level 0 index block is decremented to two. The resulting contents of index and data blocks after the deletion of 107 is illustrated in Figure 9.9.

A number of changes must take place during the deletion of the first record from a data block that is the first block referenced in a level 0 index block. For example, if the record with the key 101 is deleted from the file in Figure 9.9, the other records and keys in the data block move toward the ends of the data block (Figure 9.10), and the number of entries in the header becomes 1. Since 101 was the first record in the data block, the key-address entry for the block starting with 101 in the level 0 index block must be changed to reveal that 104 is the starting record in the data block. Similarly, since 101 is the first key-address entry in the level 0 index block, and it is changed to 104, the level 1 index block that is the parent must have the corresponding entry changed from 101 to 104. All levels of index blocks that contain record 101 must be changed to 104 to indicate the deletion of 101 from the data file.

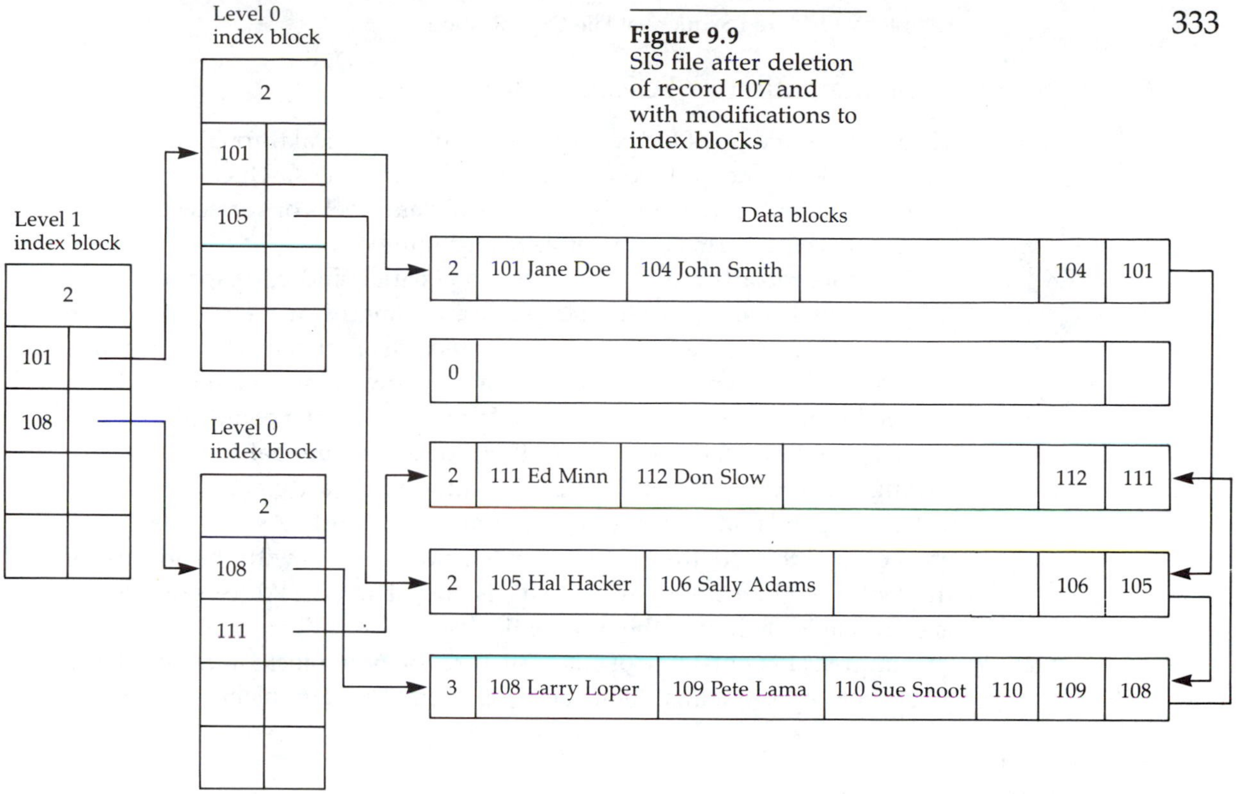

Level 0
index block

Figure 9.9
SIS file after deletion
of record 107 and
with modifications to
index blocks

2	
101	
105	

Level 1
index block

2	
101	
108	

Data blocks

| 2 | 101 Jane Doe | 104 John Smith | | | 104 | 101 |

| 0 | | | | |

Level 0
index block

2	
108	
111	

| 2 | 111 Ed Minn | 112 Don Slow | | | 112 | 111 |

| 2 | 105 Hal Hacker | 106 Sally Adams | | | 106 | 105 |

| 3 | 108 Larry Loper | 109 Pete Lama | 110 Sue Snoot | 110 | 109 | 108 |

Level 0
index block

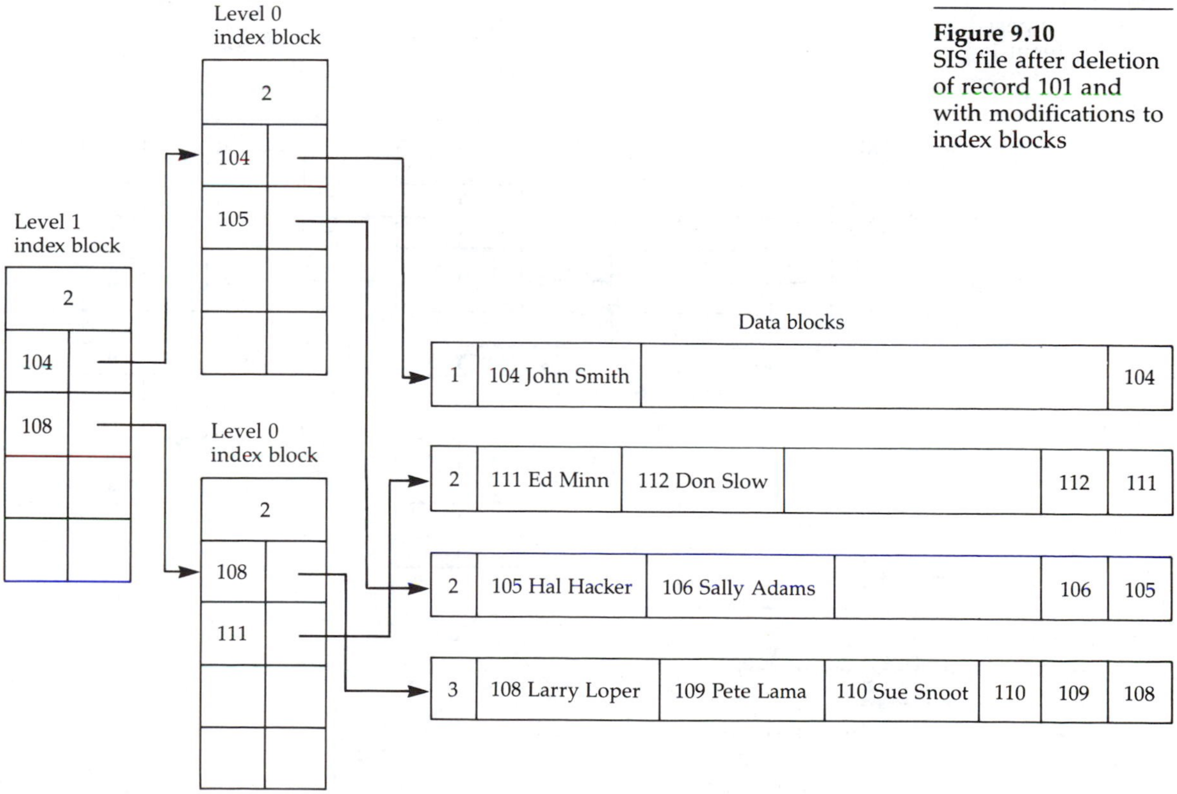

Figure 9.10
SIS file after deletion
of record 101 and
with modifications to
index blocks

2	
104	
105	

Level 1
index block

2	
104	
108	

Data blocks

| 1 | 104 John Smith | | 104 |

| 2 | 111 Ed Minn | 112 Don Slow | | | 112 | 111 |

Level 0
index block

2	
108	
111	

| 2 | 105 Hal Hacker | 106 Sally Adams | | | 106 | 105 |

| 3 | 108 Larry Loper | 109 Pete Lama | 110 Sue Snoot | 110 | 109 | 108 |

Implementation in TURBO Pascal

The implementation of indexed sequential files in Pascal through the index-and-data-blocks method requires the use of relative files, which allow rapid access to individual records. The address of data blocks or surfaces is stored in the indexes in terms of a relative record number.

The data records are fixed in size, so separate and corresponding key fields for each record in the data block are unnecessary. Each data block contains a fixed number of fixed-size data records. Each index block contains a fixed number of entries. Without knowing how many data records there will be in the file, the number of levels of index blocks could continue to grow beyond storage capacity. As the indexed sequential file is created, storing data records in data blocks, the index blocks are created as well. As a data block fills, an entry is stored in an index block. As the data blocks are stored in the file, the B^+-tree of index blocks grows with the address of the root saved in memory until the file is built. Then the address of the root is stored in location 0 of the B^+-tree file.

Figure 9.11 is a diagram of data structures of index blocks and data blocks as an indexed sequential file is being created. The data blocks are labeled

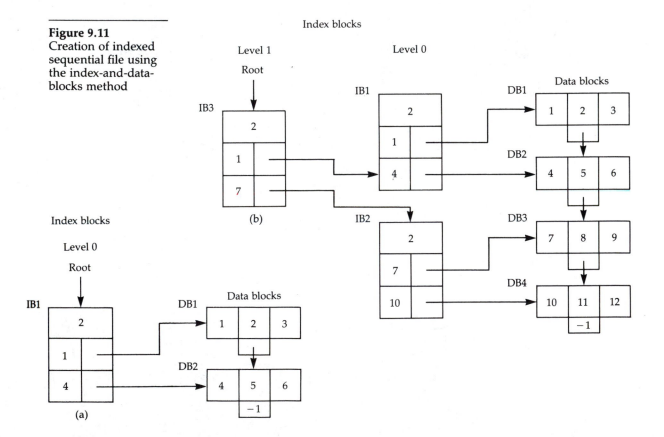

Figure 9.11
Creation of indexed sequential file using the index-and-data-blocks method

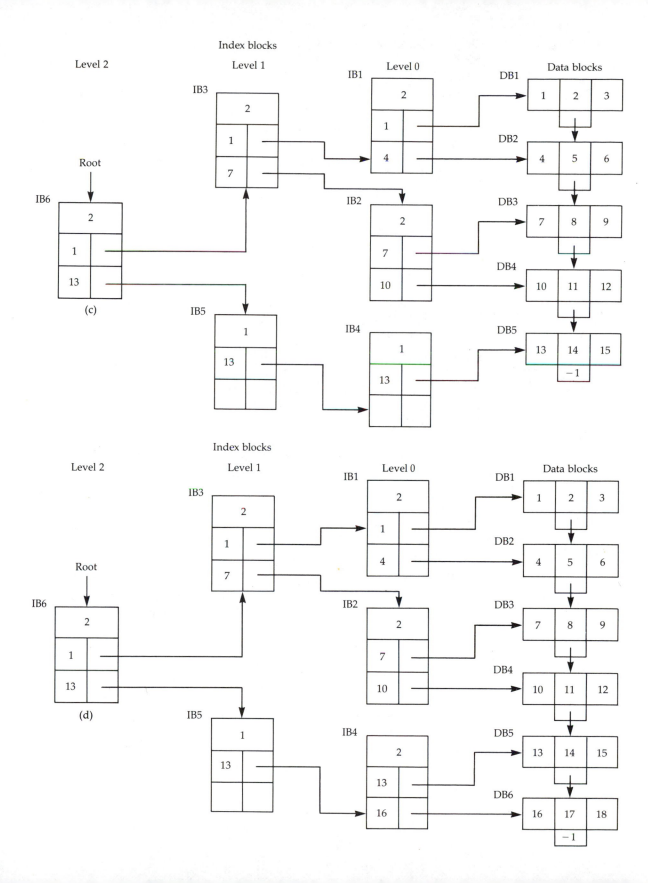

DB*d*, where *d* indicates the location where the block will be stored in the relative data file. The index blocks are labeled IB*i*, where *i* indicates that the index block is written to location *i* of the index block file. The address of the index block at the root of the index structure is written to location 0 of the index blocks file for easy retrieval.

The maximum number of entries for each data block is three. The maximum number of entries for each index block is two, and each entry has a key field and an address field as shown in Figure 9.12. As each data block is filled, the first key in the data block and the address of the data block form the key-address entry, which is added to the tree structure of index blocks. The index block structure is basically a B^+-tree with no minimum requirements for the number of entries in the index blocks. As index blocks fill, a split occurs at the point where the last key-address is inserted, and a sibling level 0 index block is created.

Figure 9.11(a) illustrates the data and index blocks created after two data blocks have been written to the file. Figure 9.11(b) shows the indexed sequential file after four data blocks have been created. The index structure now has two levels. As the fifth data block is written to the data file (Figure 9.11(c)), a new level 0 index block is created, causing a new index block at level 1 (IB5) and level 2 (IB6). Adding a sixth data block to the file (Figure 9.11(d)), adds a new key address entry to the level 0 index block, and the index structure retains the same number of blocks.

The pseudocode for creating an indexed sequential file using the index-and-data-blocks method is presented in Algorithm 9.1. The routine Insert_Into_Index_Blocks is a modification of the insertion algorithm for B-trees.

To search the indexed sequential file created by Algorithm 9.1, the top-level index block is input and scanned first to locate the address of the next lower-level index block. The next lower-level index block is input, and index blocks are scanned until the lowest-level index block is searched and yields the address of a data block. The data block is input and searched for a particular record. The index block numbers and the particular entry selected

Figure 9.12
Index block and data
block layout

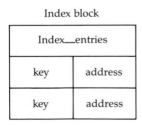

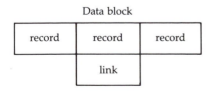

Algorithm 9.1   Create Indexed Sequential File

```
            root ← −1
            db ← 0
            data_block_number ← 1
            next_index_location ← 2
            While Not end of input
                input (record)
                db ← db + 1
                data_block [db] ← record
                If db = MAX_DATA_ENTRIES
                    Data_Block_Full
                    db ← 0


            If db <> 0
                Data_Block_Full
                { change link of last data block to −1 }
            Input (data_blocks_file, data_block, data_block_number − 1)
            data_block.link ← −1
            Output (data_blocks_file, data_block, data_block_number − 1)


            next_available_data_block_location ← data_block_number
            Output (data_blocks_file, next_available_data_block_location, 0)


            Output (index_blocks_file, next_index_location, 1)



    Algorithm Data_Block_Full

            data_block.data_entries ← db
            data_block.link ← data_block_number + 1
            Output (data_blocks_file, data_block, data_block_number)

            hold_tuple.key ← data_block [1].record_key
            hold_tuple.addr ← data_block_number
            Insert_Into_Index_Blocks (hold_tuple, root)
            data_block_number ← data_block_number + 1



    Algorithm Insert_Into_Index_Blocks (hold_tuple, root)

            Search (hold_tuple, root, insert_required)
            If insert_required
                        {
                            new root contains hold_tuple with old root as
                            tuple[1]; tuple = (key, addr[key])
                        }
                    New_Root
```

Algorithm New_Root

```
If root  =  −1   { no root exists yet }
    new_node.level_0_index_block ← TRUE
    new_node.tuple [1] ← hold_tuple
    new_node.entries ← 1
Else
    Input (index_blocks_file, root_node, root)
    new_node.tuple[1].key ← root_node.tuple[1].key
    new_node.tuple[1].addr ← root
    new_node.tuple[2] ← hold_tuple
    new_node.entries ← 2


Output (index_blocks_file, newnode, next_index_location)
root ← next_index_location
Output (index_blocks_file, root, zero)
next_index_location   ← next_index_location  +  1
```

Algorithm Search (VAR hold_Tuple; p; VAR insert_required)

```
If p  =  0
    insert_required ← TRUE
Else
    Input (index_blocks_file, node, p) { node ← contents of p }
    i ← 1
    found ← FALSE
    done ← FALSE
    While Not done And Not found And (i <= node.entries)
        If hold_tuple.key < node.tuple[i].key
            done ← TRUE
            i ← i − 1
        Else
            If hold_tuple = node.tuple[i].key
                found ← TRUE
            Else { > }
                i ← i + 1

If found
    Output ('duplicate entry')
Else { done }
    If node.level_0_index_block
        Insert (hold_tuple, node, p, i, insert_required)
                { hold_tuple into position i + 1 of node }
    Else
        Search (hold_tuple, node.tuple[i].addr, insert_required)

        If insert_required
            Insert (hold_tuple, node, p, i, insert_required)
                { hold_tuple into position i + 1 of node }
```

Algorithm Insert (hold_tuple, node, p, i, insert_required)

```
If node.n < M − 1 { resulting node is large enough for addition }
    insert_required ← FALSE
    For count ← node.n DownTo i + 1
        node.tuple [count + 1] ← tuple [count]

    node.n ← node.n + 1
    tuple [i + 1] ← hold_tuple
    Output (index_blocks_file, node, p)
Else
    { node is full so addition will cause a split }
    Split
```

Algorithm Split

```
new_node.tuple[1] ← hold_tuple
j ← 1
For count ← i + 1 To node.entries
    j ← j + 1
    new_node.tuple[j] ← node.tuple[count]

new_node.entries ← j

new_node.level_0_index_block ← node.level_0_index_block

node.entries ← i − 1
hold_tuple.key ← new_node.tuple[1].key
hold_tuple.addr ← index_block_number

Output (index_blocks_file, newnode, next_index_location)

Output (index_blocks_file, node, p)
next_index_location ← next_index_location  + 1
{ insert_required remains TRUE upon return }
```

for moving on to a lower-level index block are pushed onto a stack. (Each level of the index is being scanned in case changes need to be made in the index blocks.) By stacking the index block numbers and entry values, the search routine can be used by an insertion routine or a deletion routine to modify all index nodes on the path to a selected record in a data block. Algorithm 9.2 presents the search routine in pseudocode.

Maintenance of the indexed sequential file involves changes to existing records, additions of new records to the file, and deletions of existing records. Changes to existing records require that the record to be changed be located through the use of Algorithm 9.2, that the data block containing the located record be input, that the specified changes be made to the record,

Algorithm 9.2   Search for a Record in File

Find (trans_key, data_block_number, location, successful)

    Input (index_blocks_file, root, 0)
    Search_Indexes (transkey, root, successful, data_block_number)
    If successful
        Input (data_block, data_block_number)
        Search_Data_Block (successful)

Algorithm Search_Indexes (key, index_block_number, successful, data_block_number)

    found ← false
    Input (index_blocks_file, index_block, index_block_number)
    i ← 1
    While i ($<=$index_block.entries)
    And Not found
        If key $>$ index_block.tuple[i].key
            i ← i + 1
        Else
            If key $=$ index_block.tuple[i].key
                found ← TRUE
            Else
                found ← TRUE
                i ← i − 1

    If i $>$ index_block.entries
            {
                key was $>$ last key in index block so look in
                last address
            }
        found ← TRUE
        i ← i − 1

    Push (index_block_number, i)
    If found
        If i $=$ 0
            {
                key was $<$ first key in index block so is not
                in the file
            }
            data_block_number ← 0
            found ← FALSE
        Else
            {
                search next level down
            }
            index_block_number ← index_block.tuple[i].addr
            If not index_block.level_0_index_block
            {
                next level down is an index block
            }
            Search_Indexes (successful, data_block_number)
            {

```
                Else next level down is a data block
                    }

    successful ← found

Search_Data_Block (found)

    continue ← TRUE
    found ← FALSE
    i ← 1
    While i <=data_block.entries
    And Not found
    And continue
        If trans_key < data_block.key[i]
                {
                    transkey not found in data block so return i as the
                    location of the first entry > transkey
                    transkey belongs immediately prior to location i
                }
            continue ← FALSE
        Else
            If trans_key = data_block.key[i]
                found ← TRUE
            Else { > }
                i ← i + 1

    location ← i
```

Algorithm 9.3   Change Indexed Sequential File Created in 9.1

```
        Input (data_blocks_file, next_data_location, 0)
        Input (index_blocks_file, root, 0)
        Input (index_blocks_file, next_index_location, 0)
        While Not end of transfile
            Input (transfile, trans_record)
            Find (trans_key, data_block_number, location, found)
            If found
                Make_Changes_In_Data_Block (location)
                Output (data_block, data_block_number)

            Else
                Output ('not found')

        While Not stack_empty
            Pop (p, i)
```

and that the data block containing the record changed be output back to
the same location in the data file from which the record was input. The
pseudocode for changing existing records in the indexed sequential file built
in Algorithm 9.1 is presented in Algorithm 9.3.

Algorithm 9.4 is an expansion of Algorithm 9.3. It allows additions to the existing file as well as changes to existing records. When an addition causes a data block to split, the first key of the new data block is inserted as an entry into the index blocks. The search routine stacked up the index block numbers during the scan of the index blocks to locate a particular

Algorithm 9.4   Change and Add Records in Indexed Sequential File

```
Input (data_blocks_file, next_data_location, 0)
Input (index_blocks_file, root, 0)
Input (index_blocks_file, next_index_location, 1)

While Not end of transfile
    Input (transfile, trans_record)
    Find (trans_key, data_block_number, location, found)
    If found
        Case update_code
            'C': Make_Changes_In_Data_Block (location)
                 Output (data_lock, data_block_number)
                 While Not stack_empty
                 Pop (p, i)

            'A': Output ('duplicate add transaction'
                 While Not stack_empty
                 Pop (p, i)

    Else
        Case update_code
            'C': Output ('no matching record')
                 While Not stack_empty
                 Pop (p, i)

            'A' : If data_block.data_entries = MAX_DATA_ENTRIES
                      new_block.record[1] ← trans_record
                      Split_Data_Block (location)
                      Output (data_blocks_file, new_block, next_data_location)
                      next_data_location ← next_data_location + 1
                  Else
                      With data_block
                          entries ← entries + 1
                          For i ← entries Downto location + 1
                              record [i] ← record [i − 1]
                          record [location] ← trans_record

                  Output (data_blocks_file, data_block, data_block_number)

    Output (data_blocks_file, next_data_location, 0)
    Output (index_blocks_file, root, 0)
    Output (index_blocks_file, last_index_location, 1)
```

Algorithm Split_Data_Block (location)

```
entry ← 1
For i ← location To data_block.entries
      entry ← entry + 1
      new_block.record [entry] ← data_block.record [i]

new_block.entries ← entry
data_block.entries ← location − 1

new_block.link ← data_block.link
data_block.link ← next_data_location

hold_tuple.key ← new_block.key[1]
hold_tuple.addr ← next_data_location

successful ← FALSE
Search_Indexes (hold_tuple.key, root, successful, data_block_number)
                { Search_Indexes from Algorithm 9.2 }
If Not successful
      insert_required ← TRUE
      While Not stack_empty { pop off ancestors }
            Pop (p, i)
                  {
                      p is the address of the index_block at the
                      next higher level; insert into position i + 1
                  }
            If insert_required
                  Input (index_blocks_file, node, p)
                  Insert (hold_tuple, node, p, i, insert_required)
                  { Insert from Algorithm 9.1 }

      If insert_required
                  {
                      new root contains hold_tuple with old root as
                      tuple[1]; tuple = (key, addr[key])
                  }
      New_Root   { New_Root from Algorithm 9.1 }
```

record. The level 0 index block (on top of the stack) is popped off the stack, and the new entry inserted. If an insertion of an entry into an index block causes a split, the flag insert required is returned to indicate that an insertion is required at the parent level.

Deletion of records from the data blocks only affects the index blocks if the first record in a data block is deleted or if a record that is the only record in a data block is deleted. If the first record in a data block is deleted, the key in the index blocks should be replaced by the key of the next record in the data block. If the record deleted is the only record in a data block, the key entry should be removed from all index blocks that contain that key.

For example, consider the index blocks and data blocks from Figure 9.11(d). If the record with key 12 is deleted, no change occurs in the index blocks (Figure 9.13(a)). On the other hand, if the record with key 7 is deleted, all key-address entries in the index blocks that reference key 7 must be changed to reflect the new lowest key in the data block. Key 8 is now the lowest key in data block 3, so the first entry in index block 2 (IB2) references key 8 in data block 3 (DB3), and the second entry in index block 3 (IB3) references key 8 in index block 2 (IB2). Figure 9.13(b) illustrates the index blocks and data blocks after deleting key 7.

If the records with keys 1, 2, and 3 are deleted from the data blocks file, data block 1 (DB1) is left empty. The first entry in the level 0 index block (IB1) that references DB1 is deleted, leaving only one entry in the index block to DB2 (Figure 9.13(c)). Since the first entry of IB1 has been deleted, the first entry in level 1 index block IB3 must be changed to reference the new first entry in IB1, namely key 4. Similarly, the first entry in level 2 index block (and root) IB6 must be replaced by a reference to key 4.

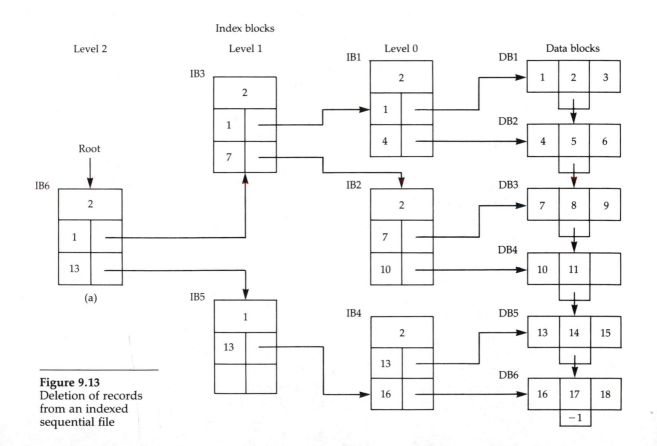

Figure 9.13
Deletion of records from an indexed sequential file

Index blocks

Level 2   Level 1   Level 0   Data blocks

(b)

(c)

Consider the situation where enough deletions have been made to delete all entries from an index block. Suppose that the records with keys 4, 5, and 6 have been deleted from the data blocks file. The single entry in level 0 index block IB1 is now empty. The first key-address entry in level 1 index block IB3 is removed, leaving only a single reference to key 8 in IB3. Since the first entry in IB3 was removed, the reference to key 4 in level 2 index block (the root) must be replaced with the new first entry of IB3, namely a reference to the key 8. The results of deleting the records with keys 4, 5, and 6 are shown in Figure 9.13(d). The information from the index blocks could be stored in fewer index blocks, but the SIS file organization refrains from moving data around any more than necessary. After a number of deletions, the indexed sequential file may need to be reorganized by listing all the records in sequential order and recreating a new SIS file with full data and index blocks.

Algorithm 9.5 is an expansion of Algorithm 9.4 (with new statements indicated with a † to the left). Algorithm 9.5 allows deletions and changes to existing records as well as additions to the existing file.

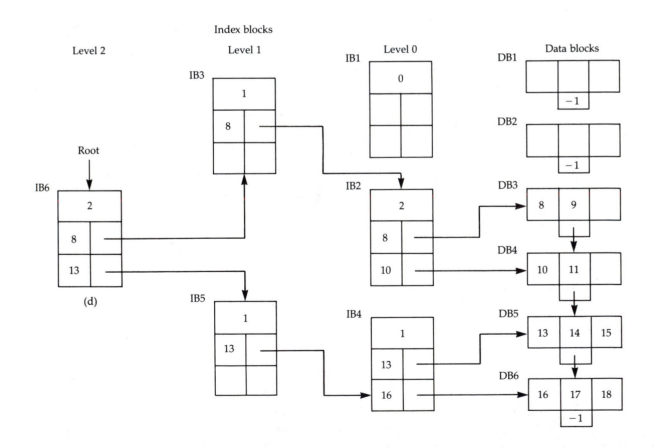

Algorithm 9.5   Change, Add, and Delete Records in Indexed Sequential File

       Input (data_blocks_file, last_data_location, 0)
       Input (index_blocks_file, root, 0)
       Input (index_blocks_file, next_index_location, 1)

       While Not end of transfile
           Input (transfile, trans_record)
           Find (trans_key, data_block_number, location, found)
           If found
               Case update_code
                   'C': Make_Changes_In_Datablock (location)
                       Output (data_blocks_file, data_block, data_block_number)
                       While Not stack_empty
                       Pop (p, i)

                   'A' : Output ('duplicate add transaction')
                       While Not stack_empty
                       Pop (p, i)

  †   'D': key ← data_block.key[1]
  †   If data_block.entries = 1 { delete only entry }
  †   Delete_Index_Entry (DELETE, key, hold_tuple)
  †
  †   Else
  †   For i ← location + 1 To data_block.entries
  †   record [i − 1] ← record [i]
  †
  †   data_block.entries ← data_block.entries − 1
  †   Output (data_blocks_file, data_block, data_block_number)
  †
  †   If location = 1 { delete first entry }
  †   hold_tuple.key ← data_block.key[1]
  †   hold_tuple.addr ← data_block_number
  †   { replace key with hold_tuple entry in parent }
  †   Delete_Index_Entry (REPLACE, key, hold_tuple)

            Else { not found }
               Case update_code
                   'C': Output ('no matching record')

                   'A' : If data_block.entries = MAX_DATA_ENTRIES
                      new_block.record[1] ← trans_record
                      Split_Data_Block (location)
                      next_data_location ← next_data_location + 1
                      Output (data_blocks_file, new_block, next_data_location)

```
                                Else
                                    With  data_block
                                        entries ← entries + 1
                                        For i ← entries Downto location + 1
                                            record [i] ← record [i − 1]

                                        record [location] ← trans_record

                                    Output (data_blocks_file, data_block, data_block_number)

†                           'D': Output ('no matching record')
†                                While Not stack_empty
†                                Pop (p, i)

        Output (data_blocks_file, next_data_location, 0)

        Output (index_blocks_file, root, 0)
        Output (index_blocks_file, next_index_location, 1)


† Algorithm Delete_Index_Entry (action, key, hold_tuple)
†
†       While Not stack_empty
†            Pop (p, i)
†            Input (index_blocks_file, index_block, p)
†            Case action
†                REPLACE : Replace (key, hold_tuple, index_block, p, i, action)
†
†                DELETE   : Delete (key, index_block, p, i, action)
†
†       If action = DELETE { last data block has been deleted }
†            root ← −1


† Algorithm Replace (key, hold_tuple, index_block, p, i, action)
†
†       If index_block.tuple[i].key = key
†            index_block.tuple[i] ← hold_tuple
†            Output (index_blocks_file, index_block, p)
†            action ← REPLACE


† Algorithm Delete (key, index_block, p, i, action)
†
†       key ← index_block,tuple[1].key
†       If index_block.entries = 1 { delete only entry }
†            action ← DELETE
†                      { link around deleted data block }
†            previous ← index_block.tuple[i − 1].addr
†            Input (data_blocks_file, data_block, previous)
†            data_block.link ← index_block.tuple[i + 1].addr
†            Output (data_blocks_file, data_block, previous)
†
```

```
†        Else
†                index_block.entries ← index_block.entries − 1
†                For count ← i To index_block.entries
†                        index_block.tuple[count] ← index_block.tuple[count + 1]
†                Output (index_blocks_file, index_block, p)
†                If i = 1
†                        hold_tuple.key ← index_block.key[1]
†                        hold_tuple.addr ← p
†                                { replace key with hold_tuple entry in parent }
†                        action ← REPLACE
```

CASE STUDY 9.1: THE CAR-RENTAL AGENCY

The same data used in previous chapters will be stored in a SIS file for comparison. The transaction file T1 in Figure 5.2 contains the initial records to be loaded to the file. The records are in sequential order and are loaded to data blocks of size 3 with index blocks holding three entries. Figure 9.14 shows three snapshots of loading the records to the SIS file. Any record can be accessed by first retrieving the root from location 0 of the index blocks file, then retrieving and searching two levels of index blocks, and a final retrieval of a data block. The search for a record that does not exist in the SIS file involves the same process.

The transaction file T2 contains only a single addition of the record with key GM6. The key GM6 should be inserted into data block 4, which is already full (Figure 9.14(c)). As a result, data block 4 is split to data block 6

Figure 9.14
Creation of car-rental agency indexed sequential master file using the index-and-data-blocks method

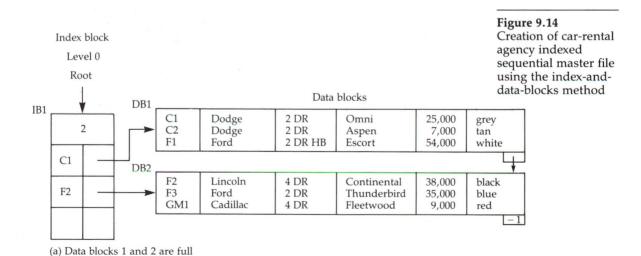

(a) Data blocks 1 and 2 are full

Index blocks

Level 1   Level 0

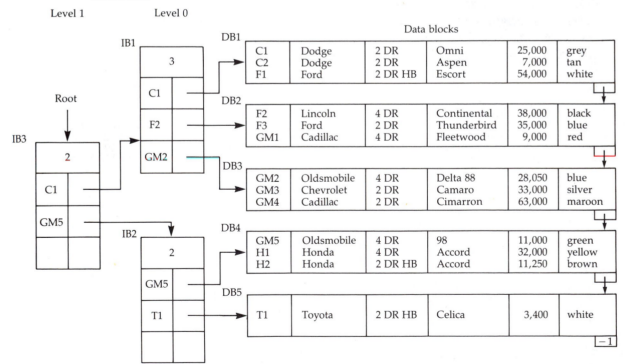

(b) Four full data blocks

Index blocks

Level 1   Level 0

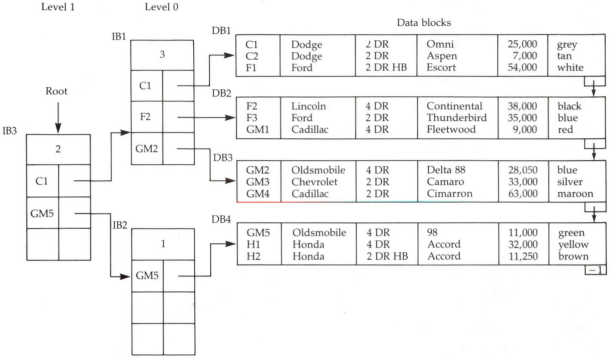

(c) Five data blocks and three index blocks

at the point of insertion, causing a new entry to be added to parent index block IB2 (Figure 9.15).

Transaction file T3 contains several transactions, the net effect of which is shown in Figure 9.16. The record with key F1 is deleted from data block 1, which causes no change in the index block structure. The addition of GM7 into data block 6, which is full, causes a split into data block 7. The key GM7 is inserted into index block 2, causing a split into index block 4 of keys GM7 and T1, with the key GM7 also being inserted into the root index block. A subsequent deletion of the record with the key T1 leaves index block 4 with only one entry and data block 5 empty. Figure 9.16 shows the results of applying transaction file T3.

The car-rental agency master file in Figure 9.16 has two levels of index blocks. Searching for a record in the file involves an input operation to retrieve the location of the root of the index blocks structure, an input operation for an index block on each of the two levels of the structure, and

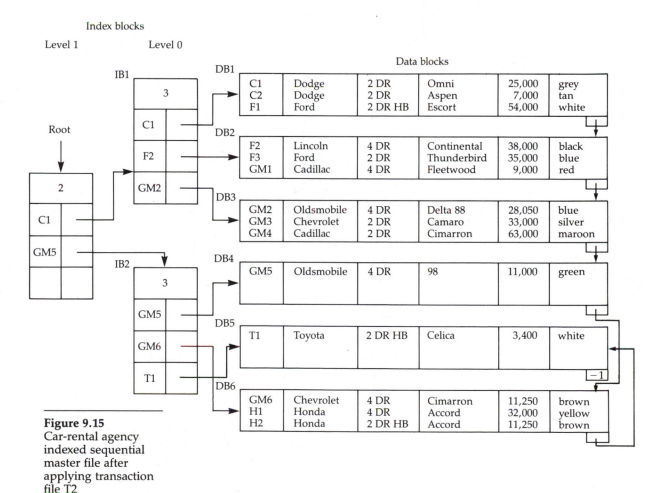

Figure 9.15
Car-rental agency indexed sequential master file after applying transaction file T2

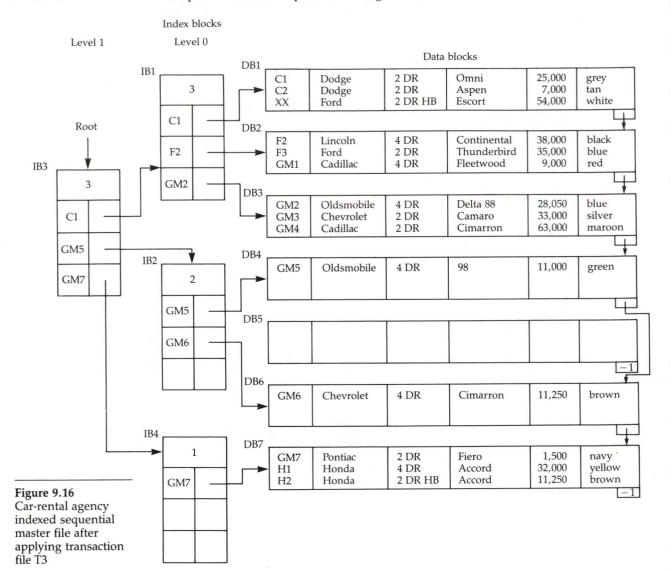

Figure 9.16
Car-rental agency
indexed sequential
master file after
applying transaction
file T3

a fourth input operation to input a data block. Therefore, the search time for accessing a record in the file involves four input operations from secondary memory. Sequentially accessing the indexed file to list the car records in sequence by key involves an inorder traversal of the tree of index blocks as was the case for the B-tree structures in Chapter 8. One of the major advantages of the indexed sequential file organization over relative file organization (in addition to the fact that indexed sequential organization provides both sequential and random access to the data) is that data records are stored in data blocks rather than one data record per record location. The data in the indexed sequential file in Figure 9.16 can be retrieved in sequential order with only six input operations (one input operation per data block). The relative file in Figure 7.34 (which contains the same data) can be retrieved sequentially using the B-tree in Figure 8.49 with 13 input operations (one input operation per record). Of course the index blocks of the index tree need to be input with one input operation per index block, which adds to the number of input operations. But clearly, the structure of indexed sequential files allows the use of blocking, which improves the access time.

CYLINDER-AND-SURFACE INDEXING METHOD

The **cylinder-and-surface indexing method** used on IBM computers is known as Indexed Sequential Access Method **(ISAM) file organization** and is based on the physical characteristics of a magnetic disk. An ISAM file consists of three areas: (1) an index area containing an index to the cylinders of data, (2) a prime data area containing data records, and (3) an independent overflow area. The data of the ISAM file are stored in several cylinders, each consisting of a **surface index** (secondary-level index) to data records stored within the cylinder, **a prime data area** of data records stored sequentially by a primary key, and a **cylinder overflow area**. The surface index is usually stored on surface 0, the prime data area is usually stored on surfaces 1 through $n - 1$, and the cylinder overflow area is usually surface n of the cylinder. Each surface of the prime data area is fixed in size and contains data records stored in ascending order by a primary key value. The first cylinder of the ISAM file contains only the **cylinder indexes** (top-level indexes), and the last cylinder contains the **independent overflow area**. The prime data area resides between the first and last cylinders. Figure 9.17 is a layout

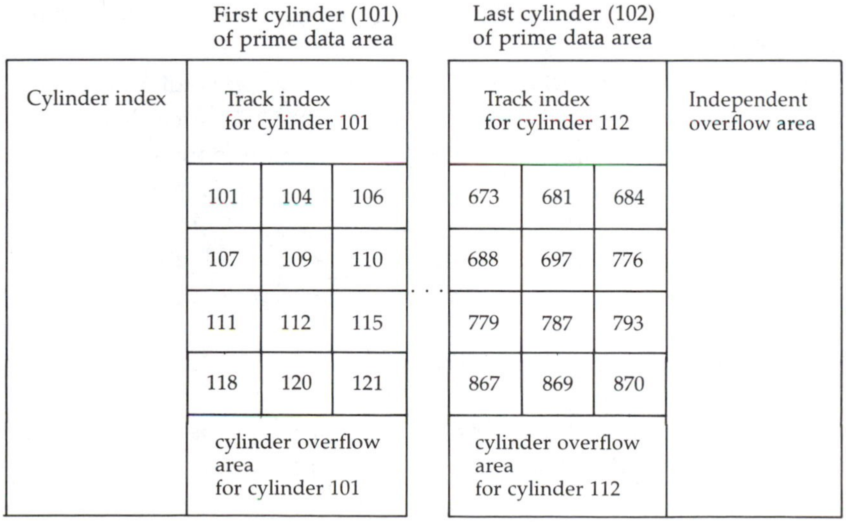

Figure 9.17
Layout of ISAM file of 14 cylinders (six surfaces per cylinder and three records per surface)

Cylinder index	Track index for cylinder 101			Track index for cylinder 112			Independent overflow area
	First cylinder (101) of prime data area			Last cylinder (102) of prime data area			
	101	104	106	673	681	684	
	107	109	110	688	697	776	
	111	112	115	779	787	793	
	118	120	121	867	869	870	
	cylinder overflow area for cylinder 101			cylinder overflow area for cylinder 112			

of an ISAM file on a disk with six surfaces per cylinder and three records per surface. The file consumes 14 cylinders. Only the key values are shown for the data records stored in the prime data area.

The cylinder overflow area at the end of each cylinder is reserved for overflow of records from the prime area caused by the addition of new records. The cylinder overflow area, also termed **embedded overflow** (since the overflow area is embedded within prime data areas of the file), eliminates many of the problems associated with adding new records to a sequential file. The addition of a record to a full track in the prime data causes the last record on the track to be moved to the cylinder overflow area to allow the records on the prime data track to be stored in sequential order. The record moved to overflow is linked with the prime data track from which it was moved in the cylinder and track overflow indexes. Should the cylinder overflow area fill up, an independent overflow area (independent since it follows the prime data areas), is usually reserved.

The advantage of the cylinder (embedded) overflow area is that the area is on the same cylinder as the prime data area from which the overflow occurs; no additional seeks are necessary to access the embedded overflow. The disadvantage is that the embedded overflow area is usually the same for all cylinders (usually one or two tracks), even though the number of additions to all cylinders may not be the same. Some cylinders are used while others are empty and just waste space.

The advantage of the independent overflow area is that the last one or two tracks of each cylinder do not have to be reserved for possible overflow. As a result all additions can be made to the independent overflow area at the end of the file (on the last cylinder). The disadvantage of the independent overflow area is that an additional seek is necessary each time the area is accessed. The common approach is a compromise whereby cylinder overflow areas are reserved for the average number of overflows to the cylinder, and an independent overflow area is reserved in case the cylinder overflow areas become full.

The records in the first cylinder of the prime data area all have lower key values than in the second cylinder of the prime data area. When the ISAM file is created, the data records are stored in contiguous locations on contiguous surfaces within the prime data area of the first cylinder. After the prime data area of the first cylinder is full, the prime data area of the second cylinder is filled in the same manner. The physical ordering of the records in the prime data area along with the surface indexes allows the sequential access of data from the file.

The surface index for a cylinder contains two index entries (normal and overflow) for each surface of the prime data area of the cylinder. Each normal entry indicates the address of a surface in the prime data area and the highest key of all the records on that surface. Each overflow entry indicates the address of the next overflow record in sequence (if any) for that prime data area surface and the highest key of all the records in overflow assigned to that surface. The key in the normal entry is lower than the key in the overflow entry for any surface and

Nkey 1 < Okey 1 < Nkey 2 < Okey 2 < . . . < Nkey n < Okey n

Nkey i is the key of the normal entry and Okey i is the key of the overflow entry for prime data surface i. In searching for a particular record, the keys Nkey i and the keys Okey i are scanned in sequence as shown above until the first key larger than the key of the record being sought is found. Assuming the cylinder overflow areas are empty, the surface index (also called **track index**) for cylinder 101 of the ISAM file from Figure 9.17 is presented in Figure 9.18. (Si is surface i.) Data records are maintained in sequence by ascending key values on a surface and within the prime data areas. Additions of records to a surface cause the expansion of records from the surface into the cylinder overflow area. The overflow entry, when different from the normal entry for a surface, indicates that an expansion of the surface has occurred and shows where the records that overflowed from the surface may be found.

The cylinder index for an ISAM file consists of an entry for each cylinder of the prime data area. Each entry consists of the highest key in the cylinder and the address of the cylinder. The cylinder index of the ISAM file of 14 cylinders from Figure 9.17 is presented in Figure 9.19. (Ci is cylinder i.) To access a record randomly with key k, the entries in the cylinder index are

Surface index
for cylinder 101

Normal entry		Overflow entry	
Highest key	Address	Highest key	Address
106	S1	106	S1
110	S2	110	S2
115	S3	115	S3
121	S4	121	S4

Cylinder index

Highest key	Address
121	C101
⋮	⋮
870	C112

Figure 9.18
Surface index for cylinder 101 of Figure 9.17

Figure 9.19
Cylinder index for the ISAM file

scanned until the first key larger than key k is located. The corresponding address indicates the cylinder to be scanned. The normal and overflow entries of the surface index of the cylinder are scanned until the first key larger than key k is found. The corresponding address is the surface on which the record with key k should be found. The surface is scanned sequentially to locate the record.

Given the cylinder index shown in Figure 9.19, suppose a record with key 105 is added to the file. To decide where the record should be added, the searching routine used to locate an existing record is performed. The first key in the cylinder index larger than 105 is the first entry with a key of 121 and an address of cylinder 101.

A search of the cylinder 101 surface index (Figure 9.20) determines that surface 1 has keys as large as 106, so 105 should be stored on surface 1 if there is room. Because the file was created by storing records in contiguous locations, surface 1 is full. To maintain the sequence of records by key values on a surface, record 105 should be stored between record 104 and record 106. The last record on the surface is moved to the cylinder overflow area (surface 5, record 0), and the overflow entry for surface 1 becomes: 106, S5R0. Record 105 is stored in sequence at the end of the surface. The normal entry for surface 1 becomes: 105, S1. Cylinder 101 with the specified changes is presented in Figure 9.21.

Suppose a record with the key 108 is added to the ISAM file in Figure 9.21. A search of the cylinder index yields cylinder 101 as the cylinder for inserting the record 108. A search of the cylinder 101 surface index yields surface 2 as the location for inserting the record 108. Surface 2 is full with keys 107, 109, and 110. The record with key 108 should be stored between record 107 and record 109. The last record on the surface is moved to the next available location in the cylinder overflow area (surface 5, record 1), and the overflow entry for surface 2 becomes: 110, S5R1. Record 109 is moved to the end of the surface to allow record 108 to be stored in sequence. The normal entry for surface 2 becomes: 109, S2. Cylinder 101 now contains the data presented in Figure 9.22.

Notice that the records stored in the cylinder overflow area are expansions from all of the surfaces in the prime data area. The physical ordering of the records in the overflow area has no meaning, but the records in overflow are referenced from the surface indexes. Each record that is moved to the cylinder overflow area as a surface is expanded and linked in a list to allow sequential access of all records in the ISAM file by the primary key value.

To illustrate the linked list of records in the cylinder overflow area, suppose a record with key 102 is added to the ISAM file above. A search of the cylinder index determines that cylinder 101 is where the insertion should take place. A search of the cylinder 101 surface index indicates that surface

Surface index
for cylinder 101

Normal entry		Overflow entry	
Highest key	Address	Highest key	Address
106	S1	106	S1
110	S2	110	S2
115	S3	115	S3
121	S4	121	S4

Surface index
for cylinder 101

Normal entry		Overflow entry	
Highest key	Address	Highest key	Address
105	S1	106	S5R0
110	S2	110	S2
115	S3	115	S3
121	S4	121	S4

Prime data area
for cylinder 101

S1	101	104	106
S2	107	109	110
S3	111	112	115
S4	118	120	121
(Overflow) S5			

Prime data area
for cylinder 101

S1	101	104	105
S2	107	109	110
S3	111	112	115
S4	118	120	121
(Overflow) S5	106		

Figure 9.20
Cylinder 101 of the
ISAM file

Figure 9.21
Cylinder 101 with
record 105

1 has keys as large as 105, so record 102 should be inserted on surface 1. A scan of surface 1 indicates that record 102 should be inserted between 101 and 104. The last record on the surface (105) is moved to the next available location in the cylinder overflow area (surface 5, record 2). Record 105 contains a pointer to record 106, which is also in overflow, and the overflow entry for surface 1 becomes: 106, S5R2. The overflow entry indicates that surface 1 has been expanded into the cylinder overflow area with records with keys as large as 106 and that the linked list of all records expanded from surface 1 begins in location surface 5, record 2. Record 104 is moved to the end of the surface to allow record 102 to be stored in sequence between record 101 and record 104. The normal entry for surface 1 is changed to reflect the new highest key on the surface: 104, S1. The new cylinder 101 is presented in Figure 9.23.

Surface index
for cylinder 101

Normal entry		Overflow entry	
Highest key	Address	Highest key	Address
105	S1	106	S5R0
109	S2	110	S5R1
115	S3	115	S3
121	S4	121	S4

Prime data area
for cylinder 101

S1	101	104	105
S2	107	108	109
S3	111	112	115
S4	118	120	121
(Overflow) S5	106	110	

Figure 9.22
Cylinder 101 with
record 108 added

Surface index
for cylinder 101

Normal entry		Overflow entry	
Highest key	Address	Highest key	Address
104	S1	106	S5R2
109	S2	110	S5R1
115	S3	115	S3
121	S4	121	S4

Prime data area
for cylinder 101

S1	101	102	104
S2	107	108	109
S3	111	112	115
S4	118	120	121
(Overflow) S5	106	110	105

Figure 9.23
Cylinder 101 with
record 102

Should another record be added to cylinder 101, the cylinder overflow area is full, and the independent overflow area in the last cylinder is used to expand the cylinder overflow area. The overflow entry for an expanded surface contains CcSsRr as the address, which indicates cylinder c, surface s, record r.

Deletion of records from an ISAM file does not cause the records to be physically removed. Instead deletion causes the record to be "marked" as deleted. The deleted record may be marked by moving a very high value into the key field or by including a delete field in each record that is initialized to NO when the record is added to the file and changed to YES when the record is deleted. If the record with key 108 is deleted from the ISAM file in Figure 9.23, the key could be replaced with Xs as shown in Figure 9.24. This static approach to deletions requires that sequential access

Surface index
for cylinder 101

Normal entry		Overflow entry	
Highest key	Address	Highest key	Address
104	S1	106	S5R2
109	S2	110	S5R1
115	S3	115	S3
121	S4	121	S4

Figure 9.24
Cylinder 101 after
deletion of record 108

Prime data area
for cylinder 101

S1	101	102	104
S2	107	XXX	109
S3	111	112	115
S4	118	120	121
(Overflow) S5	106	110	105

to the ISAM file skip over marked records and that random access to the ISAM file skip marked records.

The disadvantage to the static approach is the wasted space for deleted records that still reside within the ISAM file and are merely marked as logically deleted. If the marked records begin to account for a large amount of space, a reorganization of the ISAM file may be in order. The organization entails sequentially accessing the ISAM file, skipping marked records, and copying all other records to another file. The reorganization essentially recreates the ISAM files to physically delete marked records from the file. The advantage to the static approach is that the "garbage collection" of deleted records need not take place with each deletion. If a marked record resides in a prime data area, the space may be used for the next addition to the surface. If a record to be deleted is in the cylinder overflow area, the record can be marked and logically deleted from the linked list of records. The address of the marked record is stored on a free-space list to be used the next time a record is moved into the cylinder overflow area.

Implementation in TURBO Pascal

This section presents a simplified, machine-independent version of the cylinder-and-surface indexing method for the implementation of an indexed sequential file in Pascal. Rather than two levels of indexes (cylinder and surface indexes), only one level of index will be used. The implementation of ISAM files in Pascal requires the use of relative files, which allow rapid access to individual records. The addresses of surfaces are stored in the indexes in terms of relative record numbers.

One index is used for the entire file, and each entry is comprised of a normal entry and an overflow entry. Each prime data block contains a fixed number of fixed-size data blocks. Prime data records are maintained in sequence by ascending key values within a data block and within the index. Overflow blocks contain a record spilled from a prime data block and the address of the next overflow block in the linked list.

For each prime data block in the file, the index contains a normal entry and an overflow entry. The normal entry contains the address of the prime data block and the largest key in the prime data block. The overflow entry, if different from the normal entry, indicates that records have been added in sequence to the prime data block. The added records cause spilling of data records from the prime data block into overflow blocks. The overflow entry contains: (1) the address of the first block in a linked list of overflow blocks, and (2) the largest key of all the overflow blocks in the linked list. The data records are maintained in sequence from the beginning to the end of a linked list of overflow blocks.

Figure 9.25(a) is a diagram of the data structures (index, and prime data blocks) of an indexed sequential file. The maximum number of entries for each prime data block is three. The diagrams in parts (b) through (e) of the

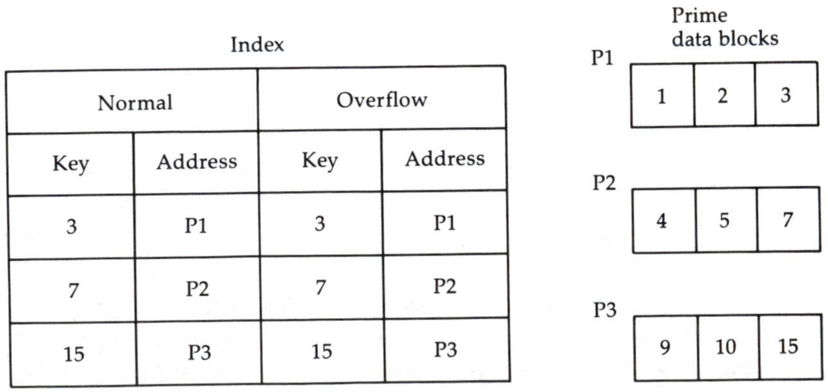

Figure 9.25
Indexed sequential file using the cylinder-and-surface indexing method with one level of indexes

Index					Prime data blocks
Normal		Overflow			
Key	Address	Key	Address	P1	1 │ 2 │ 3
3	P1	3	P1		
7	P2	7	P2	P2	4 │ 5 │ 7
15	P3	15	P3	P3	9 │ 10 │ 15

(a) ISAM file with one index

figure show the changes in the file as records are added and deleted. Adding key 11 causes key 15 to be moved into overflow. The normal key becomes 11, and the overflow address becomes V1 (Figure 9.25(b)). The link field of −1 in the overflow block V1 indicates the end of the linked list.

The addition of the key 6 into prime data block P2 causes key 7 to be moved to an overflow block (V2). The normal key of the index changes to 6, and the overflow address of the index to indicate V2 has an overflow record (Figure 9.25(c)). If the key 8 is added next, the indexes are scanned. The scan looks at the normal key and then at the overflow key for each entry to find that the largest key in prime data block P3 is 11. Key 8 is added to prime data block P3, which is full. As a result the last key in the prime

Index

Normal		Overflow	
Key	Address	Key	Address
3	P1	3	P1
7	P2	7	P2
11	P3	15	V1

Prime data blocks

P1

1	2	3

P2

4	5	7

P3

9	10	11

Overflow blocks

V1

15	−1

(b) ISAM file with key 11

Index

Normal		Overflow	
Key	Address	Key	Address
3	P1	3	P1
6	P2	7	V2
11	P3	15	V1

Prime data blocks

P1

1	2	3

P2

4	5	6

P3

9	10	11

Overflow blocks

V1

15	−1

V2

7	−1

(c) ISAM file with key 6

data block, key 11, is moved to overflow (Figure 9.25(d)). Notice that prime data block P3 already has key 15 in overflow block V1. Key 11 is stored in the next available overflow block, V3. The link field of overflow block V3 becomes the overflow address from the index, V1. In consequence all records that have overflowed from prime data block P3 are linked (11 points to 15). The address of the beginning of the linked list, V3, is stored in the overflow address in the index for prime data block P3. The normal key in the index is changed to key 10.

The deletion of the last key in a prime data block causes the normal key of an index entry to be changed. In contrast the deletion of key 5—which is in the middle of the prime data block—causes the deleted record to be marked but causes no changes in the index (Figure 9.25(e)).

Index

Normal		Overflow	
Key	Address	Key	Address
3	P1	3	P1
6	P2	7	V2
10	P3	15	V3

Prime data blocks

P1: | 1 | 2 | 3 |
P2: | 4 | 5 | 6 |
P3: | 8 | 9 | 10 |

Overflow blocks

V1: | 15 | −1 |
V2: | 7 | −1 |
V3: | 11 | V1 |

(d) ISAM file with key 8

Index

Normal		Overflow	
Key	Address	Key	Address
3	P1	3	P1
6	P2	7	V2
10	P3	15	V3

Prime data blocks

P1: | 1 | 2 | 3 |
P2: | 4 | X | 6 |
P3: | 8 | 9 | 10 |

Overflow blocks

V1: | 15 | −1 |
V2: | 7 | −1 |
V3: | 11 | V1 |

(e) ISAM file after deletion of key 5

The pseudocode for creating an indexed sequential file using the cylinder-and-surface indexing method shown in Figure 9.25 is presented in Algorithm 9.6.

The algorithm for searching the indexed sequential file is much simpler than the search for the previous indexed sequential file. The one-level index is input into an array in memory, and the normal and overflow entries for each prime data block are scanned until the first key larger than the key sought is found. The corresponding address is the location of the data block (in prime or overflow). The data block is input to further search for the record being sought. Algorithm 9.7 presents the search routine.

Maintenance of the indexed sequential file involves changes to and deletions of existing records in the file as well as additions of new records to

Algorithm 9.6 Create ISAM with One Normal Index, One Overflow Index

Algorithm Create_ISAM

```
        index_count ← 0
        db ← 0
        prime_data_block_number ← 0
        While Not end of input
            Input (a_record)
            db ← db + 1
            data_block [db] ← a_record
            If db = MAX_DATA_ENTRIES
                prime_data_block_number ← prime_data_block_number + 1
                Data_Block_Full
                db ← 0

        If db <> 0
            prime_data_block_number ← prime_data_block_number + 1
            Data_Block_Full

        Output (data_blocks_file, prime_data_block_number, 0)

        Output_Indexes { sequentially }

Algorithm Data_Block_Full

        Output (data_blocks_file, data_block, prime_data_block_number)
        index_count ← index_count + 1

        normal [index_count].key ← data_block.key [db]
        normal [index_count].address ← location

        overflow [index_count].key ← normal [index_count].key
        overflow [index_count].address ← normal[index_count].address
```

Algorithm 9.7 Search Algorithm for Locating a Record in File

```
Algorithm Find


    If Search_Indexes
        previous ← 0
        If status = overflow
            Find ← Search_Overflow_Data
        Else { status = normal }
            Find ← Search_Prime_Data
    Else          {
                        key larger than any currently in the file so add to the
                        next available data block and add new entry to indexes
                  }
        data_block [1] ← trans_record
        Output (data_blocks_file, data_block, last_prime_location)
        index_count ← index_count + 1


        normal [index_count].key ← data_block.key [1]
        normal [index_count].address ← last_prime_location


        overflow [index_count].key ← normal [index_count].key
        overflow [index_count].address  ← normal [index_count].address
        last_prime_location ← last_prime_location + 1


Algorithm Search_Indexes


    found ← FALSE
    count ← 1
    While (count <= SIZE_OF_INDEXES)
    And Not found
        If trans_key <= normal [count].key
            found ← TRUE
            status ← normal
            index_location ← count
            data_block_number ← normal [count].address


        Else { trans_key > normal }
            If trans_key <= overflow [count].key
                found ← TRUE
                index_location ← count
                data_block_number ← overflow [count].address
                status ← overflow
            Else
                count ← count + 1


    Search_Indexes ← found
```

Algorithm Search_Prime_Data

```
Input (data_blocks_file, prime_data_block, data_block_number)
found ← FALSE
continue ← TRUE
i ← 1
While (i <= SIZE_OF_PRIME_DATA_BLOCK)
And Not found
And continue
    If prime_data_block.key[i] Not marked
        If trans_key < prime_data_block.key [i]
            {
                trans_key not found in prime_data_block so return i
                as location of first entry greater than transkey.
                trans_key belongs immediately prior to location i.
            }
          continue ← FALSE
        Else
            If trans_key = prime_data_block.key [i]
                found ← TRUE
            Else { trans_key > key[i] }
                i ← i + 1
        Else
            i ← i + 1
    location ← i
    Search_Prime_Data ← found
```

Algorithm Search_Overflow_Data

```
Input (overflow_blocks_file, overflow_block, data_block_number)
If trans_key < overflow_data_block.key [i]
    found ← FALSE

Else
    If transkey = overflow_data_block.key [i]
        found ← TRUE

    Else { transkey > key [i] }
        previous_block ← overflow_block
        previous ← data_block_number
        data_block_number ← overflow.next_block
        found ← Search_Overflow_Data

Search_Overflow_Data ← found
```

the file. Algorithm 9.8 is the maintenance algorithm for changing existing records. Algorithm 9.9 is an expansion of Algorithm 9.8 that allows additions of new records as well as changes to existing records. Algorithm 9.10

is a further expansion of Algorithm 9.9 (with new statements indicated with a † to the left). Algorithm 9.10 allows deletions, changes, and additions to the existing file.

Algorithm 9.8   Change Indexed Sequential File Created in Algorithm 9.6

```
Input_Indexes
Input (data_blocks_file, last_prime_location, 0)
Input (overflow_blocks_file, last_overflow_location, 0)
While Not end of transfile
      Input (trans_record)
      If Find
            Changes
      Else
            output ('not found')
Output_Indexes {sequentially}

Output (data_blocks_file, last_prime_location, 0)

Output (overflow_blocks_file,  last_overflow_location ,0)
```

Algorithm Changes

```
If status ← overflow
      Make_Changes_In_Overflow_Block (data_location)
      Output (overflow_blocks_file, overflow_block, data_block_number)
Else
      Make_Changes_In_Prime_block (data_location)
      Output (data_blocks_file, prime_data_block, data_block_number)
```

Algorithm 9.9   Change and Add Records to Indexed Sequential File

```
Input_Indexes
Input (data_blocks_file, last_prime_location, 0)
input (overflow_blocks_file, last_overflow_location, 0)
While Not end of transfile
      input (trans_record)
      If Find
            Case update_code
                  'C' : Changes
                  'A' : output ('duplicate add transaction')
      Else { not found }
            Case update_code
                  'C' : output ('no matching record')
                  'A' : Adds (trans_record)
Output_Indexes {sequentially}

Output (data_blocks_file, last_prime_location, 0)

Output (overflow_blocks_file, last_overflow_location, 0)
```

Algorithm Changes

    If status = overflow
        Make_Changes_In_Overflow_Block (data_location)
        Output (overflow_blocks_file, overflow_block, data_block_number)
    Else
        Make_Changes_In_Prime_Block (data_location)
        Output (data_blocks_file, prime_data_block, data_block_number)

Algorithm Adds (new_record)

    If status = normal
        Insert_Normal
    Else { status = overflow }
        Insert_Overflow

Algorithm Insert_Normal

        If prime_data_block full
            {
                data_block full
            }
        last ← MAX_DATA_ENTRIES
        hold_record ← prime_data_block.record [last]

        If overflow [index_location].key = normal [index_location].key
            Insert_Into_Block
              {
                get new overflow block
              }
            new_over_record.next_record ← NIL
            new_over_record.record ← hold_record
            last_overflow_location ← last_overflow_location + 1
            overflow [index_location].address ← last_overflow_location
            Output (overflow_blocks_file, new_over_record, last_overflow_location)

        Else
            Insert_Into_Block
            trans_key ← hold_record.key
            If Not Find
                Adds (hold_record)
      Else { block not full}
            Insert_Into_Block

Algorithm Insert_Overflow

        new_over_record.record ← new_record
        last_overflow_location ← last_overflow_location + 1
        If data_block_number = overflow [index_location].address
            {
                add to front of linked list
            }
        new_over_record.next_record ← overflow [index_location].address
        overflow [index_location].address ← last_overflow_location

```
            Else
                    {
                        add  to  middle  of  linked  list
                    }
                new_over_record.next_record  ←  previous_block.next_record
                previous_block.next_record  ←  last_overflow_location
                Output  (overflow_blocks_file,  previous_block,  previous)

            Output  (overflow_blocks_file,  new_over_record,  last_overflow_location)

    Algorithm  Insert_Into_Block

        For  i  ←  MAX_DATA_ENTRIES  Downto   data_location  +  1
            prime_data_block.record  [i]  ←  prime_data_block.record  [i  −  1]

        prime_data_block.record  [data_location]  ←  new_record
        normal  [index_location].key  ←  prime_data_block.record[MAX_DATA_ENTRIES]
        Output  (data_blocks_file,  prime_data_block,  data_block_number)
```

Algorithm 9.10 Change, Add, and Delete Records in Indexed Sequential File

```
        Input_Indexes
        Input  (data_blocks_file,  last_prime_location,  0)
        Input  (overflow_block,  last_overflow_location,  0)
        While  Not  end  of  transfile
            Input  (trans_record)
            If  Find
                Case  update_code
                    'C'  :  Changes
                    'A'  :  Output  ('duplicate  add  transaction')
 †                  'D'  :  Deletes
            Else  {  not  found  }
                Case  update_code
                    'C'  :  Output  ('no  matching  record')
                    'A'  :  Adds  (trans_record)
 †                  'D'  :  Output  ('no  matching  record')
 †  Algorithm  Deletes
 †
 †    If  status  =  normal
 †        prime_data_block.key  [data_location]  ←  'XXX'
 †        If  trans_key  =  normal  [index_location].key
 †                {
 †                    last  one  in  block
 †                }
 †            If  data_location  >  1
 †                {
 †                    will  not  delete  the  last  one  in  the  block  from  indexes
 †                }
 †                If  normal  [index_location].key  =  overflow  [index_location].key
 †                    overflow  [index_location].key  ←
 †                                            prime_data_block.key  [data_location  −  1]
 †                    normal  [index_count].key   ←
 †                                            prime_data_block.key  [data_location  −  1]
 †        Output  (data_blocks_file,  prime_data_block,  data_block_number)
 †
```

```
†
†   Else { status  =  overflow }
†        If overflow [index_location].address  =  data_block_number
†                {
†                    first one in linked list
†                }
†            overflow [index_location].address ← overflow_block.next_record
†
†       Else
†                {
†                    middle or last of linked list
†                }
†            previous_block.next_record ← overflow_block.next_record
†            If overflow_block.next_record  =  0
†                {
†                    last of list so change overflow.key
†                }
†                overflow [index_location].key ← previous_block.key
†            Output (overflow_blocks_file, previous_block, previous)
```

CASE STUDY 9.2: THE CAR-RENTAL AGENCY

The car-rental agency data used in previous file organizations will be stored in an ISAM file for comparison. The transaction file T1 in Figure 5.2 contains the records to be loaded to the file in sequential order. Each track holds three records. Figure 9.26 shows the ISAM master file after creation. The records are stored sequentially in each prime data block, sequentially in contiguous prime data blocks, and the largest key in each block is recorded in the indexes. Any record can be accessed by searching the cylinder index (not shown) to identify the cylinder to seek, then searching the track index to identify the prime data block (surface), and finally searching through the data block to locate the record. Locating a record in the prime data area involves:

1. seeking the cylinder index
2. scanning the cylinder index
3. seeking the cylinder
4. scanning the track index to identify the prime data block
5. scanning the prime data block (surface)

Accessing the ISAM file sequentially involves scanning the cylinder indexes in order. Each cylinder also scans the track indexes in order. The result is a list of all the records in prime data block $P(i)$, all the overflow blocks for this prime block, all the records in prime data block $P (i + 1)$, all the overflow blocks for this prime block, and so on until all prime data blocks and embedded overflow blocks have been listed in sequential order.

Figure 9.26
Creation of car-rental
agency indexed
sequential master file
using cylinder-and-
surface indexing
method

Index

Normal		Overflow	
Key	Address	Key	Address
F1	P1	F1	P1
GM1	P2	GM1	P2
GM4	P3	GM4	P3
H2	P4	H2	P4
T1	P5	T1	P5

Prime data blocks

P1

C1	Dodge	2 DR	Omni	25,000	grey
C2	Dodge	2 DR	Aspen	7,000	tan
F1	Ford	2 DR HB	Escort	54,000	white

P2

F2	Lincoln	4 DR	Continental	38,000	black
F3	Ford	2 DR	Thunderbird	35,000	blue
GM1	Cadillac	4 DR	Fleetwood	9,000	red

P3

GM2	Oldsmobile	4 DR	Delta 88	28,050	blue
GM3	Chevrolet	2 DR	Camaro	33,000	silver
GM4	Cadillac	2 DR	Cimarron	63,000	maroon

P4

GM5	Oldsmobile	4 DR	98	11,000	green
H1	Honda	4 DR	Accord	32,000	yellow
H2	Honda	2 DR HB	Accord	11,250	brown

P5

T1	Toyota	2 DR HB	Celica	3,400	white

Transaction file T2 contains a single addition to the file, GM6. A search of the indexes indicates that GM6 should be added in prime data block P4, which is full. The last record, H2, from P4 is moved into overflow (V1) and initialized with a link field of −1 (Figure 9.27). The records in the prime data block are moved to allow GM6 to be stored in sequential order in the block. The indexes are changed to reflect the movement of records: The normal key for P4 is now H1, and the overflow address for P4 is now V1.

The transaction file T3 contains several transactions, and they are applied to the file in Figure 9.27. The record with key F1 is to be deleted. A search

Index

Normal		Overflow	
Key	Address	Key	Address
F1	P1	F1	P1
GM1	P2	GM1	P2
GM4	P3	GM4	P3
H1	P4	H2	V1
T1	P5	T1	P5

Figure 9.27
Car-rental agency indexed sequential master file after applying transaction file T2

Prime data blocks

P1

C1	Dodge	2 DR	Omni	25,000	grey
C2	Dodge	2 DR	Aspen	7,000	tan
F1	Ford	2 DR HB	Escort	54,000	white

P2

F2	Lincoln	4 DR	Continental	38,000	black
F3	Ford	2 DR	Thunderbird	35,000	blue
GM1	Cadillac	4 DR	Fleetwood	9,000	red

P3

GM2	Oldsmobile	4 DR	Delta 88	28,050	blue
GM3	Chevrolet	2 DR	Camaro	33,000	silver
GM4	Cadillac	2 DR	Cimarron	63,000	maroon

P4

GM5	Oldsmobile	4 DR	98	11,000	green
GM6	Chevrolet	4 DR	Cimarron	11,250	brown
H1	Honda	4 DR	Accord	32,000	yellow

P5

T1	Toyota	2 DR HB	Celica	3,400	white

Overflow blocks

V1

H2	Honda	2 DR HB	Accord	11,250	brown	− 1

of the indexes indicates that F1 resides in P1. The key field is marked with Xs to indicate deletion, and, since F1 was the last key in the block, the normal key entry changes to C2 (Figure 9.28). GM7 is added to P4, causing H1 to move to overflow with a link field from the overflow address of P4—

Figure 9.28
Car-rental agency
indexed sequential
master file after
applying transaction
file T3

Index

Normal		Overflow	
Key	Address	Key	Address
C2	P1	C2	P1
GM1	P2	GM1	P2
GM4	P3	GM4	P3
GM7	P4	H2	V2
XXX	P5	XXX	P5

Prime data blocks

P1

C1	Dodge	2 DR	Omni	25,000	grey
C2	Dodge	2 DR	Aspen	7,000	tan
XX	Ford	2 DR HB	Escort	54,000	white

P2

F2	Lincoln	4 DR	Continental	38,000	black
F3	Ford	2 DR	Thunderbird	35,000	blue
GM1	Cadillac	4 DR	Fleetwood	9,000	red

P3

GM2	Oldsmobile	4 DR	Delta 88	28,050	blue
GM3	Chevrolet	2 DR	Camaro	33,000	silver
GM4	Cadillac	2 DR	Cimarron	63,000	maroon

P4

GM5	Oldsmobile	4 DR	98	11,000	green
GM6	Chevrolet	4 DR	Cimarron	11,250	brown
GM7	Pontiac	2 DR	Fiero	1,500	navy

P5

XXX	Toyota	2 DR HB	Celica	3,400	white

Overflow blocks

V1

H2	Honda	2 DR HB	Accord	11,250	brown	−1

V2

H1	Honda	4 DR	Accord	32,000	yellow	V1

namely, V1. H1 is, therefore, linked to H2. The address of H1, which is the beginning of the linked list, is stored in the overflow address for P4 (V2). GM7 is inserted at the end of the prime data block P4, and its key is recorded in the normal key of the entry for P4. The final transaction deletes T1, which is in P5. Since it is the only record in the block, it is marked as deleted, and the normal and overflow entries for P5 in the index are also marked as deleted. Figure 9.28 illustrates the master file after applying transaction file T3.

Access to a record in overflow involves:

1. seeking the cylinder index
2. scanning the cylinder index
3. seeking the cylinder
4. scanning the track index to identify the overflow
5. scanning the overflow block
6. If the record is not located, use the link field to find the next overflow block and continue with step 5 until the record is located or a link of -1 is found.

Searching for H2 involves scanning the cylinder index, seeking the cylinder, scanning the track index, scanning the overflow block V2, and scanning the overflow block V1 until the record is found. A record in overflow, H2, takes six steps to locate; a record in the prime data area takes only five steps to locate. In fact the number of steps translates to I/O operations, and the number increases as the linked list of overflow blocks increases.

After a great many additions and deletions to the file, a number of records are in overflow blocks, and a number of deleted (marked) records are taking up space in the prime data area. The file can be accessed more efficiently if all the records are in the prime data area. Periodic reorganization of ISAM files is required to ensure efficient access to the data in the file. Reorganization involves accessing the file in sequential order and recreating the ISAM file with all the records stored in prime data blocks and new indexes created.

VSAM FILE ORGANIZATION

The cylinder-and-surface indexing method used on IBM machines (ISAM) was replaced in 1972 by Virtual Sequential Access Method **(VSAM) file organization** on virtual machines. A VSAM file consists of four areas: (1) **control intervals**, which contain data records; (2) **control areas**, which contain several control intervals; (3) a **sequence set**, which is an index of a control area; and (4) an **index set**, which is a tree containing up to three levels of index blocks. The lowest-level index blocks point to sequence sets. Figure 9.29 illustrates the relationships of the four parts of a VSAM file.

A control interval contains one or more data records, much as the data records are stored in a block in the SIS files or in a single track in the ISAM files. Figure 9.30 depicts the format of a control interval that contains data records at the beginning, free space for later additions, record definition fields **(RDFs)** for each record in the control interval, and finally a control interval definition field **(CIDF)**. The RDF of each record contains the relative byte address **(RBA)** relative to the beginning of the file. The CIDF contains

Figure 9.29
VSAM file structure

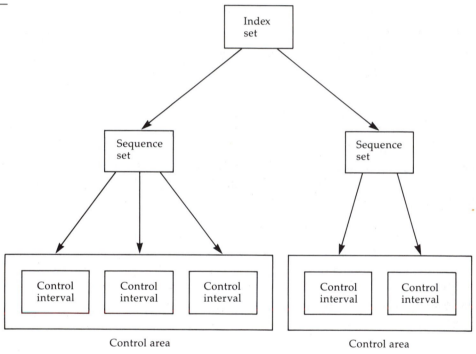

Figure 9.30
Control interval format for a VSAM file

Record 1	Record 2		Record 3	Record 4
Record 5	Record 6		FREE SPACE	
FREE SPACE			RDF 6	RDF 5
RDF 4	RDF 3	RDF 2	RDF 1	CIDF

the length in bytes of the free space within the control interval and the position of the free space. The ith RDF contains the length in bytes of the ith record within the control interval.

Records are stored physically within the control interval according to the keys of the records. Record 1 is stored at the beginning of the control interval, and the RDF for record 1 is stored to the left of the CIDF. Record 2 is stored to the right of record 1, with the corresponding RDF for record 2 being stored to the left of the RDF for record 1. Thus, the logical records and corresponding RDFs are stored in the control interval as two stacks of information growing toward each other. This method of storing records in one end of the control interval and RDFs in the other end allows the free space to reside in the middle of the control interval. Additions and deletions to the control interval move records and RDFs within the control interval to ensure that all the free space is in contiguous locations.

A control area, which is a collection of control intervals, is synonymous with a cylinder in the ISAM method; it is a collection of tracks. The maximum key in each control interval within a control area is stored in the lowest level of the index known as a sequence set. The control intervals for a given control area need not be physically stored in ascending order by maximum key values. Why? The sequence set has an ordered list of all the maximum key values of all control intervals in the control area along with the address of each control interval. The sequence set elements have pointers to siblings to facilitate easy sequential access.

The index set is a tree structure consisting of index blocks containing key-pointer pairs. The key-pointer pair is the maximum key in an index block at the next lower level in the tree and a pointer to the index block. The lowest level of the index set points to a sequence set. The key-pointer pairs within an index block are stored in order by the key values to facilitate sequencing through the file.

A VSAM file that stores records in order by a key value (a **key-sequenced VSAM file**) must be created sequentially so that the records may be stored physically in order within a control interval. The keys for control intervals may be ordered within sequence sets, and the keys for sequence sets may be ordered within the index set. At the time of creation of a VSAM file, free space is allocated within each control interval to allow for additions to the file later. This space is called **embedded space** or **distributed free space**. Empty control intervals may be allocated at the end of each control area much like the cylinder overflow areas for ISAM files. Figure 9.31 presents a sample VSAM file with two levels of index blocks.

Key-sequenced VSAM files may be accessed sequentially, skip-sequentially, or randomly. Sequential access involves searching through the index to identify the RBA of the first control interval in the file. The linked list formed by the elements of the sequence set is traversed retrieving each

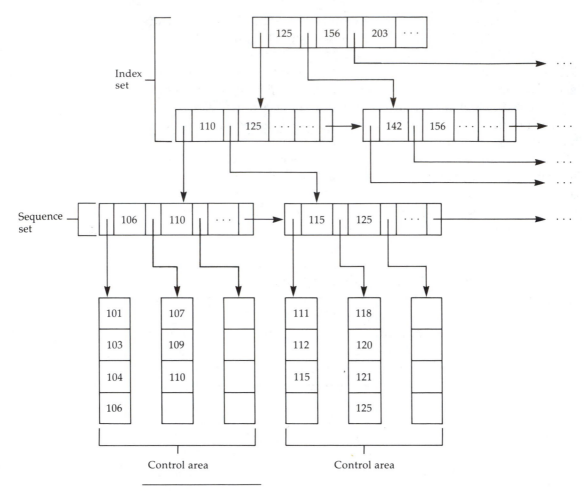

Figure 9.31
Sample VSAM file

control interval referenced. The sequential access need not start with the first record but may start with a specific record key and retrieve sequentially from that point to the end of the file.

Skip-sequential access involves a subset of the records in the file in key order. For a given set of keys that is a subset of the keys in the file, the sequence set is scanned (using the links between sequence set elements) for the RBA of the control interval containing the next key in the given set.

Random access to records in the key-sequenced VSAM involves traversing the index set down to the sequence set in the same way the B^+-trees in Chapter 8 were traversed to locate information in the leaf nodes. The sequence set identifies the RBA of the control interval to be retrieved that contains the record to be located. Random access may be used to retrieve a record with a specific key, to retrieve the record with the next largest key, and to retrieve the first record to satisfy a generic key. The general form of record retrieval makes VSAM a powerful access mechanism.

Addition of records to the VSAM file involves moving records within the control interval so the records remain in sequence by the key values. If the free space does not contain enough room to add a record, a **control interval split** takes place. The full control interval is split (by moving half of the records) into one of the empty control intervals at the end of the control area. The control intervals may no longer be in order physically, but the sequence set (index) retains the order for sequencing the control intervals within the control area. If no empty control intervals exist within the control area, a **control area split** occurs. Half of the control intervals in the full control area are moved into an empty control area at the end of the file. As with the control interval split, the control areas are no longer in order physically, but the sequence set elements retain the order of control areas.

Suppose a record with the key of 105 is added to the sample VSAM file in Figure 9.31. The search routine scans the top-level index blocks (which are linked for sequencing through the file) for the first key larger than 105. The first entry is 125 with a pointer to the second-level index block. Scanning the second-level index block reveals the key 110 with a pointer to a sequence set. Searching the sequence set for the first key larger than 105 finds a key of 106 with a pointer to a control interval. The control interval containing records with keys 101, 103, 104, and 106 is the block into which record 105 should be added, but there is not sufficient room. The control interval is split, leaving records 101, 103, and 104; 105 is stored in an empty control interval at the end of the control area. Record 106 moves into the same control interval as record 105. Figure 9.32 shows the VSAM file with record 105 inserted. The sequence set for this control area has been modified to include a pointer and the maximum key value of the split control interval. Notice that the keys in the sequence set are moved to maintain the key order.

Suppose that a record with the key 108 is added to the file. A search of the index set and sequence set leads to the same control area. The control interval containing 107, 109, and 110 should now contain 108. Since there is some free space within the control interval, records 110 and 109 are moved toward the end of the control interval so record 108 can be inserted physically in order (Figure 9.33). No changes to the sequence set are necessary.

Deletion of records from the VSAM file involves moving all records in the control interval with keys larger than the deleted record up toward the beginning of the control interval (just as we moved the SIS files on the CDC). As a result the deleted space is joined with the free space in the middle of the control interval. Suppose that the record with key 120 is deleted from the VSAM file in Figure 9.33. The records in the control inter-

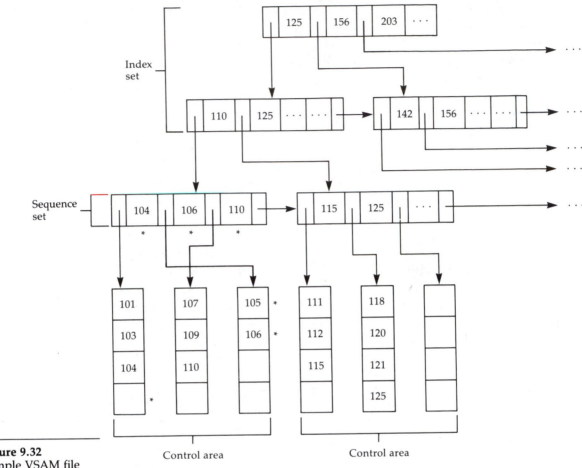

Figure 9.32
Sample VSAM file
with record 105

Control area   Control area

*Indicates changes

val with keys larger than 120 are moved toward the beginning of the control
interval, so all the empty space resides in contiguous positions within the
control interval. Figure 9.34 shows the file after the records in the control
interval are moved. If the record with key 125 is deleted, the second entry
in the second sequence set record and the second entry in the first index
set record have to be changed to reflect that 121 is now the largest key in
the control interval.

VSAM also supports **entry-sequenced files** and **relative record files**. An
entry-sequenced file is simply a sequential file. The order of the records in
the file is determined by the sequence in which records are entered into
the file. VSAM keeps no index structure for entry-sequenced files but simply returns to the user the RBA of each record as it is loaded into the file.
The user could then use this RBA to build an index to the file.

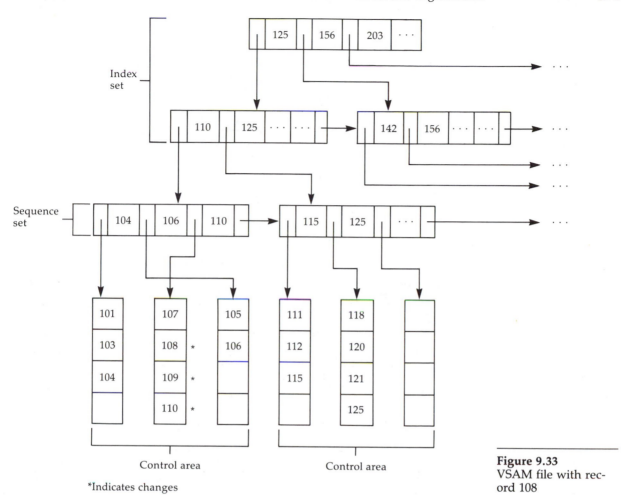

Figure 9.33
VSAM file with record 108

*Indicates changes

Relative record files in VSAM are identical to the relative files presented in Chapter 7. VSAM stores records in a relative file in control intervals according to the record's relative record number—a number that is assigned by the user. No index is constructed for relative record files. All records must be fixed in length so that the number of records in each control interval is identical. For example, suppose that each control interval can hold eight relative records. The relative record numbers for the first control interval are 1 through 8, the locations in the succeeding control interval are relative record numbers 9 through 16, and so on for the whole file.

VSAM performs better than ISAM for two reasons: (1) VSAM does not distinguish between prime data areas and overflow areas and (2) VSAM automatically combines space left after deleting a record with existing free space within the control interval. By using a B$^+$-tree structure for the index,

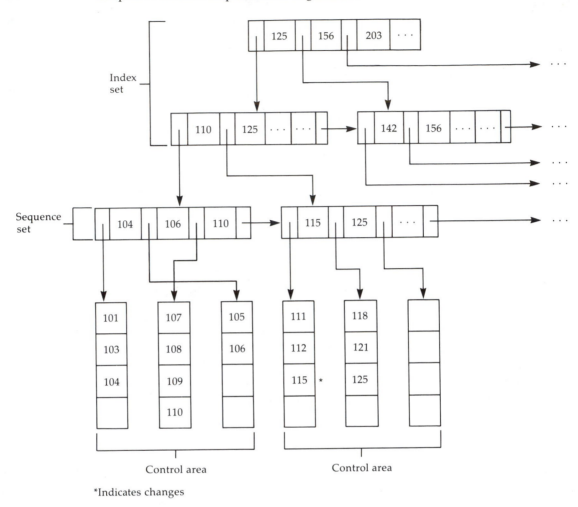

Figure 9.34
VSAM file after dele-
tion of record 120

VSAM is able to split control intervals into free control intervals that are
not physically contiguous. By reclaiming deleted record spaces and keeping
control information (such as RBAs) on each record in the control interval,
variable records can be stored in the control intervals quite easily.

CASE STUDY 9.3: THE CAR-RENTAL AGENCY

The data used in case studies in previous chapters will be stored in a VSAM
file for comparison. The transaction file T1 in Figure 5.2 contains the initial

records for creation of the master file. The records are in key order and are loaded into control intervals of size 4 (Figure 9.35). Each control area contains three control intervals, one of which is empty at the time of creation for use in control interval splits. The index entry in the sequence set elements is the largest key in each control interval in the control area. The index entry in the index set is the largest key in each sequence set element.

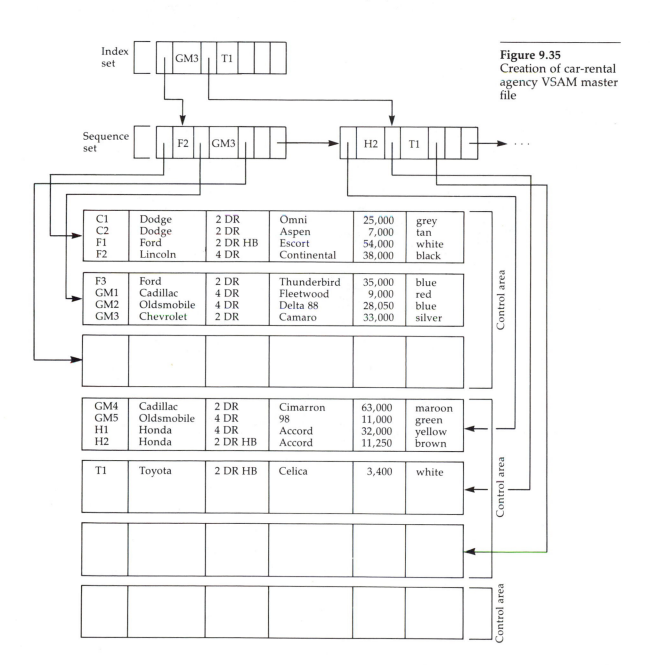

Figure 9.35
Creation of car-rental agency VSAM master file

The transaction file T2 contains a single addition of a record with key GM6. The key GM6 should be stored in the first control interval of the second control area, but the control interval is full. A control interval split occurs: The record to be added, GM6, is stored in the empty control interval in the control area (Figure 9.36), and the keys larger than GM6 are split into the same control interval as GM6. This split moves half of the records out of the original control interval. An index entry for the original control inter-

Figure 9.36
VSAM master file after applying transaction file T2

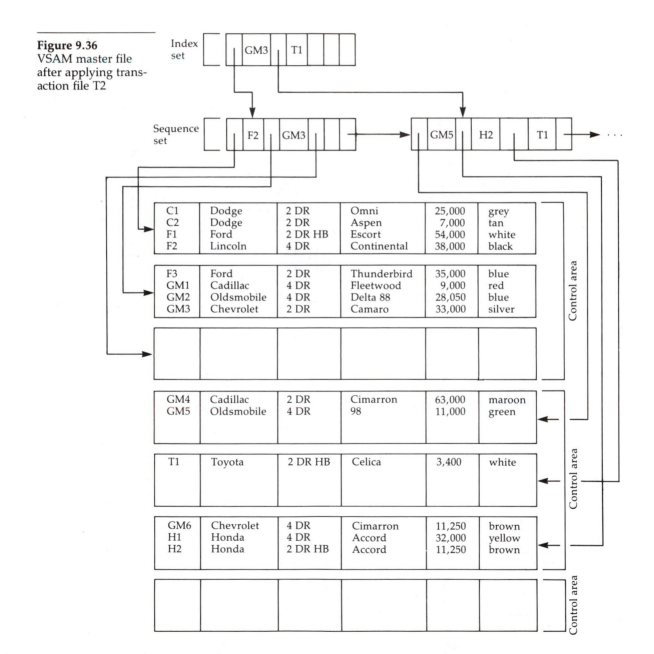

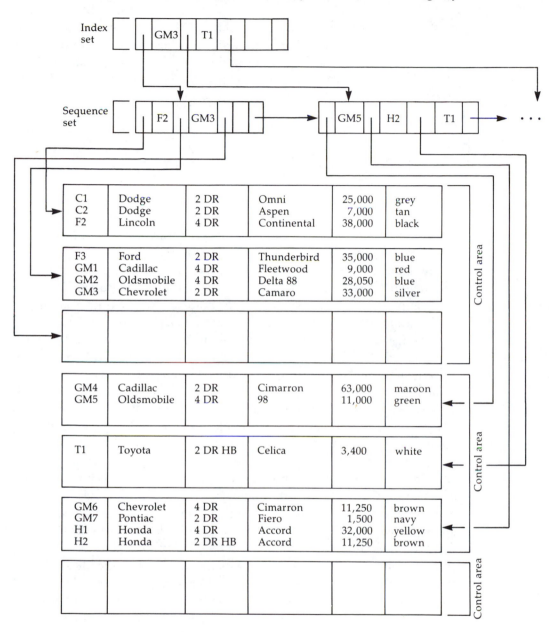

val (the largest key is GM5) is inserted into the second sequence set element. Figure 9.36 shows the VSAM file after the addition of GM6.

The transition file T3 contains several changes that result in the deletion of the record with key F1, the addition of a new record with key GM7, and the deletion of the record with key T1. The record with the key F1 is deleted from the first control interval in the first control area, and the records in the same control interval with larger keys are moved forward. As a result all the empty space is left in one large block (Figure 9.37). The record with

Figure 9.37
VSAM master file after applying transaction file T3 and a control area split

key GM7 is added into the third control interval in the second control area. The record with the key T1 is deleted from the second control interval of the second control area. The entries in the sequence set elements for these two control areas are adjusted accordingly. Figure 9.37 illustrates the VSAM after applying the transactions in transaction file T3.

SUMMARY

Indexed sequential file organization for a collection of records in a file provides sequential access to the records in the file by one primary key field as well as random access to an individual record by the same primary key field. Two common methods exist for structuring indexed sequential files: (1) the index-and-data-blocks method (used by CDC computers), and the cylinder-and-surface indexing method (used by IBM computers).

The index-and-data-blocks method organizes the file into data blocks and index blocks. The data blocks contain a fixed number of data records that are maintained in sequence within each data block. The lowest primary key value in each data block is recorded in an index block, which contains a fixed number of references to data blocks. Each reference in an index block contains the lowest key value and the address (relative record number) of a data block. Random access is achieved by searching through several levels of index blocks to locate the one data block that contains the record being sought. Sequential access is achieved by using the indexes to list the file in order by the primary key field. Additions of records to the file cause a data block to split to maintain the sequencing by the primary key field within data blocks. The split of the data block could cause index blocks to split to maintain the sequencing for the whole file. Deletions of records from the file cause movement of records within a data block—movements that keep the unused locations of a data block in one free space.

The cylinder-and-surface indexing method is based on the physical characteristics of a magnetic disk. The indexed file using this method (an ISAM file) consists of an index area, a prime data area, and an independent overflow area. The data are stored sequentially by a primary key field in consecutive cylinders on the magnetic disk. Each cylinder contains a surface index (secondary-level index) to data records stored within the cylinder, a prime data area, and a cylinder overflow area. The first cylinder of the file contains the cylinder index (primary-level index) to the cylinders of data in the file. Each entry in the cylinder indexes contains the largest key value stored in that cylinder. Similarly, each entry in the surface index contains the largest key value stored on that surface. Each entry also contains the largest key value stored in the overflow area that was expanded from that surface of the prime data area. Random access is achieved by first searching the cylinder index to locate the particular cylinder in which the record may reside, then searching the surface index within that cylinder to determine whether the record resides in the prime data area or in the cylinder overflow area. Once the particular area has been determined, that area is searched sequentially to locate the record. Additions of records to the file cause a surface of the prime data area to expand into the cylinder overflow area. The movement of key values is recorded in the surface indexes. Deletions of records from the file cause the record location to be marked for deletion; the record space is wasted until the next reorganization retrieves the unused space.

VSAM file organization is a replacement for ISAM file organization. VSAM organization uses dynamic structures for indexing a data file that resemble the structures used by SIS file organization on CDC computers (a B$^+$-tree structure). The car-rental agency case study was repeated for each of the three indexed sequential implementations presented in this chapter.

Key Terms

CIDF	index-and-data-blocks method
control areas	index set
control area split	indexed sequential file organization
control intervals	ISAM file organization
control interval split	key-sequenced VSAM file
cylinder-and-surface indexing method	prime data area
	RBA
cylinder indexes	RDFs
cylinder overflow area	relative record files
data block split	sequence set
distributed free space	SIS file organization
embedded overflow	surface index
entry-sequenced files	track index
independent overflow area	VSAM file organization

Exercises

1. What do sequential and indexed sequential files have in common?

2. What facilities do indexed sequential files have for accessing data and updating data files that sequential files do not have?

3. Why is insertion of records into indexed sequential files a problem in theory?

4. List two approaches for handling insertions into an indexed sequential file.

5. Show the SIS file in Figure 9.11(c) after the insertion of keys 19 and 20.

6. Show the SIS file in Figure 9.13(d) after the deletion of keys 10 and 11.

7. Show the ISAM file in Figure 9.25(d) after the insertion of keys 14 and 12.

8. Show the ISAM file in Figure 9.25(e) after the deletion of keys 3 and 11.

9. Show the VSAM file in Figure 9.33 after the addition of keys 123 and 113.

10. Show the VSAM file in Figure 9.34 after the deletion of keys 115 and 105.

11. Why does an ISAM file have to be reorganized more often than a SIS or VSAM file? What is meant by the reorganization of an ISAM file?

12. Why are fewer accesses expected to a SIS file or a VSAM file as compared to an ISAM file?

13. Identify the exact number of accesses necessary to retrieve a record from an ISAM file.

14. Identify the exact number of accesses necessary to retrieve a record from an SIS file.

15. Identify the exact number of accesses necessary to retrieve a record from a VSAM file.

16. Why is a B^+-tree a better choice than a B-tree for the index structure of an indexed sequential file?

17. Compare the advantages and disadvantages of the index-and-data-blocks method and the cylinder-and-surface indexing method.

18. Describe the actions required to access an SIS file sequentially.

19. Describe the actions required to access an ISAM file sequentially.

20. Describe the actions required to access a VSAM file sequentially.

21. Compare your answers from exercises 18 through 20; which organization is the most efficient?

22. Assume that the maximum time for a seek to a disk is 20 ms and that to search a track is 50 ms. What is the maximum time to access a record in a prime data area in an ISAM file stored on this disk? Assume the ISAM file has two levels of indexes: cylinder and track.

23. Assume that the maximum time to input an index or data block from an SIS file on disk is 30 ms. If the file has three levels of index blocks, what is the maximum time to access a record in the SIS file.

24. Repeat exercise 23 for a VSAM file with a one-level index set.

25. Rewrite Algorithms 9.1 through 9.5 to implement VSAM file organization.

Programming Problems

1. From a nontext sequential master file create an indexed sequential master file that describes an inventory of parts. The input file should contain:

sequential master file
   key field = part number
   A nontext file of part data containing the following in each record:
      part number (10 characters)
      part description (26 characters)
      part price (real)

The output files should consist of:

a. Scope Indexed Sequential master file

   key field = part number
   a relative file stores the data physically in sequential order in data blocks. Each relative address should contain the following declaration:

```
TYPE
    Char10 = Packed Array [1..10] Of Char;
    Char26 = Packed Array [1..26] Of Char;
    Isamrecord =
        Record
            part_number : Char10;
            part_description : Char26;
            part_price : Real
        End;
    Isamblock =
        Record
            part : Array [1..3] Of Isamrecord;
            link : Integer
        End;
```

two levels of indexes in which each node contains the largest key in five data blocks with a link to each data block (see the diagram that follows). Write the level-one index nodes to a file (INDEX1) at the end of the program. Write the level-two index nodes to a file (INDEX2) at the end of the program. Each node of the indexes should contain the following declaration:

```
TYPE
    IndexEntry = Record
                       key : Char10;
                       datablock : Integer
                 End;
    Indexnode : Array [1..5] of IndexEntry;
VAR
    index1,
    index2 : Indexnode;
    index1file,
    index2file : File of Indexnode;
```

b. a list produced from a dump of the indexes and data blocks

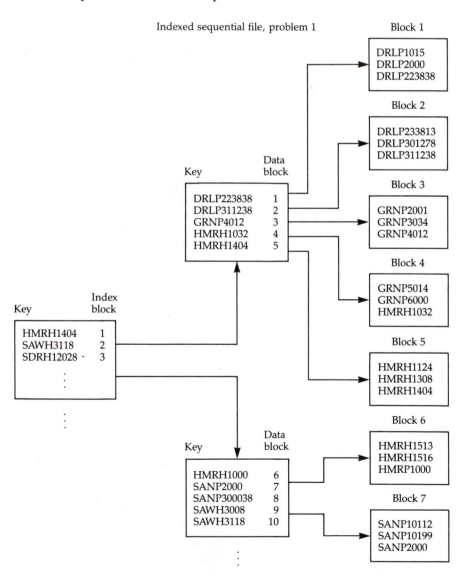

2. In problem 2, you will update the Scope Indexed Sequential master file created in problem 1 with input transaction records. Produce an updated indexed sequential master file (on disk) and an audit/error list (on the printer). Use the SIS you created in problem 1. The transaction file should have the following characteristics:

a. key fields = part number (major)
update code (minor)

b. a text file of update information containing several different formats:

    additions
        update code (A)
        part number (10 characters)
        part description (26 characters)
        part price (real)
    changes
        description
            update code (C)
            part number (10 characters)
            change id (D)
            new description (26 characters)
        price
            update code (C)
            part number (10 characters)
            change id (P)
            new price (real)
    deletions
        update code (D)
        part number (10 characters)

The output will consist of:

a. updated indexed sequential master file

b. audit/error list

    For each transaction key list:
        update code
        transaction key
        action taken (an addition, a change, a deletion, or an error)
        error message if necessary

Your program should perform the following steps:

a. Read each input transaction record (without using INPUT). Validate each transaction to ensure that it contains one of the following update codes:

    A for add
    C for change
    D for delete

b. Create a master record for each valid add transaction.

c. Change the appropriate master field for each valid change transaction.

d. Delete the master record for each valid delete transaction.

e. Identify the following error conditions.

ERROR CONDITION	ERROR MESSAGE
Add a transaction that is already on the master file	INVALID ADD-ALREADY ON MASTER
Change a transaction that is not on the master file	INVALID CHANGE-NOT ON MASTER
Delete a transaction that is not on the master file	INVALID DELETE-NOT ON MASTER
Invalid update code	INVALID UPDATE CODE

Employ the following hints to achieve exemplary program style and clarity:

Tally master and transaction record counts and print after audit/error list.

Input the new master file and list on the printer to make sure the information is right.

Count the number of lines output on the page and reprint headings and page numbers at the top of each new page rather than printing across the page perforations.

3. Repeat problem 1, but—this time—create a VSAM key-sequenced file.

4. Repeat problem 2 to update the VSAM file you created in problem 3.

5. Create an ISAM master file from a nontext sequential part master file. The ISAM input file should be like the input file in problem 1. The output files should consist of:

a. ISAM master file

   key field = part number
   a relative prime data file stores the data physically in sequential order (initially) in data blocks. Each relative address should contain the following declaration:

```
CONST
    MAX_DATA_ENTRIES = 5;
TYPE
    Char10 = Packed Array [1..10] Of Char;
    Char26 = Packed Array [1..26] Of Char;
    Part_Record =
        Record
            part_number : Char10;
            part_description : Char26;
            part_price : Real
        End;
```

```
      Prime_Data_Block =
          Record
              data_entries : Integer;
              prime_record : Array [1..MAX_DATA_ENTRIES] Of Part_Record;
          End;
VAR
      data_file : File of Prime_Data_Block;
```

a relative overflow data file that stores records expanded from the prime data file. Link all records expanded from one prime data block in a singly linked list in sequential order. The overflow linked list for one prime data block should contain records with keys greater than the largest in the prime data block. Each record in the overflow data file should contain the following declaration:

```
TYPE
    Overflow_Block =
        Record
            over_record : Part_Record;
            next_overflow : Integer
        End;
VAR
    over_file : File of Overflow_Block;
```

one level of indexes where each entry in the indexes contains the largest key in one prime data block (normal entry) and the largest key in the overflow file (over entry) that corresponds to the one prime data block with a link to each data block (see the diagram that follows). The indexes should be stored in an array while the indexed sequential file is being built, then written to a sequential data file. Each entry of the indexes should contain the following declaration:

```
TYPE
    Key_Field = Packed Array [1..10] Of Char;
    An_Entry = Record
                    key : Key_Field;
                    address : Integer
                End;
    Index_Entries =
        Record
            normal : An_Entry;
            over   : An_Entry
        End;
VAR
    indexes    : Array [1..30] of Index_Entries;
    index_file : File of Index_Entries;
```

Indexed sequential file, problem 9

Indexes

Normal key	Address	Overflow key	Address
DRLP301278	1	DRLP301278	1
GRNP5014	2	GRNP5014	2
HMRH1404	3	HMRH1404	3
SANP10199	4	SANP10199	4
SAWH116314	5	SAWH116314	5
SAWH3118	6	SAWH3118	6
SAWP43012	7	SAWP43012	7
SAWP5012	8	SAWP5012	8
SDRH12028	9	SDRH12028	9
SDRH215612	10	SDRH215612	10
SDRH25184	11	SDRH25184	11
WWOP5000	12	WWOP5000	12

Prime data blocks

Block 1

```
        5
DRLP1015
DRLP2000
DRLP223838
DRLP233813
DRLP301278
```

Block 2

```
        5
DRLP311238
DRLP2001
GRNP3034
GRNP4012
GRNP5014
```

Block 3

```
        5
GRNP6000
HMRH1032
HMRH1124
HMRH1308
HMRH1404
```

   b. a listing produced from a dump of the indexes and data blocks

6. Access the ISAM master file you created in problem 5 to retrieve certain records. A sequential transaction text file contains the keys of those records to be retrieved and each record contains a part number (10 characters). The ISAM master file has the following characteristics:

   a. key field = part number

b. a relative file with three records and a link field stored in a block in each relative address. Each relative address should contain the following declaration:

```
TYPE
    Char10 = Packed Array [1..10] Of Char;
    Char26 = Packed Array [1..26] Of Char;
    Isamrecord = Record
                    part_number : Char10;
                    part_description : Char26;
                    part_price : Real
                 End;
    Isamblock = Record
                    part : Array [1..3] Of Isamrecord;
                    link : Integer
                 End;
```

c. two levels of indexes in which each node contains the largest key in five data blocks and the relative record address of each data block. Each node of the indexes should contain the following declaration:

```
TYPE
    Entre = Record
                key : Char10;
                address : Integer
            End;
    Indexnode = Array [1..5] Of Entre;
VAR
    index1 : Indexnode;
    index2 : Array [1..4] Of Indexnode;
    index1file : File of Indexnode;
    index2file : File of Indexnode;
```

d. the address field of the index1 node contains a subscript referencing an indexnode in index2

e. output should contain a list of each transaction key followed by:

the record with a matching key retrieved from the indexed sequential file using the indexes or
an error message to the effect that the record is not on the master file

7. Repeat problem 2, but—this time—update the ISAM file created in problem 5.

8. Repeat problem 1 but—this time—build a Scope Indexed Sequential file that contains data about vendors. The input file should contain:

a. key field = vendor number (major)
              vendor data due (minor)

   b. a file of vendor data, where each record contains:

> vendor number (8 characters)
> vendor data due (yymmdd)
> vendor name (20 characters)
> vendor amount due (real)

9. Repeat problem 2, but—this time—update the file created in problem 8 with a transaction file that contains vendor transactions. The input file has the properties:

   a. key field = vendor number (major)
                  vendor date due (minor)

   b. a text file of update data that contains several different formats:

> additions
>   update code (A)
>   vendor number (8 characters)
>   vendor date due (yymmdd)
>   vendor name (20 characters)
>   vendor amount due (real)
> changes
>   name
>   update code (C)
>   vendor number (8 characters)
>   vendor date due (yymmdd)
>   change id (N)
>   new name (20 characters)
>   amount due
>   update code (C)
>   vendor number (8 characters)
>   vendor date due (yymmdd)
>   change id (A)
>   new amount due (real)
> deletions
>   update code (D)
>   vendor number (8 characters)
>   vendor date due (yymmdd)

10. Using the guidelines in problem 1, build a VSAM file using the vendor data in problem 8.

11. Update the VSAM file in problem 10 as you did in problem 9.

12. Using the guidelines in problem 5, build an ISAM file using the vendor data described in problem 12.

13. Update the ISAM file in problem 12 as you did in problem 9.

14. Using the guidelines in problem 1, build a SIS file where the input is now employee data. The file should have the properties:

   a. key field = employee number

b. a file of employee data in which each record contains:

    section id (3 characters)
    department number (integer)
    employee number (integer)
    last name (12 characters)
    first name (9 characters)
    middle initial (1 character)
    sex code (1 character)
    marital status (1 character)
    number of exemptions (integer)
    pay rate (real)
    earnings (real)
    year-to-date earnings (real)

15. Repeat problem 2, but—this time—update the file built in problem 14 with a transaction file containing employee transactions. The input file should have the properties:

a. key field = employee number

b. a file of employee transactions where each record contains one of the following formats:

    additions
        update code (A)
        section id (3 characters)
        department number (integer)
        employee number (integer)
        last name (12 characters)
        first name (9 characters)
        middle initial (1 character)
        sex code (1 character)
        marital status (1 character)
        number of exemptions (integer)
        pay rate (real)
        earnings (real)
        year-to-date earnings (real)
    changes
        employee number (integer)
        one of the following changes:

CHANGE ID	FIELD
L	last name (12 characters)
F	first name (9 characters)
M	middle initial (1 character)
X	sex code (1 character)
S	marital status (1 character)
E	number of exemptions (integer)
P	pay rate (real)

      deletions
        update code (D)
        employee number (integer)
        last name (12 characters)

16. Using the guidelines in problem 1, build a VSAM file with the employee data described in problem 14.

17. Repeat problem 2, but—this time—update the file created in problem 16.

18. Using the guidelines in problem 1, build an ISAM file with the employee data described in problem 14.

19. Repeat problem 2, but—this time—update the file created in problem 18.

PART V

LIST-STRUCTURED FILE ORGANIZATION

Chapter 10
Multiple-Key File Organization

Chapter 10

CHAPTER CONTENTS

Multiple-Key File Organization

PREVIEW

THIS CHAPTER INVESTIGATES OTHER TYPES of file organization that use linked lists or tree structures to provide multiple-key access to random-access data files. Included in this chapter is a discussion of inverted files and multilist files along with creation and manipulation algorithms. The discussion employs the car-rental agency data to illustrate the inverted file and the use of multilist files to provide access by several keys. Quantitative measures of access times provide a basis for comparison to other types of file organization.

TYPES OF MULTIPLE-KEY FILE ORGANIZATION

The field of a record that uniquely identifies the record is known as the **primary key** field. Indexed sequential file organization provides sequential and random access to the records in a file by one primary key field. Many applications require access of records in a file by more than one key field. When using random-access file organization, we can locate a record of data containing a particular key value by specifying that key value. The other fields of a record, which may be used to access the record in **multiple-key file organization**, are known as **secondary key** fields. Two types of multiple-key file organization provide access to the records in a file by several key fields: **inverted file organization** and **multilist file organization**.

Single-key file organization (sequential, random, and indexed sequential) provides access to the data in the record by one primary key field. Given the primary key of a record, the data from the record can be accessed. To locate all records with a given attribute for a field other than the primary key field, all records must be accessed sequentially.

Multiple-key file organizations provide an inverse relationship between the data in a record and the primary key of the record that uniquely identifies it. Multiple-key files allow access to the data file by fields other than the primary key, just as an index for a book allows access to the information within the book by any key word listed in the index. Like the index for a book that lists the page numbers where a particular key word may be found, the multiple-key file index lists the primary keys of all the records in the data file that contain a particular secondary key value. The primary keys are then used to access the records from the data file. In other words, given an attribute for a secondary key field, the primary key field of the records containing the attribute can be found; the records can be accessed.

It is important to realize that the secondary key indexes discussed in this chapter are an additional structure in the sense that the data file is organized according to some underlying structure—either an indexed sequential or relative file—to which the primary key provides access. The secondary key indexes access records according to a particular secondary key value related to a set of primary keys.

The two common approaches to multiple-key file organizations, inverted files and multilist files, both build an index (directory) for each secondary key field that is much like an index for a book. The difference between these two approaches is in the way in which the list of primary keys for a particular secondary key value is stored. Access to data from a file by secondary keys is achieved in inverted file organization by using a directory of all possible attributes for each secondary key field and the address (primary key) of all records containing those attributes. With multilist file organization, the directory contains all possible attributes for each secondary key

Primary key	Secondary keys		Nonindexed data		
Id no.	Make	Style	Model	Mileage	Color
C1	Dodge	2 DR	Omni	25,000	grey
H1	Honda	4 DR	Accord	32,000	yellow
F1	Ford	2 DR HB	Escort	54,000	white
GM1	Cadillac	4 DR	Fleetwood	9,000	red
GM2	Oldsmobile	4 DR	Delta 88	28,050	blue
H2	Honda	2 DR HB	Accord	11,250	brown
F2	Lincoln	4 DR	Continental	38,000	black
C2	Dodge	2 DR	Aspen	7,000	tan
F3	Ford	2 DR	Thunderbird	35,000	blue
GM3	Chevrolet	2 DR	Camaro	33,000	silver
GM4	Cadillac	2 DR	Cimarron	63,000	maroon
GM5	Oldsmobile	4 DR	98	11,000	green
T1	Toyota	2 DR HB	Celica	3,400	white

Figure 10.1
Sample inventory of a car-rental agency

field and a pointer to a linked list of all records containing that attribute.

Apply multiple-key access to our car-rental agency example. The agency has records for all cars in their inventory and needs access to the inventory data by a unique identification number, by make, and by style. The sample inventory in Figure 10.1 will be used in all examples in this chapter. The primary key of the data is the unique car identification number (id number). The primary key provides access to the actual record of data within the file. The secondary keys that are to be used to access the file are the make and style of the cars. The other data fields in the file are nonindexed but are necessary for inventory purposes.

INVERTED FILE ORGANIZATION

The **inversion index** for a record key of a data file contains all the values that the key field contains and a pointer to the records in the file that contain those key values. The data file is considered to be inverted on that key. The index for a book can be considered an inversion on the pages of the book since it lists all the topics contained in the book along with page numbers where the topics can be found.

An inverted file contains two areas: (1) a directory and (2) a data record area. The data records could be stored in a relative file and the primary key hashed to randomly access the records, or the records could be stored in an indexed sequential file to provide random access by the primary key field. The data record area can be organized in any manner as long as random access to the records is provided. The directory contains an inverted list for each secondary key field to be used in accessing the data records in the data record area. The directory provides access to the records in the file using a secondary key field by adding a higher level of indexing over the organization of the data file. A **partially inverted file** is one in which an inverted list is built for each of a number of selected fields. A **fully inverted file** has an inverted list for every field in the record, and entries for all attributes in the file. A fully inverted file provides access to the data by any field in the record.

The inverted list for each secondary key field can be stored in individual files or all inverted lists can be stored in one directory file. Each entry in an inverted list for a secondary key field contains an attribute found in the secondary key field in the file and a list of addresses of records in the file in which this attribute appears. The entries may vary in length because the number of addresses in the list may vary depending on the number of records in the file containing the attribute. Storing the inverted lists for several secondary key fields in one file may be difficult since variable-length records are needed. Therefore, the inverted list for a single secondary key field can be stored in an individual file. Rather than using variable-length records for storage of inverted lists, each entry is fixed in length and allocated space for the maximum number of addresses for any given entry. Then all inverted lists for an inverted file are stored as a sequential or indexed sequential file.

CASE-STUDY 10.1: THE CAR-RENTAL AGENCY

The process of creating an inverted file from a set of data is called **inverting a data file.** As each record in the data file in this case study is input, the values in the make and style fields are compared to the inverted lists. If the make of the record is not already present in the make inverted list, it is inserted. If the style of the record is not already present in the style inverted list, it is inserted. Once the values for make and style are present in the inverted lists, the primary key of the record input is inserted in the inverted list in the list of addresses for the appropriate secondary key value. After accessing the first record in the data file, the inverted list for make contains the entry Dodge C1, and the style inverted list contains the entry 2 DR C1. Each record in the data file is input in turn, and the make and style values along with the primary keys are inserted into the inverted lists.

Figures 10.2 through Figure 10.10 show several snapshots of the creation of make and style inverted lists. The lists are created by reading a record from the data file in Figure 10.1 and entering the make, style, and primary key values into the inverted directories. Boldface indicates the changes

Make	Primary key(s)
Dodge	C1

(a) Make of car

Make	Primary key(s)
Dodge	C1
Honda	**H1**

(a) Make of car

Make	Primary key(s)
Dodge	C1
Honda	H1
Ford	**F1**

(a) Make of car

Style	Primary key(s)
2 DR	C1

(b) Style of car

Figure 10.2
Inverted file directories for make and style with attributes for record with key C1

Style	Primary key(s)
2 DR	C1
4 DR	**H1**

(b) Style of car

Figure 10.3
Inverted file directories for make and style with attributes for record with key H1

Style	Primary key(s)
2 DR	C1
4 DR	H1
2 DR HB	**F1**

(b) Style of car

Figure 10.4
Inverted file directories for make and style with attributes for record with key F1

from the previous snapshot. The complete inverted directories for secondary keys make and style are presented in Figure 10.10.

The inverted list for make of car contains eight key values: Dodge, Honda, Toyota, Ford, Cadillac, Lincoln, Oldsmobile, and Chevrolet. The values are entered into the inverted index as they are encountered. For each key value in the inverted list for make, the primary keys of those records containing the corresponding make of car are listed. Two records in the file contain data concerning cars of the make Dodge; namely, the records with primary keys C1 and C2. Five records in the inverted file contain data concerning two-door (2 DR) cars; namely, the records with primary keys C1, C2, F3, GM3, and GM4.

One of the advantages of an inverted file is the ease of answering queries. In answer to the query "What cars are available with a make of Dodge?" the make inverted list is scanned for the make of Dodge. The scan results in a list of two primary keys, C1 and C2. The records C1 and C2 can be

Make	Primary key(s)
Dodge	C1,
Honda	H1
Ford	F1
Cadillac	**GM1**

(a) Make of car

Style	Primary key(s)
2 DR	C1
4 DR	H1, **GM1**
2 DR HB	F1

(b) Style of car

Figure 10.5
Inverted file directories for make and style with attributes for record with key GM1

Make	Primary key(s)
Dodge	C1
Honda	H1
Ford	F1
Cadillac	GM1
Oldsmobile	**GM2**

(a) Make of car

Style	Primary key(s)
2 DR	C1
4 DR	H1, GM1, **GM2**
2 DR HB	F1

(b) Style of car

Figure 10.6
Inverted file directories for make and style with attributes for record with key GM2

accessed from the file, and the answer to the query is that a grey two-door Dodge Omni with 25,000 miles and a tan two-door Dodge Aspen with 7,000 miles are available. Once the secondary key value (make = Dodge) is located in the inverted list, only one access per primary key in the list is needed to satisfy the query.

Consider an intersecting query such as "How many two-door Dodges are available?" The algorithm searches for the list of all Dodge cars (C1, C2), then searches for the list of all 2 DR cars (C1, C2, F3, GM3, GM4). The intersection of the two lists (C1, C2) satisfies the query with the answer, which is two. If the query is "List all two-door Dodges," the records with the primary keys in the intersection (C1, C2) are accessed. An intersecting

Make	Primary key(s)
Dodge	C1
Honda	H1, **H2**
Ford	F1
Cadillac	GM1
Oldsmobile	GM2

(a) Make of car

Make	Primary key(s)
Dodge	C1
Honda	H1, H2
Ford	F1
Cadillac	GM1
Oldsmobile	GM2
Lincoln	**F2**

(a) Make of car

Style	Primary key(s)
2 DR	C1
4 DR	H1, GM1, GM2
2 DR HB	F1, **H2**

(b) Style of car

Figure 10.7
Inverted file directories for make and style with attributes for record with key H2

Style	Primary key(s)
2 DR	C1
4 DR	H1, GM1, GM2, **F2**
2 DR HB	F1, H2

(b) Style of car

Figure 10.8
Inverted file directories for make and style with attributes for record with key F2

query can be answered by the intersection of lists of primary keys from the secondary key entries so that only the records that match the qualifications of the query are accessed from the file. Fewer input and output operations are performed to answer the queries than with other file organizations. If space permits, searching is faster if the inverted lists are retained in main memory during the access of the inverted file.

Another advantage of inverted file organization is the space saved in storing data in the file. Those fields of the records that are primary or secondary keys need not be stored in the data file. The primary key is the

Make	Primary key(s)
Dodge	C1, **C2**
Honda	H1, H2
Ford	F1
Cadillac	GM1
Oldsmobile	GM2
Lincoln	F2

(a) Make of car

Style	Primary key(s)
2 DR	C1, **C2**
4 DR	H1, GM1, GM2, F2,
2 DR HB	F1, H2

(b) Style of car

Figure 10.9
Inverted file directories for make and style with attributes for record with key C2

Figure 10.10
Inverted file directories for make and style with all records

Make	Primary key(s)
Dodge	C1, C2
Honda	H1, H2
Ford	F1, **F3**
Cadillac	GM1, **GM4**
Oldsmobile	GM2, **GM5**
Lincoln	F2
Chevrolet	**GM3**
Toyota	**T1**

(a) Make of car

Style	Primary key(s)
2 DR	C1, C2, **F3, GM3, GM4**
4 DR	H1, GM1, GM2, F2, **GM5**
2 DR HB	F1, H2, **T1**

(b) Style of car

address of the record in the file—it does not necessarily need to be stored in the file; it will only be stored in the inverted lists. The actual values for the secondary key fields make and style are stored in the inverted lists with addresses of all records having those values. Storing data about make and style in the inverted lists as well as in the file is a duplication of data. The actual data record need only contain the nonindexed data: model, mileage, and color. Figure 10.11 presents the inverted lists for make and style of car along with the data file that contains only the nonindexed data. The inverted lists and the data file comprise the total data concerning all the cars described by the file.

Make	Primary key(s)
Dodge	C1, C2
Honda	H1, H2
Ford	F1, F3
Cadillac	GM1, GM4
Oldsmobile	GM2, GM5
Lincoln	F2
Chevrolet	GM3
Toyota	T1

Data file contents

Primary key	Model	Mileage	Color
C1	Omni	25,000	grey
H1	Accord	32,000	yellow
F1	Escort	54,000	white
GM1	Fleetwood	9,000	red
GM2	Delta 88	28,050	blue
H2	Accord	11,250	brown
F2	Continental	38,000	black
C2	Aspen	7,000	tan
F3	Thunderbird	35,000	blue
GM3	Camaro	33,000	silver
GM4	Cimarron	63,000	maroon
GM5	98 ·	11,000	green
T1	Celica	3,400	white

Style	Primary key(s)
2 DR	C1, C2, F3, GM3, GM4
4 DR	H1, GM1, GM2, F2, GM5
2 DR HB	F1, H2, T1

Figure 10.11
Inverted lists and data records with no duplication of data

Conserving space in this manner presents a problem if the data file is to be accessed in a sequential manner since the inverted lists for the secondary keys contain only part of the data for the records in the file. Both the data file and the indexes need to be accessed to list all data for all the cars. For example, the first record in the data file contains the primary key C1. To identify the make and style of the car with primary key C1, the lists of primary keys under each value in the inverted directory for make of car are searched sequentially for the primary key C1. C1 is found under the value Dodge. Similarly, the lists of primary keys under each value in the inverted directory for style of car need to be searched to locate the primary key C1 to determine the style. This searching entails a great deal of time, so in this case it is hardly worthwhile to avoid duplicating data in the data file and the inverted directories.

One disadvantage to inverted file organization is the storage of the inverted lists. Each entry contains a secondary key value and a list of record addresses that contain the key value. The list of record addresses varies in length, so it is difficult to store the entries in a file of fixed-length records. For this reason the inverted list for a single secondary key is often stored as an individual file. Access time to the data in the inverted list could be shortened by storing the data as a B-tree rather than a sequential table. Additions and deletions to the file entail additions and deletions to the inverted lists for each secondary key field. If the inverted list is a tree, these operations are easier to handle.

Additions to the inverted file result in modifications to the inverted lists. For example, suppose a record is added to the inverted file. The primary key is GM6, the make is Chevrolet, and the style is 4 DR. The modifications to the inverted lists in Figure 10.10 are shown in Figure 10.12. Since Chevrolet already exists as an attribute in the inverted list for make, GM6 is added to the list of addresses containing the attribute Chevrolet for make. Likewise, 4 DR already exists as a style, so GM6 is added to the list of addresses containing 4 DR for style. The addition of a record with attributes that exist in the inverted lists requires that the address (primary key) of the new record be added to the present list of addresses for each secondary key field.

Suppose an addition of a record with primary key GM7, make of Pontiac, and style of 2 DR is made to the file. Since Pontiac as a make attribute is not present in the inverted list, the new attribute Pontiac must be added to the inverted list for make of car. The primary key GM7 is added as the address of a record with the make Pontiac. Figure 10.13 presents the inverted lists from Figure 10.12 with the addition of GM7. The style 2 DR presently exists in the inverted list for style, so the address GM7 is added to the list of addresses.

Deletions from the inverted file result in deletions of attributes and/or addresses in the inverted lists. When deleting a record with an attribute that occurs several times in the file, the address of the record to be deleted is removed from each inverted list in which it occurs. If the record with primary key F1 is deleted, all occurrences of F1 are removed from the inverted lists. The make of the car F1 is Ford and the style is 2 DR HB. Under the attribute Ford in the make inverted list and under the attribute 2 DR HB in the style inverted list, F1 is deleted. The asterisks in Figure 10.14 indicate that data has been deleted for an attribute in order to delete F1 from the inverted file.

On the other hand, deleting a record with unique attributes in secondary key fields results in the deletion of an entire entry from an inverted list. If the record with primary key T1 is deleted, all occurrences of T1 are removed from the inverted lists. The make of the car T1 is Toyota and the style is 2

Make	Primary key(s)
Dodge	C1, C2
Honda	H1, H2
Ford	F1, F3
Cadillac	GM1, GM4
Oldsmobile	GM2, GM5
Lincoln	F2
Chevrolet	GM3, **GM6**
Toyota	T1

(a) Make of car

Style	Primary key(s)
2 DR	C1, C2, F3, GM3, GM4
4 DR	H1, GM1, GM2, F2, GM5, **GM6**
2 DR HB	F1, H2, T1

(b) Style of car

Figure 10.12
Inverted file directories for make and style from Figure 10.10 with GM6

Figure 10.13
Inverted file directories for make and style with GM7

Make	Primary key(s)
Dodge	C1, C2
Honda	H1, H2
Ford	F1, F3
Cadillac	GM1, GM4
Oldsmobile	GM2, GM5
Lincoln	F2
Chevrolet	GM3, GM6
Toyota	T1
Pontiac	**GM7**

(a) Make of car

Style	Primary key(s)
2 DR	C1, C2, F3, GM3, GM4, **GM7**
4 DR	H1, GM1, GM2, F2, GM5, GM6
2 DR HB	F1, H2, T1

(b) Style of car

DR HB. The changes to the inverted lists to delete T1 are presented in Figure 10.15. The make Toyota is unique to record T1, so the entire entry for attribute Toyota is removed from the make inverted list. T1 is removed from the list of addresses for 2 DR HB. Only one 2 DR HB remains in the file (primary key H2).

Make	Primary key(s)
Dodge	C1, C2
Honda	H1, H2
* Ford	F1, F3
Cadillac	GM1, GM4
Oldsmobile	GM2, GM5
Lincoln	F2
Chevrolet	GM3, GM6
Toyota	T1
Pontiac	GM7

(a) Make of car

Figure 10.15
Inverted file directories for make and style after deletion of T1

Make	Primary key(s)
Dodge	C1, C2
Honda	H1, H2
Ford	F1, F3
Cadillac	GM1, GM4
Oldsmobile	GM2, GM5
Lincoln	F2
Chevrolet	GM3, GM6
*	
Pontiac	GM7

(a) Make of car

Style	Primary key(s)
2 DR	C1, C2, F3, GM3, GM4, GM7
4 DR	H1, GM1, GM2, F2, GM5, GM6
* 2 DR HB	H2, T1

(b) Style of car

*Site of latest deletion

Style	Primary key(s)
2 DR	C1, C2, F3, GM3, GM4, GM7
4 DR	H1, GM1, GM2, F2, GM5, GM6
* 2 DR HB	H2

(b) Style of car

*Site of latest deletion

Figure 10.14
Inverted file directories for make and style after deletion of F1

Inverted Files in TURBO Pascal

The implementation of inverted files in Pascal requires some mechanism for storing the address list for each key value, which may vary in length. One approach for storing the inverted lists is to use a linked-list structure rather than a static structure such as an array. The linked-list structure facilitates the addition and deletion of key values into the index and the address list. The make inverted list from Figure 10.10, for example, is stored in the linked structure shown in Figure 10.16.

The variant record in Pascal could be used to store the inverted lists if the nodes in the linked structure are stored in one of the two formats shown in Figure 10.17. The first node in the link structure in Figure 10.16 is stored in format (a); the key value is Dodge and the next value field contains a pointer to another format of the same kind. (The second format contains Honda for a key value.) The first key field contains a pointer to the linked list of format (b) records, which contains the primary keys C1 and C2.

The inverted list is built as a linked structure in main memory as the data file is created. At the close of the program, the linked structure containing the inverted list is converted from pointer values to integer record

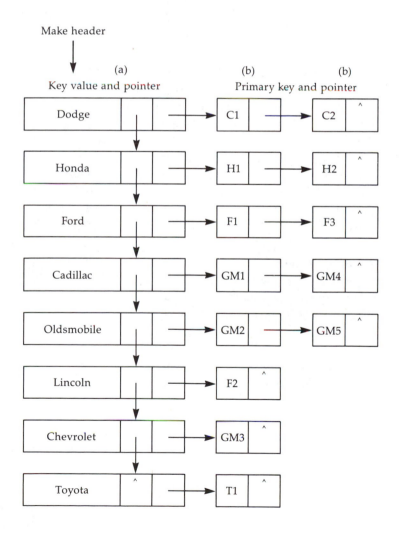

Figure 10.16
Inverted list of car makes in linked storage structure

Key value	Next value	First key

(a) format for storing a key value and a pointer
    to the first primary key in the address list

Key value	First address

(a) format for storing a key value and a record
    address of a format (b) record from the
    index file of the first primary key in the
    address list

Primary key	Next key

(b) format for storing a primary key and a pointer
    to the next primary key in the address list

Primary key	Next address

(b) format for storing a primary key and a record
    address of a format (b) record from the index
    file of the next primary key in the address list

Figure 10.17
Storage formats for a
linked structure of an
inverted list

Figure 10.18
Storage formats for
storing an inverted
list on external files

addresses, then stored in a file using the formats shown in Figure 10.18. The first format (a) node, which contains the key value Dodge, is written to record location 1. The first address is record location 2. The first format (b) node (which Dodge points to) contains the primary key C1. The node is stored in record 2, and the next address field is record 3. The last address in the address list has a next address value of −1. For example, if the data in the inverted list in Figure 10.16 is written to an external file, the resulting record contents appear as presented in Table 10.1. The first record in the file contains the value Dodge and an address of record 2. Record 2 contains the primary key C1 with a pointer to record 3. Record 3 has the primary key C2 with a pointer that is −1, indicating the end of the primary key linked list for the make of Dodge. In this way the file is read back into main memory and stored in the linked structure pictured in Figure 10.16.

Locating a certain make of car usually involves searching half the nodes in the linked structure, since the values for make of car are inserted in the order in which they appear in the file. With eight different car makes the average search visits four nodes to successfully locate the primary keys for that make. An unsuccessful search for the make Audi, for example, searches the entire list of eight nodes.

The pseudocode for creating an inverted file using the formats and structures described above is presented in Algorithm 10.1. The id_no is the primary key for the car data and is stored in the linked structure of the inverted list. The primary keys are in ascending order to answer intersecting queries more easily.

The pseudocode for modifying the inverted lists by adding a record to the data file or deleting a record from the data file as discussed previously

Table 10.1   File contents of inverted file in Figure 10.16

Format	Record No.	File Contents	
a	1	Dodge	2
b	2	C1	3
b	3	C2	−1
a	4	Honda	5
b	5	H1	6
b	6	H2	−1
a	7	Ford	8
b	8	F1	9
b	9	F2	−1
a	10	Cadillac	11
b	11	GM1	12
b	12	GM4	−1
a	13	Oldsmobile	14
b	14	GM2	15
b	15	GM5	−1
a	16	Lincoln	17
b	17	F2	−1
a	18	Chevrolet	19
b	19	GM3	−1
a	20	Toyota	21
b	21	T1	−1

Format a	Key value	First address	
Format b	Primary key	Next address	

Algorithm 10.1   Build Inverted Index As Data File Is Created

```
header [MAKE_INDEX] ← NIL
header [STYLE_INDEX] ← NIL
record_no ← 1 { first available record location in data_file }
Output (data_file, record_no, 0)

While Not Eof (input)
    Input (new_record ← id_no, make, style, non_indexed_items)
    Build_Index (MAKE_INDEX, new_record.make)
    Build_Index (STYLE_INDEX, new_record.style)
                {
                    output new_record to data_file
                }
    Output (data_file, new_record, record_no)
    record_no ← record_no + 1
    Output (data_file, record_no, 0)
    Output_Indexes (MAKE_INDEX, make_file)
    Output_Indexes (STYLE_INDEX, style_file)
```

Algorithm Build_Index (index, second_key)
                {
                    index indicates which index is to be built:
                            MAKE_INDEX or STYLE_INDEX
                    second_key is either the make or style that was read
                        into new_record
                }
        Search_List (where_found)
        If found
            Add_To_Key_List (where_found)
        Else
            Add_To_Index

Algorithm Search_List_(where_found)
                {
                    where_found returns NIL if second_key is not found
                    in index and returns a pointer to the node in the linked
                    structure if found
                }
        where_found ← header [index]
        found ← FALSE
        While (where_found <> NIL)
        And   Not found
            If where_found^.key_value = second_key
                found ← TRUE
            Else
                where_found ← where_found^.next_value

Algorithm Add_To_Key_List_(where_found)
                {
                    add the record location of new_record to the list of
                    addresses for the key_value pointed to by where_found
                    the primary keys in the key list are stored in
                    ascending order to facilitate searching
                }
        New (address_ptr)
        address_ptr^.primary_key ← id_no
        j ← where_found^.first_key
        previous ← where_found
        found ← FALSE
        While (j <> NIL)
        And   Not found
                {
                    search for the first primary key larger than the new id_no
                    in order to insert the new id_no in ascending order
                }
            If   j^.primary_key <= new_record.id_no
                previous ← j
                j ← j^.next_key

```
            Else
                found ← TRUE

        address_ptr^.next_key ← j
        If previous = where_found
                    {
                        insert  the  address  of the  primary  key  of new_record
                        at the front of  linked structure,   i.e., the first_key of
                        the list of primary keys
                    }
            previous^.first_key ← address_ptr


        Else
            previous^.next_key ← address_ptr

Algorithm Add_To_Index
                    {
                        add  the  second_key  as  a new value in the linked  structure
                        with  the  address  of  the  primary  key  of new_record  as the
                        first_key
                    }
        New (address_ptr)
        address_ptr^.primary_key ← id_no
        address_ptr^.next_key ← NIL
        New (key_value_ptr)
        key_value_ptr^.key_value ← second_key
        key_value_ptr^.next_value ← header [index]
        key_value_ptr^.first_key ← address_ptr
        header [index] ← key_value_ptr


Algorithm Output_Indexes (index, index_file)
                    {      .
                        output either  the  MAKE_INDEX or the  STYLE_INDEX (index)
                        sequentially to an external file for storage
                        all pointers  must be  converted to record
                        addresses and all "NIL" pointer values must be
                        converted to  −1
                    }
        record_no ← 1
        i ← header [index]

        While i <> NIL
            index_record.key_value ← i^.key_value
            index_record.first_address ← record_no + 1
                    {
                        output index_record to record_no location of index_file
                    }
            Output (index_file, index_record, record_no)
            record_no ← record_no + 1
            j ← i^.first_key
```

```
While   j <> NIL
       index_record.primary_key ← j^.primary_key

       If j^.next_key <> NIL
           index_record.next_key ← record_no + 1

       Else
           index_record.next_key ← −1

       Output (index_file, index_record, record_no)
       record_no ← record_no + 1
       j ← j^.next_key

   i ← i^.next_value
```

is presented in Algorithm 10.2. Algorithm 10.2 employs the same formats and structures as Algorithm 10.1. The inverted file is input into a linked structure at the beginning of the algorithm, modified as additions and deletions are made, and output at the end of the algorithm.

Use of a B-tree provides another approach to storing the inverted lists. A B-tree facilitates modifications but does not require that the structure be built before accessing the data file. The use of a B-tree of some appropriate order reduces the number of nodes required to store the inverted data for make or style of car, thus reducing the number of disk accesses required to search the inverted list. The B-tree is appropriate for an inverted list of a larger, more realistic file that is too large to fit into main memory. Instead of the linked list structure shown in Figure 10.16, the B-tree structure in

Algorithm 10.2 Modify Inverted Index (Additions and Deletions)

```
Input (data_file, record_no)
Input_Indexes (make_file, MAKE_INDEX);
Input_Indexes (style_file, STYLE_INDEX);

While Not Eof (input)
     Input (transaction_code)
     Case transaction_code
        'A' : Input(new_record ← id_no, make, style, non_indexed items)
              Build_Index (MAKE_INDEX, new_record.make)
              Build_Index (STYLE_INDEX, new_record.style)
              Output (data_file, new_record, record_no)
              record_no ← record_no + 1
```

```
'D' : Input (id_no)
            {
                input record from data file with id = id_no
            }
        Input (data_file, new_record, id_no)
        Delete_Index (MAKE_INDEX, new_record.make)
        Delete_Index (STYLE_INDEX, new_record.style)


Output_Indexes (MAKE_INDEX, make_file)
Output_Indexes (STYLE_INDEX, style_file)


Algorithm Input_Indexes (index_file, index)
                {
                    input the external file containing the key values and
                    address pointers into a linked structure
                    all record addresses must be converted to pointers
                    and all −1 pointer values must be converted to NIL
                }
    Input (index_file, index_record)
    New (key_value_ptr)
    header [index] ← key_value_ptr
    Link_Key_Value_Entry


Algorithm Link_Key_Value_Entry
                {
                    link the key value input from the record with the primary
                    keys in the list of addresses that follow
                    the end of the list of records with primary keys for this
                    key value is noted as a −1 for the next_address field of
                    the record
                }
    key_value_ptr^.key_value ← index_record.key_value
    If index_record.first_address <> −1
        Input (index_file, index_record)
        New (address_ptr)
        address_ptr^.primary_key ← index_record.primary_key
        key_value_ptr^.first_key ← address_ptr


        While index_record.next_address <> −1
                {
                    input and build list of addresses
                }
            Input(index_file, index_record)
            New (next_address_ptr)
            address_ptr^.next_key ← next_address_ptr
            next_address_ptr^.primary_key ← index_record.primary_key
            address_ptr ← next_address_ptr
```

```
                        address_ptr^.next_key ← NIL
                        If Not Eof (index_file)
                                {
                                    input next key value
                                }
                            Input (index_file, index_record)
                            New (next_key_value_ptr)
                            key_value_ptr^.next_value ← next_key_value_ptr
                            key_value_ptr ← next_key_value_ptr
                            Link_Key_Value_Entry
                        Else
                                key_value_ptr^.next_value ← NIL
                                Return


            Algorithm Delete_Index (index, second_key)
                            {
                                index indicates which index is to have a deletion:
                                        MAKE_INDEX or STYLE_INDEX
                                second_key is either the make or style that is
                                        to be deleted from the index
                            }
                    Search_List (where_found)
                    If found
                        If where_found^.first_key^.primary_key = id_no
                                {
                                    delete first key
                                }
                            where_found^.first_key ← where_found^.first_key^.next_key
                            If where_found^.first_key = NIL
                                {
                                    delete entire entry since the only id_no has been deleted
                                }
                                If previous = NIL { first key value in linked structure }
                                    header [index] ← where_found^.next_value
                                Else
                                        previous^.next_value ← where_found^.next_value


                    Else
                            j ← where_found^.first_key^.next_key
                            i ← where_found^.first_key
                            found ← FALSE
                            While (j <> NIL)
                            And Not found        { search for id_no in list of addresses }
                                If j^.primary_key <> id_no
                                    i ← j
                                    j ← j^.next_key

                                Else
                                        found ← TRUE

                        If Not found
                            Print 'Not found'
```

```
            Else
                i^.first_key  ←  j^.next_key

        Else
            Print 'not found'

Algorithm Search_List (where_found)
                    {
                        where_found returns NIL if second_key is not found
                        in index, and returns a pointer to the node in
                        the linked structure if found
                        previous contains the pointer to the node previous to
                        the node containing the second_key in case a
                        deletion is to be made
                    }
        previous  ←  NIL
        where_found  ←  header [index]
        found  ←  FALSE
        While (where_found <> NIL)
        And      Not found
            If where_found^.key_value  =  second_key
                found  ←  TRUE
            Else
                previous  ←  where_found
                where_found  ←  where_found^.next_value
```

Figure 10.19 is built externally, and each node of the B-tree represents a disk access. When the B-tree inverted structure for make of car is complete, it already resides in a disk file. The linked structure, as you recall, was built in main memory and had to be copied to a disk file for storage. The B-tree structure that stores the inverted list for style of car is presented in Figure 10.20.

Each tuple in the nodes of the B-tree contains a make value, the address of a record containing the list of primary keys for this make of car, and the address of the record that is the root of the subtree containing values greater than this make of car. For example, the first tuple in the root node in Figure 10.19 contains the make Dodge, a pointer to the record with primary keys C1 and C2, and a pointer to the record that contains the tuple Ford.

The algorithms for building a B-tree and making additions and deletions of values in the B-tree are presented in Chapter 8. The algorithms can easily be modified to efficiently store the data in the inverted lists. To retrieve data concerning a certain make of car requires, in the worst case, only three accesses: two accesses to visit the two levels of the B-tree and a third access to retrieve the linked list of primary keys for that make of car. This method certainly represents a savings over the previous design in terms of access time, building time, and the time necessary for modification.

Figure 10.19
B-tree of order 4 stor-
ing inverted list from
Figure 10.16

Figure 10.20
B-tree of order 4 stor-
ing inverted list of car
styles from Figure
10.10 (b)

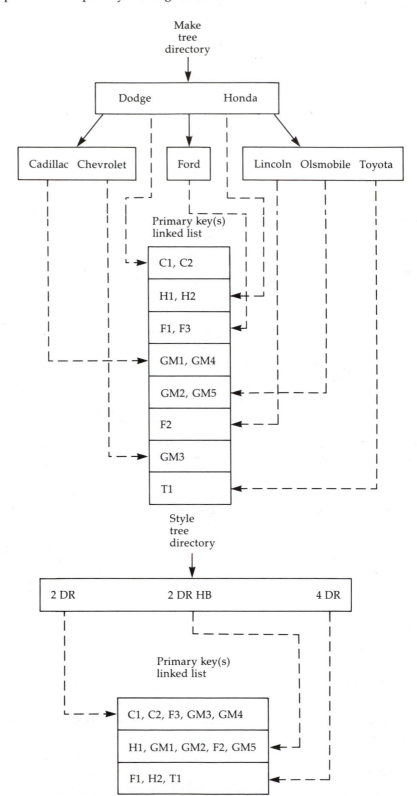

MULTILIST FILE ORGANIZATION

Because the length of a list of addresses may vary, the length of an entry in an inverted list may vary. As a previous section discussed, this variance often necessitates storing a single secondary key inverted list in an individual file.

One solution to the difficulty of storing a varying list of addresses with the same secondary key value is linking the elements in a list. The address of the first record in the linked list is stored in the directory. A file that links data records with identical secondary key values is organized as a **multilist file**. A multilist file contains two areas: (1) a directory and (2) a data record area. The directory contains an inverted list for each secondary key field to be used in accessing the data records in the data record area. The data records are organized in any manner that provides random access to the records.

As in inverted file organization, each entry in the directory for a secondary key field contains an attribute found in this secondary key field in the file. Unlike inverted files however, each entry in the directory contains the primary key of only one record in the file rather than a list of primary keys of all records containing the attribute. All data records containing the same attribute in a secondary key field are linked in the data file. So the one primary key in the directory is the primary key of the first record in a linked list of records. The list contains the same attribute for a particular secondary key field, and each directory entry also contains an integer indicating the number of records in the linked list for this attribute. If directories are built to provide access to a number of secondary key fields, each data record contains a link field for each secondary key field.

CASE STUDY 10.2: THE CAR-RENTAL AGENCY

The multilist file directory that provides secondary key access by make and style for the sample car-rental agency data is found in Figure 10.10, and so is the corresponding data file for the multilist file organization, expanded to contain link fields for make and style.

Each entry in the directory for make of car contains the make, the primary key of the first record in the linked list of all records containing this make, and the length of the linked list (the number of records in the linked list). As the directory for the inverted file indicates, two records in the file contain data concerning cars of the make Dodge. The first record for a Dodge contains the primary key C1. The record in the multilist data file with the primary key C1 needs to be input so that the link field for make can be accessed to identify the second record in the file for a Dodge. The data record with primary key C1 contains a link field for make of car with the value C2. The record with primary key C2 does contain data for a Dodge,

Figure 10.21
Multilist file directories and file with link fields for car-rental agency data

Multilist file directories

(a) Make of car

Make	Primary key	Length
Dodge	C1	2
Honda	H1	2
Ford	F1	2
Cadillac	GM1	2
Oldsmobile	GM2	2
Lincoln	F2	1
Chevrolet	GM3	1
Toyota	T1	1

(a) Make of car

Style	Primary key	Length
2 DR	C1	5
4 DR	H1	5
2 DR HB	F1	3

(b) Style of car

Multilist data file

Primary key	Secondary keys				Nonindexed data
Id no.	Make	Link	Style	Link	
C1	Dodge	C2	2 DR	C2	
H1	Honda	H2	4 DR	GM1	
F1	Ford	F3	2 DR HB	H2	
GM1	Cadillac	GM4	4 DR	GM2	
GM2	Oldsmobile	GM5	4 DR	F2	
H2	Honda	^	2 DR HB	T1	
F2	Lincoln	^	4 DR	GM5	
C2	Dodge	^	2 DR	F3	
F3	Ford	^	2 DR	GM3	
GM3	Chevrolet	^	2 DR	GM4	
GM4	Cadillac	^	2 DR	^	
GM5	Oldsmobile	^	4 DR	^	
T1	Toyota	^	2 DR HB	^	

and the link field for make is nil (^), which indicates the end of the linked list. Record C1 also contains a style link of C2. Record C2 contains a style link of F3, and record F3 contains a style link of GM3. Record GM3 contains a style link of GM4, and GM4 contains a nil style link, which indicates that records C1, C2, F3, GM3, and GM4 all have the same style (2 DR). The directory indicates that, in fact, the file contains five 2 DR cars beginning with record C1.

One of the advantages of the multilist file over the inverted file is the fixed length of the entries in the directory. The disadvantage created by the fixed-length directory entries is the increase in the number of record accesses to satisfy queries. Questions that ask "How many Fords are available" can be answered by retrieving the length field of the index entry for the make of Ford.

If the query is "How many two-door Dodges are available," the primary keys in the intersection of (1) the list of all Dodges and (2) the list of all two-door cars is the answer. The primary key of one Dodge is listed in the directory for make (C1), but the primary key of the second Dodge can be located only by retrieving the make link field of record C1. The primary key of one 2 DR car is listed in the directory for style (C1), but the primary key of all other 2 DR cars can be located only by retrieving all records in the following linked list: The style link of record C1 is C2, the style link of record C2 is F3, the style link of record F3 is GM3, the style link of record GM3 is GM4, and the style link of GM4 is nil. The intersection of the list for (1) all Dodges (C1, C2) and the list for (2) all 2 DR cars (C1, C2, F3, GM3, GM4) tells how many two-door Dodges are available. The answer is two: C1 and C2.

With inverted file organization, the primary key of all cars having the attribute Dodge for make are listed in the directory as well as cars having the attribute 2 DR for style. In consequence the data file is not accessed to answer a query involving make and style. With multilist file organization, the primary key of one record is listed in the directory, but primary keys of all other records having the attributes Dodge for make and 2 DR for style must be retrieved from link fields of data records. With multilist file organization, the number of data records that must be retrieved to answer an intersecting query is five: one to retrieve primary keys of all Dodge cars and four to retrieve primary keys of all 2 DR cars. With inverted file organization no retrievals are required.

Additions to the multilist file result in modifications not only to the directory but to the link fields of records in the data file. For example, suppose a record with key fields GM6, Chevrolet, and 4 DR is added to the multilist file. For those attributes that exist in the directories, the length field is incremented. The new record is added to the data file, a make link in the file is changed to include GM6 in the linked list of Chevrolet cars, and a style link in the file is changed to include GM6 in the linked list of 4 DR cars. The required changes are indicated in Figure 10.22 with asterisks.

Additions of records to the file with new attributes for secondary key fields result in the new attributes being added as new entries in the directory. If the record with keys GM7, Pontiac, 2 DR HB is added to the multilist file, Pontiac is a new attribute for car make. Figure 10.23 presents the multilist file and directory with GM7 added. Pontiac is added as a new entry in the directory for make and GM7 as the first key. The length is 1, and the make link for GM7 is nil. Since 2 DR exists in the directory for style, the length is incremented, and the style link field of the record in the file is changed to include GM7.

When adding a record to a linked list, the last record in the linked list is changed to contain the address of the newly added record; the record with key GM4, the last 2 DR car prior to adding GM7, now has a link of

Figure 10.22
Multilist file directo-
ries and file with link
fields after addition
of GM6 Chevrolet 4
DR

Multilist file directories

Make	Primary key	Length
Dodge	C1	2
Honda	H1	2
Ford	F1	2
Cadillac	GM1	2
Oldsmobile	GM2	2
Lincoln	F2	1
Chevrolet	GM3	2*
Toyota	T1	1

(a) Make of car

Style	Primary key	Length
2 DR	C1	5
4 DR	H1	6*
2 DR HB	F1	3

(b) Style of car

Multilist data file

Primary key	Secondary keys				Nonindexed data
Id no.	Make	Link	Style	Link	
C1	Dodge	C2	2 DR	C2	
H1	Honda	H2	4 DR	GM1	
F1	Ford	F3	2 DR HB	H2	
GM1	Cadillac	GM4	4 DR	GM2	
GM2	Oldsmobile	GM5	4 DR	F2	
H2	Honda	^	2 DR HB	T1	
F2	Lincoln	^	4 DR	GM5	
C2	Dodge	^	2 DR	F3	
F3	Ford	^	2 DR	GM3	
GM3	Chevrolet	GM6*	2 DR	GM4	
GM4	Cadillac	^	2 DR	^	
GM5	Oldsmobile	^	4 DR	GM6*	
T1	Toyota	^	2 DR HB	^	
GM6*	Chevrolet*	^ *	4 DR*	^ *	*

*latest additions

GM7. Adding to the end of the linked list requires input of records C1, C2, F3, GM3, and GM4 to change the style link of GM4. Rather than using five input operations to find the end of the linked list and one output operation to store GM4 back to the file, GM7 could have been added at the beginning of the linked list. Let the style link GM7 be the primary key from the entry for 2 DR in the style directory (C1), and store GM7 as the primary key in the style directory. Storing the new addition in the beginning of the linked list requires only a change in the directory—no records need be input. It takes one change to the directory and one output operation to add GM7 at the beginning of the linked list as opposed to five inputs and one output to add GM7 at the end of the linked list.

Multilist file directories

Make	Primary key	Length
Dodge	C1	2
Honda	H1	2
Ford	F1	2
Cadillac	GM1	2
Oldsmobile	GM2	2
Lincoln	F2	1
Chevrolet	GM3	2
Toyota	T1	1
Pontiac*	GM7*	1*

(a) Make of car

Style	Primary key	Length
2 DR	C1	6*
4 DR	H1	6
2 DR HB	F1	3

(b) Style of car

Figure 10.23
Multilist file directory and file with link fields after addition of GM7 Pontiac 2 DR

Multilist data file

Primary key	Secondary keys				Nonindexed data
Id no.	Make	Link	Style	Link	
C1	Dodge	C2	2 DR	C2	
H1	Honda	H2	4 DR	GM1	
F1	Ford	F3	2 DR HB	H2	
GM1	Cadillac	GM4	4 DR	GM2	
GM2	Oldsmobile	GM5	4 DR	F2	
H2	Honda	^	2 DR HB	T1	
F2	Lincoln	^	4 DR	GM5	
C2	Dodge	^	2 DR	F3	
F3	Ford	^	2 DR	GM3	
GM3	Chevrolet	GM6	2 DR	GM4	
GM4	Cadillac	^	2 DR	GM7*	
GM5	Oldsmobile	^	4 DR	GM6	
T1	Toyota	^	2 DR HB	^	
GM6	Chevrolet	^	4 DR	^	
GM7*	Pontiac*	^ *	2 DR*	^ *	*

*latest additions

Deletions to the multilist file result in deletions of keys and/or attributes in the directory as well as changes in the linked lists for all secondary key fields that included the deleted record. If the primary key of the deleted record occurs in the directory, it is deleted, and the next record in the linked list for that attribute is placed in the directory with the length of the list reduced by one. If the primary key of the deleted record does not occur in the directory, the length of the attribute is reduced by one to indicate the removal of one record.

If the record with primary key F1 in Figure 10.23 is deleted, the record is deleted from the linked list of all cars with make Ford and from the linked list of all cars with style 2 DR HB. The directory for make indicates that

Ford occurs in record F1 and that there are two records with Ford. The record F1 is the first record in the linked list, and the make link field of record F1 contains the value F3, (Figure 10.23). Since F1 is the first record in the linked list and is to be deleted, the value in the make link field of record F1 (F3) is placed in the directory for make of Ford (Figure 10.24). The number of records of Ford make (length) is reduced from two (in Figure 10.23) to one (in Figure 10.24). The first record in Figure 10.23 with the style of 2 DR HB is F1, and three records have that attribute. Since F1 is the first record in the linked list and is to be deleted, the value in the style link field of record F1 (H2) is placed in the directory for style 2 DR HB, and the entry

Figure 10.24
Multilist file directories and file with link fields after deletion of F1

Multilist file directories

Make	Primary key	Length
Dodge	C1	2
Honda	H1	2
Ford	F3*	1*
Cadillac	GM1	2
Oldsmobile	GM2	2
Lincoln	F2	1
Chevrolet	GM3	2
Toyota	T1	1
Pontiac	GM7	1

(a) Make of car

Style	Primary key	Length
2 DR	C1	6
4 DR	H1	6
2 DR HB	H2*	2*

(b) Style of car

Multilist data file

Primary key	Secondary keys				Nonindexed data
Id no.	Make	Link	Style	Link	
C1	Dodge	C2	2 DR	C2	
H1	Honda	H2	4 DR	GM1	
*	*	*	*	*	*
GM1	Cadillac	GM4	4 DR	GM2	
GM2	Oldsmobile	GM5	4 DR	F2	
H2	Honda	^	2 DR HB	T1	
F2	Lincoln	^	4 DR	GM5	
C2	Dodge	^	2 DR	F3	
F3	Ford	^	2 DR	GM3	
GM3	Chevrolet	GM6	2 DR	GM4	
GM4	Cadillac	^	2 DR	GM7	
GM5	Oldsmobile	^	4 DR	GM6	
T1	Toyota	^	2 DR HB	^	
GM6	Chevrolet	^	4 DR	^	
GM7	Pontiac	^	2 DR	^	

*site of deletion

in the length column changes from 3 (Figure 10.23) to 2 (Figure 10.24). The record F1 is deleted from the data file.

Deleting a record with unique attributes for secondary key fields results in the deletion of an entire entry from the directory of the multilist file. Consider deleting T1 from Figure 10.24. T1 contains the make Toyota, the style 2 DR HB and has a length of 1, which indicates that T1 is the only Toyota in the data file. The entire entry is deleted from the make directory. The style 2 DR HB is not unique, so H2—which links to T1—remains the address in the style directory. The length is reduced from 2 to 1, and the style link field of record H2 is changed from T1 to nil. The changes made when deleting T1 from the multilist file are shown in Figure 10.25.

Multilist file directories

Make	Primary key	Length
Dodge	C1	2
Honda	H1	2
Ford	F3	1
Cadillac	GM1	2
Oldsmobile	GM2	2
Lincoln	F2	1
Chevrolet	GM3	2
*	*	*
Pontiac	GM7	1

(a) Make of car

Style	Primary key	Length
2 DR	C1	6
4 DR	H1	6
2 DR HB	F1	1*

(b) Style of car

Figure 10.25
Multilist file directories and file with link fields after deletion of T1

Multilist data file

Primary key	Secondary keys				Nonindexed data
Id no.	Make	Link	Style	Link	
C1	Dodge	C2	2 DR	C2	
H1	Honda	H2	4 DR	GM1	
F1	Ford	F3	2 DR HB	H2	
GM1	Cadillac	GM4	4 DR	GM2	
GM2	Oldsmobile	GM5	4 DR	F2	
H2	Honda	^	2 DR HB	^	
F2	Lincoln	^	4 DR	GM5	
C2	Dodge	^	2 DR	F3	
F3	Ford	^	2 DR	GM3	
GM3	Chevrolet	GM6	2 DR	GM4	
GM4	Cadillac	^	2 DR	GM7	
GM5	Oldsmobile	^	4 DR HB	GM6	
*	*	*	*	*	*
GM6	Chevrolet	^	4 DR	^	
GM7	Pontiac	^	2 DR	^	

*site of deletion

Multilist Files in TURBO Pascal

The implementation of multilist files in Pascal is similar to that of inverted files previously discussed in this chapter. The directories are stored in a linked structure to facilitate the addition and deletion of key values into the directory. With each key value in the linked structure is also stored the first primary key in the linked list of records that has the same key value and a length field containing the number of records in the linked list. The make directory (Figure 10.21(a)) is stored in a linked structure as shown in Figure 10.26.

Unlike the inverted files discussed earlier, variant records are not needed because the nodes of the linked structure all have three fields. The nodes

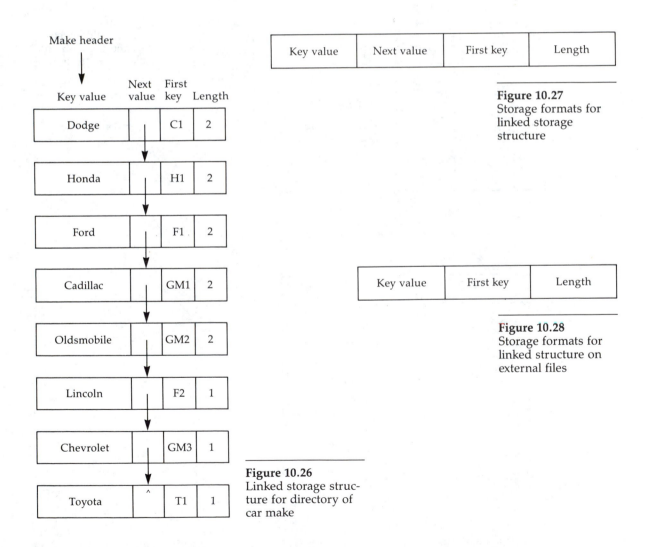

Figure 10.27
Storage formats for linked storage structure

Figure 10.28
Storage formats for linked structure on external files

Figure 10.26
Linked storage structure for directory of car make

are stored in the format shown in Figure 10.27. A node of the linked structure with the key value Dodge contains the next value field with a pointer to another node of the same format. The first key field contains the primary key C1, and a length of 2.

The directory of the multilist file is built as a linked structure in main memory as the data file is created. At the close of the program, the linked structure containing the directory is stored in a file using the format shown in Figure 10.28. The next value field is dropped, and the nodes from the linked structure are stored sequentially. Each directory is stored in an individual file since the key value field may vary from one secondary key field to another. For example, the data in the linked storage structure in Figure 10.26 are written to an external file. The resulting record contents are presented in Table 10.2.

Locating a certain make of car involves searching, on the average, half the nodes in the linked structure. In other words the average search visits four nodes to successfully locate the beginning of a linked list of records for that make. Once the beginning of the linked list for a make of car is located, the data file must be accessed to search, on the average, half-way through the linked list of records. This search through the linked list of records is the expensive characteristic of a multilist file. Just as in the inverted list, an unsuccessful search—a search for Audi, for example—requires the search of the entire multilist make directory.

The pseudocode for creating a multilist file using the formats and structures described above is presented in Algorithm 10.3. The id_no is the primary key for the car data. The records in a single linked list are linked in ascending order by primary key to answer intersecting queries more easily.

Table 10.2   File contents of multilist file in figure 10.26

Record No.	File Contents		
1	Dodge	C1	2
2	Honda	H1	2
3	Ford	F1	2
4	Cadillac	GM1	2
5	Oldsmobile	GM2	2
6	Lincoln	F2	1
7	Chevrolet	GM3	1
8	Toyota	T1	1

| **Format** | Key value | First key | Length |

Algorithm 10.3   Build Multi-List Index As Data File Is Created

```
header [MAKE_INDEX] ← NIL
header [STYLE_INDEX] ← NIL
record_no ← 1 { first available record location in data_file }
Output (data_file, record_no, 0)

While Not Eof (input)
    Input (new_record ← id_no, make, style, non_indexed_items)
    new_record.make_link ← −1
    new_record.style_link ← −1
    Build_Index (MAKE_INDEX, new_record.make, new_record.make_link)
    Build_Index (STYLE_INDEX, new_record.style, new_record.style_link)
                    {
                        output new_record to data_file
                    }
    Output (data_file, new_record)
    record_no ← record_no + 1

Output (data_file, record_no, 0)
Output_Indexes (MAKE_INDEX, make_file)
Output_Indexes (STYLE_INDEX, style_file)

Algorithm Build_Index (index, second_key, link)
                    {
                        index indicates which index is to be built:
                            MAKE_INDEX or STYLE_INDEX
                        second_key is either the make or style that was read
                            into new_record
                        link is either the make_link or style_link of
                            new_record
                    }
    Search_List (where_found)
    If found
        Add_To_Key_List (where_found)
    Else
        Add_To_Index

Algorithm Search_List (where_found)
                    {
                        where_found returns NIL if second_key is not found in
                        index and returns a pointer to the node in the
                        linked structure if found
                    }
    where_found ← header [index]
    found ← FALSE
    While (where_found <> NIL) And Not found
        If where_found^.keyvalue = second_key
            found ← TRUE
        Else
            where_found ← where_found^.next_value
```

```
Algorithm Add_To_Key_List (where_found)
                    {
                        add the primary key of new_record to the list of primary
                        keys for the key_value pointed to by where_found
                        the primary keys in the key list are stored in ascending
                        order to facilitate searching
                    }
    where_found^.length ← where_found^.length + 1
    j ← where_found^.first_key
    previous := j
    done ← FALSE
    While (j <> −1) And Not done
                    {
                        search for the first id_no larger than the new id_no in
                        order to insert the new id_no in ascending order
                    }
        input (data_file, hold_record, j)
        If hold_record.id_no > new_record.id_no
            done ← TRUE
        Else
            previous ← j
            prev_record ← hold_record
            Case index
                MAKE_INDEX  : j ← hold_record.make_link
                STYLE_INDEX : j ← hold_record.style_link


    link ← j { new_record linked to next larger id_no }
    If previous = j
                    {
                        insert the primary key of new_record at the front of the
                        linked structure, i.e., the first_key of the list
                        of primary keys
                    }
        where^.first_key ← id_no
    Else
        Case index
            MAKE_INDEX  : prev_record.make_link ← id_no
            STYLE_INDEX : prev_record.style_link ← id_no


        Output (data_file, prev_record, previous)


Algorithm Add_To_Index
                {
                    add the second_key as the new value in the linked structure
                    with the primary key of new_record as the first_key
                }
```

```
                    New  (key_value_ptr)
                    key_value_ptr^.key_value  ←  second_key
                    key_value_ptr^.next_value  ←  header [index]
                    key_value_ptr^.first_key  ←  id_no
                    key_value_ptr^.length  ←  1
                    header [index]  ←  key_value_ptr

Algorithm Output_Indexes (index, index_file)
                              {
                                   output either the MAKE_INDEX or the STYLE_INDEX (index)
                                   sequentially to an external file for storage
                              }
         i ← header [index]
         While (i <> NIL)
              index_record.key_value  ←  i^.key_value
              index_record.first_key  ←  i^.first_key
              index_record.length  ←  i^.length
              Output (index_file, index_record)
              i  ←  i^.next_value
```

The pseudocode for modifying the multilist file when adding a record to the data file or deleting a record from the data file is presented in Algorithm 10.4. Algorithm 10.4 uses the same formats and structures as Algorithm 10.3. The directory is input at the beginning of the algorithm into the linked structures, modified as additions and deletions are made, and output at the end of the algorithm.

The B-tree presented in Chapter 8 is an appropriate structure in which to store the multilist index. The B-tree allows secondary key values to be stored to facilitate faster searching and easier modification. As with the inverted list, the number of nodes in the B-tree can be reduced by increasing the order of the tree, thus reducing the number of disk accesses to search the multilist directory.

Algorithm 10.4   Modify Multi-listed Index (Additions and Deletions)

```
Input (data_file, record_no)
Input_Indexes (make_file, MAKE_INDEX)
Input_Indexes (style_file, STYLE_INDEX)

While Not Eof (input)
     Input (transaction_code)
     Case (transaction_code)
          'A' : Input (new_record ← id_no, make, style, non_indexed items)
                Build_Index (make_index, new_record.make, new_record.make_link)
                Build_Index (style_index, new_record.style, new_record.style_link)
                Output (data_file, new_record, record_no)
                record_no ← record_no + 1
```

```
    'D' : Input (id_no)
                {
                    input record from data_file
                }
            Input (data_file, new_record, id_no)
            Delete_Index (MAKE_INDEX, new_record.make)
            Delete_Index (STYLE_INDEX, new_record.style)

Output_Indexes (MAKE_INDEX, make_file)
Output_Indexes (STYLE_INDEX, style_file)

Algorithm Input_Indexes (index_file, index)
                    {
                        input the external file containing the key values, the
                        first key, and the length into a linked structure
                    }
    Input (index_file, index_record)
    New (key_value_ptr)
    header [index] ← key_value_ptr
    Link_Key_Value_Entry

Algorithm Link_Key_Value_Entry

    key_value_ptr^.key_value ← index_record.key_value
    key_value_ptr^.first_key ← index_record.first_key
    key_value_ptr^.length ← index_record.length
    If Not Eof (index_file)
                {
                    input next key value
                }
        Input (index_file, index_record)
        New (next_key_value_ptr)
        key_value_ptr^.next_value ← next_key_value_ptr
        key_value_ptr ← next_key_value_ptr
        Link_Key_Value_Entry
    Else
        key_value_ptr^.next_value ← NIL
        Return

Algorithm Delete_Index (index, second_key)

    Search_List (where_found)
    If found
        If where_found^.first_key = id_no
                {
                    delete first key
                }
        If where_found^.length = 1 { delete entire entry }
            If previous = NIL { first entry }
                header [index] ← where_found^.next_value
```

```
                              Else
                                    previousˆ.next_value ← where_foundˆ.next_value

                        Else { find next primary key to become first_key }
                              Input (data_file, hold_record, where_foundˆ.first_key)
                              Case index
                                    MAKE_INDEX   :
                                          where_foundˆ.first_key ← hold_record.make_link
                                    STYLE_INDEX :
                                          where_foundˆ.first_key ← hold_record.style_link

                              where_foundˆ.length ← where_foundˆ.length  −  1

                  Else { id_no not  =  first_key }
                        previous ← where_foundˆ.first_key
                        Input (data_file, hold_record, previous)
                        Case index
                              MAKE  : j ← hold_record.make_link
                              STYLE : j ← hold_record.style_link

                        found ← FALSE
                        While (j <> NIL)
                        And Not found
                              { search for id_no in linked list of records }
                              If j <> id_no
                                    previous ← j
                                    prev_record ← hold_record
                                    Case index
                                          MAKE  : j ← hold_record.make_link
                                          STYLE : j ← hold_record.style_link

                              Else
                                    found ← TRUE

                        If Not found
                              Print 'not found'
                        Else
                              Case index
                                    MAKE  : prev_record.make_link ← hold_record.make_link
                                    STYLE : prev_record.style_link ← hold_record.style_link
                              where_foundˆ.length ← where_foundˆ.length  −  1
            Else
                  Print 'not found'

Algorithm Search_List (where_found)
                  {
                        where_found returns NIL if second_key is not found in
                        index and returns a pointer to the node in the linked
                        structure if found
                        previous contains the pointer to the node previous to the
                        node containing the second_key in case a deletion is
                        to be made
                  }
```

```
previous ← NIL
where_found ← header [index]
found ← FALSE
While (where_found <> NIL)
And    Not found
   If where_found^.key_value = second_key
         found ← TRUE
   Else
         previous ← where_found
         where_found ← where_found^.next_value
```

The data in the multilist directories in Figure 10.21 can be stored in a B-tree structure as pictured in Figures 10.29 and 10.30. The B-tree is stored externally, and each node represents a disk access. The whole structure is much simpler than the structure for the inverted list, since each tuple contains the data found in the multilist directory pertaining to one make or style of car. The first tuple in the root node in Figure 10.29 contains the same information found in one entry of the multilist directory of Figure 10.21(a): the make Dodge, the first primary key of the linked list (C1) and the length of the linked list (2). The B-tree also contains a pointer to the record (node) that contains the tuple Ford.

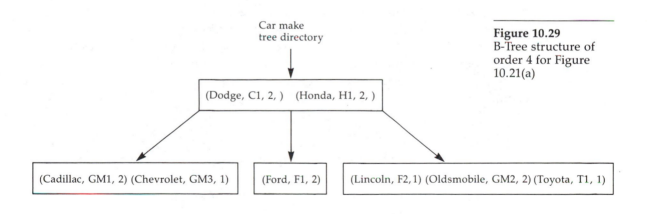

Figure 10.29
B-Tree structure of order 4 for Figure 10.21(a)

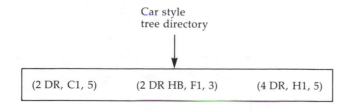

Figure 10.30
B-tree structure of order 4 for Figure 10.21(b)

SUMMARY

Multiple-key file organization provides access to a data file by one or more secondary key fields in addition to access by a primary key field. Two types of multiple-key file organization are inverted file organization and multilist file organization.

Inverted file organization uses an inverted index of all attributes in the data file for each secondary key field. Each attribute is accompanied by a list of addresses (primary keys) of all records in the data file containing the attribute. Inverted files may be partially inverted (some of the fields in the record are secondary key fields with inverted lists available) or fully inverted (all fields in the record are secondary key fields with inverted lists available). Most queries, including intersecting queries, can be answered from data in the inverted lists for the secondary key fields without access to the data file itself. Additions and deletions to the file require changes to the directory. The disadvantage of inverted file organization is the variance in length of the list of addresses in the inverted lists.

Multilist file organization overcomes the disadvantage of inverted file organization by linking records in the data file with the same attribute for a secondary key field. Multilist files also retain in the directory the attribute, the address (primary key) of the first record in the linked list, and the length of the linked list. The directory now has fixed-length entries, which are easier to store. However, more space is used for the data file since each field that is a secondary key is accompanied by a link field. A major disadvantage of multilist files is the number of file accesses necessary to answer a query. Since only one primary key is stored in the directory, retrieval of all records in a linked list requires accessing the data file—one record at a time—to retrieve the link field, which specifies the next record in the list. Additions and deletions to the file require manipulation of all linked lists to properly insert or remove a record.

Key Terms

fully inverted file	multiple-key file organization
inversion index	partially inverted file
inverted file organization	primary key
multilist file	secondary key
multilist file organization	

Exercises

1. List the advantages and disadvantages of an inverted index for a multiple-key file.

2. List the advantages and disadvantages of a multilist index for a multiple-key file.

3. Describe the kinds of queries that can be answered by searching the inverted index without searching the data file. Describe the actions necessary to answer the same queries for a multilist index.

4. Describe several applications that might require secondary key access.

5. Of what use is the length field (length of the linked list) in a multilist file?

6. Design an algorithm for answering intersecting queries for the make and style secondary key fields in the car-rental agency data file. A query might be, for example, "List all the four-door Chevrolets," where four-door (4 DR) and Chevrolet are secondary key values for the make and style fields, respectively. Assume that inverted files are used for secondary key access.

7. Repeat exercise 6, but—this time—assume that multilist files are used for secondary key access.

8. Using the inverted files for make and style of car in Figure 10.10, assume the inverted directories are stored in main memory, and assume each record in the data file requires a disk access for retrieval. State the number of disk accesses required to answer the following queries:

   a. How many four-door Oldsmobiles are in the data file?

   b. List all the four-door cars.

   c. What are the colors of the two-door Dodges?

   d. Are there any 2-door hatchbacks in the data file?

   e. What is the mileage of each of the four-door Cadillacs?

9. Repeat exercise 8 assuming the inverted files for make and style of car are stored as an indexed sequential file, and each attribute requires a disk access. Compare your answers with those to exercise 8.

10. Repeat exercise 8 assuming the inverted files for make and style of car are stored as B-trees as pictured in Figures 10.19 and 10.20. Compare your answers with those to exercises 8 and 9.

11. Repeat exercise 8 assuming the car-rental agency data file is stored with sequential organization and that no secondary key access is available. Compare your answers with those to exercises 8 through 10.

12. Repeat exercises 8 through 11 assuming a multilist file is available for secondary keys make and style of car for a multiple-key car-data file.

13. Use the following data records about a hospital to build inverted lists for secondary key access by the doctor's name and the patient's ward.

PRIMARY KEY	PATIENT'S NAME	WARD	ROOM NUMBER	DOCTOR'S NAME	CURRENT MEDICATION
121	Novak, T. R.	G	102	White	Hypoch
231	Drew, R. W.	I	123	Rollins	Sulph-3
243	Black, H. J.	I	124	Brown	Sulph-3
354	James, J. K.	P	213	Taylor	Cryol
365	Tasher, R. E.	R	312	Watson	Neoben
467	Andrews, T. B.	G	103	Rollins	Hypoch
587	Black, T. Y.	M	154	Taylor	Tylph
678	McCarry, C. M.	P	215	Taylor	Cryol
767	Jones, T. T.	I	126	Brown	Sulph-3
876	Smith, D. W.	R	313	Watson	Neoben

ward legend: G = general ward
P = pediatric ward
I = intensive care unit
M = maternity ward
R = recovery room

14. Using the inverted list from exercise 13, how many disk accesses are necessary to answer the following queries? (Assume the inverted list is in main memory.)

   a. What are the names of the patients in the recovery room?

   b. How many patients are currently in the maternity ward?

   c. Is Tom Jones a patient at the hospital?

   d. What drugs are the patients of Dr. Taylor currently taking?

15. Using the hospital data file in exercise 13, draw a multilist file for doctor's name and patient's ward. Also draw the data file with the links included.

16. Repeat exercise 14 for the multilist file built in exercise 15.

Programming Problems

1. Write a program to build an inverted file for the indexed sequential employee data file created in programming problem 14, 16, or 18 in Chapter 9 to provide secondary key access to department number, section id, and marital status. Use the linked structure example shown in Figure 10.16 for the inverted lists, then copy the information to an external file.

2. Repeat problem 1 using a B-tree of order 5 for inverted lists.

3. Write a program to build a multilist file for the indexed sequential employee data file created in programming problem 14, 16, or 18 in Chapter 9 to provide secondary key access to department number, section id, and marital status.

4. Repeat problem 3 using a B-tree of order 5 for the multilists.

5. Write a program to update the file and secondary key indexes created in problem 1.

6. Write a program to update the file and secondary key indexes created in problem 2.

7. Write a program to update the file and secondary key indexes created in problem 3.

8. Write a program to update the file and secondary key indexes created in problem 4.

9. Write a program to count the number of accesses to the file built in problem 1.

10. Modify the program written in problem 1 to eliminate secondary key values from the indexed sequential file.

11. Write a program to count the number of accesses to the file built in problem 10. Compare your answers to those in problem 9.

12. Repeat problem 9 for the file built in problem 3 and compare the counts.

Appendix A

Simulating Random-Access Files in Standard Pascal

Random access can easily be simulated in versions of Pascal that closely follow the ISO standard. The simulation is achieved by storing the records of data in a sequential file, reading the entire file into an array in internal memory at the beginning of the program that randomly accesses the data records, using procedures that simulate a random read and random write, then writing the array of records to a sequential file at the close of the program that randomly updates the data. The routines for simulating random access to a file of data assume the following data type and structure declarations:

```
CONST
     FILE_SIZE = some constant;
TYPE
     Record_Type =  Record
                         .
                         .
                         .
                       End;
     Array_Type = Array [1..FILE_SIZE] of Record_Type;
     File_Type = File of Record_Type;
VAR
     filename : File_Type;
     records : Array_Type;
```

The entire file must be read in at the beginning of the program before any access to the file of data. The Reset statement

```
    Reset (internal_name)
```

should be replaced by a call to the procedure Reset_Random_File

```
    Reset_Random_File (internal_name, records)
```

The random read, which consists of the following two statements:

```
Seek (internal_name, location)
Read (internal_name, a_record)
```

should be replaced by a call to the procedure Random_Read

```
Random_Read (location, a_record)
```

The random write, which consists of the following two statements:

```
Seek (internal_name, location)
Write (internal_name, a_record)
```

should be replaced by a call to the procedure Random_Write

```
Random_Write (location, a_record)
```

After all accesses to the data in the array, a call to the Close procedure

```
Close (internal_name)
```

should be replaced by a call to the procedure Close_Random_File so that any changes to the array of data can be written back to the external sequential file

```
Close_Random_File (internal_name, records)
```

The routines listed above follow.

```
PROCEDURE Reset_Random_File (VAR internal_name : File_Type;
                             VAR records : Array_Type);
VAR
    i : Integer;
BEGIN
    Reset (internal_name);
    i := 0;
    While Not Eof (internal_name) Do
    Begin
        Read (internal_name, records [i])
        i := i + 1;
    End;
    Close (internal_name)
END;
```

```
PROCEDURE Random_Read (location : Integer;
                       VAR a_record : Record_Type);

BEGIN
     a_record := records [location]
END;

PROCEDURE Random_Write (location : Integer;
                        VAR a_record : Record_Type);

BEGIN
     records [location] := a_record
END;

PROCEDURE Close_Random_File (internal_name : File_Type;
                             VAR records : Array_Type);
VAR
    i : Integer;
BEGIN
    Rewrite (internal_name);
    For i := 0 To FILE_SIZE Do
        Write (internal_name, records [i]);
    Close (internal_name)
END;
```

Appendix B

Random Access in Different Versions of Pascal

TURBO Pascal

Random Open

An external file may be opened for random access by using the `Assign` procedure followed by either a call to `Rewrite` (if the file does not exist) or a call to `Reset` (to access an existing file). If the file does not exist, it must be created sequentially before it can be accessed randomly.

The formats of the `Assign`, `Reset`, and `Rewrite` calls follow:

```
Assign (internal_file_name, 'external_file_name')
Reset (internal_file_name)
Rewrite (internal_file_name)
```

`Assign` associates `internal_file_name` with an actual `external_file_name`. The `Reset` opens the file for access, and the file buffer receives the first component of the file. The `Rewrite` opens the file for output only and writes an end-of-file marker in the file. If the file referenced in the `Rewrite` is an existing file, it will be destroyed.

Random Read

Random input from an external file is achieved by the use of two procedures: `Seek` and `Read`. Random input is valid only after the external file has been created (with `Assign`, `Rewrite`, `Write`, and `Close`) and opened for random access (with `Assign` and `Reset`). The formats of the calls to the `Seek` and `Read` procedures follow:

```
Seek (internal_file_name, location)
Read (internal_file_name, component)
```

The `Seek` positions the file pointer to the component specified by the variable `location`, where `location` is the relative record number ($> = 0$).

443

The Read fills the second parameter with the component specified by the file pointer.

Random Write

Random output to an external file is produced through the use of two procedures: Seek and Write. Random output is valid only after the external file has been opened for output with an Assign and a Rewrite. The formats of the calls to the Seek and Write procedures follow:

```
Seek (internal_file_name, location)
Write (internal_file_name, component)
```

The Seek positions the file pointer to the component specified by the variable location, where location is the relative record number ($>=0$). The Write moves the data in the variable component to the file buffer and physically writes the file buffer contents to the external file.

Random Close

An external file must be closed before being opened again with a Reset or Rewrite. The format for the Close procedure call follows:

```
Close (internal_file_name)
```

The Close procedure closes the file and stores the external file name in the directory.

UCSD Pascal

Random Open

An external file may be opened for random access by either a call to the Rewrite procedure (if the file does not exist) or a call to the Reset procedure (to access an existing file). If the file does not exist, it must be created sequentially before it can be accessed randomly.

The format of the Reset and Rewrite calls follow:

```
Reset (internal_file_name, 'external_file_name')
Rewrite (internal_file_name, 'external_file_name')
```

The Reset associates internal_file_name with an actual external_file_name, opens the file for access, and moves the first component into the file buffer. The `Rewrite` associates the `internal_file_ name` with an actual `external_file_name`, opens the file for output only, and writes an end-of-file marker in the file. If the file referenced in the `Rewrite` is an existing file, it will be destroyed.

Random Read

Random input from an external file is achieved by the use of two procedures: `Seek` and `Get`. Random input is valid only after the external file has been created (with `Rewrite`, `Write`, and `Close`) and opened for random access (with `Reset`). The formats of the calls to the `Seek` and `Get` procedures follow:

```
Seek (internal_file_name, location)
Get (internal_file_name)
```

The `Seek` positions the file pointer to the component specified by the variable `location`, where `location` is the relative record number ($>=0$). The `Get` fills the file buffer (referenced `internal_file_name`) with the component specified by the file pointer. An assignment statement may then access the file buffer to store the contents in a program variable.

Random Write

Random output to an external file is produced through the use of two procedures: `Seek` and `Put`. Random output is valid only after the external file has been opened for output with a `Rewrite`. The formats of the calls to the `Seek` and `Put` procedures follow:

```
Seek (internal_file_name, location)
Put (internal_file_name)
```

The `Seek` positions the file pointer to the component specified by the variable `location`, where `location` is the relative record number ($>=0$). The data to be written to the file must have been moved to the file buffer (`internal_file_name`) previously. The `Put` physically writes the file buffer contents to the external file.

Random Close

An external file must be closed before being opened again with a `Reset` or `Rewrite`. The formats for the `Close` procedure call follow:

```
Close (internal_file_name)
Close (internal_file_name ,lock)
```

A Close procedure call with only one parameter closes the file. If the file had previously opened as output (with a Rewrite), the file will be destroyed. The Close procedure call with two parameters closes the file and stores the external file name in the directory.

VAX-11 Pascal

After a file is opened with the Open procedure with access_method := direct, the procedures Find, Locate, and Update may be used for random access to an external file.

Random Open

The format of the Open procedure call follows:

```
Open (internal_file_name, 'external_file_name',
      history := <history parameter>,
      access_method := direct)
```

where <history parameter> can be one of the following:

new—if an output file is to be created
old—if an existing file is to be accessed
readonly—if an existing file is to be opened for input only
unknown—VAX operating system will assign old if the file exists, otherwise new will be assigned.

Random Read

The procedure Find positions the file pointer to a specified component of the file. The format of the call is:

```
Find (internal_file_name, component_number)
```

where component_number is a positive integer expression. The file is positioned to the specified component, the file buffer assumes the value of the specified component, and the file mode is set to inspection.
    The Find may be followed by:

```
Read (internal_file_name, record_name)
```

which moves the buffer contents into the variable record_name.

Random Write

The `Locate` procedure positions the file pointer to a specified component of the file so a subsequent `Put` procedure can modify that component. The format of the call is

```
Locate (internal_file_name, component_number)
```

For example:

```
Locate (file_name, n);
file_name^ := a_record;
Put (file_name)
```

positions the file referenced by `file_name` to the *n*th component so that the contents of `a_record` can be written into the file in component n.

The `Update` procedure writes the file buffer contents into the component referenced by the current file pointer. The format of the call is:

```
Update (internal_file_name)
```

The file must be in `inspection` mode (in other words, the `Update` call must be preceded by a `Find` or `Get` to position the file pointer to a specified component and place the file in `inspection` mode.

Random Close

An external file must be closed before being opened again with a `Reset` or `Rewrite`. The format for the `Close` procedure call follows:

```
Close (internal_file_name, disposition := <d_parameter>)
```

where `<d_parameter>` is either:

save—if the file is to become a permanent file, or
delete—if the file is to be deleted

For external files, the default disposition is `save`.

Answers to Selected Exercises

Chapter 1

1. b   3. g   5. h   7. i

9. d   11. a   13. b

15. sequential and random

17. to choose the best organization for the application and accesses needed

19. random; to provide rapid key access by flight number

21. sequential; read into memory to use

Chapter 2

1. a. 4 bytes. b. 16 bytes. c. 28 bytes. d. 12 bytes.

3. 4 bytes. 5. LEGAL. 7. ILLEGAL, type mismatch.

9. a. `worker [6]` is a record of type `Employee`.

   b. `worker [13].age` is an `Integer`.

   c. `worker [62].name [3]` is a `Char`.

   d. `worker [71].name` is a `Packed Array` of 30 characters.

11. ```
    worker [i].name := family.man.name;
    worker [i].age := family.man.age;
    worker [i].sex := MALE
    ```

13. ```
    TYPE
         Aid_Record = Record
                      name : Packed Array [1..30] Of Char;
                      Case financial_aid : Boolean Of
                           TRUE : (current : Integer;
                                   total : Integer);
                           FALSE : ()
                End;
    ```

15. b. 17. a.

19. True. 21. True.

23. `Eof` = Text, Non-text
    `Eoln` = Text
    `Get` = Text, Non-text
    `Put` = Text, Non-text
    `Read` = Text
    `Readln` = Text
    `Reset` = Text, Non-text
    `Rewrite` = Text, Non-text
    `Write` = Text
    `Writeln` = Text

25. c   27. b   29. b   31. a   33. c

35. `identifier := filename^;`
    `Get (filename);`

Chapter 3

1. A logical file component is the amount of data logically input, logically output, or processed by a program at any one time. A physical file component is the amount of data physically input from or physically output to a file. A physical file component may contain one or several logical file components.

3. The purpose of blocking is to reduce the number of file accesses.

5. size of main memory available, size of main memory needed for each program that accesses the file, accesses to a file (to input a block to access one component of the block), and characteristics of the external storage devices used to store the file

7. The `Reset` procedure in Pascal fills the buffer with the first component of the file and initializes the location indicator of the buffer to 1, so the first `Read` statement simply accesses the filled buffer and refills the buffer. The `Rewrite` procedure in Pascal initializes the file with an <eof> marker and the location indicator for the buffer to 0 in preparation for the first `Write` statement.

9. main storage

11. number of logical accesses
    = 1 access/component $\times$ 1 component/block $\times$ nb blocks/file
    = nb accesses
    number of physical accesses
    = 1 access/block $\times$ nb blocks/file
    = nb accesses

13. block length in bytes = 120 bytes/record $\times$ 25 records/block
    = 3,000 bytes
    file buffer with single buffering = 3,000 bytes
    file buffer with double buffering = 6,000 bytes or 2 blocks

15. a. total time = 962 × (input time + processing time)
           = 962 × (53.05 ms + 25 ms)
           = 126,118.2 ms
           = 126.1182 sec
           = 2.10 min

    b. total time = (1924 × input time) + 1 × processing time
           = (1924 × 51.52 ms) + 25 ms
           = 99,149.4 ms
           = 99.1494 sec
           = 1.65 min

    c. total time = 490 × (input time + processing time)
           = 490 × (53.07 ms + 25 ms)
           = 38,254.3 ms
           = 38.2543 sec
           = 0.67 min

    d. total time = (979 × input time) + 1 × processing time
           = (979 × 51.53 ms) + 25 ms
           = 50,472.87 ms
           = 50.47287 sec
           = 0.84 min

    e. total time = 5637 × (input time + processing time)
           = 5637 × (53.02 ms + 25 ms)
           = 439,798.74 ms
           = 439.79874 sec
           = 7.33 min

    f. total time = (11,273 × input time) + 1 × processing time
           = (11,273 × 51.51 ms) + 25 ms
           = 580,697.23 ms
           = 580.69723 sec
           = 9.68 min

    g. total time = 235 × (input time + processing time)
           = 235 × (53.07 ms + 25)
           = 18,346.45 ms
           = 18.34645 sec
           = 0.31 min

    h. total time = (469 × input time) + 1 × processing time
           = (469 × 51.53 ms) + 25 ms
           = 24,141.04 ms
           = 24.14104 sec
           = 0.41 min

    i. total time = (708 × input time) + 1 × processing time
           = (708 × 51.01 ms) + 25 ms
           = 36,140.08 ms
           = 36.14008 sec
           = 0.6 min

Chapter 4

1. tape—to allow the tape to start moving up to the transfer speed before beginning of block is located and to stop over nondata; disk—to locate block before transfer begins

3. Tapes provide sequential access; disks provide sequential and random access.

5. no seek with fixed-head disk

7. c. rotational delay; no seek, and head activation time is almost nil

9. sequential access—accesses next physically contiguous component of a file; random access—accesses next component based on the component's address within the file (not necessarily the next contiguous component)

11. The higher the blocking factor, the fewer the IBGs, so tape capacity is increased. As the blocking factor is increased, more data can be read for each start and stop, so less total time is required to transfer the entire file.

13. even parity—track 9: 0110110
    odd parity—track 9: 1001001

15. a. $\text{time to read 1 block} = \dfrac{\text{block length in inches}}{\text{transfer speed}} + \text{start time} + \text{stop time}$

$$= \dfrac{0.375\,\text{inch}}{50\,\text{inch/sec}} + 0.01\,\text{sec} + 0.01\,\text{sec}$$

$$= 0.0075 + 0.01 + 0.01$$

$$= 0.0275\,\text{sec/block}$$

$\text{time to read tape} = (\text{time to read 1 block}) \times (\text{number of blocks})$

$$= 0.0275\,\text{sec/block} \times 32{,}913\,\text{blocks}$$

$$= 905.1075\,\text{sec}$$

$$= 15.09\,\text{min}$$

b. $\text{time to read 1 block} = \dfrac{\text{block length in inches}}{\text{transfer speed}} + \text{start time} + \text{stop time}$

$$= \dfrac{1.125\,\text{inch}}{50\,\text{inch/sec}} + 0.01\,\text{sec} + 0.01\,\text{sec}$$

$$= 0.0225 + 0.01 + 0.01$$

$$= 0.0425\,\text{sec/block}$$

$\text{time to read tape} = (\text{time to read 1 block}) \times (\text{number of blocks})$

$$= 0.0425\,\text{sec/block} \times 17{,}722\,\text{blocks}$$

$$= 753.185\,\text{sec}$$

$$= 12.55\,\text{min}$$

c. time to read 1 block = $\dfrac{\text{block length in inches}}{\text{transfer speed}}$ + start time + stop time

$$= \dfrac{1.875\,\text{inch}}{50\,\text{inch/sec}} + 0.01\,\text{sec} + 0.01\,\text{sec}$$

$$= 0.0375 + 0.01 + 0.01$$

$$= 0.0575\,\text{sec/block}$$

time to read tape = (time to read 1 block) × (number of blocks)

$$= 0.0575\,\text{sec/block} \times 12{,}126\,\text{blocks}$$

$$= 697.245\,\text{sec}$$

$$= 11.62\,\text{min}$$

17. block length = logical record length × blocking factor
     (in bytes)   = 120 bytes/record × 45 records/block
                  = 5,400 bytes/block

number of blocks = $\dfrac{\text{number of records}}{\text{blocking factor}}$

$$= \dfrac{50{,}000\,\text{records}}{45\,\text{records/block}}$$

$$= 1{,}111\,\text{blocks (1111.1111 is truncated)}$$

block length = $\dfrac{\text{block length in bytes}}{\text{density}}$

$$= \dfrac{5{,}400\,\text{bytes/block}}{1{,}600\,\text{bytes/inch}}$$

$$= 3.375\,\text{inches/block}$$

tape length = (number of blocks × (block length + IBG)) + IBG

$$= (1{,}111 \times (3.375 + 0.5)) + 0.5$$

$$= (1111 \times 3.875) + 0.5$$

$$= 4305.625\,\text{inches}$$

19. highest—

blocking factor = $\dfrac{1{,}000\,\text{bytes/buffer}}{92\,\text{bytes/record}}$

$$= 10\,\text{records/block (10.87 is truncated)}$$
with density of 1,600 bpi

lowest—
blocking factor = 1 record/block with density of 800 bpi

21. 21 seeks

23. a. 6,000 rev = 1 min

1 rev $= \dfrac{1\,\text{min} \times 60\,\text{sec/min}}{6{,}000\,\text{rev}}$

$$= 0.01\,\text{sec}$$

$$= 10\,\text{ms}$$

latency = 10 ms

b. sectors/cylinder = 20 sectors/track × 5 tracks/cylinder
                    = 100 sectors/cylinder

25. Fixed-head disks have a read/write head per track per surface, eliminating the seek time from the access time computation. Removable disks have a read/write per surface that must serve all tracks on a surface.

Chapter 5

1. If the master file is stored on tape and copied to a new master file on a second tape, the old master file is an automatic backup already on tape. Then the transaction file is on disk, which is a better device for sorting the transactions prior to the maintenance run.

3.
$$\text{file activity ratio} = \frac{3\,\text{changes}}{10\,\text{master records}} = 33\%$$

$$\text{file volatility ratio} = \frac{6\,\text{additions and deletions}}{10\,\text{master records}} = 60\%$$

5. file update should be frequent for—
   high rate of data change
   high file activity ratio
   high urgency for current data
   small size file
   Frequent updates increase processing costs and improve data quality.

7. Batch processing allows data on master file to become outdated between update runs.

9. The disk file can be updated randomly, which means the transactions need not be sorted.

Chapter 6

1.

File 1	File 2	File 3	File 4	File 5
1	2	3	4	5
6	7	8	9	
10	11	12	13	14
15	16	17		
18	19	20	21	22
23	24	25	26	27
28	29	30	31	
32	33			

3. Two-way sort/merge

	Number of runs on		
	File 1	File 2	File 3
Sort phase	16	15	0
Merge pass 1	0	0	16
redistribution	8	8	0
Merge pass 2	0	0	8
redistribution	4	4	0
Merge pass 3	0	0	4
redistribution	2	2	0
Merge pass 4	0	0	2
redistribution	1	1	0
Merge pass 5	0	0	1

Balanced two-way sort/merge

	Number of runs on			
	File 1	File 2	File 3	File 4
Sort phase	16	15	0	0
Merge pass 1	0	0	8	8
Merge pass 2	4	4	0	0
Merge pass 3	0	0	2	2
Merge pass 4	1	1	0	0
Merge pass 5	0	0	1	0

Balanced k-way sort/merge ($k = 3$)

	Number of runs on					
	File 1	File 2	File 3	File 4	File 5	File 6
Sort phase	11	10	10	0	0	0
Merge pass 1	0	0	0	4	4	3
Merge pass 2	2	1	1	0	0	0
Merge pass 3	0	0	0	1	1	0
Merge pass 4	1	0	0	0	0	0

Polyphase sort/merge ($p = 3$)

	Number of runs on			
	File 1	File 2	File 3	File 4
Sort phase	13	11	7	0
Merge pass 1	6	4	0	7
Merge pass 2	2	0	4	3
Merge pass 3	0	2	2	1
Merge pass 4	1	0	0	0

5. 1 record access $= 50\,\text{ms} + 20\,\text{ms} + 1\,\text{ms}$
$\qquad\qquad\qquad = 71\,\text{ms}$

31 record accesses $= 71\,\text{ms} \times (31)$
(whole file) $\qquad = 2{,}201\,\text{ms} = 2.201\,\text{sec}$

1 pass $=$ input and output entire file
$\qquad\quad = 2.201\,\text{sec} \times (2)$
$\qquad\quad = 4.402\,\text{sec}$

two-way sort/merge $= 10\,\text{passes} \times 4.402\,\text{sec}$
$\qquad\qquad\qquad\quad = 44.02\,\text{sec}$

balanced two-way sort/merge $= 6\,\text{passes} \times 4.402\,\text{sec}$
$\qquad\qquad\qquad\qquad\qquad\quad = 26.412\,\text{sec}$

balanced k-way sort/merge $= 5\,\text{passes} \times 4.402\,\text{sec}$
$\qquad\qquad\qquad\qquad\qquad = 22.01\,\text{sec}$

polyphase sort/merge $= 4.475\,\text{passes} \times 4.402\,\text{sec}$
$\qquad\qquad\qquad\qquad = 19.699\,\text{sec}$

7. Two-way sort/merge

	Number of runs on		
	File 1	File 2	File 3
Sort phase	13	12	0
Merge pass 1	0	0	13
redistribution	7	6	0
Merge pass 2	0	0	7
redistribution	4	3	0
Merge pass 3	0	0	4
redistribution	2	2	0
Merge pass 4	0	0	2
redistribution	1	1	0
Merge pass 5	0	0	1

Balanced two-way sort/merge

	Number of runs on			
	File 1	File 2	File 3	File 4
Sort phase	13	12	0	0
Merge pass 1	0	0	7	6
Merge pass 2	4	3	0	0
Merge pass 3	0	0	2	2
Merge pass 4	1	1	0	0
Merge pass 5	0	0	1	0

Balanced k-way sort/merge ($k = 3$)

	Number of runs on							
	File 1	File 2	File 3	File 4	File 5	File 6	File 7	File 8
Sort phase	7	6	6	6	0	0	0	0
Merge pass 1	0	0	0	0	2	2	2	1
Merge pass 2	1	1	0	0	0	0	0	0
Merge pass 3	0	0	0	0	1	0	0	0

Polyphase sort/merge ($p = 3$)

	Number of runs on				
	File 1	File 2	File 3	File 4	File 5
Sort phase	8	7	6	4	0
Merge pass 1	4	3	2	0	4
Merge pass 2	2	1	0	2	2
Merge pass 3	1	0	1	1	1
Merge pass 4	0	1	0	0	0

9. The number of passes reflects I/O activity, and the number of comparisons reflects CPU activity. Most of the time I/O activity is considered more expensive than CPU activity.

11. The balanced k-way sort/merge continues merging until all input files have ended, which sometimes means copying the runs from the last file without merging. The polyphase sort/merge continues merging until one input file has ended, which eliminates needless copying of one file. Each pass is always merging k files and never less.

Chapter 7

1. PAY: 215193232 Mod 101 = 6
   AGE: 193199197 Mod 101 = 34
   RATE: 217193227197 Mod 101 = 5
   NUMBER: 213228212194197217 Mod 101 = 89

3.
location	contents	
1	PAY	
2	RATE	(synonym of 1)
3	TAX	(displaced from 2)
4	PENSION	
5	SALARIED	(synonym of 8)
6		
7		
8	DEDUCT	
9	STATUS	(synonym of 8)
10	DEPENDENTS	(synonym of 8)
11	SEX	(synonym of 8)

5. When overflow from one bucket spills into a nearby bucket, the same problems occur as with linear probing: Synonyms may be stored some distance from the hashed bucket and displacements may occur.

7. directory lookup table in memory—
   advantages: 1. Searching lookup table first results in exactly one access to the file.
                  2. Changes to the file mean changing lookup table to keep in agreement with file.
   disadvantages: 1. Lookup table requires memory space.
                  2. Size of lookup table must be known prior to allocation.

9. on the degree of uniformity of the hashing distribution and the number of synonyms produced

11. prime-number division remainder

13. By storing synonyms in a separate area, the home locations contain only keys that have hashed to home locations.

15. consecutive spill addressing—Synonyms are stored in the nearest bucket with available locations. bucket chaining—An overflow area is used for storing all synonyms, usually in individual locations rather than in buckets, and the overflow locations are chained to the home bucket for easy and fast access.

Chapter 8

1. Each node of a binary search tree may point to at most two other nodes; each node in an *m*-way search tree may point to at most *m* other nodes.

3. Each node may contain a maximum of 16 subtree pointers and 15 keys.

5. root node = 2 <= subtree pointers <= m
              = 2 <= subtree pointers <= 9
              = 1 <= keys <= 8
  interior nodes = $\lceil m/2 \rceil$ <= subtree pointers <= m
               = 5   <= subtree pointers <= 9
               = 4   <= keys <= 8

7. for a B-tree of order 4:
  interior nodes = $\lceil m/2 \rceil$ <= subtree pointers <= m
             = 2   <= subtree pointers <= 4
  The number of nodes accessed in the worst case is
      $\log_2 (243 + 1) = 8$

9. insert 9:   insert 28:

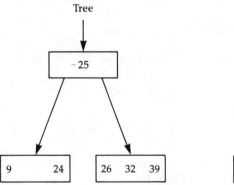

insert 45:   insert 13:

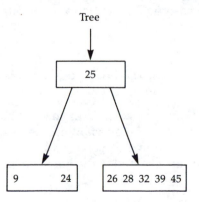

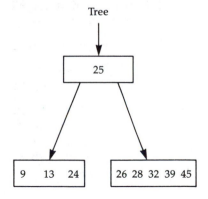

11. B-tree from exercise 10:

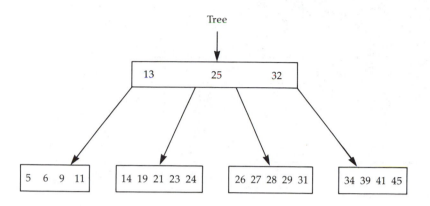

delete 26:

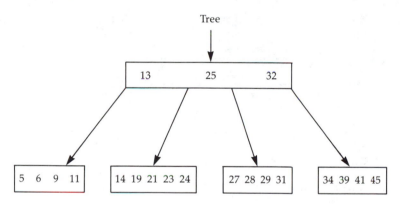

delete 21:

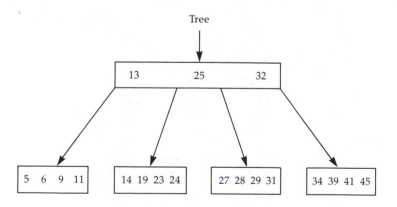

delete 11:

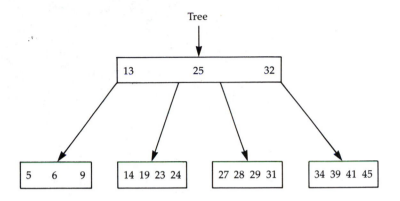

delete 9:

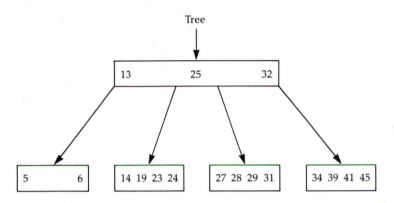

delete 45:

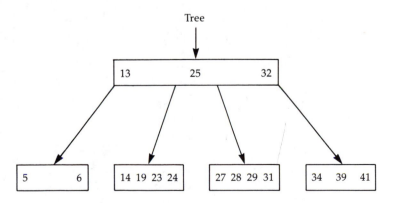

delete 13:

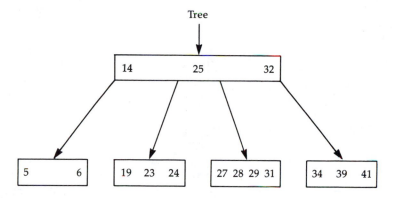

delete 39:

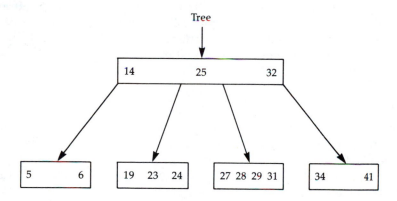

delete 6:

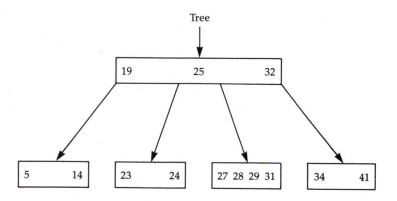

delete 6:

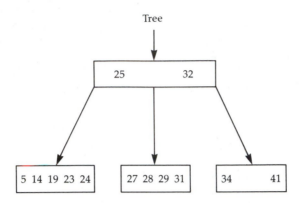

13. The nodes of a B-tree are at least half-full, but the nodes of the B*-tree are at least two-thirds full. The B$^+$-tree is significantly different from the other two types of trees in that all the keys and address of the records with those keys are stored in the terminal nodes, and the largest key in each terminal node is also stored in the parent node.

Chapter 9

1. The data records are stored sequentially. In the sequential file the records are stored sequentially with respect to the entire file. In the indexed sequential files, the records are stored sequentially with respect to each data block or track, and an index indicates the order of access of the data blocks for sequential access.

3. In theory the records are stored sequentially, so they should present the same problems as the insertion of records into a sequential file.

5.

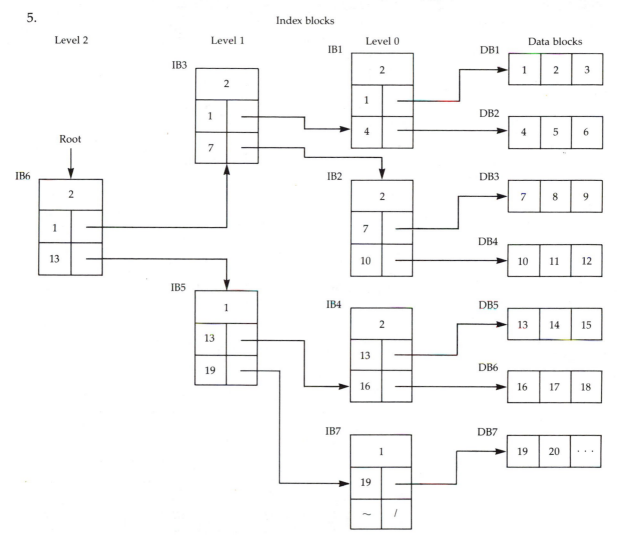

Figure 9.11(d) after insertion of 19 and 20

7.

Index				Prime data blocks		Overflow blocks

Index

Normal		Overflow	
Key	Address	Key	Address
3	P1	3	P1
6	P2	7	V2
10	P3	15	V3

Prime data blocks

P1

1	2	3

P2

4	5	6

P3

8	9	10

Overflow blocks

V1

15	−1

V2

7	−1

V3

11	V5

V4

14	V1

V5

12	V4

Figure 9.25(d) after insertion of 14 and 12

9.

Figure 9.33 with 123 and 113 added

11. Insertions into a track cause a record to split into a cylinder overflow area that holds such splits from all tracks in the cylinder. The other organizations discussed in the chapter split records into an area unique for the split block. Reorganization entails accessing the ISAM file sequentially and creating a new ISAM file with all the data records stored in prime data blocks (prime data area or tracks) and nothing in overflow.

13. access the cylinder index   = 1 access
    access the track index   = 1 access
    access the prime track   = <u>1 access</u>
    number of accesses for prime = 3

or

    access the cylinder index   = 1 access
    access the track index   = 1 access
    access each record in overflow = n accesses
    number of accesses for overflow = $n + 2$
       (n = number in overflow)

15. access the index set   = 3 accesses (maximum)
    access the sequence set   = 1 access
    access the control interval   = <u>1 access</u>
    number of accesses to VSAM = 5 accesses

17. From the answers to questions thirteen and fifteen, the index-and-data-blocks method ensures that the number of accesses for any record in the file is the same, even after insertions and deletions, by modifying the indexes to indicate the logical order rather than physically linking the records in order (as is done with the cylinder-and-surface indexing method). As presented in the answer to question eleven, reorganization is necessary periodically with the cylinder-and-surface indexing method and is never necessary with the index-and-data-blocks method.

19. For each entry in the cylinder index
     For each entry in the surface index
        list each record in the prime surface
        list each record in overflow that was split from this surface

21. VSAM is more efficient since each control interval is linked to the next control interval containing the next higher keys. Once the control interval with the lowest keys is found, the index set and sequence set need not be accessed; only control intervals, in order, are accessed.

23.   access 3 index blocks   = 3 × 30 ms
  + access one data block   = <u>1 × 30 ms</u>
     number of accesses to SIS   = 4 × 30 ms   = 120 ms

Chapter 10

1. advantages: 1. Many queries can be answered by scanning the inverted index and without accessing the file of data records.
   2. No additional fields are needed in the file of data records to invert the data file.

   disadvantage: The variance in length of the list of addresses in the inverted index presents a problem in storing the index.

3. questions of the nature: How many records have one or more particular characteristics? Are there any records with certain characteristics? For the multilist file, the index indicates the first record in a linked list, and each record in the list must be accessed.

5. The length field in a multilist file allows questions of the nature: How many . . . to be answered without accessing the data records, provided only the secondary key in the field is accessed. (This is not true of intersection queries.)

7. address1 ← first_address of entry with make key = Chevrolet
   address2 ← first_address of entry with style key = 4 DR
   { Search through the two linked lists }
   If address1 < address 2
      input record at location address1 into "record"
      address 1 ← record.make_pointer
   Else
      If address1.record_key = address2.record_key
        output record_key
      Else
        input record at location address2 into "record"
        address2 ← record.style_pointer

9. a. two accesses to inverted directory
   b. one access to inverted directory and five to access data records
   c. one access to inverted directory and five to access data records
   d. one access to inverted directory
   e. two accesses to inverted directory and one access to a data record

11. The entire file must be read to answer all queries.

13.

Doctor's name	Primary key(s)
Brown	243, 767
Rollins	231, 467
Taylor	354, 587, 678
Watson	365, 876
White	121

Ward	Primary key(s)
G	121, 467
I	231, 243, 767
M	587
P	354, 678
R	365, 876

15.

Directory for doctor's name		
Doctor's name	First key	Length
Brown	243	2
Rollins	231	2
Taylor	354	3
Watson	365	2
White	121	1

Directory for Ward		
Ward	First key	Length
G	121	2
I	231	3
M	587	1
P	354	2
R	365	2

Multilist data file of records

Primary key	Patient's name	Ward	Ward link	Room number	Doctor's name	link	Current medication
121	Novak, T.R.	G	467	102	White	^	Hypoch
231	Drew, R.W.	I	243	123	Rollins	467	Sulph-3
243	Black, H.J.	I	767	124	Brown	767	Sulph-3
354	James, J.K.	P	678	213	Taylor	587	Cryol
365	Tasher, R.E.	R	876	312	Watson	876	Neoben
467	Andrews, T.B.	G	^	103	Rollins		Hypoch
587	Black, T.Y.	M	^	154	Taylor	678	Tylph
678	McCarry, C.M.	P	^	215	Taylor	^	Cryol
767	Jones, T.T.	I	^	126	Brown	^	Sulph-3
876	Smith, D.W.	R	^	313	Watson	^	Neoben

Glossary

absolute address A machine-dependent address consisting of a cylinder number, surface number, and record number for cylinder-addressable devices and a sector number and record number for sector-addressable devices.

activity of a file A measure of the percentage of existing master file components changed during a maintenance run.

adding records See *additions*.

additions Transactions that cause a new record to be added to an existing master file.

ancestor A node that is at one or more levels higher than the current node.

array A collection of data items of the same type, each accessed by a name and an index. See *record*.

ASCII A 7-bit code for representing characters.

associated value hashing A perfect hashing function.

audit/error listing One output of a maintenance run that includes all transactions processed, update actions (additions, changes, deletions) taken for each transaction (audit portion) and any errors that occurred during the run (error portion).

AVL tree A height-balanced binary tree introduced by Adelson–Velskii and Landis in 1962.

B-tree An m-way search tree, stored externally, in which all nodes (except the root node) have at least half as many keys and subtree pointers as the maximum (indicated by the order).

B*-tree An m-way search tree, stored externally, in which all nodes (except the root node) have at least two-thirds as many keys and subtree pointers as the maximum (indicated by the order).

B$^+$-tree A B-tree with interior nodes that contain only keys and subtree pointers and with addresses of records in terminal nodes only.

balance factor of a node The difference between the height of the left subtree and the height of the right subtree of a node (equals 0 if both heights are the same).

balanced k-way sort/merge Each cycle involves merging sorted runs from k files into larger sorted runs stored alternately on k empty files. The cycle is repeated until all data are in one sorted run.

balanced tree Tree in which the height is a minimum for the number of nodes.

balanced two-way sort/merge Each cycle involves merging sorted runs from two files into larger sorted runs stored alternately on two empty files. The cycle is repeated until all data are in one sorted run.

batch processing Updates to a master file are accumulated over time in a transaction file, then periodically sorted into the same order as the master file and applied to the master file in a maintenance run. See *maintenance run*.

binary search tree   A tree in which each node contains a left pointer to a subtree with lower values and a right pointer to a subtree with higher values than the current node.

block   The smallest amount of data that can be input from or output to a secondary storage device during one access.

blocking   The software interface between a program and a blocked file that groups several components into a block with memory accesses to be output to a file during one output operation.

blocking routine   See *blocking*.

bucket addressing   A collision-resolution method where a group of record locations is associated with one hash address.

bucket chaining   Synonyms that overflow a bucket are stored in a separate overflow area, and the overflow location is linked to the home bucket for easy access.

buffering   The software interface between a program that accesses one component of a file at a time and a file of blocked components. See *blocking* and *deblocking*.

ceiling of x   The next larger integer greater than x.

changes   Transactions that cause data in an existing master record to be changed.

child   A node that is one level below and pointed to by the current node.

CIDF   Control interval definition field.

clustering   Grouping components, that are accessed within a short time of each other, into one block.

collision   Occurs when the hashing function results in the same relative address for two keys that are not the same.

component of a file   The amount of data accessed with each I/O statement.

consecutive spill addressing   Used with bucket addressing. Overflow from one bucket spills into the nearest bucket with available locations.

control file   An output of a maintenance run containing information concerning the run.

cylinder   A collection of vertically aligned tracks on a disk pack.

deblocking   The software interface that inputs one block of file components from a blocked file and allows a program to access only one component at a time with memory accesses.

deblocking routine   See *deblocking*.

degree of a node   The number of subtrees pointed to by the node.

degree of a tree   The maximum degree of the nodes in a tree.

deleting records   See *deletions*.

deletions   Transactions that cause existing master records to be deleted from a file.

dense keys   Consecutive keys are close together in value.

descendant   A node that is one or more levels below the current node.

digit extraction   A hashing function.

direct file organization   A file organization in which there exists a predictable relationship between the key used to identify an individual component and that component's position in an external file. The position is a device-specific absolute address. See *random file organization*.

disk pack   A collection of aluminum platters attached to and rotating on a center spindle. A secondary storage device.

displacement   Occurs with linear probing when a synonym of location i is stored in location k, displacing a later record that hashes to location k, where i and k are different. The displaced record is displaced by a nonsynonym.

double buffering   Allocating two file buffer variables for a file instead of one to improve the access time.

double hashing   A collision-resolution method where a second hash function is applied to synonyms and added to the first hash value to distribute synonyms into a separate overflow area. Eliminates searching sequentially for an available location.

double-sided disk   Data are recorded on both sides of a floppy disk. See *single-sided disk*.

dummy runs   Empty or null runs that are added to files during the sort phase (initial distribution of sorted runs) of the Polyphase Sort/Merge to obtain an nth-level perfect Fibonacci distribution.

dynamic hashing   A collision-resolution method that dynamically changes the hashing function to access a hashed file that increases in size as records are added.

EBCDIC   An 8-bit code for representing characters.

editing   The process of identifying invalid data values in a transaction file prior to the maintenance run so that the invalid values can be corrected. Thus more transactions will be accepted during the maintenance run.

end-of-tape marker   A reflective aluminum strip near the end of a tape indicating the end of recordable surface, followed by a section of leader for winding around the tape reel. The marker is sensed by the tape drive so that the tape does not unwind from the reel.

even parity   Employs the parity bit to make sure the number of 1 bits in each character is even.

external files   A collection of data stored on nonvolatile secondary storage devices.

field   A component of a record data structure.

file buffer   Contains one component of a file. The buffer is initialized to the first file component by the `Reset` procedure, filled with a file component by the `Get` procedure, and accessed by the `Put` procedure (referenced by `filename^` where `filename` is the internal file name).

file header label   Precedes every file on tape or disk and contains file identification data.

file maintenance program   See *maintenance run*.

file trailer label   Follows every file on tape or disk and contains record and block counts for the file.

file organization   Refers to the way in which components are stored on an external file and determines the type of access.

file size   Determined by the number of components in the file and the length (in bytes) of each component.

fixed-head disk   A disk with a permanently sealed pack and a read/write head for every track. See *removable disk*.

floor of x The largest integer contained in x.

floppy disk   A single plastic platter that resembles a 45-rpm phonograph record and is a common secondary storage device for microcomputers. See *single-sided disk* and *double-sided disk*.

folding   A hashing function.

frequency of file use   An important factor in file design.

fully inverted file   An inverted list exists for every field in the record.

hard disk   A collection of rigid aluminum platters stacked to form a disk pack. It is a common secondary storage device for large-scale computers; also, a single rigid platter on microcomputers.

hard-sectored floppy disk   A floppy disk containing a ring of tiny index holes, one at each sector boundary, punched near the center of the disk. A beam of light senses the holes to determine the beginning of a sector.

hashing   The application of a function to a key value that will result in mapping the range of possible key values into a smaller range of relative (or absolute) addresses.

head activation time   Time necessary to electrically switch on the read/write head for a particular track on a disk to be accessed. Essentially, head activation time = 0 relative to other factors relating to access time.

head settle time   Time necessary for the read/write heads to settle onto the floppy disk surface and make contact. Settling occurs before access is possible.

height   The number of levels of nodes contained in a tree.

height-balanced binary tree   Tree in which the height of the subtrees of each node are the same.

history file   A collection of the old master files, old transaction files, and control files from past maintenance runs.

immediate predecessor   The largest value in the left subtree of the current node.

immediate successor   The smallest value in the right subtree of the current node.

indexed sequential file organization   A file organization that combines the sequential access and ordering of file components provided in sequential file organization and the random-access capabilities of random file organization.

inorder traversal   Visit the left subtree, visit the root, then visit the right subtree of a binary tree.

interblock gap (IBG)   Separates blocks of data on tape and disk. The IBG allows the tape to start and stop between read/write requests without stopping on data and allows data to be processed by the CPU before the next block is accessed from disk.

interrecord gap (IRG)   Another term for interblock gap.

inversion index   Contains all the values that the key field contains and a pointer to the records in the file that contain those key values.

inverted file organization   Contains an inversion index for each secondary key field.

I/O-bound   A program or computer system that is limited in processing speed by its I/O devices.

I/O channel   The part of the operating system that provides input and output control to peripheral devices. See *processor-bound*.

key   Key field.

key field   A field of a record with a unique value used for identification.

kilobyte   1,024 bytes.

latency   Rotational delay; time required for the beginning of the block to be accessed to rotate around to the read/write heads on removable disks.

leaf nodes   Nodes that point to no other nodes. See *terminal nodes*.

level   The distance of a node from the root of the tree. If the root is on level 1, the root's child nodes are on level 2, and so on.

lg x   The logarithm to the base 2 of x.

linear probing   A collision-resolution method in which the file is scanned sequentially until an empty location is found for a synonym.

LL rotation   Rotation performed to balance an AVL tree that has had an insertion in the left subtree of the left subtree of the root, causing the tree to no longer be height-balanced.

load factor   The ratio of the number of key values to be stored in a relative file to the number of file positions allocated for the file.

load-point marker   A reflective aluminum strip following a section of leader at the beginning of a tape indicating the beginning of recordable surface. The marker is sensed by a beam of light when loading a tape into a tape drive.

location indicator   Specifies the current component of the file being accessed.

logical read   Accessing a file buffer in memory rather than the external file.

logical record   The amount of data requested and processed by a program at a time. A logical record is grouped into blocks for more efficient use of space and access time on tape and disk. See *physical record*.

logical write   See *logical read*.

LR rotation   Rotation performed to balance an AVL tree that has had an insertion in the right subtree of a node that is the left child of its parent node, causing the tree to no longer be height-balanced.

***m*-way search tree**   A balanced search tree in which all nodes are of degree m or less.

magnetic disk   A direct-access storage device (DASD) that allows a particular record to be accessed randomly and without reference to preceding records.

magnetic tape   A sequential-access storage device in which blocks of data are stored serially along the length of the tape and can only be accessed in a serial manner.

maintenance run   The application of transactions (additions, changes, and deletions) to a master file to keep the master file current.

master file   Contains permanent data.

maximum seek time   The time it takes the access arm to move from the outermost or innermost track to the farthest track.

megabyte   1,048,576 bytes.

merge phase   The second of two phases of an external sort/merge algorithm. The merge phase involves merging the sorted runs produced by the sort phase repeatedly until all data are in one sorted run. See *sort phase*.

mid-square   A hashing function.

millisecond   1/1,000 of a second.

minimum seek time   The time needed to move the access arm to an adjacent track.

movable-head disk   Removable disk.

multikey file organization   Allows access to a data file by several different key fields.

multilist file organization   A file that links data records with identical secondary key values and contains an inversion index.

nontext file   A file of components, each component being the same type, with noncharacter data stored in internal (computational) form.

nth-level distribution   A distribution of sorted runs on file where n indicates the number of passes of the merge cycle that must be performed to merge all data into one run.

odd parity   Employs the parity bit to make sure the number of 1 bits in each character is odd.

order of a tree   The maximum degree of any node in the tree.

overflow technique   A technique used in B*-trees of rotating keys from a full node into a sibling node that is less than full. It is used instead of splitting.

packing density   See *load factor*.

packing factor   See *load factor*.

parent   The node in a tree that points to the current node or the node at one level higher in the tree.

parity bit   An addition bit for each character that is used to detect errors that occur when reading or writing data. Even parity makes the parity bit 1, so the number of bits for a character is even and 0 if the number of bits is already even. Odd parity ensures each character has an odd number of bits by making the parity bit 1 when necessary.

partially inverted file   An inverted list exists for each of a number of selected fields in the record.

perfect Fibonacci distribution   The distribution of sorted runs to files that ensures that there is only one run on each of *k* files to be merged during the last merge pass of the Polyphase Sort/Merge, regardless of the number of initial runs.

perfect hashing function   A hashing function that provides a one-to-one mapping from a key into a position.

physical read   Accessing the external file. See *logical read*.

physical record   The amount of information that can be transferred at any one access. See *block*.

physical write   See *physical read, logical write*.

polyphase sort/merge   Each cycle involves merging sorted runs from *k* files into one empty file until one file becomes empty. The empty file becomes the output file for the next cycle. The merge is most efficient when the *p*th order perfect Fibonacci distribution is used in the sort phase. See *pth order Fibonacci distribution*.

primary key   The field in a record that uniquely identifies the record.

prime-number division remainder method   A hashing function.

processor-bound   A program or computer system that is limited in processing speed by the speed of the CPU. See *I/O bound*.

pth order Fibonacci distribution   The distribution of sorted runs to files where the *n*th term in the *p*th order Fibonacci series is computed as the sum of the previous *p* terms.

quotient reduction   A perfect hashing function.

radix conversion   A hashing function.

random file organization   A file organization in which there exists a predictable relationship between the key used to identify an individual component and that component's position in an external file. See *direct file organization, relative file organization*.

random update   The maintenance process consists of randomly locating the master record that matches the transaction key, applying the transaction, and rewriting the updated master record to the original location from which it was read. The transaction need not be in the key order. Random updating is available only on direct-access storage devices (disks). See *sequential update*.

randomizing scheme   See *hashing*.

RBA   Relative byte address.

RDF   Record definition field.

readable radius   The radius of the readable portion of the surface of a disk. The outermost track is not on the very edge of the disk and the innermost track is not on the very center of the disk, so the distance between the two is the readable portion. (See Figure 4.9).

reciprocal hashing   A perfect hashing function.

record   A collection of data items of similar or different types accessed by a single name. See *array*.

record data structure   See *record data type*.

record data type   A collection of data items of different types accessed by a single identifier.

recording density   The number of characters or bytes of data that can be stored in 1 inch of storage media.

relative file organization   A common implementation of random file organization in which a component's location is specified as an integer number relative to the beginning of the file.

relative files   Those with relative file organization.

relative record number   An address relative to the beginning of the file representing the location of a record within a file.

remainder reduction   A perfect hashing function.

removable disk   A disk pack that may be mounted on the disk drive to access data and subsequently unmounted for storage. It contains movable read/write heads, one per surface. See *fixed-head disk*.

report file   A file containing data drawn from a master file that has been prepared for a user.

RL rotation   A rotation performed to balance an AVL tree that has had an insertion in the left subtree of a node that is the right child of its parent node, causing the tree to no longer be height-balanced.

root   The top node of a tree that is pointed to by no other node in the tree except an external pointer.

root of a subtree   A node that is neither the root of the tree nor a terminal node.

rotational delay   Latency.

rotational time   The time for one revolution of a disk.

RR rotation   Rotation performed to balance an AVL tree that has had an insertion in the right subtree of the right subtree of the root, causing the tree to no longer be height-balanced.

run   A group of records from a file to be sorted. The file is larger than main memory and requires an external sort.

secondary collision   The second collision that occurs when looking for an empty location for a synonym. It may occur during linear probing and double hashing.

secondary key   A field in a record other than the primary key, which may be used to access a record.

sector   A portion of a track on a disk pack. Each has a unique address for access.

seek procedure   A Pascal procedure that positions the file location indicator to the beginning of a record whose relative record number is given as a parameter. It allows random access by the subsequent Get or Put.

seek time   The time needed to move the read/write heads (access arm) to a particular track on movable-head disk drives with removable disk packs. Seek time is eliminated for fixed-head disks.

sentinel value   A value that is higher than any key occurring on the file.

separate overflow area A collision-resolution method where a storage separate from the home area is allocated for synonyms, so displacement is eliminated. It is an alternative to linear probing.

sequential file organization A file organization in which components are written and accessed consecutively. The physical order of data is the same as the logical order.

sequential update The maintenance process that is restricted to sequential access whereby the transactions must be in the same sorted order as the master file. It is similar to a file merge process. See *random update*.

serially One record stored after another in succession.

sibling nodes Nodes in a tree that are at the same level of the tree.

single-sided disk Data are recorded on only one side of a floppy disk. See *double-sided disk*.

skewed tree A tree with more levels of nodes in one subtree of a node than in the other subtree.

soft-sectored floppy disk A floppy disk with one index hole for allowing the read/write heads to access the disk where the boundaries between sectors are determined by the computer software.

sort phase The first of two phases of a sort/merge algorithm. It involves accessing groups of records from the file to be sorted into main memory on which an internal sort is applied. The sorted result is written to one or more files as a sorted run. See *merge phase*.

spanned record A block that is stored on a sector-addressable disk with the block length longer than a sector.

spill addressing Used with bucket addressing. An overflowed bucket spills over into the next bucket.

start/stop time The time necessary to start the tape and move it up to speed to access a block of data, or the time necessary to stop the tape after accessing a block of data. Usually the stop time and start time are equal to the amount of time it takes to traverse an IBG.

synonym chaining A collision-resolution method where synonyms are linked to provide faster access with fewer I/O accesses.

synonyms Two or more keys that have hashed to the same relative address.

table file A file containing a table of data that is static and referenced by other files.

tag field A field within a variant part of a record data structure whose value determines which, if any, of the variant part is present.

terminal nodes Nodes in a tree that point to no other nodes in the tree. See *leaf nodes*.

text file A file of characters grouped into lines. Each line is terminated by an end of line marker.

track   A row of bits on a tape that is parallel to the edges of the tape. A circle of bits on a disk contains the bits for characters stored serially along the track.

transaction file   Contains changes, additions, and deletions to be applied to a master file.

transfer rate   Time to transfer data to or from a disk.

transfer time   The time required for the entire block of data to pass under the read/ write head.

two-way sort/merge   Each cycle merges two files containing sorted runs into one output file. The runs from the output file are redistributed back to the input file, and the cycle repeats until all data are in one sorted run.

update code   A code in each transaction indicating the type of update.

variant part   A portion of a record data structure that varies in the number of fields allocated depending upon the value of a tag field.

variant record   A record data structure containing a variant part.

volatility of a file   A measure of the number of file components added and deleted during a maintenance run compared to the number of components in the file originally.

volume label   Contains the serial number of the tape or disk and other identifying data for the reel or pack.

Winchester disk   A hard disk used with microcomputers that consists of one platter that is sealed in the drive and offers higher densities, higher storage capacities, and faster access speeds than floppy disks.

Bibliography

Alberte–Hallam, Teresa; Hallam, Stephen F.; and Hallam, James. *Microcomputer Use: Word Processors, Spreadsheets, and Data Bases.* Academic Press, Orlando, FL, 1985.

Bayer, R. and McCreight, E. "Organization and maintenance of large ordered indexes," *Acta Informatica*, 1(3):173–189, 1972.

Bradley, James. *File and Data Base Techniques.* Holt, Rinehart & Winston, New York, 1981.

Buchholz, W. "File organization and addressing," *IBM Systems Journal*, 2(6):86–111, 1963.

Chang, C. C. "The study of an ordered minimal perfect hashing scheme," *Communications of the ACM*, 27(4):384–387, 1984.

Chaturvedi, Atindra. "Tree structures: A tutorial on using tree structures for random data storage and retrieval," *PC Tech Journal*, (2):78–87, 1985.

Chaturvedi, Atindra. "Tree structures: part 2," *PC Tech Journal*, (3):131–142, 1985.

Cichelli, R. J. "Minimal perfect hash functions made simple," *Communications of the ACM*, 23(1):17–19, 1980.

Claybrook, Billy G. *File Management Techniques.* John Wiley, New York, 1983.

Cook, C. R. "A letter oriented minimal perfect hashing function," *Sigplan Notices*, 17(9):18–27, 1982.

Dijkstra, E. W. *A Discipline of Programming.* Prentice–Hall, Englewood Cliffs, NJ, 1976.

Dwyer, Barry. "One more time—how to update a master file," *Communications of the ACM*, 24(1):3–8, 1981.

Fagin, R. et al. "Extendable hashing: A fast access method for dynamic files," *ACM Transactions on Database Systems*, 4(3):315–344, 1979.

Finger, Susan and Finger, Ellen. *Pascal with applications in science and engineering.* D. C. Heath, Lexington, MA, 1986.

Ghosh, S. P. and Lum, V. Y. "An analysis of collisions when hashing by division," IBM Research Report RJ1218, May 1973.

Guibas, L. U. "The analysis of hashing techniques that exhibit k-ary clustering," *Journal of ACM*, 25(4):544–555, 1978.

Hanson, Owen J. *Design of Computer Data Files.* Computer Science Press, Rockville, MD, 1982.

Helman, Paul and Veroff, Robert. *Intermediate Problem Solving and Data Structures.* Benjamin/Cummings Publishing, Menlo Park, CA, 1986.

Horowitz, Ellis and Sahni, Sartaj. *Fundamentals of Data Structures in Pascal.* Computer Science Press, Rockville, MD, 1984.

Introduction to IBM Direct Access Storage Devices and Organization Methods. IBM Manual No. GC 20-1649-10.

Jackson, M. A. *Principles of Program Design.* Academic Press, New York, 1975.

Jaeschke, G. and Osterburg, G. "On Cichelli's minimal perfect hash functions method," *Communications of the ACM,* 23(12):728–729, 1980.

Jaeschke, G. "Reciprocal hashing: A method for generating minimal perfect hashing functions," *Communications of the ACM,* 24(12):829–833, 1981.

Jensen, Kathleen and Wirth, Nicklaus. *Pascal User Manual and Report Third Edition.* Revised by Andrew B. Mickel and James F. Miner. Springer–Verlag, New York, 1985.

Johnson, Leroy F. and Cooper, Rodney H. *File Techniques for Data Base Organization in COBOL.* Prentice–Hall, Englewood Cliffs, NJ, 1981.

Knott, G. D. "Hashing functions," *Computer Journal,* 18(3):265–278, 1975.

Knuth, Donald E. *The Art of Computer Programming Vol. 3, Sorting and Searching.* Addison–Wesley, Reading, MA, 1973.

Litwin, W. "Virtual hashing: A dynamically changing hashing," *Proceedings of the Fourth Conference on Very Large Databases,* West Berlin, September 1978, 517–523.

Loomis, Mary E. S. *Data Management and File Processing.* Prentice–Hall, Englewood Cliffs, NJ, 1983.

Lum, V. Y. "General performance analysis of key-to-address transformation methods using an abstract file concept," *Communications of the ACM,* 16(10):603–612, 1973.

Lum, V. Y. and Yuen, P.S.T. "Additional results on key-to-address transform techniques," *Communications of the ACM,* 15(11):996–997, 1972.

Lum, V. Y. et al. "Key-to-address transform techniques," *Communications of the ACM,* 14(4):228–229, 1971.

Maurer, W. D. and Lewis, T. G. "Hash table methods," *ACM Computing Surveys,* 7(1):5–20, 1975.

Microcomputer Interfaces Handbook. Digital Equipment Corporation, Marlboro, MA, 1981.

OS/VS1 and VS2 Access Method Services. IBM manuals No. GC 26-3840 and GC 26-3841.

Powers, Michael J.; Adams, David R.; and Mills, Harlan D. *Computer Information Systems Development: Analysis and Design.* South-Western Publishing, Cincinnati, 1984.

Programming in VAX Pascal. Order # AA-L369B-TE. Digital Equipment Corporation, Maynard, MA, 1985.

Scholl, M. "New file organization based on dynamic hashing," *ACM Transactions on Database Systems,* 6(1):194–211, 1981.

Sloan, M. E. *Computer Hardware and Organization.* Science Research Associates, Chicago, 1983.

Sprugnoli, R. "Perfect hashing functions: A single probe retrieving method for static sets," *Communication of the ACM*, 11(10):841–850, 1977.

Stone, Harold S., editor. *Introduction to Computer Architecture*. Science Research Associates, Chicago, 1980.

Tremblay, Jean–Paul and Sorenson, Paul G. *An Introduction to Data Structures with Applications*. McGraw–Hill, New York, 1984.

Welburn, Tyler. *Advanced Structured COBOL, Batch, On-line, and Data-Base Concepts*. Mayfield Publishing, Palo Alto, CA, 1983.

Wirth, Nicklaus. *Algorithms + Data Structures = Programs*. Prentice–Hall, Englewood Cliffs, NJ, 1976.

Zaks, Rodnay. *Introduction to Pascal (Including UCSD PASCAL)*. Sybex, Inc., Berkeley, CA, 1981.

INDEX